3rd Workshop on Advances in Language and Vision Research (ALVR 2024)

Bangkok, Thailand
16 August 2024

ISBN: 979-8-3313-0155-2

Printed from e-media with permission by:

Curran Associates, Inc.
57 Morehouse Lane
Red Hook, NY 12571

Some format issues inherent in the e-media version may also appear in this print version.

Printed with permission by Curran Associates, Inc. (2024)

Association for Computational Linguistics
209 N. Eighth Street
Stroudsburg, Pennsylvania 18360

Phone: 1-570-476-8006
Fax: 1-570-476-0860

acl@aclweb.org

Additional copies of this publication are available from:

Curran Associates, Inc.
57 Morehouse Lane
Red Hook, NY 12571 USA
Phone: 845-758-0400
Fax: 845-758-2633
Email: curran@proceedings.com
Web: www.proceedings.com

ALVR 2024

The 3rd Workshop on Advances in Language and Vision Research

Proceedings of the Workshop

August 16, 2024

Introduction

Welcome to the 3rd Workshop on Advances in Language and Vision Research. Co-located with ACL 2024, the workshop is scheduled for August 16, 2024. To facilitate the participation of the global NLP and CV community, we continue running the workshop in a hybrid format.

Language and vision research has attracted great attention from both natural language processing (NLP) and computer vision (CV) researchers. Gradually, this area is shifting from passive perception, templated language, and synthetic imagery/environments to active perception, natural language, and photo-realistic simulation or real-world deployment. The workshop covers (but is not limited to) the following topics:

- Self-supervised vision and language pre-training;
- New tasks and datasets that provide real-world solutions in language and vision;
- Text-to-image/video generation and text-guided image/video editing;
- External knowledge integration in visual and language understanding;
- Visually-grounded natural language understanding and generation;
- Language-grounded visual recognition and reasoning;
- Language-grounded embodied agents, e.g., vision-and-language navigation;
- Visually-grounded multilingual study, e.g., multimodal machine translation;
- Shortcomings of the existing large vision & language models on downstream tasks and solutions;
- Ethics and bias in large vision & language models;
- Multidisciplinary study that may involve linguistics, cognitive science, robotics, etc.;
- Explainability and interpretability in large vision & language models.

Our agenda features keynote speeches, hybrid talk sessions both for long and short papers, and poster sessions. This year we received 35 submissions, and after a thorough peer-review process, 31 papers were accepted. Among the accepted papers, 18 are archive papers and 13 are non-archive papers.

We would like to deeply thank all the authors, committee members, keynote speakers, and participants for helping us grow this research community both in quantity and quality.

Workshop Chairs

Jing Gu, UC Santa Cruz
Tsu-Jui Fu, UC Santa Barbara
Drew Hudson, Google DeepMind
Asli Celikyilmaz, Fundamentals AI Research @ Meta
William Wang, UC Santa Barbara

Organizing Committee

General Chair

Jing Gu, University of California Santa Cruz, USA
Tsu-Jui (Ray) Fu, Apple, USA
Drew Hudson, Google DeepMind, USA
Asli Celikyilmaz, Fundamentals AI Research (FAIR) @ Meta, USA
William Wang, University of California Santa Barbara, USA

Program Committee

Reviewers

Arjun Reddy Akula, Google Research
Asma Ben Abacha, Microsoft, USA
Yupeng Cao, Stevens Institute of Technology
Zhi Chen, Stevens Institute of Technology
Dhivya Chinnappa, Thomson Reuters
Zhiyang Deng, Stevens Institute of Technology
Simon Dobnik, University of Gothenburg
Yue Fan, University of California, Santa Cruz
Zhe Gan, Apple
Cristina Garbacea, University of Michigan - Ann Arbor
Ran Gong, University of California, Los Angeles
Xueying Jia, Carnegie Mellon University
Huaizu Jiang, Northeastern University
Yuechen Jiang, New Jersey Institute of Technology
Yiqiao Jin, Georgia Institute of Technology
Liqiang Jing, University of Texas at Dallas
Haohang Li, Stevens Institute of Technology
Zikai Lin, University of Michigan - Ann Arbor
Tianrui Liu, StubHub
Yujie Lu, UC Santa Barbara
Ziqian Luo, Oracle
Bohan Lyu, Tsinghua University
Loitongbam Sanayai Meetei, National Institute of Technology Silchar
Yulei Niu, ByteDance Inc.
Udita Patel, Amazon
Zhejian Peng, Snap Inc. and Georgia Institute of Technology
Vikas Raunak, Microsoft
Anthony Reyna, University of California, Santa Cruz
Arka Sadhu, University of Southern California
Shubham Shukla, Nordstrom
Thoudam Doren Singh, National Institute of Technology Silchar
Alok Singh, University of Oxford
Alessandro Suglia, Heriot-Watt University
Dachun Sun, Department of Computer Science, University of Illinois at Urbana-Champaign
Ece Takmaz, Utrecht University
Hao Tan, Adobe Systems
Yunlong Tang, University of Rochester
Jingxiao Tian, University of California, San Diego
Tianshi Wang, Department of Computer Science, University of Illinois at Urbana-Champaign
Zheng Wang, Stanford University
Yiming Xie, Northeastern University
Qi Xin, University of Pittsburgh
Wei Xiong, Adobe
Qingyang Xu, Massachusetts Institute of Technology
Qianqi Yan, University of California, Santa Cruz
Tiankai Yang, University of Southern California

Peiyan Zhang, Hong Kong University of Science and Technology
Siqiao Zhao, Morgan Stanley
Kaizhi Zheng, University of California, Santa Cruz
Chang Zhou, Columbia University
Wanrong Zhu, University of California, Santa Barbara
Fangrui Zhu, Northeastern University

Table of Contents

Program

Friday, August 16, 2024

09:00 - 09:15	*Welcome Speech*
09:15 - 10:15	*Invited Talk by Dr. Alane Suhr*
10:15 - 10:30	*Poster Session 1*
10:30 - 11:00	*Coffee Break*
11:00 - 12:00	*Invited Talk by Dr. Angel Chang*
12:00 - 13:00	*Invited Talk by Dr. Daniel Fried*
13:00 - 13:45	*Lunch Break*
13:45 - 14:45	*Invited Talk by Roozbeh Mottaghi*
14:45 - 15:45	*Invited Talk by Dr. Heng Ji*
15:45 - 16:15	*Coffee Break*
16:15 - 17:15	*Invited Talk by Xin (Eric) Wang*
17:15 - 17:45	*Poster Session 2*
17:45 - 18:00	*Closing Remarks*

WISMIR3
A Multi-Modal Dataset to Challenge Text-Image Retrieval Approaches

Florian Schneider and **Chris Biemann**
Language Technology Group, Department of Informatics
Universität Hamburg, Germany
{florian.schneider-1, biemann}@uni-hamburg.de

Abstract

This paper presents WISMIR3, a multi-modal dataset comprising roughly 300K text-image pairs from Wikipedia. With a sophisticated automatic ETL pipeline, we scraped, filtered, and transformed the data so that WISMIR3 intrinsically differs from other popular text-image datasets like COCO and Flickr30k. We prove this difference by comparing various linguistic statistics between the three datasets computed using the pipeline. The primary purpose of WISMIR3 is to use it as a benchmark to challenge state-of-the-art text-image retrieval approaches, which already reach around 90% Recall@5 scores on the mentioned popular datasets. Therefore, we ran several text-image retrieval experiments on our dataset using current models, which show that the models, in fact, perform significantly worse compared to evaluation results on COCO and Flickr30k. In addition, for each text-image pair, we release features computed by Faster-R-CNN and CLIP models. With this, we want to ease and motivate the use of the dataset for other researchers.

1 Introduction

Current multi-modal text-image retrieval approaches already reach over 90% Recall@5 on popular evaluation sets (Wang et al., 2023). The reason for this is definitely due to the advances in visio-linguistic approaches implemented by state-of-the-art models like UNITER (Chen et al., 2020), TERAN (Messina et al., 2021), CLIP (Radford et al., 2021), or BEiT3 (Wang et al., 2023). However, we argue that this is not solely due to the model's architecture but also because of the simplicity of the widely used training data and its similarity to the evaluation data. Although more recent datasets exist, the most popular datasets used to train and evaluate state-of-the-art text-image retrieval methods are still COCO (Lin et al., 2014) and Flickr30k (Young et al., 2014). Both datasets comprise short and simple captions created by crowdsourcing workers for Flickr images showing everyday scenes. Schneider et al. (2021) showed that recent multi-modal transformer-based approaches trained on these popular datasets cannot generalize well on out-of-domain data with more complexity and variety. In the mentioned work, two preliminary datasets were introduced. However, during detailed data analysis, we found multiple issues in these preliminary datasets, which we address in this work.

The main contribution of this work is the release of WISMIR3 (**WI**kiCaps **S**ubset for **M**ulti-Modal Text-**I**mage **R**etrieval v**3**)[1], a clean multi-modal dataset, thought of as a benchmark to challenge state-of-the-art text-image retrieval models. WISMIR3 contains more than 300K text-image pairs from Wikipedia, scraped, filtered, transformed, and statistically analyzed by a sophisticated automatic ETL pipeline tool. Further, we provide a detailed overview, discuss and release linguistic statistics of the comprised data, and compare it to COCO and Flickr30K. Additionally, we release pre-computed image features from a popular pre-trained Faster-R-CNN (Ren et al., 2016) model and image and text embeddings from pre-trained CLIP models employing ViT (Dosovitskiy et al., 2021) as the image encoder. With this, we aim to ease the use of the dataset to train, finetune, or evaluate models on the WISMIR3 dataset. By evaluating different state-of-the-art text-image retrieval approaches on WISMIR3 and comparing the results with their performance on COCO and Flickr30k, we show that these models indeed perform much worse on our dataset.

2 Related Work

State-of-the-art approaches for multi-modal text-image retrieval are typically trained on text-image

[1] https://github.com/floschne/wismir3
https://huggingface.co/datasets/floschne/wismir3

Proceedings of the 3rd Workshop on Advances in Language and Vision Research, pages 1–6
August 16, 2024 ©2024 Association for Computational Linguistics

pairs. Despite their age, the most popular datasets to train and evaluate models on this task are still COCO (Lin et al., 2014) and Flickr30k (Young et al., 2014). COCO is a well-known dataset for various Computer Vision tasks like object detection, object segmentation, image captioning, keypoint detection, human pose estimation, and text-image retrieval. Besides labels and annotations, the dataset contains about 123K carefully selected images from Flickr with five descriptive captions each. Flickr30k contains about 30K icon photographs of everyday activities, events, and scenes from Flickr, where also five different captions describe each image. Both COCO and Flickr30k are datasets designed by researchers and handcrafted by crowdsourcing workers to describe the images with short, simple, and descriptive captions.

Less popular but larger datasets like SBU Captions (Ordonez et al., 2011), Conceptual Captions (Sharma et al., 2018), or Visual Genome (Krishna et al., 2017) are primarily designed for tasks like image-captioning, visual question answering, or visual entailment. However, since they comprise text-image pairs, the datasets are often part of the training data for text-image retrieval approaches. Visual Genome contains about 108K images collected from an intersection of MS COCO and YFCC-100M (Thomee et al., 2016) with captions created by crowdsourcing workers. SBU Caption contains about 1M photos and their captions from Flickr. Conceptual Captions contains approximately 3.3M text-image pairs scraped from billions of websites and automatically transformed and filtered by a sophisticated pipeline.

Further, WIT (Srinivasan et al., 2021) and LAION-5B (Schuhmann et al., 2022) are huge text-image datasets suitable for pre-training vison-language foundation models like CLIP (Radford et al., 2021), ALIGN (Jia et al., 2021), or BLIP2 (Li et al., 2023). The WIT dataset contains about 37.5M text-image pairs, comprising 11.5M unique images with captions from Wikipedia across 108 different languages. The LAION-5B dataset contains about 5B non-curated text-image pairs scraped from Common Crawl dumps.

Another text-image dataset is WikiCaps (Schamoni et al., 2018), containing about 3.8M text-image pairs from Wikipedia. Captions are taken from the associated Wikimedia image descriptions, mainly in English. This dataset is the basis of WISMIR3 and is of particular interest in this work because the data is from random Wikipedia articles.

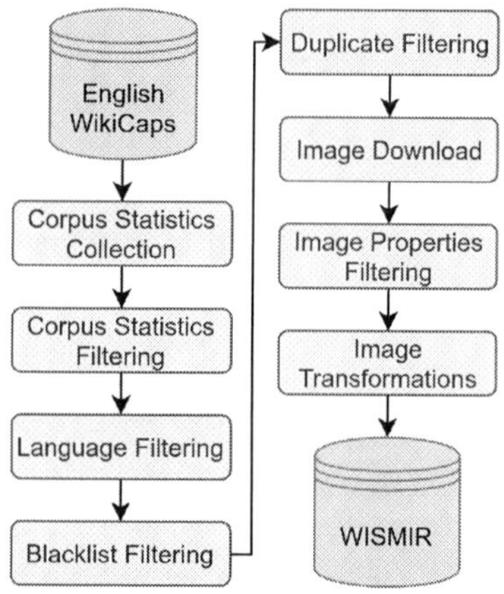

Figure 1: A schematic overview of the pipeline used to collect the WISMIR3 dataset.

Therefore, the captions and images cover a wide range of different topics and concepts.

3 Data Collection Pipeline

A schematic overview of the pipeline used to collect the WISMIR3 dataset, presented by this work, is shown in Figure 1. In the following, more details about the single steps are described.

The input to the pipeline is a CSV file released by the WikiCaps authors, containing 3.8M Wikimedia image file IDs and the corresponding English captions. Since this file format is unhandy to compute statistics or apply transformations, it is converted into a pandas DataFrame, used throughout the whole pipeline.

In the first stage, extensive corpus statistics are collected for each caption using a spaCy pipeline with the "en_core_web_lg" model. These statistics include, for example, the number of tokens and sentences, POS tags of each token, counts of the Universal Dependency tags (Nivre et al., 2020), the language of each sentence, named entities, and ratios between the number of all tokens and nouns or named entities.

The DataFrame is then filtered based on these statistics, as described in the following. Samples are dropped if

- the caption consists of less than 10 or more than 300 tokens
- the caption consists of less than 1 or more than 7 sentences
- the number of tokens in a sentence in the caption is less than 5

- the ratio between all tokens and tokens that are part of named entities does not exceed 0.8

Further samples were removed if the language of every sentence in the caption was not English.

Moreover, since the purpose of this dataset is to challenge text-image retrieval approaches, it is essential that most of the words in an image description are also represented in the image. Hence, we created a blocklist of non-depictable words like "URL", "Sarcasm", "Confusion" and filtered out every sample that contains one or more of these terms.

In the next pipeline stage, the duplicate filtering stage, we remove duplicate captions so that one caption describes at most five different images. This decision was inspired by COCO or Flickr30k, where it is the other way round, i.e., five different captions describe one image.

With the mentioned filtering stages, we reduced the 3.8M WikiCaps samples by about 92% to 304317 samples. After downloading the images, we removed 3431 that were too small or had erroneous data format. We applied the following transformations to every image in the final pipeline stage.

- converting to RGB if it was grayscale before
- resizing while keeping the aspect ratio with bicubic interpolation so that the maximum width and maximum height do not exceed 640 pixels
- compressing to a max of 72 DPI
- converting to and persisting as PNG

The final output of the pipeline is the WISMIR3 dataset, comprising 300886 text-image pairs. A detailed overview is described in the following sections.

4 Dataset Structure and Statistics

4.1 Structure

The textual data of the WISMIR3 is released in two pandas DataFrames[2], one for the training set and one for the test or evaluation set. In addition to the "raw" format, we also release the dataset on HuggingFace[3]. The training and test split comprises 295886 and 5000 randomly chosen text-image pairs, respectively. Besides the caption and the corresponding image filename, both DataFrames contain various linguistic statistics of the caption, as described in Table 1. To compute these statistics, we used spaCy[4] with the "en_core_web_lg" model.

Column Name	Description
wikicaps_id	The row index in the original WikiCaps CSV file
wikimedia_file_id	The Wikimedia File ID of the original image
caption	The caption of the image
tokens	The list of tokens in the caption
num_tok	The number of tokens in the caption
sentence_spans	A list of tuples containing the start and end index of the sentences w.r.t. the list of tokens
num_sents	The number of sentences in the caption
min_sent_len	The minimum length of the sentences in the caption
max_sent_len	The maximum length of the sentences in the caption
num_ne	The number of named entities in the caption
ne_types	A list of the named entity types in the caption
ne_texts	A list of the named entity surface forms in the caption
num_nouns	The number of tokens tagged as NOUN
num_propns	The number of tokens tagged as PROPN
num_conj	The number of tokens tagged as CONJ
num_verb	The number of tokens tagged as VERB
num_sym	The number of tokens tagged as SYM
num_num	The number of tokens tagged as NUM
num_adp	The number of tokens tagged as ADP
num_adj	The number of tokens tagged as ADJ
ratio_ne_tok	The ratio of tokens that belong to named entities versus all tokens of the caption
ratio_noun_tok	The ratio of tokens tagged as NOUN versus all tokens of the caption
ratio_propn_tok	The ratio of tokens tagged as PROPN versus all tokens of the caption
ratio_all_noun_tok	The ratio of tokens tagged as NOUN or PROPN versus all tokens of the caption
image_id	The filename of the image corresponding to this sample
clip_embs_id	The ID of the CLIP image and text embeddings of this sample in the CLIP embeddings tensor
frcnn_embs_id	The filename of the Faster-R-CNN image embedding of this sample

Table 1: The extensive list of the columns and their descriptions contained in WISMIR3.

The images related to the samples are released as single PNG files. Further, we released 36 bounding boxes for regions of interest with corresponding feature vectors extracted by a pretrained Faster-R-CNN (Ren et al., 2016; Yu et al., 2020) model for each image as single NumPy archive files. Additionally, we computed and published the caption and image embedding for each sample computed with two pretrained CLIP (Radford et al., 2021) models employing 16x16 and 32x32 patch ViT (Dosovitskiy et al., 2021), respectively.

Three random samples of WISMIR3, i.e., the images with their corresponding captions, are shown in Figure 2.

4.2 Statistics

In this section, we present a statistical overview of WISMIR3 in Table 2 and, based on this, discuss the contrasts between the dataset and COCO or Flickr30k.

An appreciable difference between WISMIR3, COCO, and Flickr30k becomes apparent when comparing these statistics between the respective datasets. For example, in COCO and Flickr30k, the respective average number of tokens per caption is

[2]https://github.com/floschne/wismir3

[3]https://huggingface.co/floschne/wismir3

[4]`https://spacy.io`

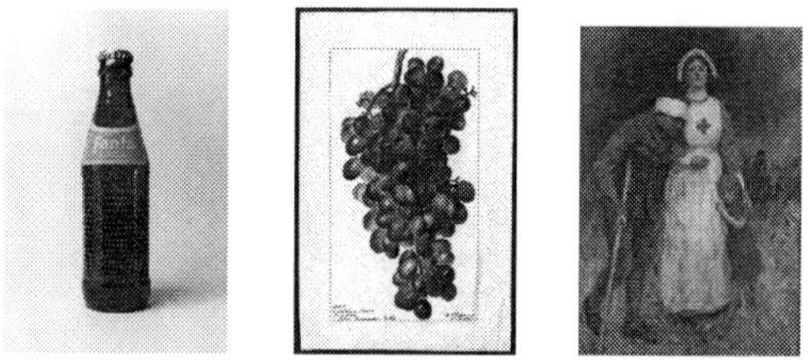

(a) (b) (c)

Figure 2: Randomly chosen images and their captions included in WISMIR3. (a) *Fanta Klassik, 75th anniversay edition of the Fanta soft drink, 2015. Front view of the bottle.* (b) *Image of the Sultanina Rosea variety of grapes (scientific name: "Vitis"), with this specimen originating in Niles, Fremont, Alameda County, California, United States. Source: U.S. Department of Agriculture Pomological Watercolor Collection. Rare and Special Collections, National Agricultural Library, Beltsville, MD 20705.* (c) *"The painting is a design for a poster." image: Three figures dominate the image. A Red Cross nurse stands in the centre. A wounded soldier with a crutch and bandaged head leans on her right arm. On her left a small child in a red dress clings to her skirts; the nurse has her hand resting reassuringly on the child's shoulder. There is the ruin of a building in the background.*

	min	**max**	**avg**
Number of tokens	12	294	59.8
Number of sentences	1	6	2.71
Ratio of NOUN or PROPN tokens	0.0	0.92	0.44
Ratio of named entity tokens	0.0	0.79	0.31
Cosine similarity of caption and image embeddings	0.04	0.53	0.32

Table 2: Various aggregated per-caption statistics in WISMIR3. The cosine similarity was computed using a CLIP model with a ViT using 16x16 patches.

11.34 and 13.49, which is close to the minimum number of tokens and about 4 to 5 times smaller than the average number of tokens per caption in WISMIR3.

Further, by looking at the average ratio of named entity tokens of COCO and Flickr30k, which are 0.02 and 0.03, respectively, it becomes clear that there are almost no named entities in the two datasets. However, in WISMIR3, this ratio lies at 0.44 on average. We argue that in real-world image-retrieval systems, users search for images of specific entities, e.g., with textual queries like "The Eifel Tower at night." instead of general images with queries like "A large iron tower at night". Hence, the training and evaluation data for models powering these real-world systems should contain named entities.

Another difference between WISMIR3 and COCO or Flickr30k is the number of nouns per caption. In COCO and Flickr30k, the average ratio of noun tokens compared to all tokens of a caption is 0.33 and 0.31, respectively, while, in WISMIR3, it is 0.44.

Furthermore, we computed Flesch-Kincaid (Farr et al., 1951) (FK) and Dale-Chall (Chall and Dale, 1995) (DC) readability scores for the captions in the three datasets, which are similar for COCO and Flickr30k but much higher for WISMIR3 (c.f. Figure 3). This suggests a much higher textual com-

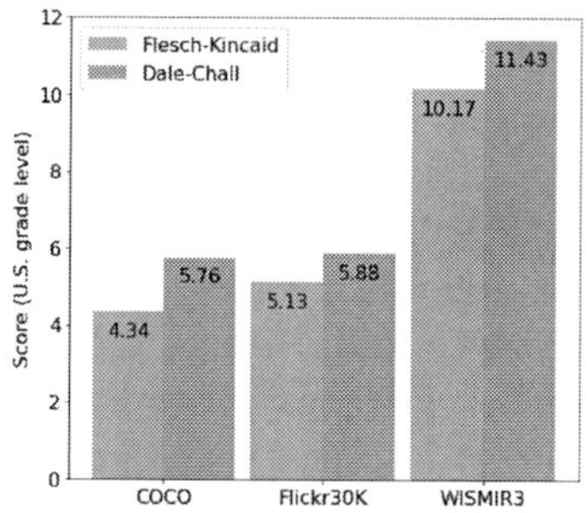

Figure 3: Comparison of Flesch-Kincaid (FK) and Dale-Chall (DC) readability scores of COCO (C), Flickr30k (F), and WISMIR3 (W) captions containing $10^6 \pm 0.1\%$ characters.

plexity of WISMIR3 compared to the two other datasets. That is, COCO and Flickr30k should be easily understood by an average 4th to 6th-grade US student, while WISMIR3 captions are recommended for college students.

We further computed the text-image cosine similarity for each sample in WISMIR3 using a pretrained CLIP model. With the average similarity of 0.32 being above the minimum threshold of the LAION-400M dataset, we consider the text-image alignment in WISMIR3 as acceptable.

5 Image Retrieval Experiments

This section presents text-image retrieval evaluation results of various recent models on the WISMIR3 dataset and compares them to the models' performances on COCO and Flickr30k. As listed in Table 3, evaluation scores of all listed models on the WISMIR3 (W3) evaluation set are significantly worse compared to the models' performances on COCO (C) and Flickr30k (F30K).

Further observed is that COCO and Flickr30k data did not contribute anything meaningful during TERAN training processes when evaluating the

Model	Data	R@1	R@5	R@10
	Text-Image Retrieval (t2i)			
$\text{CLIP}_{\text{ViT-B-16}}$	W3	**47.9**	**72.42**	**80.32**
TERAN_{W3}	W3	15.3	39.6	53.1
$\text{UNITER}_{\text{base}}$	W3	8.76	21.84	29.54
$\text{TERAN}_{\text{COCO}}$	W3	1.1	3.7	5.6
$\text{TERAN}_{\text{F30K}}$	W3	0.9	2.7	4.4
$\text{CLIP}_{\text{ViT-B-16}}$	COCO	**58.4**	**81.5**	**88.1**
$\text{UNITER}_{\text{base}}$	COCO	50.33	78.52	87.16
$\text{TERAN}_{\text{COCO}}$	COCO	42.6	72.5	82.9
$\text{CLIP}_{\text{ViT-B-16}}$	F30K	68.7	90.6	95.2
$\text{UNITER}_{\text{base}}$	F30K	**72.52**	**92.36**	**96.08**
$\text{TERAN}_{\text{F30K}}$	F30K	59.4	84.8	90.5

Table 3: Recall@K evaluation results of different models and evaluation sets on text-image retrieval on the WISMIR3 test set. "W3" stands for WISMIR3. In the model column, the subscript datasets indicate the training data of the TERAN model. For evaluation on COCO, we used the 5k evaluation set. Further, we used CLIP or UNITER in a zero-shot setting without fine-tuning on WISMIR3.

models on WISMIR3. However, one noticeable finding is that the CLIP model[5] performs exceptionally well on WISMIR3 compared to UNITER and even the TERAN model trained on the WISMIR3 training set. Also, UNITER performs much better than TERAN on WISMIR3. Since CLIP was trained on a very large-scale dataset containing more than 400M text-image pairs scraped from random websites, its training data is probably relatively similar to the data contained in WISMIR3 or even comprises the data. Moreover, UNITER was trained on much larger datasets of roughly 5.6M samples compared to WISMIR3.

These findings show that current text-image retrieval approaches perform significantly worse on WISMIR3 than COCO and Flickr30k.

6 Conclusion

This paper presents WISMIR3, a clean multi-modal dataset containing roughly 300K text-image pairs. The dataset comprises images with corresponding captions from Wikipedia using WikiCaps as the source dataset. By implementing a sophisticated automatic ETL pipeline tool, we scraped, filtered, and transformed the data so that WISMIR3 differs from popular datasets like COCO and Flickr30k. We prove this difference by comparing linguistic statistics between the three datasets also computed using the tool. The purpose of WISMIR3 is to use it as a hard benchmark to challenge state-of-the-art text-image retrieval approaches, which already reach 90% Recall@5 scores on the mentioned popular datasets. With the experiments in this paper, we show that the text-image retrieval performance of the current models on WISMIR3 is much lower than on COCO or Flickr30k, as anticipated.

7 License

The dataset is licensed under the Creative Commons Attribution-ShareAlike 4.0 International (CC BY-SA 4.0) [6]. This allows copying and redistributing the data in any medium or format when appropriate credit is given and a link to the license is given. Further, it is allowed to mix, transform, or extend the dataset for any purpose. However, every change has to be indicated.

References

Jeanne S. Chall and Edgar Dale. 1995. *Readability Revisited: The New Dale-Chall Readability Formula*. Brookline Books, U.S.

Yen-Chun Chen, Linjie Li, Licheng Yu, Ahmed El Kholy, Faisal Ahmed, Zhe Gan, Yu Cheng, and Jingjing Liu. 2020. UNITER: UNiversal Image-TExt Representation Learning. In *European Conference on Computer Vision (ECCV)*, pages 104–120, Online.

Alexey Dosovitskiy, Lucas Beyer, Alexander Kolesnikov, Dirk Weissenborn, Xiaohua Zhai, Thomas Unterthiner, Mostafa Dehghani, Matthias Minderer, Georg Heigold, Sylvain Gelly, Jakob Uszkoreit, and Neil Houlsby. 2021. An Image is Worth 16x16 Words: Transformers for Image Recognition at Scale. In *9th International Conference on Learning Representations, ICLR 2021, Virtual Event, Austria, May 3-7, 2021*.

James N. Farr, James J. Jenkins, and Donald G. Paterson. 1951. Simplification of Flesch Reading Ease Formula. *Journal of applied psychology*, 35(5):333.

Chao Jia, Yinfei Yang, Ye Xia, Yi-Ting Chen, Zarana Parekh, Hieu Pham, Quoc V Le, Yunhsuan Sung, Zhen Li, and Tom Duerig. 2021. Scaling Up Visual and Vision-Language Representation Learning With Noisy Text Supervision. *arXiv preprint arXiv:2102.05918*.

Ranjay Krishna, Yuke Zhu, Oliver Groth, Justin Johnson, Kenji Hata, Joshua Kravitz, Stephanie Chen, Yannis Kalantidis, Li-Jia Li, David A. Shamma, et al. 2017. Visual Genome: Connecting Language and Vision Using Crowdsourced Dense Image Annotations. *International Journal of Computer Vision (IJCV)*, 123(1):32–73.

[5]https://huggingface.co/openai/clip-vit-base-patch16

[6]https://creativecommons.org/licenses/by-sa/4.0/

Junnan Li, Dongxu Li, Silvio Savarese, and Steven Hoi. 2023. BLIP-2: Bootstrapping Language-Image Pre-training with Frozen Image Encoders and Large Language Models. *arXiv preprint arXiv:2301.12597.*

Tsung-Yi Lin, Michael Maire, Serge Belongie, James Hays, Pietro Perona, Deva Ramanan, Piotr Dollár, and C. Lawrence Zitnick. 2014. Microsoft COCO: Common Objects in Context. In *European Conference on Computer Vision (ECCV)*, pages 740–755, Zurich, Switzerland.

Nicola Messina, Giuseppe Amato, Andrea Esuli, Fabrizio Falchi, Claudio Gennaro, and Stéphane Marchand-Maillet. 2021. Fine-grained Visual Textual Alignment for Cross-Modal Retrieval using Transformer Encoders. *ACM Transactions on Multimedia Computing, Communications, and Applications (TOMM)*, 17(4):1–23.

Joakim Nivre, Marie-Catherine de Marneffe, Filip Ginter, Jan Hajivc, Christopher D Manning, Sampo Pyysalo, Sebastian Schuster, Francis Tyers, and Daniel Zeman. 2020. Universal Dependencies v2: An Evergrowing Multilingual Treebank Collection. *arXiv preprint arXiv:2004.10643.*

Vicente Ordonez, Girish Kulkarni, and Tamara Berg. 2011. Im2Text: Describing Images Using 1 Million Captioned Photographs. In *Advances in Neural Information Processing Systems (NIPS)*, volume 24, pages 1143–1151, Granada, Spain.

Alec Radford, Jong Wook Kim, Chris Hallacy, Aditya Ramesh, Gabriel Goh, Sandhini Agarwal, Girish Sastry, Amanda Askell, Pamela Mishkin, Jack Clark, et al. 2021. Learning Transferable Visual Models from Natural Language Supervision. *arXiv preprint arXiv:2103.00020.*

Shaoqing Ren, Kaiming He, Ross Girshick, and Jian Sun. 2016. Faster R-CNN: Towards Real-Time Object Detection with Region Proposal Networks. *IEEE Transactions on Pattern Analysis and Machine Intelligence (TPAMI)*, 39(6):1137–1149.

Shigehiko Schamoni, Julian Hitschler, and Stefan Riezler. 2018. A Dataset and Reranking Method for Multimodal MT of User-Generated Image Captions. In *Proceedings of the 13th Conference of the Association for Machine Translation in the Americas*, pages 140–153, Boston, MA, USA.

Florian Schneider, Özge Alaçam, Xintong Wang, and Chris Biemann. 2021. Towards Multi-Modal Text-Image Retrieval to Improve Human Reading. In *Proceedings of the 2021 Conference of the North American Chapter of the Association for Computational Linguistics: Student Research Workshop (NAACL SRW)*, Mexico City, Mexico (Online).

Christoph Schuhmann, Romain Beaumont, Richard Vencu, Cade Gordon, Ross Wightman, Mehdi Cherti, Theo Coombes, Aarush Katta, Clayton Mullis, Mitchell Wortsman, et al. 2022. LAION-5B: An Open Large-Scale Dataset for Training Next Generation Image-Text Models. *Advances in Neural Information Processing Systems (NeurIPS)*, 35:25278–25294.

Piyush Sharma, Nan Ding, Sebastian Goodman, and Radu Soricut. 2018. Conceptual Captions: A Cleaned, Hypernymed, Image Alt-text Dataset For Automatic Image Captioning. In *Proceedings of the 56th Annual Meeting of the Association for Computational Linguistics*, pages 2556–2565, Melbourne, Australia.

Krishna Srinivasan, Karthik Raman, Jiecao Chen, Mike Bendersky, and Marc Najork. 2021. WIT: Wikipedia-based Image Text Dataset for Multimodal Multilingual Machine Learning. In *Proceedings of the 44th International ACM SIGIR Conference on Research and Development in Information Retrieval (SIGIR)*, Online.

Bart Thomee, David A Shamma, Gerald Friedland, Benjamin Elizalde, Karl Ni, Douglas Poland, Damian Borth, and Li-Jia Li. 2016. YFCC100M: The New Data in Multimedia Research. *Communications of the ACM*, 59(2):64–73.

Wenhui Wang, Hangbo Bao, Li Dong, Johan Bjorck, Zhiliang Peng, Qiang Liu, Kriti Aggarwal, Owais Khan Mohammed, Saksham Singhal, Subhojit Som, et al. 2023. Image as a Foreign Language: BEiT Pretraining for Vision and Vision-Language Tasks. In *Proceedings of the IEEE/CVF Conference on Computer Vision and Pattern Recognition*, pages 19175–19186, Vancouver, Canada.

Peter Young, Alice Lai, Micah Hodosh, and Julia Hockenmaier. 2014. From Image Descriptions to Visual Denotations: New Similarity Metrics for Semantic Inference Over Event Descriptions. *Transactions of the Association for Computational Linguistics (TACL)*, 2:67–78.

Zhou Yu, Jing Li, Tongan Luo, and Jun Yu. 2020. A PyTorch Implementation of Bottom-Up-Attention. `https://github.com/MILVLG/bottom-up-attention.pytorch`.

mBLIP: Efficient Bootstrapping of Multilingual Vision-LLMs

Gregor Geigle[1,2] **Abhay Jain**[3*] **Radu Timofte**[2] **Goran Glavaš**[1]
[1]WüNLP, [2]Computer Vision Lab, CAIDAS, University of Würzburg,
[3]Indian Institute of Technology (BHU), Varanasi, India
gregor.geigle@uni-wuerzburg.de

Abstract

Modular vision-language models (Vision-LLMs) align pretrained image encoders with (frozen) large language models (LLMs) and post-hoc condition LLMs to 'understand' the image input. With the abundance of readily available high-quality English image-text data as well as strong monolingual English LLMs, the research focus has been on English-only Vision-LLMs. Multilingual vision-language models are still predominantly obtained via expensive end-to-end pretraining, resulting in comparatively smaller models, trained on limited multilingual image data supplemented with text-only multilingual corpora. We present mBLIP, the first Vision-LLM leveraging multilingual LLMs, which we obtain in a computationally efficient manner on consumer-level hardware. To this end, we *re-align* an image encoder previously tuned to an English LLM to a new, multilingual LLM using only a few million multilingual training examples derived from a mix of vision-and-language tasks, which we obtain by machine-translating high-quality English data to 95 languages. On the IGLUE benchmark and XM3600, mBLIP yields results competitive with state-of-the-art models and it greatly outperforms strong English-only Vision-LLMs like Llava 1.5. We release our model, code, and train data at https://github.com/gregor-ge/mBLIP.

1 Introduction

The success of model and data scaling in NLP from BERT (Devlin et al., 2019) to more recent Large Language Models (LLMs) (Brown et al., 2020; Zhang et al., 2022; Touvron et al., 2023, *inter alia*) has prompted similar endeavors in vision-language pretraining from 'small' BERT-size models (Chen et al., 2020; Li et al., 2020, 2021, 2022) trained on a few million image-text pairs to billion-parameter models trained with billions of examples (Wang et al., 2021; Yu et al., 2022; Wang et al., 2022; Chen et al., 2022, 2023). The prohibitive cost of such end-to-end (pre)training, however, has resulted in increased interest in efficient modular methods that leverage existing large language models (LLMs). These align the output of a pretrained image encoder to the LLM's input representation space (Tsimpoukelli et al., 2021; Alayrac et al., 2022; Li et al., 2023a), resulting in a Vision-LLM.

Pretraining vision-language models from scratch requires a massive amount of high-quality image-text data, which is only available in English. Because of this, multilingual pretraining of vision-language models (Ni et al., 2021; Zhou et al., 2021; Zeng et al., 2023; Shan et al., 2022; Li et al., 2023c) commonly supplements limited-size multilingual image-text data with multilingual text-only data (the amount of which often surpasses that of image-text data) to achieve strong results, despite initialization with weights of multilingual text encoders such as XLM-R (Conneau et al., 2020).

In this work, we recognize modular Vision-LLM methods as a potential solution to this problem, observing that: (1) once an image encoder is aligned to one LLM, it requires significantly less data to re-align it to another LLM (Zhang et al., 2023; Zhu et al., 2023) and (2) since image encoding is, in principle, language-agnostic, it may be possible to successfully re-align the image encoder to a strong multilingual LLM, even if it was initially aligned only with English image-text data. Based on these observations, we present mBLIP, the first massively multilingual modular Vision-LLM, which we obtain by (re-)aligning an image encoder to a multilingual LLM. Putting together a range of recent advances in multimodal representation learning, we efficiently bootstrap a massively multilingual Vision-LLM using only ~2.5 million images (and without any additional multilingual text-only data), training only 124 million parameters on consumer-grade hardware. We achieve this efficiency by: 1)

*Work done during an internship at WüNLP

bootstrapping our model from a) an "English" image encoder (Li et al., 2023a), previously aligned to a monolingual English LLM and b) a strong instruction-tuned multilingual LLM (Xue et al., 2021; Scao et al., 2022; Muennighoff et al., 2022); 2) leveraging recent advances in massively multilingual machine translation (Costa-jussà et al., 2022), which we use to translate high-quality English data—both classic captions as well as task instructions (Dai et al., 2023)—to 95 languages; and finally 3) coupling parameter-efficient training methods (Hu et al., 2022) together with quantization (Dettmers et al., 2022, 2023) to enable training on consumer-grade hardware.

We extensively evaluate mBLIP on different multilingual vision-language tasks to confirm the efficacy of our approach: for multilingual image captioning, mBLIP (with mT0-XL) surpasses (zero-shot) PaLI-X (a model with 55B parameters, trained with billions of examples) (Chen et al., 2023) on the XM3600 (Thapliyal et al., 2022). On the visual reasoning and QA tasks of the IGLUE benchmark (Bugliarello et al., 2022), mBLIP matches or surpasses the performance of state-of-the-art models, despite training far fewer parameters on far less pretraining data. We consistently outperform state-of-the-art English Vision-LLMs outside of English, highlighting the multilingual prowess of our model.

2 Related Work

2.1 LLMs and Images

The success of scaling up training data and model parameters has resulted in large vision-language models with billions of parameters (Wang et al., 2021; Yu et al., 2022; Wang et al., 2022). However, with the number of parameters in single-digit billions, these are still an order of magnitude smaller than text-only models (Brown et al., 2020); the compute necessary to pretrain comparably large vision-language models, however, is available only to select few (Chen et al., 2022, 2023).

Instead, much of the vision-language research turned to approaches that can leverage the power of existing LLMs by training an image encoder to map an image into a sequence of tokens in the LLM embedding space (Tsimpoukelli et al., 2021; Alayrac et al., 2022; Li et al., 2023a), while the LLM is kept as-is or is only partially tuned (Alayrac et al., 2022). Most recently, the release of strong publicly available LLMs such as Llama (Touvron et al., 2023) and the success of conversational instruction tuning (Ouyang et al., 2022; Taori et al., 2023; Chiang et al., 2023; Xu et al., 2023), has led to a body of work (Zhu et al., 2023; Liu et al., 2023b; Ye et al., 2023; Dai et al., 2023; Gao et al., 2023; Liu et al., 2023a; Bai et al., 2023) that tries to replicate the vision-language skills of GPT-4 (OpenAI, 2023). The vast majority of research focused on English, where both an abundance of high-quality image-text data and strong LLMs exist. To the best of our knowledge, we are the first to extend a massively multilingual LLM with "vision capabilities".

2.2 Multilingual Vision-Language Models

While the majority of research on vision-language models targets English only, a number of multilingual models have been proposed too. M3P (Ni et al., 2021), the first transformer-based (Vaswani et al., 2017) multilingual vision-language model, adopts the architecture and pretraining objectives of English counterparts (Chen et al., 2020; Li et al., 2020). but trains on (i) the code-switched image-text data in which words in English image captions are replaced with translations from various languages as well as (ii) additional text-only multilingual corpora. UC2 (Zhou et al., 2021) uses a similar architecture and a mix of training objectives but instead of code-switching, it machine translates the 3M captions of CC3M (Sharma et al., 2018) to 5 languages (German, French, Czech, Japanese, and Chinese). Li et al. (2023c) and CCLM (Zeng et al., 2023), which adopt the ALBEF architecture (Li et al., 2021) that incorporates additional contrastive learning objectives, use the same translated CC3M data but they additionally supplement 19M parallel sentences (pairing English with all of the languages spanned by their respective downstream evaluation tasks). ERNIE-UniX2 (Shan et al., 2022), with an encoder-decoder architecture, adopts the same pretraining objectives but scales up the data to more translated captions and more text-only data (both aligned and monolingual). Finally, PaLI (Chen et al., 2022) (17B parameters) and PaLI-X (Chen et al., 2023) (55B parameters) represent two huge encoder-decoder models trained using a mixture of vision-and-language tasks, with billions of web-crawled multilingual captions, machine translated data, automatically extracted data (e.g., OCR and object detection), and generated visual QA (VQA) examples. With the exception of the PaLI models and ERNIE-UniX2 – both of which are not publicly available – all other multilingual vision-language models represent encoder-only architectures, which cannot perform image captioning out of the box.

3 mBLIP

We first briefly describe the modular BLIP-2 architecture (Li et al., 2023a) which we adopt in this work, followed by the description of training tasks and data, which we translate to 95 languages.

3.1 Architecture

We follow the modular BLIP-2 architecture (Li et al., 2023a) depicted in Figure 1: A Query-Former (Q-Former) is an encoder-only transformer (Vaswani et al., 2017) with 32 learned query tokens as input: it contextualizes the query tokens – via the cross-attention mechanism – with the representations of the image patches encoded by a large (frozen) Vision Transformer (ViT) (Dosovitskiy et al., 2020). The visual tokens that are the output of the Q-Former are then projected into the LLM embedding space with a single linear projection matrix $\mathbf{W}_P \in \mathbb{R}^{h_v \times h_l}$, with h_v and h_l as hidden dimensions (i.e., embedding dimensionality) of the Q-Former and LLM, respectively.

During training, only the the Q-Former (including the 32 query tokens) and the linear projection $\mathbf{W}_P$ are updated; all ViT and LLM parameters are kept frozen. Although the Q-Former and projection have initially been aligned to a monolingual English LLM, they only produce *visual* tokens: we believe that as such they are not overly tailored to English and can therefore be effectively re-aligned to a different, multilingual LLM.

Because the LLM is frozen in the BLIP-2 training, its parameters cannot adapt to task-specific idiosyncrasies, e.g., in fine-tuning for VQA or for instruction-following (Dai et al., 2023). Instead, task-specific fine-tuning of BLIP-2 requires that the text input is not just fed into the LLM but also into the Q-Former in order to enable encoding of *task-specific* visual information from the input. The Q-Former, however, is based on the English BERT (Devlin et al., 2019), preventing the application of this same approach in the multilingual setting (i.e., we cannot feed the text in other languages into the Q-Former nor efficiently make it massively multilingual, i.e., without a large multilingual pretraining effort). Because of this, we opt for a different approach: instead of feeding the text of the image-text instance (e.g., in VQA) to the Q-Former, we partially update the LLM with the parameter-efficient LoRA (Hu et al., 2022), which trains low-rank reparametrization of the LLM matrices.

3.2 Training Tasks and Data

We create a small but high-quality mix of tasks for our re-alignment training. We start from existing high-quality English data and machine-translate it to 95 languages in order to obtain multilingual training data for re-alignment of the Q-Former to the multilingual LLM.[1] We hypothesized that the re-alignment to a new LLM can be done with significantly less data than what is needed to train the original Q-Former (Zhu et al., 2023; Zhang et al., 2023). Accordingly, we create a small, high-quality English datasets and make it multilingual via MT rather than training with large-scale but very noisy multilingual image-caption datasets like LAION5B (Schuhmann et al., 2022). In addition, in line with findings from language-only instruction-tuning (Sanh et al., 2022; Muennighoff et al., 2022; Chung et al., 2022) and vision-language training (Dai et al., 2023; Liu et al., 2023b,a; Bai et al., 2023), we expect the training on a mixture of vision-and-language tasks (as opposed to training only for image captioning), with different task instructions, to result in better generalization abilities of the model and improve its (zero-shot) downstream performance and usability.

Task Mix: We select below the tasks and datasets used to create our training mix for re-alignment (naturally, we ensure that the data does not overlap with our downstream evaluation data; see §4.1). For every task, we create a set of instruction templates with which we generate the training examples (we provide the templates in §D.1 in the Appendix, along with additional details about the training data). In total, across all tasks, we use 5.1M examples encompassing 2.7M unique images.

1. Image Captioning: We use MSCOCO (Lin et al., 2014) along with 2.3 million examples sampled from the synthetic CapFilt dataset (Li et al., 2022) with the noun phrase method by Liu et al. (2023b) to ensure concept diversity. Additionally, we use LLaVA-Instruct-Detail (Liu et al., 2023b), which contains longer and more detailed captions.

2. Visual Question Answering and Generation: For VQA and the inverse task of question generation (given the answer, the model is supposed to

[1]Training with only English data, even without LoRA, results in the LLM producing only English output.

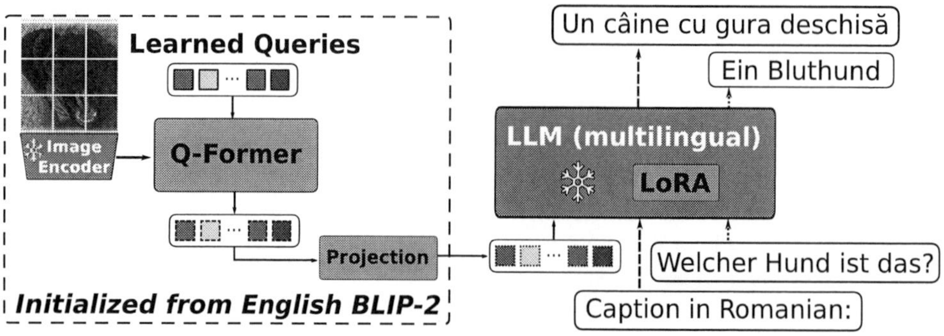

Figure 1: The mBLIP architecture: A Q-Former encodes the image in learned query tokens which are projected to the LLM space. We initialize the Q-Former from a BLIP-2 model and *re-align* it to the multilingual LLM with a multilingual task mix. The image encoder and LLM (aside from LoRA weights) are frozen during training.

produce the question), we use VQAv2 (Goyal et al., 2017). Additionally, we split the conversations from LLaVA-Instruct-Conversation into separate VQA pairs. We use A-OKVQA (Schwenk et al., 2022), a knowledge-intensive VQA dataset with rationales behind the answers, to create data for two additional task variants: 1) given the question, generate the answer and the rationale behind it, 2) given the question and the answer, generate the rationale. Finally, we use ImageNet (Deng et al., 2009) with the multilingual labels from Babel-ImageNet (Geigle et al., 2023) framed as an open-ended QA task (with questions like *"What is in the image?"* and no predefined answer choices).

3. Matching: Inspired by image-text matching (Lu et al., 2019), where an encoder has to classify if caption and image match, we propose a *yes/no* matching task so that the model learns what is and what is not in the image to reduce hallucinations when interrogating for image content (Li et al., 2023b). For this, we use the Web CapFilt captions for "standard" caption matching with hard negatives. We also use the ImageNet examples with multilingual class labels, where the model has to predict if a given class is in the image or not.

Machine Translation: We translate the above English data with NLLB (Costa-jussà et al., 2022) (*nllb-200-distilled-1.3B*), a recent massively multilingual MT model that exhibits strong performance also for low(er)-resource languages. To extend the utility of mBLIP to languages beyond what is covered by existing multilingual evaluation benchmarks, we translate the English data to all languages from the mC4 corpora (Xue et al., 2021),[2] excluding only a handful of languages not supported by NLLB.[3] Our final training dataset thus covers 96 languages (English and 95 translation languages). Translating all English training instances to every target language would result in a 96 times larger dataset (w.r.t. the original English data) and, consequently, prohibitively expensive re-alignment training. We thus translate English instances to target languages in proportion to the languages' representation in mC4 (e.g., we translate 6% of English instances to German, because German represents 6% of the mC4 corpus). We do not translate the short answers in A-OKVQA nor most VQAv2 examples[4] because translating them without context is overly error-prone.

Output Language: Essential for multilingual models is control over the output language and minimizing language hallucinations (,i.e., output in an unwanted language) (Xue et al., 2021; Vu et al., 2022; Pfeiffer et al., 2023; Li and Murray, 2023). We achieve this by combining English prompts that explicitly specify the target language (e.g., *"Answer in French."*) and translating the instructions for image captioning and LLaVA (Liu et al., 2023b) to the target languages (other templates contain placeholders that make translation difficult).

4 Experiments

4.1 Evaluation Tasks and Setup

We evaluate our model on a range of languages on (1) classification-style VQA and image understanding tasks, where the model generates a short answer in response to a question or premise and (2) image captioning tasks, where the model de-

[2] tensorflow.org/datasets/catalog/c4#c4multilingual

[3] Excluded are (ISO-1/3 codes): *fy*, *haw*, *hmn*, *la*, and *co*.

[4] See §D.1 for details. In short, we limit to the top-1500 answers and use consistency with back-translations to filter incorrect translation. We also still use English half the time.

scribes an image. For VQA and image captioning, we ensured that no evaluation instances were used in re-alignment training. In contrast to VQA and image captioning, the model was not exposed to image understanding during re-alignment: these tasks thus test the model's cross-task generalization abilities. To generate outputs, we use beam search with the beam width of 5 and a length penalty of -1 for classification-style tasks to encourage short answers. We provide the exact instruction-tuning templates for each task/dataset in §D.2.

Image Captioning: XM3600 (Thapliyal et al., 2022) is a captioning dataset covering 36 languages, 3600 images, and $\sim$2 captions per image and language. xFlickrCo (Bugliarello et al., 2022) combines the 1000 Flickr30k (Plummer et al., 2015) test images with 1000 images from the MSCOCO (Lin et al., 2014) test split[5] and provides one new caption for each image in 8 languages. For the English xFlickrCo results, we use the standard Flickr30k test split (i.e., without MSCOCO images and with 5 reference captions per image). We use CIDEr (Vedantam et al., 2015) as the evaluation metric[6] For Chinese, Japanese, and Thai, which do not use white space for tokenization, we use the default spaCy 3.5.3 segmenter for the respective languages; our results on those languages are thus *not directly comparable* to previous work – which, unfortunately, does not disclose the used tokenizer (Thapliyal et al., 2022; Chen et al., 2022, 2023).

VQA: we leverage xGQA (Pfeiffer et al., 2022) and MaXM (Changpinyo et al., 2022), two VQA datasets with 8 and 7 languages, respectively. While answers in xGQA are in English (as only the original GQA (Hudson and Manning, 2019) questions were translated), answers in MaXM are in the language of the question. We evaluate our model in zero-shot inference (i.e., without any additional fine-tuning other than the VQA training included in the re-alignment mix) on both datasets. For xGQA, we additionally fine-tune the model on the training portion of the English GQA and perform cross-lingual zero-shot transfer.[7] We use exact match accuracy with open generation, that is, we do not constrain the generation to a fixed set of labels like, e.g., Zeng et al. (2023). For MaXM, an exact match to any one of the answer candidates is correct, as proposed by Changpinyo et al. (2022).

Image Understanding: XVNLI (Bugliarello et al., 2022; Xie et al., 2019) is a visual entailment task that covers 5 languages: given an image and a statement, the model has to decide if the image entails, contradicts or is neutral to the statement. MaRVL (Liu et al., 2021) is based on NLVR2 (Suhr et al., 2019) with new images and concepts spanning different cultures in 6 languages: given two images, the model has to decide if a statement is true or false. We *separately* encode the two images with the Q-Former and then concatenate their visual tokens together as input for the LLM. Like for xGQA, we evaluate the models on XVNLI and MaRVL with (1) zero-shot inference (i.e., no fine-tuning for XVNLI and MaRVL) and (2) supervised cross-lingual transfer: we fine-tune the re-aligned model on the English training portions (of XVNLI and NLVR2, respectively) and evaluate its performance on the test portions of target languages. We report the results in terms of exact match accuracy.

4.2 Implementation Details

Architecture: We initialize the mBLIP's ViT (EVA CLIP ViT-g/14 (Fang et al., 2022)) and Q-Former with the BLIP-2 Flan-T5-XL checkpoint. For the multilingual LLM, we experiment with mT0-XL and BLOOMZ-7B (Muennighoff et al., 2022), the instruction-tuned versions of mT5-XL (Xue et al., 2021) and BLOOM-7B (Scao et al., 2022). We use 8/4-bit quantization (Dettmers et al., 2022, 2023).

Warmup: Similar to Zhang et al. (2023); Liu et al. (2023b), we first train only the linear projection between the Q-Former and LLM. with 1M captions.

Re-Alignment Training: We train on the re-alignment task mixture for 80k steps (2 epochs), which takes 4 days (mT0) and 6 days (BLOOMZ) with 4 consumer-grade NVIDIA RTX 3090 cards.

Fine-tuning: We train 3 runs—reporting their average—and select the optimal checkpoint based only on the English validation data for *true* zero-shot cross-lingual transfer (Schmidt et al., 2022).

Full hyperparameters are listed in Appendix A.

4.3 Results

Baselines. We compare with various multilingual baselines: PaLI (Chen et al., 2022), PaLI-X (Chen et al., 2023), Thapliyal et al. (2022), LMCap (Ramos et al., 2023), UC2 (Zhou et al., 2021), Li et al. (2023c), CCLM (Zeng et al.,

[5]These captions were created from scratch and not by translating existing MSCOCO captions so this does not constitute leakage from the MSCOCO data of the training mix.

[6]Implementation: pycocoeval

[7]Note that by zero-shot cross-lingual transfer here we refer to the fact that the model has been fine-tuned only on the English GQA data; in re-alignment training, however, it has been exposed to VQA from other datasets.

Model	Train P.	Total P.	XM3600 en	XM3600 35-avg
Thapliyal et al. (2022) †	0.8B	0.8B	57.60	28.90
PaLI-3B †	3B	3B	92.80	47.00
PaLI-17B †	17B	17B	**98.10**	**53.60**
PaLI-X †	55B	55B	94.20	53.10
PaLI-X 0-shot	55B	55B	48.80	22.70
LMCap (Ramos et al., 2023)	0	3B	45.20	17.60
InstructBLIP Flan-T5-XL	107M	4.1B	85.22	1.10
Llava 1.5 7B	7B	7.3B	55.87	9.78
mBLIP mT0-XL	124M	4.9B	80.17	26.77
mBLIP BLOOMZ-7B	124M	8.3B	76.40	21.87

(a) mBLIP outperforms all models except those fine-tuned on MSCOCO translated to all 36 languages (†). Different tokenizers for *zh, ja, th* make results not perfectly comparable.

Model	Train P.	Total P.	xFlickrCo en	xFlickrCo 7-avg
InstructBLIP Flan-T5-XL	107M	4.1B	**84.71**	1.46
Llava 1.5 7B	7B	7.3B	64.47	22.23
mBLIP mT0-XL	124M	4.9B	77.00	**44.39**
mBLIP BLOOMZ-7B	124M	8.3B	76.75	42.11

(b) No multilingual baseline on xFlickrCo exists at the time of writing but mBLIP is competitive with English models.

Table 1: Captioning results (CIDEr) on XM3600 and xFlickrCo for English and other languages.

2023), Ernie-UniX2 (Shan et al., 2022), Changpinyo et al. (2022); and also evaluate two strong English Vision-LLMs (InstructBLIP (Dai et al., 2023) and Llava 1.5 (Liu et al., 2023a) (LLM is Vicuna 1.5 (Touvron et al., 2023; Chiang et al., 2023))).

Image Captioning. Table 1 summarizes our image captioning results. On XM3600 (Table 1a), mBLIP mT0 outperforms the (training-free) captioning pipeline LMCap (Ramos et al., 2023) as well as PaLI-X (in zero-shot inference): these results are very encouraging, considering that PaLI-X trains orders of magnitude more parameters (55B vs. 124M for mBLIP), on billions of multilingual vision-and-language examples. mBLIP, however, substantially trails the performance of the PaLI models fine-tuned on MSCOCO *with full translations to all 35 languages* (yielding 3× more training examples than we do from our entire re-alignment task mix). While mBLIP is also trained on MSCOCO with translated captions, PaLI models consume orders of magnitude more data in most languages, especially the low-resource ones. With proportionally less mBLIP training for lower-resource languages (according to the language-specific corpus portions in mC4), this yields especially large gains for PaLI models for low-resource languages; mBLIP is more competitive for high-resource languages like Spanish or German.

The English models show strong English results (as expected) but fail for other languages as they either do not generate captions in the target language or, for high-resource languages like German where captioning works, still underperform mBLIP.

We additionally evaluate on xFlickrCo (Table 1b). While we are the first to use it for multilingual captioning (in Bugliarello et al. (2022), it is used for image-text retrieval), on the English Flickr30k captions, mBLIP achieves performance that is comparable to that of the English LLMs while outclassing them for other languages.

Finally, between the two mBLIP models, the mT0 variant beats the BLOOMZ variant. We believe this is due to the fact that mT5 (the base LLM from which mT0 was derived) was trained on almost 3 times more text (1 trillion tokens vs. 366 billion) and in nearly twice as many languages as BLOOM (the LLM of BLOOMZ). On a handful of languages like Indonesian or Hindi, however, BLOOMZ outperforms mT0, suggesting that the choice of the mBLIP variant is language-specific.

VQA and Image Understanding. Table 2 summarizes the results on VQA and image understanding tasks. On xGQA, mBLIP (zero-shot) outperforms the UC2 model that has been fine-tuned on the GQA data (Zhou et al., 2021; Bugliarello et al., 2022) *for all target languages*. When fine-tuned, our mBLIP variants are only outperformed by CCLM (large) (Zeng et al., 2023); CCLM (large) trains nearly nine-times more parameters and leverages more multilingual pretraining data[8]. Crucially, however, CCLM resorts to constrained generation w.r.t. the available answers, which is an easier yet computationally much more demanding evaluation protocol than our open generation. mBLIP exhibits relatively poor zero-shot XVNLI performance, as it fails to predict the neutral class. After fine-tuning for XVNLI, however, mBLIP mT0 yields multilingual performance (over 4 languages) comparable to that of CCLM (large). The MaRVL zero-shot performance of mBLIP variants is surprisingly good, considering that they were never trained for any task involving multiple images as input; Zero-shot performance of mBLIP mT0 on MaRVL is comparable to that of multiple fine-tuned baselines. When also fine-tuned, mBLIP achieves state-of-the-art MaRVL results, on par with CCLM (large).

[8]CCLM is also initialized with the English X2-VLM (Zeng et al., 2022a) which is trained on >1B images; the BLIP-2 weights, from which we start the mBLIP training, in contrast, were trained using only 129M images.

Model	Train P.	Total P.	XVNLI en	XVNLI 4-avg	MaRVL en	MaRVL 5-avg	xGQA en	xGQA 7-avg	MaXM en	MaXM 6-avg
Fine-tuned on train split										
UC2 (Bugliarello et al., 2022)	270M	270M	76.38	62.05	70.56	57.28	55.19	29.35	—	—
Li et al. (2023c)	330M	330M	—	69.50	—	62.10	—	42.10	—	—
CCLM (4M) †	520M	520M	—	73.32	83.22	67.17	—	46.24	—	—
CCLM base	420M	420M	—	74.78	—	68.49	—	48.12	—	—
CCLM large	970M	970M	—	**78.95**	—	74.83	—	**56.25**	—	—
Ernie-UniX2	910M	910M	**87.73**	77.42	—	—	56.68	45.25	—	—
mBLIP mT0-XL	124M	4.9B	82.41	76.41	85.20	**75.13**	56.54	47.71	—	—
mBLIP BLOOMZ-7B	124M	8.3B	75.45	66.96	**86.69**	73.94	**57.89**	44.91	—	—
Zero-shot										
Changpinyo et al. (2022) ‡	1.5B	1.5B	—	—	—	—	41.50	39.44	36.60	42.42
PaLI-17B ‡	17B	17B	—	—	—	—	54.20	**50.77**	**56.40**	**57.27**
InstructBLIP Flan-T5-XL	107M	4.1B	**62.09**	48.65	—	—	48.23	18.63	55.03	1.4
Llava 1.5 7B *	7B	7.3B	56.43	49.33	—	—	***57.37**	*27.53	52.01	16.22
mBLIP mT0-XL	124M	4.9B	60.61	**57.65**	**67.26**	**66.66**	42.55	39.20	47.99	41.04
mBLIP BLOOMZ-7B	124M	8.3B	58.26	55.46	62.26	58.61	43.35	37.73	55.70	27.91

Table 2: VQA and image understanding results for English and averaged over all other languages: The metric is (exact match) accuracy with open generation for mBLIP & PaLI and constrained generation to a set of labels for CCLM on xGQA. **Bold** indicates the best score in each column. †: From (Zeng et al., 2022b) v1 (arXiv). ‡: Fine-tuned on VQAv2 translated to all MaXM & xGQA languages. *: GQA included in training data.

On MAXM, mBLIP mT0 (zero-shot) performs comparably to the 1.5B parameter baseline model of Changpinyo et al. (2022) but falls short of the performance of the huge PaLI-17B model. mBLIP BLOOMZ exhibits strong English performance, but surprisingly poor results for other languages. We should emphasize here that training on the translated VQAv2 answers is crucial: without it, the LLM consistently generate answers in English. Even though only ~25% of examples in VQAv2 have non-English answers, this is already sufficient to eliminate language hallucination, where the model only answers in English regardless of the instruction language[9].

The English Vision-LLMs, like in captioning, show strong results for English but fall behind in other languages. This is particular evident in MAXM, which has non-English answers (unlike xGQA and XVNLI) that the models fail to consistently generate. For high-resource languages like German, mBLIP still outperforms them, highlighting its strong multilingual capabilities.

Looking at results for individual languages on the three IGLUE tasks in Figure 2, we see that mBLIP with mT0 greatly improves cross-lingual transfer over prior work, especially for lower-resource languages: while CCLM and Ernie-UniX2 exhibit a gap of 20-25% on xGQA between the best and worst language (German and Bengali), the same gap is only 5% for our fine-tuned mBLIP. Similarly, on MaRVL, CCLM has a gap of 11% between Indonesian and Tamil, while the largest gap for mBLIP amounts to 2%. The same holds for XVNLI, but to a lesser degree: the largest gap between languages for mBLIP (mT0) is 4%, compared to 8% for CCLM/Ernie-UniX2. The BLOOMZ-based variant, however, exhibits much weaker transfer ability and has in fact larger gaps than prior work; this highlights the importance of deriving mBLIP from a strong multilingual LLM.

5 Ablation

We ablate the various components and design decisions for mBLIP, namely: 1) using our instruction mix compared to the 'classic' setting used for BLIP-2 with only image-caption data (using the 2M Web CapFilt examples as training data) and compared to the instruction mix translated following the mT5 language distribution, 2) using LoRA on (all) LLM matrices to better align the LLM to the visual input, and 3) using the warm-start where the projection between Q-Former and LLM is trained briefly in a preliminary stage before the full re-alignment training. We use the zero-shot results on xGQA, XVNLI, and XM3600 for evaluation. Results are shown in Table 3. In §C.1, we provide an additional ablation that investigates the effect of adding the

[9]Training with only English VQAv2 answers during re-alignment results in an mBLIP mT0 instances that achieves only 15.5% accuracy for 6-avg, due to the LLM predominantly generating English answers.

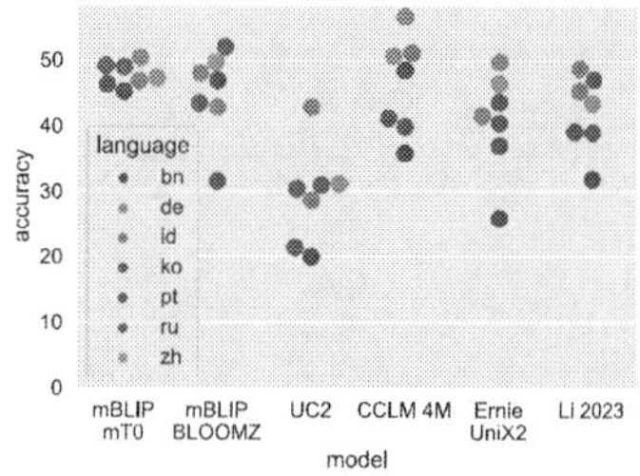

(a) xGQA

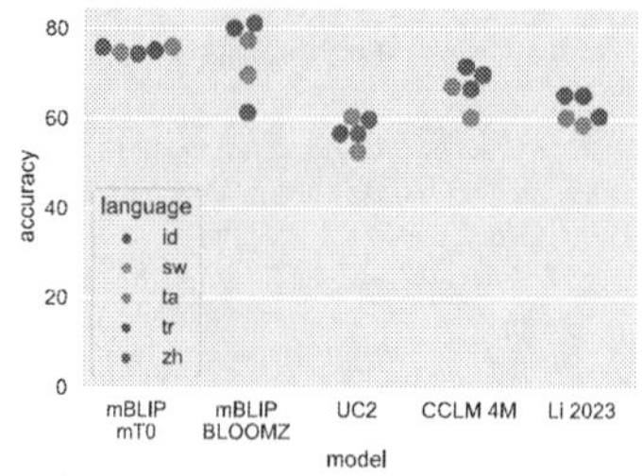

(b) MaRVL

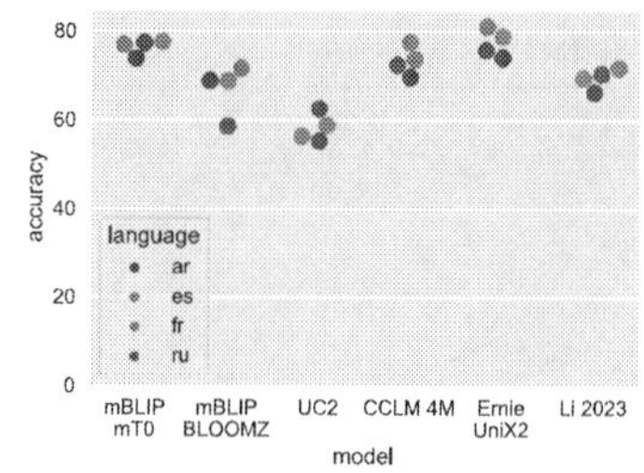

(c) XVNLI

Figure 2: Cross-lingual transfer of models fine-tuned on English. The smaller gap of mBLIP mT0 between high- and low-resource languages suggests better transfer capabilities. (CCLM 4M from (Zeng et al., 2022b) v1 on arXiv.)

matching tasks to re-alignment mix, demonstrating their effectiveness in reducing hallucinations. In §C.2, we consider the effect of our design choices on fine-tuned models (on xGQA).

Design & Training: For zero-shot xGQA and XVNLI, our complete mBLIP configuration yields the best performance. Not using LoRA (i.e., preventing any updates to the LLM) as well as training only on image captioning (compared to the full instruction task mix) both lead to substantially worse performance. Moreover, training (with LoRA) only for image captioning results in a model that does not follow instructions but merely generates captions, making it (zero-shot) useless for other tasks, barring task-specific fine-tuning. For image captioning, both the warm-start and LoRA fine-tuning boost the performance. Unsurprisingly, the re-alignment on captioning alone yields similar or slightly better captioning performance compared to re-alignment based on the full task mix (i.e., other tasks in the mix do not contribute to captioning ability of mBLIP). While the task mix brings additional quality captions from MSCOCO and LLaVA (in addition to the Web CapFilt examples), the model also has to learn the other tasks; Importantly, the ablation shows that including other tasks to re-alignment training does not harm the captioning abilities of the model.

Language Distribution: Our translation, proportional to the mC4 language distribution, results in 44% examples in English and, e.g., only 0.003% Lao examples. To test how the language distribution affects performance, we adopt another distribution: that of the mT5's pretraining corpus (reduces English to 8% and pushes Lao to 0.3%). As expected, this reduces the performance for higher-resource languages, and improves it for low(er)-resource languages. However, the changes in performance are relatively small. This would suggest that it is the language distribution of the (much larger) multilingual pretraining of the LLM that determines the downstream performance for individual languages rather than the language distribution of our (much smaller) re-alignment training.

Task Mix	LoRA	Warm-start	xGQA		XVNLI		XM3600	
			en	avg	en	avg	en	avg
✗	✗	✓	26.92	9.43	34.17	35.26	**86.78**	22.01
✗	all	✓	1.51	0.00	33.04	25.72	85.53	24.69
✓	✗	✓	37.33	33.77	52.02	54.26	84.14	21.35
✓	q,v	✓	39.83	36.50	57.91	55.22	81.45	23.46
✓	all	✗	40.89	37.88	57.74	54.50	80.68	24.38
mT5	all	✓	40.91	37.67	58.00	54.96	80.13	**25.85**
✓	all	✓	**41.98**	**38.46**	**58.87**	**56.28**	81.51	25.02

Table 3: Ablations for mBLIP (mT0) w.r.t.: (i) instruction mix (✓) vs. only captions (✗) (i.e., the 2M Web CapFilt examples) vs. instruction mix using the mT5 distribution (mT5), (ii) LoRA (no LoRA ✗, standard LoRA on query&value matrices, LoRA on all matrices), and (iii) using the warm-start where the projection between Q-Former and LLM is trained alone first. All model variants are trained (i.e., re-aligned) for 30k steps.

6 Conclusion

In this work, we presented mBLIP, the first modular and massively multilingual vision-language model based on multilingual LLMs. Using a small task mix from quality English datasets, made massively multilingual by means of MT, we re-align an English BLIP-2 model to an instruction-tuned multilingual LLM. Our approach is highly efficient in compute and data requirements and – using recent engineering advances such as 8-bit quantization – can be trained in a few days on consumer-grade hardware (e.g., NVIDIA RTX 3090 cards). We extensively evaluate mBLIP on multilingual vision-language tasks covering image captioning, visual QA, and image understanding to confirm the efficacy of our approach. Results render mBLIP comparable or better than state-of-the-art multilingual vision-language models and strong English Vision-LLMs, despite the fact that we train only a fraction of their number of parameters and on far less data.

Acknowledgements

This work was in part supported by the Alexander von Humboldt Foundation.

References

Jean-Baptiste Alayrac, Jeff Donahue, Pauline Luc, Antoine Miech, Iain Barr, Yana Hasson, Karel Lenc, Arthur Mensch, Katie Millican, Malcolm Reynolds, Roman Ring, Eliza Rutherford, Serkan Cabi, Tengda Han, Zhitao Gong, Sina Samangooei, Marianne Monteiro, Jacob Menick, Sebastian Borgeaud, Andrew Brock, Aida Nematzadeh, Sahand Sharifzadeh, Mikolaj Binkowski, Ricardo Barreira, Oriol Vinyals, Andrew Zisserman, and Karen Simonyan. 2022. Flamingo: a Visual Language Model for Few-Shot Learning. *CoRR*, abs/2204.14198. ArXiv: 2204.14198.

Jinze Bai, Shuai Bai, Shusheng Yang, Shijie Wang, Sinan Tan, Peng Wang, Junyang Lin, Chang Zhou, and Jingren Zhou. 2023. Qwen-VL: A Frontier Large Vision-Language Model with Versatile Abilities. *CoRR*, abs/2308.12966. ArXiv: 2308.12966.

Tom B. Brown, Benjamin Mann, Nick Ryder, Melanie Subbiah, Jared Kaplan, Prafulla Dhariwal, Arvind Neelakantan, Pranav Shyam, Girish Sastry, Amanda Askell, Sandhini Agarwal, Ariel Herbert-Voss, Gretchen Krueger, Tom Henighan, Rewon Child, Aditya Ramesh, Daniel M. Ziegler, Jeffrey Wu, Clemens Winter, Christopher Hesse, Mark Chen, Eric Sigler, Mateusz Litwin, Scott Gray, Benjamin Chess, Jack Clark, Christopher Berner, Sam McCandlish, Alec Radford, Ilya Sutskever, and Dario Amodei. 2020. Language Models are Few-Shot Learners. *arXiv:2005.14165 [cs]*. ArXiv: 2005.14165.

Emanuele Bugliarello, Fangyu Liu, Jonas Pfeiffer, Siva Reddy, Desmond Elliott, Edoardo Maria Ponti, and Ivan Vulic. 2022. IGLUE: A Benchmark for Transfer Learning across Modalities, Tasks, and Languages. In *International Conference on Machine Learning, ICML 2022, 17-23 July 2022, Baltimore, Maryland, USA*, volume 162 of *Proceedings of Machine Learning Research*, pages 2370–2392. PMLR.

Soravit Changpinyo, Linting Xue, Idan Szpektor, Ashish V. Thapliyal, Julien Amelot, Michal Yarom, Xi Chen, and Radu Soricut. 2022. MaXM: Towards multilingual visual question answering. *arXiv preprint arXiv:2209.05401*.

Xi Chen, Josip Djolonga, Piotr Padlewski, Basil Mustafa, Soravit Changpinyo, Jialin Wu, Carlos Riquelme Ruiz, Sebastian Goodman, Xiao Wang, Yi Tay, Siamak Shakeri, Mostafa Dehghani, Daniel Salz, Mario Lucic, Michael Tschannen, Arsha Nagrani, Hexiang Hu, Mandar Joshi, Bo Pang, Ceslee Montgomery, Paulina Pietrzyk, Marvin Ritter, A. J. Piergiovanni, Matthias Minderer, Filip Pavetic, Austin Waters, Gang Li, Ibrahim Alabdulmohsin, Lucas Beyer, Julien Amelot, Kenton Lee, Andreas Peter Steiner, Yang Li, Daniel Keysers, Anurag Arnab, Yuanzhong Xu, Keran Rong, Alexander Kolesnikov, Mojtaba Seyedhosseini, Anelia Angelova, Xiaohua Zhai, Neil Houlsby, and Radu Soricut. 2023. PaLI-X: On Scaling up a Multilingual Vision and Language Model. *CoRR*, abs/2305.18565. ArXiv: 2305.18565.

Xi Chen, Xiao Wang, Soravit Changpinyo, A. J. Piergiovanni, Piotr Padlewski, Daniel Salz, Sebastian Goodman, Adam Grycner, Basil Mustafa, Lucas Beyer, Alexander Kolesnikov, Joan Puigcerver, Nan Ding, Keran Rong, Hassan Akbari, Gaurav Mishra, Linting Xue, Ashish Thapliyal, James Bradbury, Weicheng Kuo, Mojtaba Seyedhosseini, Chao Jia, Burcu Karagol Ayan, Carlos Riquelme, Andreas Steiner, Anelia Angelova, Xiaohua Zhai, Neil Houlsby, and Radu Soricut. 2022. PaLI: A Jointly-Scaled Multilingual Language-Image Model. *CoRR*, abs/2209.06794. ArXiv: 2209.06794.

Yen-Chun Chen, Linjie Li, Licheng Yu, Ahmed El Kholy, Faisal Ahmed, Zhe Gan, Yu Cheng, and Jingjing Liu. 2020. UNITER: UNiversal Image-TExt Representation Learning. In *Computer Vision - ECCV 2020 - 16th European Conference, Glasgow, UK, August 23-28, 2020, Proceedings, Part XXX*, volume 12375 of *Lecture Notes in Computer Science*, pages 104–120. Springer.

Wei-Lin Chiang, Zhuohan Li, Zi Lin, Ying Sheng, Zhanghao Wu, Hao Zhang, Lianmin Zheng, Siyuan Zhuang, Yonghao Zhuang, Joseph E. Gonzalez, Ion Stoica, and Eric P. Xing. 2023. Vicuna: An open-source chatbot impressing gpt-4 with 90%* chatgpt quality.

Hyung Won Chung, Le Hou, Shayne Longpre, Barret Zoph, Yi Tay, William Fedus, Eric Li, Xuezhi Wang, Mostafa Dehghani, Siddhartha Brahma, Albert Webson, Shixiang Shane Gu, Zhuyun Dai, Mirac Suzgun, Xinyun Chen, Aakanksha Chowdhery, Sharan Narang, Gaurav Mishra, Adams Yu, Vincent Y. Zhao, Yanping Huang, Andrew M. Dai, Hongkun Yu, Slav Petrov, Ed H. Chi, Jeff Dean, Jacob Devlin, Adam Roberts, Denny Zhou, Quoc V. Le, and Jason Wei. 2022. Scaling Instruction-Finetuned Language Models. *CoRR*, abs/2210.11416. ArXiv: 2210.11416.

Alexis Conneau, Kartikay Khandelwal, Naman Goyal, Vishrav Chaudhary, Guillaume Wenzek, Francisco Guzmán, Edouard Grave, Myle Ott, Luke Zettlemoyer, and Veselin Stoyanov. 2020. Unsupervised Cross-lingual Representation Learning at Scale. In *Proceedings of the 58th Annual Meeting of the Association for Computational Linguistics, ACL 2020, Online, July 5-10, 2020*, pages 8440–8451. Association for Computational Linguistics.

Marta R. Costa-jussà, James Cross, Onur Çelebi, Maha Elbayad, Kenneth Heafield, Kevin Heffernan, Elahe Kalbassi, Janice Lam, Daniel Licht, Jean Maillard, Anna Sun, Skyler Wang, Guillaume Wenzek, Al Youngblood, Bapi Akula, Loïc Barrault, Gabriel Mejia Gonzalez, Prangthip Hansanti, John Hoffman, Semarley Jarrett, Kaushik Ram Sadagopan, Dirk Rowe, Shannon Spruit, Chau Tran, Pierre Andrews, Necip Fazil Ayan, Shruti Bhosale, Sergey Edunov, Angela Fan, Cynthia Gao, Vedanuj Goswami, Francisco Guzmán, Philipp Koehn, Alexandre Mourachko, Christophe Ropers, Safiyyah Saleem, Holger Schwenk, and Jeff Wang. 2022. No Language Left Behind: Scaling Human-Centered Machine Translation. *CoRR*, abs/2207.04672. ArXiv: 2207.04672.

Wenliang Dai, Junnan Li, Dongxu Li, Anthony Meng Huat Tiong, Junqi Zhao, Weisheng Wang, Boyang Li, Pascale Fung, and Steven C. H. Hoi. 2023. InstructBLIP: Towards General-purpose Vision-Language Models with Instruction Tuning. *CoRR*, abs/2305.06500. ArXiv: 2305.06500.

J. Deng, W. Dong, R. Socher, L. Li, Kai Li, and Li Fei-Fei. 2009. ImageNet: A large-scale hierarchical image database. In *2009 IEEE Conference on Computer Vision and Pattern Recognition*, pages 248–255.

Tim Dettmers, Mike Lewis, Younes Belkada, and Luke Zettlemoyer. 2022. LLM.int8(): 8-bit Matrix Multiplication for Transformers at Scale. *CoRR*, abs/2208.07339. ArXiv: 2208.07339.

Tim Dettmers, Artidoro Pagnoni, Ari Holtzman, and Luke Zettlemoyer. 2023. QLoRA: Efficient Finetuning of Quantized LLMs. *CoRR*, abs/2305.14314. ArXiv: 2305.14314.

Jacob Devlin, Ming-Wei Chang, Kenton Lee, and Kristina Toutanova. 2019. BERT: Pre-training of Deep Bidirectional Transformers for Language Understanding. In *Proceedings of the 2019 Conference of the North American Chapter of the Association for Computational Linguistics: Human Language Technologies, NAACL-HLT 2019, Minneapolis, MN, USA, June 2-7, 2019, Volume 1 (Long and Short Papers)*, pages 4171–4186. Association for Computational Linguistics.

Alexey Dosovitskiy, Lucas Beyer, Alexander Kolesnikov, Dirk Weissenborn, Xiaohua Zhai, Thomas Unterthiner, Mostafa Dehghani, Matthias Minderer, Georg Heigold, Sylvain Gelly, Jakob Uszkoreit, and Neil Houlsby. 2020. An Image is Worth 16x16 Words: Transformers for Image Recognition at Scale. *arXiv preprint*, abs/2010.11929. _eprint: 2010.11929.

Yuxin Fang, Wen Wang, Binhui Xie, Quan Sun, Ledell Wu, Xinggang Wang, Tiejun Huang, Xinlong Wang, and Yue Cao. 2022. EVA: exploring the limits of masked visual representation learning at scale. *CoRR*, abs/2211.07636.

Samir Yitzhak Gadre, Gabriel Ilharco, Alex Fang, Jonathan Hayase, Georgios Smyrnis, Thao Nguyen, Ryan Marten, Mitchell Wortsman, Dhruba Ghosh, Jieyu Zhang, Eyal Orgad, Rahim Entezari, Giannis Daras, Sarah M. Pratt, Vivek Ramanujan, Yonatan Bitton, Kalyani Marathe, Stephen Mussmann, Richard Vencu, Mehdi Cherti, Ranjay Krishna, Pang Wei Koh, Olga Saukh, Alexander Ratner, Shuran Song, Hannaneh Hajishirzi, Ali Farhadi, Romain Beaumont, Sewoong Oh, Alex Dimakis, Jenia Jitsev, Yair Carmon, Vaishaal Shankar, and Ludwig Schmidt. 2023. DataComp: In search of the next generation of multimodal datasets. *CoRR*, abs/2304.14108. ArXiv: 2304.14108.

Peng Gao, Jiaming Han, Renrui Zhang, Ziyi Lin, Shijie Geng, Aojun Zhou, Wei Zhang, Pan Lu, Conghui He, Xiangyu Yue, Hongsheng Li, and Yu Qiao. 2023. LLaMA-Adapter V2: Parameter-Efficient Visual Instruction Model. *CoRR*, abs/2304.15010. ArXiv: 2304.15010.

Gregor Geigle, Radu Timofte, and Goran Glavas. 2023. Babel-ImageNet: Massively Multilingual Evaluation of Vision-and-Language Representations. *CoRR*, abs/2306.08658. ArXiv: 2306.08658.

Y. Goyal, T. Khot, D. Summers-Stay, D. Batra, and D. Parikh. 2017. Making the V in VQA Matter: Elevating the Role of Image Understanding in Visual Question Answering. In *2017 IEEE Conference on Computer Vision and Pattern Recognition (CVPR)*, pages 6325–6334.

Edward J. Hu, Yelong Shen, Phillip Wallis, Zeyuan Allen-Zhu, Yuanzhi Li, Shean Wang, Lu Wang, and Weizhu Chen. 2022. LoRA: Low-Rank Adaptation of Large Language Models. In *The Tenth International Conference on Learning Representations, ICLR 2022, Virtual Event, April 25-29, 2022*. OpenReview.net.

Drew A. Hudson and Christopher D. Manning. 2019. GQA: A New Dataset for Real-World Visual Reasoning and Compositional Question Answering. In *IEEE Conference on Computer Vision and Pattern Recognition, CVPR 2019, Long Beach, CA, USA, June 16-20, 2019*, pages 6700–6709. Computer Vision Foundation / IEEE.

A. Karpathy and L. Fei-Fei. 2017. Deep Visual-Semantic Alignments for Generating Image Descriptions. *IEEE Transactions on Pattern Analysis and Machine Intelligence*, 39(4):664–676.

Junnan Li, Dongxu Li, Silvio Savarese, and Steven C. H. Hoi. 2023a. BLIP-2: Bootstrapping Language-Image Pre-training with Frozen Image Encoders and Large Language Models. *CoRR*, abs/2301.12597. ArXiv: 2301.12597.

Junnan Li, Dongxu Li, Caiming Xiong, and Steven C. H. Hoi. 2022. BLIP: Bootstrapping Language-Image Pre-training for Unified Vision-Language Understanding and Generation. In *International Conference on Machine Learning, ICML 2022, 17-23*

July 2022, Baltimore, Maryland, USA, volume 162 of *Proceedings of Machine Learning Research*, pages 12888–12900. PMLR.

Junnan Li, Ramprasaath R. Selvaraju, Akhilesh Deepak Gotmare, Shafiq R. Joty, Caiming Xiong, and Steven C. H. Hoi. 2021. Align before Fuse: Vision and Language Representation Learning with Momentum Distillation. *arXiv preprint*, abs/2107.07651. ArXiv: 2107.07651.

Tianjian Li and Kenton Murray. 2023. Why Does Zero-Shot Cross-Lingual Generation Fail? An Explanation and a Solution. *CoRR*, abs/2305.17325. ArXiv: 2305.17325.

Xiujun Li, Xi Yin, Chunyuan Li, Pengchuan Zhang, Xiaowei Hu, Lei Zhang, Lijuan Wang, Houdong Hu, Li Dong, Furu Wei, Yejin Choi, and Jianfeng Gao. 2020. Oscar: Object-Semantics Aligned Pre-training for Vision-Language Tasks. In *Computer Vision - ECCV 2020 - 16th European Conference, Glasgow, UK, August 23-28, 2020, Proceedings, Part XXX*, volume 12375 of *Lecture Notes in Computer Science*, pages 121–137. Springer.

Yifan Li, Yifan Du, Kun Zhou, Jinpeng Wang, Wayne Xin Zhao, and Ji-Rong Wen. 2023b. Evaluating Object Hallucination in Large Vision-Language Models. *CoRR*, abs/2305.10355. ArXiv: 2305.10355.

Zejun Li, Zhihao Fan, Jingjing Chen, Qi Zhang, Xuanjing Huang, and Zhongyu Wei. 2023c. Unifying cross-lingual and cross-modal modeling towards weakly supervised multilingual vision-language pre-training. In *Proceedings of the 61st Annual Meeting of the Association for Computational Linguistics (Volume 1: Long Papers)*, pages 5939–5958, Toronto, Canada. Association for Computational Linguistics.

Tsung-Yi Lin, Michael Maire, Serge J. Belongie, James Hays, Pietro Perona, Deva Ramanan, Piotr Dollár, and C. Lawrence Zitnick. 2014. Microsoft COCO: Common Objects in Context. In *Computer Vision - ECCV 2014 - 13th European Conference, Zurich, Switzerland, September 6-12, 2014, Proceedings, Part V*, volume 8693 of *Lecture Notes in Computer Science*, pages 740–755. Springer.

Fangyu Liu, Emanuele Bugliarello, Edoardo Maria Ponti, Siva Reddy, Nigel Collier, and Desmond Elliott. 2021. Visually Grounded Reasoning across Languages and Cultures. In *Proceedings of the 2021 Conference on Empirical Methods in Natural Language Processing, EMNLP 2021, Virtual Event / Punta Cana, Dominican Republic, 7-11 November, 2021*, pages 10467–10485. Association for Computational Linguistics.

Haotian Liu, Chunyuan Li, Yuheng Li, and Yong Jae Lee. 2023a. Improved Baselines with Visual Instruction Tuning. *CoRR*, abs/2310.03744. ArXiv: 2310.03744.

Haotian Liu, Chunyuan Li, Qingyang Wu, and Yong Jae Lee. 2023b. Visual Instruction Tuning. *CoRR*, abs/2304.08485. ArXiv: 2304.08485.

Ilya Loshchilov and Frank Hutter. 2019. Decoupled Weight Decay Regularization. In *7th International Conference on Learning Representations, ICLR 2019, New Orleans, LA, USA, May 6-9, 2019*. OpenReview.net.

Jiasen Lu, Dhruv Batra, Devi Parikh, and Stefan Lee. 2019. ViLBERT: Pretraining Task-Agnostic Visiolinguistic Representations for Vision-and-Language Tasks. In *Advances in Neural Information Processing Systems 32: Annual Conference on Neural Information Processing Systems 2019, NeurIPS 2019, December 8-14, 2019, Vancouver, BC, Canada*, pages 13–23.

Niklas Muennighoff, Thomas Wang, Lintang Sutawika, Adam Roberts, Stella Biderman, Teven Le Scao, M. Saiful Bari, Sheng Shen, Zheng Xin Yong, Hailey Schoelkopf, Xiangru Tang, Dragomir Radev, Alham Fikri Aji, Khalid Almubarak, Samuel Albanie, Zaid Alyafeai, Albert Webson, Edward Raff, and Colin Raffel. 2022. Crosslingual Generalization through Multitask Finetuning. *CoRR*, abs/2211.01786. ArXiv: 2211.01786.

Minheng Ni, Haoyang Huang, Lin Su, Edward Cui, Taroon Bharti, Lijuan Wang, Dongdong Zhang, and Nan Duan. 2021. M3P: Learning Universal Representations via Multitask Multilingual Multimodal Pre-Training. In *IEEE Conference on Computer Vision and Pattern Recognition, CVPR 2021, virtual, June 19-25, 2021*, pages 3977–3986. Computer Vision Foundation / IEEE.

OpenAI. 2023. GPT-4 technical report. *CoRR*, abs/2303.08774.

Long Ouyang, Jeffrey Wu, Xu Jiang, Diogo Almeida, Carroll L. Wainwright, Pamela Mishkin, Chong Zhang, Sandhini Agarwal, Katarina Slama, Alex Ray, John Schulman, Jacob Hilton, Fraser Kelton, Luke Miller, Maddie Simens, Amanda Askell, Peter Welinder, Paul F. Christiano, Jan Leike, and Ryan Lowe. 2022. Training language models to follow instructions with human feedback. In *NeurIPS*.

Jonas Pfeiffer, Gregor Geigle, Aishwarya Kamath, Jan-Martin O. Steitz, Stefan Roth, Ivan Vulic, and Iryna Gurevych. 2022. xGQA: Cross-Lingual Visual Question Answering. In *Findings of the Association for Computational Linguistics: ACL 2022, Dublin, Ireland, May 22-27, 2022*, pages 2497–2511. Association for Computational Linguistics.

Jonas Pfeiffer, Francesco Piccinno, Massimo Nicosia, Xinyi Wang, Machel Reid, and Sebastian Ruder. 2023. mmT5: Modular Multilingual Pre-Training Solves Source Language Hallucinations. *CoRR*, abs/2305.14224. ArXiv: 2305.14224.

Bryan A. Plummer, Liwei Wang, Chris M. Cervantes, Juan C. Caicedo, Julia Hockenmaier, and Svetlana Lazebnik. 2015. Flickr30k Entities: Collecting Region-to-Phrase Correspondences for Richer Image-to-Sentence Models. In *2015 IEEE International Conference on Computer Vision, ICCV 2015, Santiago, Chile, December 7-13, 2015*, pages 2641–2649.

Rita Ramos, Bruno Martins, and Desmond Elliott. 2023. LMCap: Few-shot Multilingual Image Captioning by Retrieval Augmented Language Model Prompting. *CoRR*, abs/2305.19821. ArXiv: 2305.19821.

Anna Rohrbach, Lisa Anne Hendricks, Kaylee Burns, Trevor Darrell, and Kate Saenko. 2018. Object Hallucination in Image Captioning. In *Proceedings of the 2018 Conference on Empirical Methods in Natural Language Processing, Brussels, Belgium, October 31 - November 4, 2018*, pages 4035–4045. Association for Computational Linguistics.

Victor Sanh, Albert Webson, Colin Raffel, Stephen H. Bach, Lintang Sutawika, Zaid Alyafeai, Antoine Chaffin, Arnaud Stiegler, Arun Raja, Manan Dey, M. Saiful Bari, Canwen Xu, Urmish Thakker, Shanya Sharma Sharma, Eliza Szczechla, Taewoon Kim, Gunjan Chhablani, Nihal V. Nayak, Debajyoti Datta, Jonathan Chang, Mike Tian-Jian Jiang, Han Wang, Matteo Manica, Sheng Shen, Zheng Xin Yong, Harshit Pandey, Rachel Bawden, Thomas Wang, Trishala Neeraj, Jos Rozen, Abheesht Sharma, Andrea Santilli, Thibault Févry, Jason Alan Fries, Ryan Teehan, Teven Le Scao, Stella Biderman, Leo Gao, Thomas Wolf, and Alexander M. Rush. 2022. Multitask Prompted Training Enables Zero-Shot Task Generalization. In *The Tenth International Conference on Learning Representations, ICLR 2022, Virtual Event, April 25-29, 2022*. OpenReview.net.

Teven Le Scao, Angela Fan, Christopher Akiki, Ellie Pavlick, Suzana Ilic, Daniel Hesslow, Roman Castagné, Alexandra Sasha Luccioni, François Yvon, Matthias Gallé, Jonathan Tow, Alexander M. Rush, Stella Biderman, Albert Webson, Pawan Sasanka Ammanamanchi, Thomas Wang, Benoît Sagot, Niklas Muennighoff, Albert Villanova del Moral, Olatunji Ruwase, Rachel Bawden, Stas Bekman, Angelina McMillan-Major, Iz Beltagy, Huu Nguyen, Lucile Saulnier, Samson Tan, Pedro Ortiz Suarez, Victor Sanh, Hugo Laurençon, Yacine Jernite, Julien Launay, Margaret Mitchell, Colin Raffel, Aaron Gokaslan, Adi Simhi, Aitor Soroa, Alham Fikri Aji, Amit Alfassy, Anna Rogers, Ariel Kreisberg Nitzav, Canwen Xu, Chenghao Mou, Chris Emezue, Christopher Klamm, Colin Leong, Daniel van Strien, David Ifeoluwa Adelani, and et al. 2022. BLOOM: A 176B-Parameter Open-Access Multilingual Language Model. *CoRR*, abs/2211.05100. ArXiv: 2211.05100.

Fabian David Schmidt, Ivan Vulić, and Goran Glavaš. 2022. Don't stop fine-tuning: On training regimes for few-shot cross-lingual transfer with multilingual language models. In *Proceedings of the 2022 Conference on Empirical Methods in Natural Language Processing*, pages 10725–10742.

Christoph Schuhmann, Romain Beaumont, Richard Vencu, Cade Gordon, Ross Wightman, Mehdi Cherti, Theo Coombes, Aarush Katta, Clayton Mullis, Mitchell Wortsman, Patrick Schramowski, Srivatsa Kundurthy, Katherine Crowson, Ludwig Schmidt, Robert Kaczmarczyk, and Jenia Jitsev. 2022. LAION-5B: An open large-scale dataset for training next generation image-text models. *CoRR*, abs/2210.08402. ArXiv: 2210.08402.

Dustin Schwenk, Apoorv Khandelwal, Christopher Clark, Kenneth Marino, and Roozbeh Mottaghi. 2022. A-OKVQA: A benchmark for visual question answering using world knowledge. In *Computer Vision - ECCV 2022 - 17th European Conference, Tel Aviv, Israel, October 23-27, 2022, Proceedings, Part VIII*, volume 13668 of *Lecture Notes in Computer Science*, pages 146–162. Springer.

Bin Shan, Yaqian Han, Weichong Yin, Shuohuan Wang, Yu Sun, Hao Tian, Hua Wu, and Haifeng Wang. 2022. ERNIE-UniX2: A Unified Cross-lingual Cross-modal Framework for Understanding and Generation. *CoRR*, abs/2211.04861. ArXiv: 2211.04861.

Piyush Sharma, Nan Ding, Sebastian Goodman, and Radu Soricut. 2018. Conceptual Captions: A Cleaned, Hypernymed, Image Alt-text Dataset For Automatic Image Captioning. In *Proceedings of the 56th Annual Meeting of the Association for Computational Linguistics (Volume 1: Long Papers)*, pages 2556–2565, Melbourne, Australia. Association for Computational Linguistics.

Alane Suhr, Stephanie Zhou, Ally Zhang, Iris Zhang, Huajun Bai, and Yoav Artzi. 2019. A Corpus for Reasoning about Natural Language Grounded in Photographs. In *Proceedings of the 57th Conference of the Association for Computational Linguistics, ACL 2019, Florence, Italy, July 28- August 2, 2019, Volume 1: Long Papers*, pages 6418–6428. Association for Computational Linguistics.

Rohan Taori, Ishaan Gulrajani, Tianyi Zhang, Yann Dubois, Xuechen Li, Carlos Guestrin, Percy Liang, and Tatsunori B. Hashimoto. 2023. Stanford alpaca: An instruction-following llama model. `https://github.com/tatsu-lab/stanford_alpaca`.

Ashish V. Thapliyal, Jordi Pont-Tuset, Xi Chen, and Radu Soricut. 2022. Crossmodal-3600: A Massively Multilingual Multimodal Evaluation Dataset. In *Proceedings of the 2022 Conference on Empirical Methods in Natural Language Processing, EMNLP 2022, Abu Dhabi, United Arab Emirates, December 7-11, 2022*, pages 715–729. Association for Computational Linguistics.

Hugo Touvron, Thibaut Lavril, Gautier Izacard, Xavier Martinet, Marie-Anne Lachaux, Timothée Lacroix,

Baptiste Rozière, Naman Goyal, Eric Hambro, Faisal Azhar, Aurélien Rodriguez, Armand Joulin, Edouard Grave, and Guillaume Lample. 2023. LLaMA: Open and Efficient Foundation Language Models. *CoRR*, abs/2302.13971. ArXiv: 2302.13971.

Maria Tsimpoukelli, Jacob Menick, Serkan Cabi, S. M. Ali Eslami, Oriol Vinyals, and Felix Hill. 2021. Multimodal Few-Shot Learning with Frozen Language Models. *arXiv:2106.13884 [cs]*. ArXiv: 2106.13884.

Ashish Vaswani, Noam Shazeer, Niki Parmar, Jakob Uszkoreit, Llion Jones, Aidan N. Gomez, Lukasz Kaiser, and Illia Polosukhin. 2017. Attention is All you Need. In *Advances in Neural Information Processing Systems 30: Annual Conference on Neural Information Processing Systems 2017, December 4-9, 2017, Long Beach, CA, USA*, pages 5998–6008.

Ramakrishna Vedantam, C. Lawrence Zitnick, and Devi Parikh. 2015. Cider: Consensus-based image description evaluation. In *IEEE Conference on Computer Vision and Pattern Recognition, CVPR 2015, Boston, MA, USA, June 7-12, 2015*, pages 4566–4575. IEEE Computer Society.

Tu Vu, Aditya Barua, Brian Lester, Daniel Cer, Mohit Iyyer, and Noah Constant. 2022. Overcoming Catastrophic Forgetting in Zero-Shot Cross-Lingual Generation. In *Proceedings of the 2022 Conference on Empirical Methods in Natural Language Processing, EMNLP 2022, Abu Dhabi, United Arab Emirates, December 7-11, 2022*, pages 9279–9300. Association for Computational Linguistics.

Wenhui Wang, Hangbo Bao, Li Dong, Johan Bjorck, Zhiliang Peng, Qiang Liu, Kriti Aggarwal, Owais Khan Mohammed, Saksham Singhal, Subhojit Som, and Furu Wei. 2022. Image as a foreign language: Beit pretraining for all vision and vision-language tasks. *CoRR*, abs/2208.10442.

Zirui Wang, Jiahui Yu, Adams Wei Yu, Zihang Dai, Yulia Tsvetkov, and Yuan Cao. 2021. SimVLM: Simple Visual Language Model Pretraining with Weak Supervision. *arXiv:2108.10904 [cs]*. ArXiv: 2108.10904.

Thomas Wolf, Lysandre Debut, Victor Sanh, Julien Chaumond, Clement Delangue, Anthony Moi, Pierric Cistac, Tim Rault, Rémi Louf, Morgan Funtowicz, Joe Davison, Sam Shleifer, Patrick von Platen, Clara Ma, Yacine Jernite, Julien Plu, Canwen Xu, Teven Le Scao, Sylvain Gugger, Mariama Drame, Quentin Lhoest, and Alexander M. Rush. 2020. Transformers: State-of-the-art natural language processing. In *Proceedings of the 2020 Conference on Empirical Methods in Natural Language Processing: System Demonstrations*, pages 38–45, Online. Association for Computational Linguistics.

Ning Xie, Farley Lai, Derek Doran, and Asim Kadav. 2019. Visual Entailment: A Novel Task for Fine-Grained Image Understanding. *arXiv preprint*, abs/1901.06706. _eprint: 1901.06706.

Canwen Xu, Daya Guo, Nan Duan, and Julian J. McAuley. 2023. Baize: An Open-Source Chat Model with Parameter-Efficient Tuning on Self-Chat Data. *CoRR*, abs/2304.01196. ArXiv: 2304.01196.

Linting Xue, Noah Constant, Adam Roberts, Mihir Kale, Rami Al-Rfou, Aditya Siddhant, Aditya Barua, and Colin Raffel. 2021. mT5: A Massively Multilingual Pre-trained Text-to-Text Transformer. In *Proceedings of the 2021 Conference of the North American Chapter of the Association for Computational Linguistics: Human Language Technologies, NAACL-HLT 2021, Online, June 6-11, 2021*, pages 483–498. Association for Computational Linguistics.

Qinghao Ye, Haiyang Xu, Guohai Xu, Jiabo Ye, Ming Yan, Yiyang Zhou, Junyang Wang, Anwen Hu, Pengcheng Shi, Yaya Shi, Chenliang Li, Yuanhong Xu, Hehong Chen, Junfeng Tian, Qian Qi, Ji Zhang, and Fei Huang. 2023. mPLUG-Owl: Modularization Empowers Large Language Models with Multimodality. *CoRR*, abs/2304.14178. ArXiv: 2304.14178.

Jiahui Yu, Zirui Wang, Vijay Vasudevan, Legg Yeung, Mojtaba Seyedhosseini, and Yonghui Wu. 2022. Coca: Contrastive captioners are image-text foundation models. *Transactions on Machine Learning Research*, 2022.

Yan Zeng, Xinsong Zhang, Hang Li, Jiawei Wang, Jipeng Zhang, and Wangchunshu Zhou. 2022a. X\(^\mbox2\)-VLM: All-In-One Pre-trained Model For Vision-Language Tasks. *CoRR*, abs/2211.12402. ArXiv: 2211.12402.

Yan Zeng, Wangchunshu Zhou, Ao Luo, Ziming Cheng, and Xinsong Zhang. 2023. Cross-View Language Modeling: Towards Unified Cross-Lingual Cross-Modal Pre-training. In *Proceedings of the 61st Annual Meeting of the Association for Computational Linguistics (Volume 1: Long Papers), ACL 2023, Toronto, Canada, July 9-14, 2023*, pages 5731–5746. Association for Computational Linguistics.

Yan Zeng, Wangchunshu Zhou, Ao Luo, and Xinsong Zhang. 2022b. Cross-View Language Modeling: Towards Unified Cross-Lingual Cross-Modal Pre-training. *CoRR*, abs/2206.00621. ArXiv: 2206.00621.

Ao Zhang, Hao Fei, Yuan Yao, Wei Ji, Li Li, Zhiyuan Liu, and Tat-Seng Chua. 2023. Transfer Visual Prompt Generator across LLMs. *CoRR*, abs/2305.01278. ArXiv: 2305.01278.

Susan Zhang, Stephen Roller, Naman Goyal, Mikel Artetxe, Moya Chen, Shuohui Chen, Christopher Dewan, Mona Diab, Xian Li, Xi Victoria Lin, et al. 2022. Opt: Open pre-trained transformer language models. *arXiv preprint arXiv:2205.01068*.

Mingyang Zhou, Luowei Zhou, Shuohang Wang, Yu Cheng, Linjie Li, Zhou Yu, and Jingjing Liu. 2021. UC2: Universal Cross-Lingual Cross-Modal Vision-and-Language Pre-Training. In *IEEE Conference on Computer Vision and Pattern Recognition, CVPR 2021, virtual, June 19-25, 2021*, pages 4155–4165. Computer Vision Foundation / IEEE.

Deyao Zhu, Jun Chen, Xiaoqian Shen, Xiang Li, and Mohamed Elhoseiny. 2023. MiniGPT-4: Enhancing Vision-Language Understanding with Advanced Large Language Models. *CoRR*, abs/2304.10592. ArXiv: 2304.10592.

A Training and Evaluation Details

Training: We use AdamW (Loshchilov and Hutter, 2019) with weight decay 0.1, learning rate 2e-4 for LoRA and 1e-5 for other parameters; 1000 warm-up steps before a cosine decay; batch size 128 (accomplished via gradient accumulation and checkpointing); we limit the max. target sequence length to 128. For LoRA, which we apply to *all* LLM matrices and not just the query and value matrices of self-attention heads, we set $r = 8, \alpha = 16$ and use dropout with the 0.05 rate.
Warmup: We use 1M captions to train for 8k steps with a learning rate of 5e-3 (and otherwise the same hyperparameters).
Fine-tuning: We train 3 runs (seeds)—reporting their average—for 5/10/20 epochs and batch size 256/128/128 for xGQA/XVNLI/MaRVL, respectively. Other hyperparameters are identical as in re-alignment training. We merge the LoRA weights obtained in instruction-based re-alignment training into the LLM before we execute LoRA fine-tuning for downstream tasks.

Implementation: We use the HuggingFace Transformers (Wolf et al., 2020) and PEFT[10] libraries for model implementation and LoRA, respectively.

B Qualitative Analysis

In addition to the quantitative evaluation on multilingual datasets of previous sections, we perform a qualitative analysis to better understand the model's visual and multilingual capabilities. As shown in Figure 3, our model can understand instructions in a wide range of languages and describe diverse images, perform simple reasoning, and correctly ground images to world knowledge in those languages. We also see some limitations. The capabilities decrease notably for lower-resource languages. The Urdu example is only a short sentence despite asking for a detailed description. Similarly, the Azerbaijani caption is completely incorrect (and non-sensical), while the model produces a meaningful caption for that same image in many other languages. The Romanian example shows the limitations of the model's world knowledge as the famous portrait of Vlad III is not recognized (neither when asked in Romanian nor in English with various prompts). Finally, the Croatian example shows the difficulty with controlling the output language that we also saw in the quantitative evaluation: despite being asked in Croatian, the model answers in (related but still distinct) Slovenian.

[10]https://github.com/huggingface/peft

	POPE						CHAIR			
	random		popular		adversarial		short		long	
	acc	yes	acc	yes	acc	yes	C_i	C_s	C_i	C_s
without matching	71.00	74%	70.40	75%	63.70	81%	3.10	4.50	14.90	54.70
with matching	87.30	48%	83.30	52%	76.10	59%	2.40	3.50	14.10	50.50

Table 4: Effect of decision tasks on object hallucination evaluated with POPE (Li et al., 2023b) and CHAIR (Rohrbach et al., 2018) metrics. POPE results improve because the yes-bias is reduced but CHAIR metrics for both short and long captions barely decrease (lower is better).

C Further Ablation Results

C.1 Matching Tasks and Object Hallucinations

We introduce the matching tasks with the aim of reducing object hallucinations. We evaluate the effectiveness of the measure using two hallucination metrics for English: POPE (Li et al., 2023b) uses interrogative questions ("Is there X in the image?") with random, popular, and adversarial negative objects (using MSCOCO images and object annotations), reporting accuracy and the portion of 'yes' answers due to a yes-bias in most models. CHAIR (Rohrbach et al., 2018) generates captions from MSCOCO images (we use 1k images from the validation split) and then counts hallucinated objects using MSCOCO object annotations. They report the ratio of hallucinated object instances C_i, that is of all occurring objects, how many are hallucinated, and the ratio of sentences with hallucinations C_s. We generate both short (Prompt: *Caption in English:*) and long captions (Prompt: *Describe the image in English with as much detail as possible.*). We train two models for 30k steps with and without the matching tasks and report results in Table 4. The matching tasks greatly improve results for POPE as they reduce the yes-bias but CHAIR metrics decrease only slightly. This seems to indicate that while matching tasks help for the interrogative POPE questions, they do not noticeably decrease

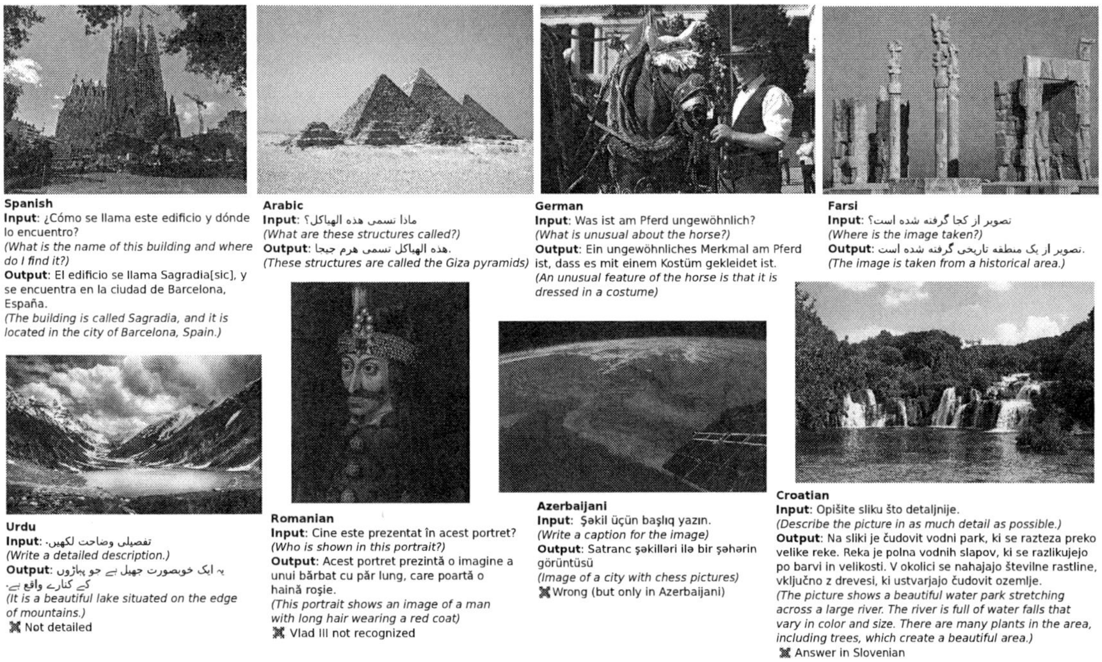

Figure 3: Multilingual examples (with translations from Google Translate in parentheses). While the first row shows that the model can handle captioning and QA in diverse languages, the second row shows some failure cases. We use beam search (5 beams) with a repetition penalty of 1.5.

Task Mix	LoRA	Warm-start	xGQA (finetune) en	avg
✗	✗	✓	**56.68**	46.50
✗	all	✓	56.55	44.78
✓	✗	✓	55.72	45.36
✓	all	✓	56.47	**46.84**

Table 5: Ablations for mBLIP (mT0) w.r.t.: (i) instruction mix (✓) vs. only captions (✗) (i.e., the 2M Web CapFilt examples) vs. instruction mix using the mT5 distribution (mT5), (ii) LoRA (no LoRA ✗, standard LoRA on query&value matrices, LoRA on all matrices), and (iii) using the warm-start where the projection between Q-Former and LLM is trained alone first. All model variants are trained (i.e., re-aligned) for 30k steps.

hallucinations when generating captions.

C.2 Fine-tuning

Looking at supervised xGQA fine-tuning, we observe that all variants exhibit similar performance, regardless of the instruction-tuning (i.e., re-alignment) design. The variants re-aligned only via captioning (first two rows of Table 3) yield even slightly better results than the variants for which VQA was included in the re-alignment training. Contradicting the findings of Dai et al. (2023), our results suggest that more 'complex' instruction-based re-alignment involving a multitude of tasks brings limited gains (if any) for downstream task with large fine-tuning data.

D Training and Evaluation Data and Template Details

D.1 Training

We present our instruction mix in more detail with Table 6 listing the datasets with additional information, and Table 7 listing the templates used to generate the examples.

D.2 Evaluation

We present the templates used for the different evaluation datasets in Table 8. Templates for XVNLI and MaRVL are selected using English validation zero-shot performance. XVNLI templates are based on Muennighoff et al. (2022).

We use the same templates for training and inference.

Dataset	Tasks	#Images	#Examples	Details
Web CapFilt (Li et al., 2022)	Image captioning	2.27m	2.27m	Subset of the CC3M+CC12M+SBU Web CapFilt dataset[11]. Like Liu et al. (2023b), we use spaCy to extract noun phrases and then sample from every phrase with at least 10 occurrences at most 30 captions for a subset covering diverse concepts.
	Caption Matching	600k	600k	Subset of our image captioning data. We use the CLIP ViT-L/14 by Gadre et al. (2023) to encode images and text to find similar examples for hard negatives. We match every image randomly with the correct caption (50% of the time) or with equal probability a random caption or the 3/10/30/100/300 most similar caption for a mix of very hard to random negatives.
MSCOCO (Lin et al., 2014)	Image Captioning	83k†	414k	Karpathy training split of MSCOCO (Karpathy and Fei-Fei, 2017) with 5 captions per image.
VQAv2 (Goyal et al., 2017)	VQA, VQG	83k†	2×443k	Question-answer pairs with ∼5 questions per image. For VQA and VQG, each example is translated to a different language to increase language diversity. We use Google Translate to translate the most common 1500 answers to the 95 languages. We then back-translate them to English and keep only the translations where the back-translation is the original answer; this is to ensure that the answer is (likely) translated correctly. We randomly use either the translated or English answer when generating examples. 83k of the 443k examples have non-English answers.
A-OKVQA (Schwenk et al., 2022)	Rational generation, VQA with rational	11k†	2×33k	Knowledge-intense VQA questions with additional answer rationals. We generate examples for all three given rationales. We only use the subset of the training split overlapping with the MSCOCO training split. A-OKVQA examples are not translated to any language.
LLaVA (Liu et al., 2023b) detail	Image captioning	23k†	23k	Subset of LLaVA instructions with detailed multi-sentence image captions.
LLaVA (Liu et al., 2023b) conversations	VQA	56k†	219k	Subset of LLaVA instructions with multi-turn dialog; we split the dialogs into independent pairs and keep all pairs with an answer length of max. 3 sentences.
ImageNet (Deng et al., 2009) and Babel-ImageNet (Geigle et al., 2023)	VQA	300k	300k	Image classification framed as open-ended VQA tasks (i.e., no answer options are given). Babel-ImageNet provides partial translations of the ImageNet classes to the 95 languages. We select one image for every class+language combination (that is, we do not use the full training set).
	Matching	300k	300k	The model has to decide if a given ImageNet class is correctly in the image. We use the correct label or a random label with equal probability. This uses the same images as the VQA examples but shuffles the image-language pairs.
Total		2.65m	5.1m	

Table 6: Detailed information about the datasets used for training. †: Dataset uses MSCOCO images.

<table>
<tr><th>Task</th><th>Templates</th></tr>
<tr><td>Image Captioning</td><td>Caption the image in $LANGUAGE.
Short $LANGUAGE image caption:
Image caption (in $LANGUAGE):
Briefly describe the image in $LANGUAGE.
Write a short $LANGUAGE image description.
Summarize the image in $LANGUAGE.
Caption the image.†
Short image caption:†
Briefly describe the image.†
Write a short image description.†
Summarize the image.†</td></tr>
<tr><td>Caption Matching
Question | Yes Answer | No Answer</td><td>Does "$CAPTION" accurately describe the image? | Yes, it does. | No, it does not.
Does the caption "$CAPTION" fit the picture? | Yes, it does. | No, it does not.
Does "$CAPTION" correctly summarize the image? | Yes, it does. | No, it does not.
Is "$CAPTION" a good image description? | Yes, it is. | No, it is not.
Is "$CAPTION" a correct caption for the picture? | Yes, it is. | No, it is not.
Is the caption "$CAPTION" a good match for the image? | Yes, it is. | No, it is not.
Decide if the following caption accurately describes the image: $CAPTION. Answer: | Yes, it does. | No, it does not.
Is this caption a good match for the picture? $CAPTION. Answer: | Yes, it is. | No, it is not.
Decide if this caption is a correct summary of the image: $CAPTION. | Yes, it is. | No, it is not.
Would "$CAPTION" be a good image summary? | Yes, it would. | No, it would not.
Would the caption "$CAPTION" fit the picture? | Yes, it would. | No, it would not.
Could you use "$CAPTION" as a caption for the image? | Yes, you could. | No, you could not.</td></tr>
<tr><td>VQA</td><td>$QUESTION. Short English answer:
Question: $QUESTION. Brief answer (in $LANGUAGE):
Give a short answer in $LANGUAGE to the following question. $QUESTION
Answer the provided question in $LANGUAGE with three words or less. $QUESTION
What is the $LANGUAGE answer to this question? $QUESTION
Briefly answer in $LANGUAGE. $QUESTION</td></tr>
<tr><td>VQG</td><td>Given the image, generate a question in $LANGUAGE whose answer is: $ANSWER. Question:
Based on the image, create a question (in $LANGUAGE) for which the answer is "$ANSWER".
From the image provided, come up with a $LANGUAGE question that leads to the reply: $ANSWER. Question:
What is a $LANGUAGE question for the image with the answer "$ANSWER"?
Given the image, what would be a $LANGUAGE question that has as answer "$ANSWER"?</td></tr>
<tr><td>VQA with rational (instruction templates)</td><td>Reason the answer to the following question. $QUESTION
Use reasoning to come to an answer for this question. $QUESTION
Think step-by-step to answer this question. $QUESTION
Answer the following question and explain your answer. $QUESTION
$QUESTION What is the answer and why?</td></tr>
<tr><td>VQA with rational (label templates)</td><td>$ANSWER. So the answer is $RATIONAL
$ANSWER so $RATIONAL
$RATIONAL. This means the answer is $ANSWER
The answer is $ANSWER because $RATIONAL.
$ANSWER because $RATIONAL.</td></tr>
<tr><td>Rational Generation</td><td>Question: $QUESTION Answer: $ANSWER. Explanation:
Question: $QUESTION: Answer: $ANSWER. The reason is because
The answer to the question "$QUESTION" is "$ANSWER". Why?
Why is the answer to the question "$QUESTION" "$ANSWER"?
Explain why the answer to the question "$QUESTION" is "$ANSWER"</td></tr>
<tr><td>ImageNet Classification</td><td>What is the main focus of the image? Short $LANGUAGE answer:
What is in the image? Answer briefly in $LANGUAGE.
This is an image of what? Answer briefly in $LANGUAGE.
What is the central object in the image? Give a short $LANGUAGE answer.
The focus of the image is on what? Short $LANGUAGE answer:
Question: This is an image of what? Answer briefly in $LANGUAGE.
What is at the center of this picture? Short $LANGUAGE answer:
Give a short answer in $LANGUAGE to the following question. What is the main thing shown in the image?
Complete the sentence in $LANGUAGE. This is a photo of a
Name the main thing of this photo in $LANGUAGE:
In less than 3 words in $LANGUAGE, what can be seen in this image?</td></tr>
<tr><td>ImageNet Matching
Question | Yes Answer | No Answer</td><td>Does this image show a $LABEL? | Yes, it does. | No, it does not.
Is there a $LABEL? | Yes, there is. | No, there is not.
Are there any $LABEL in the picture? | Yes, there are. | No, there are not.
Does the image contain a $LABEL? | Yes, it does. | No, it does not.
Yes or no, there is a $LABEL in the photo. | Yes | No
Yes or no, there is a $LABEL visible in the image. | Yes | No
Does this picture have a $LABEL in it? | Yes, it does. | No, it does not.
Can you see a $LABEL in the image? | Yes, you can. | No, you can not.</td></tr>
</table>

Table 7: Templates used for the training examples. For each example, we randomly select one template. LLaVA examples are used as is since they are already in instruction form. †: Template is translated to the 95 languages.

Dataset	Template
xFlickrCo, XM3600	Caption in $LANGUAGE:
xGQA, MaXM	Question: $QUESTION Short answer in $LANGUAGE:
XVNLI	Is it guaranteed true that "$HYPOTHESIS"? Yes, no, or maybe? Answer in English:
MaRVL	Based on the two images, is it correct to say "$STATEMENT"? Yes or no? Answer in English.

Table 8: Templates used for evaluation. XVNLI labels 'entailment', 'contradiction', and 'neutral' are remapped to 'yes', 'no', 'maybe', respectively; MaRVL labels 'true' & 'false' are remapped to 'yes', 'no', respectively.

E Image Attribution

Image attribution for Figure 3 in order of appearance from top-left to bottom-right:

- Sagrada Familia: https://de.wikipedia.org/wiki/Datei:Sagrada_Familia_8-12-21_(1).jpg. Canaan, CC BY-SA 4.0 https://creativecommons.org/licenses/by-sa/4.0, via Wikimedia Commons
- Giza: https://commons.wikimedia.org/wiki/File:All_Gizah_Pyramids.jpg. Ricardo Liberato, CC BY-SA 2.0 https://creativecommons.org/licenses/by-sa/2.0, via Wikimedia Commons
- Oktoberfest Kutsche: https://de.wikipedia.org/wiki/Datei:Oktoberfest-Kutscher.jpg. Hullbr3ach, CC BY-SA 2.5 https://creativecommons.org/licenses/by-sa/2.5, via Wikimedia Commons
- Gate of All Nations, Persepolis: https://commons.wikimedia.org/wiki/File:Gate_of_All_Nations,_Persepolis.jpg. Alborzagros, CC BY-SA 3.0 https://creativecommons.org/licenses/by-sa/3.0, via Wikimedia Commons
- Lake saif ul malook: https://en.wikipedia.org/wiki/File:Lake-saif-ul-malook_Pakistan.jpg. Ayesha.great, CC BY-SA 4.0 https://creativecommons.org/licenses/by-sa/4.0, via Wikimedia Commons
- Vlad III: https://en.wikipedia.org/wiki/File:Vlad_Tepes_002.jpg. Portrait of Vlad III the Impaler
- Satellite: https://en.wikipedia.org/wiki/File:Jaz_Murian_satellite.jpg. NASA, Public domain, via Wikimedia Commons
- Krk waterfalls: https://commons.wikimedia.org/wiki/File:Krk_waterfalls.jpg. Version13 at English Wikipedia, Public domain, via Wikimedia Commons

F Full Results

	bn	de	id	ko	pt	ru	zh
mBLIP mT0-XL (zero-shot)	38.51	40.53	38.34	38.31	40.15	39.59	38.99
mBLIP mT0-XL (finetuned)	45.21	50.32	46.80	46.28	49.12	48.94	47.28
mBLIP BLOOMZ-7B (zero-shot)	38.96	37.04	39.99	29.06	41.78	37.55	39.72
mBLIP BLOOMZ-7B (finetuned)	46.90	42.86	48.01	31.56	51.99	43.44	49.64

Table 9: Results in all languages for xGQA. Finetuned results are averaged over 3 seeds.

	ar	es	fr	ru
mBLIP mT0-XL (zero-shot)	56.26	57.57	58.52	58.26
mBLIP mT0-XL (finetuned)	73.80	77.62	76.87	77.33
mBLIP BLOOMZ-7B (zero-shot)	56.26	56.17	57.74	51.65
mBLIP BLOOMZ-7B (finetuned)	68.90	68.81	71.57	58.55

Table 10: Results in all languages for XVNLI. Finetuned results are averaged over 3 seeds.

	id	sw	ta	tr	zh
mBLIP mT0-XL (zero-shot)	64.89	64.80	69.65	68.05	65.91
mBLIP mT0-XL (finetuned)	75.09	74.61	75.93	74.32	75.72
mBLIP BLOOMZ-7B (zero-shot)	59.13	56.23	60.31	57.71	59.68
mBLIP BLOOMZ-7B (finetuned)	80.08	69.71	77.38	61.38	81.16

Table 11: Results in all languages for MaRVL. Finetuned results are averaged over 3 seeds.

	fr	hi	iw	ro	th	zh
mBLIP mT0-XL (zero-shot)	40.61	48.30	35.56	41.74	53.97	26.06
mBLIP BLOOMZ-7B (zero-shot)	22.87	52.38	18.41	31.83	17.22	24.76

Table 12: Results in all languages for MaXM.

	de	es	id	ja	ru	tr	zh
mBLIP mT0-XL (zero-shot)	58.23	64.86	47.44	33.27	41.77	35.18	29.98
mBLIP BLOOMZ-7B (zero-shot)	50.50	64.89	54.42	29.10	38.36	25.08	32.42

Table 13: Results in all languages for xFlickrCo.

	ar	bn	cs	da	de	el	es	fa	fi	fil	fr	he
mBLIP mT0-XL (zero-shot)	21.13	11.30	31.84	44.19	32.48	23.36	62.61	0.00	16.78	17.71	57.64	18.69
mBLIP BLOOMZ-7B (zero-shot)	27.78	16.12	21.77	25.25	30.04	14.12	60.03	13.84	4.69	1.99	60.42	7.16

	hi	hr	hu	id	it	ja	ko	mi	nl	no	pl	pt
mBLIP mT0-XL (zero-shot)	16.07	5.18	21.54	38.53	45.19	33.23	10.39	4.09	55.72	46.15	31.22	53.13
mBLIP BLOOMZ-7B (zero-shot)	24.91	2.13	10.99	45.29	42.40	25.43	2.54	0.02	45.54	25.01	20.65	47.79

	quz	ro	ru	sv	sw	te	th	tr	uk	vi	zh
mBLIP mT0-XL (zero-shot)	1.08	21.71	27.25	48.38	11.76	11.20	41.93	22.64	0.00	39.24	13.48
mBLIP BLOOMZ-7B (zero-shot)	0.02	17.62	22.83	31.77	8.45	8.65	8.16	14.21	8.97	54.29	14.65

Table 14: Results in all languages for XM3600.

LMPT: Prompt Tuning with Class-Specific Embedding Loss for Long-Tailed Multi-Label Visual Recognition

Peng Xia[1], **Di Xu**[2], **Ming Hu**[1], **Lie Ju**[1], **Zongyuan Ge**[1]
[1]Monash University, [2]Imperial College London
richard.peng.xia@gmail.com, zongyuan.ge@monash.edu

Abstract

Long-tailed multi-label visual recognition (LTML) task is a highly challenging task due to the label co-occurrence and imbalanced data distribution. In this work, we propose a unified framework for LTML, namely prompt tuning with class-specific embedding loss (LMPT), capturing the semantic feature interactions between categories by combining text and image modality data and improving the performance synchronously on both head and tail classes. Specifically, LMPT introduces the embedding loss function with class-aware soft margin and re-weighting to learn class-specific contexts with the benefit of textual descriptions (captions), which could help establish semantic relationships between classes, especially between the head and tail classes. Furthermore, taking into account the class imbalance, the distribution-balanced loss is adopted as the classification loss function to further improve the performance on the tail classes without compromising head classes. Extensive experiments are conducted on VOC-LT and COCO-LT datasets, which demonstrates that our method significantly surpasses the previous state-of-the-art methods and zero-shot CLIP in LTML. Our codes are fully public at https://github.com/richard-peng-xia/LMPT.

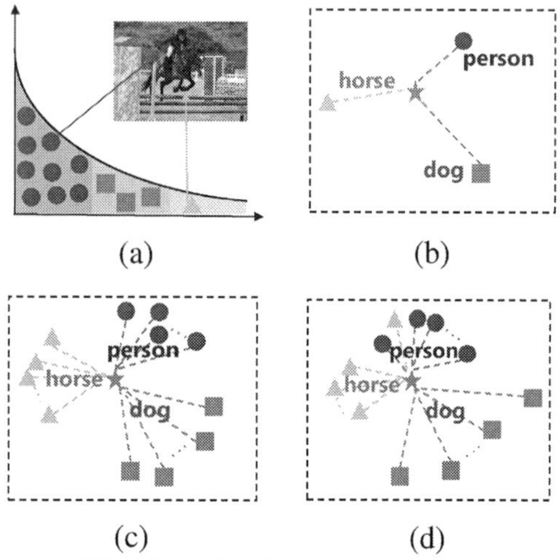

Figure 1: The class distribution is long-tailed and the VLM compares image embeddings⋆ to text embeddings●■▲ of the class, which means the closer the distance between the embeddings of different modalities, the higher the probability that the category of the text embeddings matches the image. (a) Person and horse in the image belong to the head classes and the tail classes respectively. (b) Zero-Shot CLIP. (c) Exsiting Prompt Tuning *w/o* CSE loss. (d) LMPT (Ours) *w/* CSE loss.

1 Introduction

Long-tailed multi-label visual recognition (LTML) (Wu et al., 2020; Guo and Wang, 2021) is a common and practical task owing to the highly imbalanced data distribution (Zhang et al., 2021b) and diverse objects of real-world images (Wang et al., 2017; Ju et al., 2023). Compared with long-tailed recognition and multi-label recognition tasks, LTML is more complex and challenging, because it requires capturing multiple categories and the label co-occurrence in individual images (Chen et al., 2019a), which needs to compensate for the negative impacts caused by the long-tailed distribution (i.e., *low performance on the tail classes*).

Several approaches have been proposed to address the LTML problem from different perspectives, such as re-sampling (Buda et al., 2018; Dong et al., 2017; Guo and Wang, 2021), re-weighting (Cao et al., 2019; Wu et al., 2020) and modeling more powerful structures (Chen et al., 2019a; Wang et al., 2016, 2017). Despite their great contributions, these works neglect to take into account two crucial aspects. *First of all*, the importance of semantic feature interaction between classes to capture label co-occurrence. However, these methods are limited to balancing the distribution of categories from the perspective of samples, without considering the feature correlation between different classes. *Second*, synchronous improvements in head-to-tail category performance, while some of these works improve the performance of tail classes at the expense of the head classes.

Recently, graphic models have been introduced

to model the semantic label correlation in a few works (Chen et al., 2019a; Wang et al., 2016), whereas these works are complex and are modeling label dependencies mainly based on the image modality without additional semantic information from other modal data. Vision-language models (VLMs) (Radford et al., 2021; Jia et al., 2021; Tian et al., 2022; Huang et al., 2022; Xia et al., 2024a) demonstrate the huge potential of text modality on semantic context feature for downstream visual tasks, especially for the prompt tuning methods (Schick and Schütze, 2021; Shin et al., 2020; Yao et al., 2021; Xia et al., 2023), which provide an efficient way to transfer pre-trained VLMs to downstream tasks by learning the task-specific prompts rather than finetuning the entire model. Nonetheless, the existing prompt tuning methods (Zhou et al., 2022b,a; Sun et al., 2022) for visual recognition simply minimize prediction errors using the classification loss (*e.g.*, cross-entropy loss) with respect to the learnable prompts, which may lead to learning general embeddings or inaccurate class-related embeddings. For instance, when presented with an image (Fig.1a) that contains both a head class [person] and a tail class [horse], the zero-shot method (Fig.1b) relies solely on the rich knowledge of the pre-trained VLMs to assess the similarity between the image and the word embeddings of the class names, while the existing prompt tuning method (Fig.1c) further learns more generalized prompt tokens to improve model performance. However, these methods do not consider the inter-class relationships, particularly between head and tail classes, which is a critical factor for LTML. This underscores the need for approaches that incorporate such relationships to improve performance in such scenarios.

Therefore, to address these issues, we present the class-specific embedding loss for **p**rompt **t**uning on **l**ong-tailed **m**ulti-label visual recognition, called LMPT. The abundance of image-caption data facilitates prompt learning that encompasses more nuanced and specific textual descriptions, as well as the semantic inter-dependencies between categories (Fig.1d) that share information, such as similar features or common descriptions. This attribute is particularly critical in the identification of both head and tail classes. More specifically, we propose the class-specific embedding loss to enhance the inclusivity of class-related embeddings within prompts. By gradually approaching the embeddings of the corresponding caption, our proposed approach enables prompt tokens to effectively judge the association between different classes with the aid of textual modality. Aiming for class imbalance and consistency improvements between head classes and tail classes, we integrate class-aware soft margin and re-weighting into the class-specific embedding loss, which serves to assign larger margins and more weights to tail classes. Notably, for images containing both head and tail classes, our approach outperforms visual models and current prompt tuning methods. Moreover, we adopt the distribution-balanced loss (Wu et al., 2020) as the classification loss. To sum up, the main contributions of this work include:

- We propose the LMPT framework to adapt pre-trained VLMs to tackle long-tailed multi-label visual recognition, where captions are easily accessible from public image-caption datasets or generated by powerful image-caption models (Wang et al., 2022).
- We present a novel class-specific embedding loss with class-aware soft margin and re-weighting to learn more fine-grained and class-related embeddings that build semantic relationships across head and tail classes with shared semantic information. Such design can benefit performance in tail classes and hard-to-recognize classes with the help of text modality.
- We verify the effectiveness of the proposed method by achieving new state-of-the-art (SOTA) results on two datasets, which outperform previous SOTA (Guo and Wang, 2021) by 9/6% and zero-shot CLIP by 6/2% on VOC-LT / COCO-LT.

2 Related Work

2.1 Long-Tailed Visual Recognition

Real-world training data usually exhibits long-tailed distribution (Zhang et al., 2021b), which presents a challenge for traditional methods due to the imbalanced class distribution. To address this problem, several approaches (Cui et al., 2022; Menon et al., 2020; Ouyang et al., 2016; Samuel and Chechik, 2021; Xia et al., 2024b) have been proposed from different aspects. One common method is to directly re-sample the training data to balance the class distribution (Drummond et al., 2003; Buda et al., 2018; Dong et al., 2017), by adjusting the sampling rate of head classes and tail

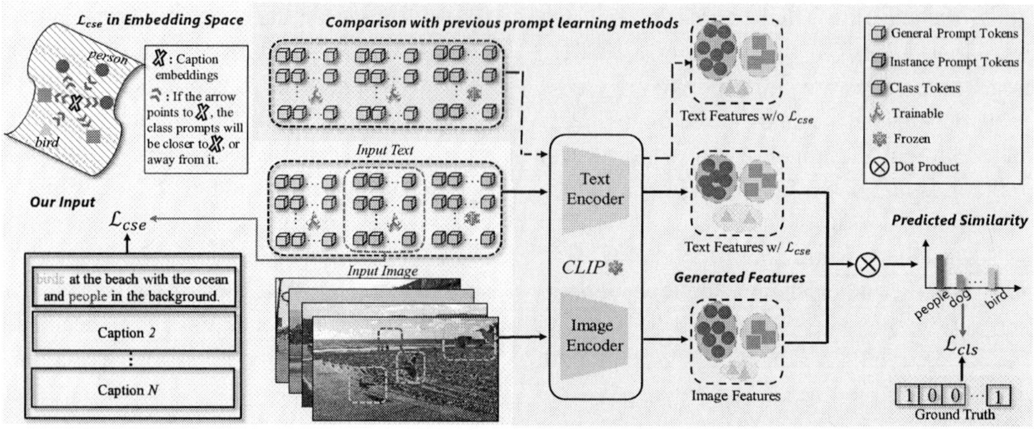

Figure 2: Overview of the architecture of our proposed method. The color blocks are defined as shown in Fig. 1.

classes, yet it might lead to the overfitting of tail classes. A better solution is to design re-weighted loss functions (Khan et al., 2017; Huang et al., 2016; Cao et al., 2019) that assign more weight to tail classes or ignore negative gradients (Tan et al., 2020) for tail classes. In addition, researchers also propose to use techniques such as transfer learning (Liu et al., 2019; Zhu and Yang, 2020) and self-supervised learning (Kang et al., 2020; Zhang et al., 2021a) to alleviate the class imbalance problem. Recently, some studies (Ma et al., 2021; Tian et al., 2022) also explore the possibility of text modality by refining visual-language representations on the long-tailed recognition tasks.

2.2 Multi-Label Visual Recognition

For multi-label visual recognition, some early methods include treating it as multiple binary image classifications (Tsoumakas and Katakis, 2007; Zhang and Zhou, 2013) or finding k-nearest neighbors (Zhang and Zhou, 2007). To locate regions of interest, some researchers (Wang et al., 2016, 2017) proposed to introduce recurrent neural networks (*e.g.*, RNN, LSTM) to learn a joint image-label embedding. In addition, Chen *et al.* (Chen et al., 2019a) proposed to model the label correlations by constructing a graph based on the label co-occurrence and Ye *et al.* (Ye et al., 2020) updated static graph to dynamic graph convolutional network (GCN) for robust representation. Wu *et al.* (Wu et al., 2020) proposed a distribution-balanced loss and Guo *et al.* (Guo and Wang, 2021) adopted collaborative training on the uniform and re-balanced samplings to alleviate the class imbalanced problem. There is also a popular trend to align between visual and textual features (Xu et al., 2022; Liu et al., 2021; Huang et al., 2022; Ridnik et al., 2023) for multi-label recognition.

2.3 Prompt Tuning for Vision-Language Models

Prompt tuning (Schick and Schütze, 2021; Shin et al., 2020; Yao et al., 2021) is a parameter-efficient technique used to utilize the representation ability of pre-trained vision-language models to achieve better performance instead of fine-tuning the whole model on downstream tasks. Meanwhile, large-scale vision-language models (*e.g.*, CLIP (Radford et al., 2021), ALIGN (Jia et al., 2021)) have demonstrated impressive power to learn visual and textual features. CoOp (Zhou et al., 2022b) learns soft prompts via minimizing the classification loss and CoCoOp (Zhou et al., 2022a) further formulates the prompts in an image-conditional way to improve its generalization to unseen classes. DualCoOp (Sun et al., 2022) firstly adapts CLIP to multi-label image recognition by learning pairs of positive and negative prompts for each class, then TaI-DPT (Guo et al., 2023) extracts both coarse-grained and fine-grained embedding by treating texts as images in prompt tuning. Different from the above work, LMPT focuses on exploring the transfer ability to address long-tailed multi-label visual recognition.

3 Methodology

In this section, we present our proposed prompting tuning method, *i.e.*, LMPT, for adapting pre-trained vision-language models for long-tailed multi-label visual recognition.

3.1 Preliminaries

Consider $\mathcal{D}$ as the dataset we use, N as the number of the dataset, C as the number of classes, and L as the fixed length of contexts for optimization. Then $(x^k, y^k, t^k) \in \mathcal{D}_{train}$, $k \in \{1, ..., N\}$, where x^k is an input single image, $y^k = [y_1^k, ..., y_C^k] \in \{0, 1\}^C$ is the multi-label ground-truth and $t^k = [t_1^k, ..., t_L^k]$ is the corresponding text embedding of text description (caption). But during the test phase, only $(x^k, y^k) \in \mathcal{D}_{test}$. Let $n_i = \sum_{k=1}^{N} y_i^k$ denote the number of training examples that contain class i. Please note that labels for computing the class-specific embedding loss need to be processed into $\tilde{y}^k = [\tilde{y}_1^k, ..., \tilde{y}_C^k] = [2 * y_1^k - 1, ..., 2 * y_C^k - 1] \in \{-1, 1\}^C$, where $\{-1, 1\}$ indicates negative and positive.

3.2 Approach Overview

In order to make effective use of the linguistic modality in the long-tailed multi-label visual recognition task, we propose a novel framework (*i.e.*, LMPT), as depicted in Fig. 2. Text encoder from the pre-trained CLIP is used to encode the prompts and text descriptions (captions) of images. Only the parameters in the prompts are optimized, while the text encoder and image encoder are both kept frozen. We introduce two sorts of trainable prompts to obtain class embedding, which are jointly optimized by the classification loss $\mathcal{L}_{cls}$ and class-specific embedding loss $\mathcal{L}_{cse}$. Details of the aforementioned loss functions will be introduced in the later sections.

3.3 Prompt Tuning

Formally, the vision-language model consists of an image encoder $\boldsymbol{f}(\cdot)$ and a text encoder $\boldsymbol{g}(\cdot)$. Following (Zhou et al., 2022a), a prompt is defined as:

$$o_i|_1^M = [\mathrm{V}]_1 [\mathrm{V}]_2 \cdots [\mathrm{V}]_m \cdots [\mathrm{V}]_M [\mathrm{CLASS}], \quad (1)$$

where $i \in \{1, ..., C\}$, $m \in \{1, ..., M\}$, the [CLASS] token is replaced by the specific class name (*e.g.*, "cat," "dog", "car"), each $[\mathrm{V}]_m$ is a learnable word embedding with the same dimension as normal word embeddings in the vocabulary (*i.e.*, 512 for CLIP), and M is a hyper-parameter specifying the number of context tokens. The prediction probability (classification output) z is then

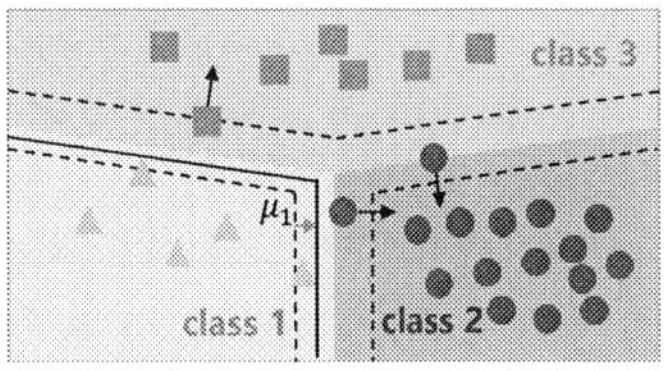

Figure 3: The class margins (dotted lines) are enforced for generated samples by updating the decision boundary with respect to class margins.

computed as:

$$p(y = i \mid x) = \frac{\exp\left(\cos\left(\boldsymbol{g}\left(o_i\right), \boldsymbol{f}\left(x\right)\right)/\tau\right)}{\sum_{j=1}^{C} \exp\left(\cos\left(\boldsymbol{g}\left(o_j\right), \boldsymbol{f}\left(x\right)\right)/\tau\right)}, \quad (2)$$

where τ is a temperature parameter learned by CLIP and $cos(\cdot, \cdot)$ represents cosine similarity.

3.4 Class-Specific Embedding Loss

We introduce the class-specific embedding (CSE) loss to optimize the trainable fine-grained instance prompts by learning from text embeddings of captions. It tries to minimize the cosine distance of matching patches and to increase the cosine distance of non-matching patches above the margin. Embedding loss is then computed as

$$\ell_{ebd} = \begin{cases} \Delta_i^k, & \text{if} \quad \tilde{y}_i^k = 1, \\ \max\left(0, \mu - \Delta_i^k\right), & \text{if} \quad \tilde{y}_i^k = -1, \end{cases} \quad (3)$$
$$\Delta_i^k = 1 - \cos\left(t_i^k, o_i|_m^M\right),$$

where μ is the margin factor. Intuitively the embedding loss penalizes positive (*i.e.*, prompts of matching classes) pairs that have large distances and negative (*i.e.*, prompts of non-matching classes) pairs that have small distance (less than μ).

LDAM (Cao et al., 2019) has inspired the development of a decision boundary that is both robust and generalizable, capable of accurately classifying features that vary within a certain range. However, when applied to long-tailed datasets characterized by a significant class imbalance, models tend to exhibit greater sensitivity to more frequent classes. As a result, the performance of these models in less frequent classes is often poor.

To address this issue, CSE loss employs the class-aware soft margin strategy to encourage the model to have the optimal trade-off between per-class margins by stimulating the minority classes to have larger margins, which can be viewed as regularization (Wei et al., 2018). More specifically, as illustrated in Fig. 3, blue samples (head classes) are classified incorrectly, and the model update gradient is shown with pointed arrows. Green samples (medium classes) are classified correctly outside of the margin and the gradient is shown. Intuitively, the embedding loss does not give special consideration to the minority categories, but with the help of class-aware soft margin, the trade-off of μ_1 (in Fig. 3) can be optimized by shifting the decision boundary to encourage the tail classes to have larger margins. So yellow samples (tail classes) are classified correctly outside of the original margin but within the enlarged margin, and the embedding loss has no gradient for these samples. Following the trade-off between the class margins, we adopt a class-aware margin for multiple classes of the form

$$\widetilde{\mu}_i \propto n_i^{-1/4} = \frac{\eta}{n_i^{1/4}}. \tag{4}$$

Here η is a hyper-parameter to be tuned. Therefore, when $y_i^k = -1$, the loss can be computed as $\max\left\{0, \widetilde{\mu}_i - \Delta_i^k\right\}$.

Meanwhile, our loss can be combined with a re-weighting strategy to be more efficient when it comes to long-tailed distribution data. We then define the reference weight based on the empirical class frequencies $\{n_1, ..., n_C\}$ on the training set:

$$w_i = \frac{(1/n_i)^\gamma}{\sum_{i=1}^{C} (1/n_i)^\gamma}, \tag{5}$$

where γ is a scale hyper-parameter to provide more flexibility. Hence, the re-weighted class-specific embedding loss is defined as:

$$\ell_{cse} = \begin{cases} w_i \Delta_i^k, & \text{if} \quad \tilde{y}_i^k = 1, \\ \max\left\{0, w_i\left(\widetilde{\mu}_i - \Delta_i^k\right)\right\}, & \text{if} \quad \tilde{y}_i^k = -1, \end{cases} \tag{6}$$

$$\mathcal{L}_{cse} = \frac{\sum_{k=1}^{N} \ell_{cse}}{N}. \tag{7}$$

The overall process of class-specific embedding loss is outlined in Algorithm 1.

3.5 Multi-Label Classification Loss

Our method can be easily combined with the existing multi-label classification loss functions (Ridnik et al., 2021; Lin et al., 2017; Cui et al., 2019; Wu et al., 2020), regardless of whether they are designed for long-tailed distributions or not. By

Algorithm 1: Class-Specific Embedding Loss

Input: Text embeddings of textual descriptions (captions) t, labels $\widetilde{y}$, prompt o

Output: Class-Specific Embedding Loss $\mathcal{L}_{cse}$

```
for k = 1, 2, ..., N do
    ℓ_cse = 0;
    for i = 1, 2, ..., C do
        Calculate class-aware soft margin μ̃_i by Eq. 4;
        Calculate weight w_i by Eq. 5;
        Calculate Δ_i^k = 1 − cos(t_i^k, o_i|_m^M);
        if ỹ_i^k = 1 then
            ℓ_cse = w_i Δ_i^k;
        else
            ℓ_cse = ReLU(w_i(μ̃_i − Δ_i^k));
Calculate L_cse by Eq. 7.
```

blending the classification loss functions with our proposed CSE loss, our method facilitates prompt learning of more refined class descriptions and semantic relationships between categories, particularly between head and tail classes.

In this study, we introduce the distribution-balanced loss (Wu et al., 2020) as the classification loss function, which can be formulated as:

$$r = \alpha + \sigma\left(\beta \times \left(\frac{\frac{1}{n_i}}{\sum_{i=1}^{C} \frac{1}{n_i}} - \theta\right)\right), \tag{8}$$

$$v_i = -\kappa \times -\log\left(\frac{1}{n_i/N} - 1\right), \tag{9}$$

$$\ell_{cls} = \begin{cases} -r\left(1 - q_i^k\right)^\gamma \log\left(q_i^k\right), & \text{if} \quad y_i^k = 1, \\ -\frac{r}{\zeta}\left(q_i^k\right)^\gamma \log\left(1 - q_i^k\right), & \text{if} \quad y_i^k = -1, \end{cases} \tag{10}$$

where $q_i^k = \sigma\left(z_i^k - v_i\right)$ is for positive instances, $q_i^k = \sigma\left(\zeta\left(z_i^k - v_i\right)\right)$ is for negative ones and $\alpha, \beta, \theta, \kappa, \zeta$ are hyperparameters. Then $\mathcal{L}_{cls} = \sum_{k=1}^{N} \ell_{cls}/N$.

Hence, the overall training loss can be written as:

$$\mathcal{L} = \lambda \mathcal{L}_{cls} + (1 - \lambda \mathcal{L}_{cse}), \tag{11}$$

where $\lambda \in [0, 1]$ is a hyperparameter to balance $\mathcal{L}_{cls}$ and $\mathcal{L}_{cse}$.

4 Experiment

4.1 Benchmark Setting

Following (Wu et al., 2020; Guo and Wang, 2021), we conduct experiments on two datasets for long-tailed multi-label visual recognition: VOC-LT and COCO-LT (Wu et al., 2020). They are artificially

Datasets	VOC-LT				COCO-LT			
Methods	total	head	medium	tail	total	head	medium	tail
RN-50								
ERM	70.86	68.91	80.20	65.31	41.27	48.48	49.06	24.25
RW	74.70	67.58	82.81	73.96	42.27	48.62	45.80	32.02
Focal Loss (Lin et al., 2017) ICCV'17	73.88	69.41	81.43	71.56	49.46	49.80	54.77	42.14
RS (Shen et al., 2016) ECCV'16	75.38	70.95	82.94	73.05	46.97	47.58	50.55	41.70
ML-GCN (Chen et al., 2019b) CVPR'19	68.92	70.14	76.41	62.39	44.24	44.04	48.36	38.96
OLTR (Liu et al., 2019) CVPR'19	71.02	70.31	79.80	64.95	45.83	47.45	50.63	38.05
LDAM (Cao et al., 2019) NeurIPS'19	70.73	68.73	80.38	69.09	40.53	48.77	48.38	22.92
CB Focal (Cui et al., 2019) CVPR'19	75.24	70.30	83.53	72.74	49.06	47.91	53.01	44.85
BBN (Zhou et al., 2020) CVPR'20	73.37	71.31	81.76	68.62	50.00	49.79	53.99	44.91
DB Focal (Wu et al., 2020) ECCV'20	78.94	73.22	84.18	79.30	53.55	51.13	57.05	51.06
LTML (Guo and Wang, 2021) CVPR'21	81.44	**75.68**	85.53	82.69	56.90	**54.13**	60.59	54.47
CLIP (Radford et al., 2021) ICML'21	84.30	63.60	88.03	97.03	56.19	35.73	60.52	68.45
CoOp (Zhou et al., 2022b) IJCV'22	81.34	65.10	81.54	93.37	54.94	38.06	56.67	67.51
CoCoOp (Zhou et al., 2022a) CVPR'22	78.63	64.33	80.51	87.94	46.02	36.02	50.57	48.82
DualCoOp (Sun et al., 2022) NeurIPS'22	81.03	66.45	80.53	92.33	53.11	40.48	55.20	62.11
TaI-DPT (Guo et al., 2023) CVPR'23	83.75	66.27	85.17	94.57	56.23	40.52	58.40	66.09
LMPT (ours)	85.44	66.62	88.11	97.86	58.97	41.87	61.60	69.60
ViT-B/16								
CLIP (Radford et al., 2021) ICML'21	85.77	66.52	88.93	97.83	60.17	38.52	65.06	72.28
CoOp (Zhou et al., 2022b) IJCV'22	86.02	67.71	88.79	97.67	60.68	41.97	63.18	73.85
CoCoOp (Zhou et al., 2022a) CVPR'22	84.47	64.58	87.82	96.88	61.49	39.81	64.63	76.42
LMPT (ours)	**87.88**	72.10	**89.26**	**98.49**	**66.19**	44.89	**69.80**	**79.08**

Table 1: mAP performance of the proposed method and comparison methods. Above the dotted line is the performance of image-only models and below is that of vision-language models.

sampled from two multi-label recognition benchmarks, PascalVOC (Everingham et al., 2015) and MS-COCO (Lin et al., 2014), respectively.

4.2 Experimental Settings

Metrics. As in (Liu et al., 2019), the classes are split into three groups by the number of their training examples: head classes each contain over 100 samples, medium classes each have between 20 and 100 samples, and tail classes with under 20 samples each. We use mean average precision (mAP) to evaluate the performance of long-tailed multi-label visual recognition for all the classes.

Implementation Details. We adopt CLIP ResNet-50 (He et al., 2016) or ViT-B/16 (Dosovitskiy et al., 2020) as the visual encoder and use the corresponding CLIP Transformer as the text encoder. During training, the parameters of both the two encoders are kept frozen, and only learnable prompts are optimized. SGD optimizer is adopted to learn prompt tokens, and the training epochs are set to 30. The learning rates for COCO-LT and VOC-LT are empirically initialized with 1e-4, 5e-4, and decay by the cosine annealing rule during training. For loss functions, η in Eq. 4, γ in Eq. 5 and λ in Eq. 11 are set as 1.0, 1.0 and 0.5, respectively. Other hyper-parameters in DB loss are set as the same as (Wu et al., 2020).

4.3 Long-Tailed Multi-Label Visual Recognition

To evaluate the effectiveness of the proposed method, firstly we compare it with previous methods of image-only models on the two long-tailed multi-label datasets. The compared methods include Empirical Risk Minimization (ERM), a smooth version of Re-Weighting (RW) using the inverse proportion to the square root of class frequency, Re-Sampling (RS) (Shen et al., 2016), Focal Loss (Lin et al., 2017), ML-GCN (Chen et al., 2019b), OLTR (Liu et al., 2019), LDAM (Cao et al., 2019), Class-Balanced (CB) Focal (Cui et al., 2019), BBN (Zhou et al., 2020), Distribution-Balanced (DB) Focal (Wu et al., 2020) and LTML (Guo and Wang, 2021). The mAP performance of different methods is shown in Table 1. The prior best performance is achieved by LTML – mAP of 81.44% over all classes on VOC-LT and 56.90% over all classes on COCO-LT.

Furthermore, we compare zero-shot and prompt

Datasets	VOC-LT			
Methods	total	head	medium	tail
BCE	82.18	64.90	83.17	94.30
MLS	84.30	64.31	84.82	97.47
Focal Loss	85.37	66.17	87.70	97.52
CB Loss	85.25	65.37	87.71	97.20
R-BCE-Focal	84.56	66.01	86.61	97.67
ASL	86.40	69.12	88.79	98.07
DB Focal	87.88	72.10	89.26	98.49
Datasets	COCO-LT			
Methods	total	head	medium	tail
BCE	58.04	41.79	58.86	73.90
MLS	61.26	41.71	64.11	74.58
Focal Loss	54.40	37.60	59.36	62.33
CB Loss	56.45	34.61	58.77	74.52
R-BCE-Focal	60.13	38.11	64.87	72.79
ASL	64.89	43.18	68.22	78.43
DB Focal	66.19	44.89	69.80	79.08

Table 2: mAP performance of the proposed method with different multi-label loss functions.

learning methods based on CLIP on the two benchmarks. The mAP performance of these methods is shown in Table 1 as well. For a fair comparison, we initialize the prompt as the default hand-crafted one "a photo of a" for all the methods. The results show that when using ViT-B/16 as the backbone, even the overall mAP performance of zero-shot CLIP reaches 85.77% and 60.17%, which outperforms previous SOTA LTML by **4.33** points (85.77% vs.81.44%) and **3.27** points (60.17% vs.56.90%) on the two datasets, respectively. Therefore, it is meaningful to explore how to use prompt tuning based on CLIP effectively for better performance. From the perspective of prompt tuning methods, when using ResNet-50 as the backbone, the performance of our method on VOC-LT is more promising, which is **4.1** points, **6.81** points, **4.41** points and **1.69** points better than CoOp, CoCoOp, DualCoOp and TaI-DPT, which are popular prompt learning methods for single-label and multi-label recognition. The performance on COCO-LT is similar to that on VOC-LT, which is **4.03** points, **12.95** points, and **5.86** points better than CoOp, CoCoOp, and DualCoOp. When replacing the backbone with ViT-B/16, the overall mAP performance of our method can further boost up to 87.88% and 66.19% on VOC-LT and COCO-LT, which is the current new **state-of-the-art** of the two datasets.

4.4 Ablation Analysis

Components Analysis. To further analyze which component makes our methods performant for LTML, we conduct a set of ablation studies and report the results in Table 3. We first conduct experiments with CLIP and the mAP performances are 85.77% on VOC-LT, 60.17% on COCO-LT, which surprisingly outperforms the prior SOTA LTML. It indicates that pre-trained VLMs demonstrate a robust capability for visual recognition, providing a solid foundation for our approach. However, the mAP performance of the tail classes outperforms the head classes by nearly 30 points on both VOC-LT and COCO-LT. Then CoOp is benefited from soft prompts and the mAP performance is improved to 86.02% on VOC-LT and 60.68% on COCO-LT, with **0.25%** and **0.51%** increments. Besides, we design the class-specific embedding loss with class-aware soft margin and re-weighting to learn more fine-grained and class-related prompts that build semantic relationships across different classes, especially for the tail classes by encouraging those classes to have larger margins and weights. The mAP performances of head, medium, and tail classes after adding the embedding loss are all significantly improved and the overall mAP surpasses CoOp by **1.26%** and **4.66%** on VOC-LT and COCO-LT, which demonstrates our embedding loss can help prompts learn fine-grained classes descriptions and semantic relationships across the classes. Finally, the integration of CASM and RW strategy further improves the mAP performance slightly, mainly for the tail performance by **0.65%** and **1.12%** on VOC-LT and COCO-LT.

Multi-Label Classification Loss Functions. We compare a number of multi-label classification loss functions, including Binary Cross-Entropy Loss (BCE), Multi-Label Soft Margin Loss (MSL), Focal Loss, CB Loss, R-BCE-Focal, Asymmetric Loss (ASL) and DB Focal. As illustrated in Table 2, DB Focal loss that takes the co-occurrence of labels and the dominance of negative labels into account works significantly better than other multi-label classification loss for the LTML task.

Effectiveness of Text Supervision. We further compare our method with fine-tuning CLIP's image encoder when using ResNet-50 as the backbone to explore whether the significant effect of our approach is due to text supervision or simply because the CLIP's image encoder is so powerful. In order to prevent interference with the trained CLIP's image encoder during the fine-tuning phase, we only fine-tune a fully connected layer added at the end of the image encoder. The results are shown in Fig. 4. Obviously, fine-tuning the image encoder shows promising results, but still largely

Soft Prompt	Embedding Loss	Class-Aware Soft Margin	Re-weighting	VOC-LT					COCO-LT				
				total	head	medium	tail	avg.Δ	total	head	medium	tail	avg.Δ
				85.77	66.52	88.93	97.83		60.17	38.52	65.06	72.28	
✓				86.02	67.71	88.79	97.67	+0.29	60.68	41.97	63.18	73.85	+0.91
✓	✓			87.28	71.07	89.01	97.84	+0.51	65.34	44.27	69.39	77.96	+5.23
✓	✓	✓		87.62	72.01	89.26	98.13	+1.99	65.81	44.90	69.71	78.76	+5.79
✓	✓	✓	✓	87.88	72.10	89.26	98.49	**+2.17**	66.19	44.89	69.80	79.08	**+5.98**

Table 3: Ablation analysis on different components of the our method. "avg.Δ" average performance improvement.

underperforms LMPT, which suggests that the gradients that went through the text encoder provide more useful information.

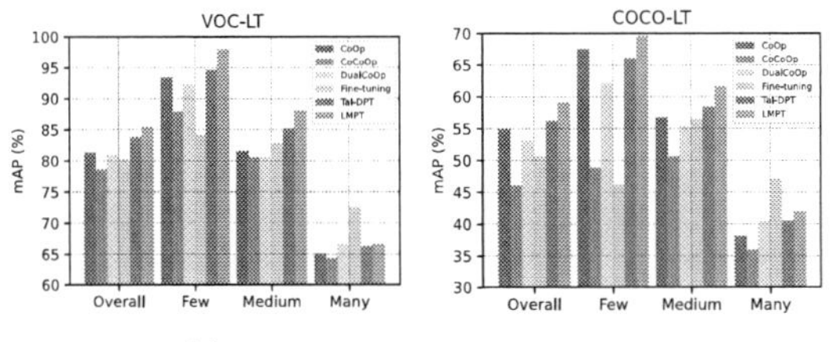

(a) (b)

Figure 4: mAP performance of different methods w/o text supervision on two datasets. (a) VOC-LT. (b) COCO-LT.

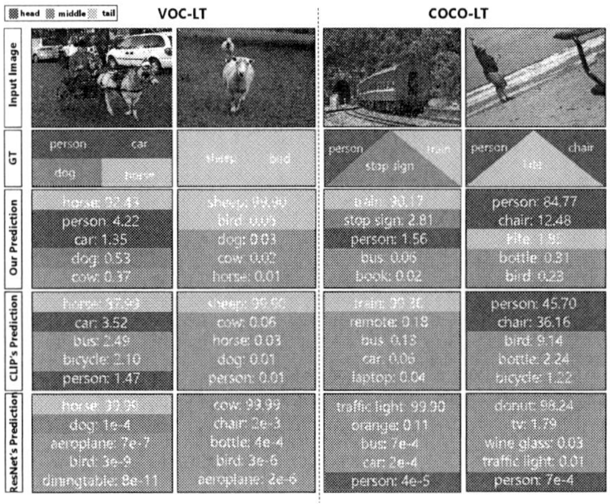

Figure 5: Example decisions from our model, CLIP, and ResNet.

4.5 Case Analysis

To better understand how our method deals with long-tailed multi-label data, we performed qualitative experiments with ResNet, CLIP, and ours on COCO-LT and VOC-LT. Fig. 5 shows several cases where the model justifies its abilities for the prediction. For example, in the third column, ResNet only recognizes [person] (belongs to head classes) and fails to classify the image to [train] (belongs to tail classes), which is a pervasive challenge encountered by image-only models. The emergence of CLIP is a great remedy for this issue, owing to its huge training data and effective text supervision. Nevertheless, simple hand-crafted templates as prompts still cannot accurately identify categories as they cannot describe the characteristics of each category. Understanding the inter-class relationships, particularly among head and tail categories, presents a formidable challenge in multi-label visual recognition, which is essential for achieving optimal performance in this domain. With the aid of our approach, utilizing prompts that learn from a large corpus of image-caption data, it has become feasible to discern the semantic relationships between categories and accurately predict the relevant categories of simple objects, even in challenging scenarios such as identifying [stop sign] from images. Therefore, our proposed method demonstrates significant advantages in effectively addressing the intricate relationship among multiple labels and the long-tailed problem with the aid of text supervision.

5 Conclusion

In this work, we propose a new view of prompt tuning for long-tailed multi-label visual recognition by learning class-specific contexts from the alignment of prompts and textual description (caption), which complements more fine-grained features and builds semantic relationships across head and tail classes. Considering the class imbalance, a novel class-specific embedding loss with the class-aware soft margin and re-weighting strategy is introduced to promote increased generalization among the tail classes. Furthermore, we integrate a distribution-balanced loss as the classification loss function in consideration of its empirical efficacy compared to alternative loss functions. Our method exhibits significant improvement over the previous state-of-the-art (SOTA) and zero-shot CLIP on VOC-LT and COCO-LT. Additionally, We hope our approach will inspire future work in this field.

Acknowledgement

We thank Monash-Airdoc Research donation Phase 2, MRFF NCRI GA89126, and MRFF AI-Eye NCRI GA89126 for their grant.

References

Mateusz Buda, Atsuto Maki, and Maciej A Mazurowski. 2018. A systematic study of the class imbalance problem in convolutional neural networks. Neural networks, 106:249–259.

Kaidi Cao, Colin Wei, Adrien Gaidon, Nikos Arechiga, and Tengyu Ma. 2019. Learning imbalanced datasets with label-distribution-aware margin loss. Advances in neural information processing systems, 32.

Tianshui Chen, Muxin Xu, Xiaolu Hui, Hefeng Wu, and Liang Lin. 2019a. Learning semantic-specific graph representation for multi-label image recognition. In Proceedings of the IEEE/CVF international conference on computer vision, pages 522–531.

Zhao-Min Chen, Xiu-Shen Wei, Peng Wang, and Yanwen Guo. 2019b. Multi-label image recognition with graph convolutional networks. In Proceedings of the IEEE/CVF conference on computer vision and pattern recognition, pages 5177–5186.

Jiequan Cui, Shu Liu, Zhuotao Tian, Zhisheng Zhong, and Jiaya Jia. 2022. Reslt: Residual learning for long-tailed recognition. IEEE Transactions on Pattern Analysis and Machine Intelligence.

Yin Cui, Menglin Jia, Tsung-Yi Lin, Yang Song, and Serge Belongie. 2019. Class-balanced loss based on effective number of samples. In Proceedings of the IEEE/CVF conference on computer vision and pattern recognition, pages 9268–9277.

Qi Dong, Shaogang Gong, and Xiatian Zhu. 2017. Class rectification hard mining for imbalanced deep learning. In Proceedings of the IEEE International Conference on Computer Vision, pages 1851–1860.

Alexey Dosovitskiy, Lucas Beyer, Alexander Kolesnikov, Dirk Weissenborn, Xiaohua Zhai, Thomas Unterthiner, Mostafa Dehghani, Matthias Minderer, Georg Heigold, Sylvain Gelly, et al. 2020. An image is worth 16x16 words: Transformers for image recognition at scale. arXiv preprint arXiv:2010.11929.

Chris Drummond, Robert C Holte, et al. 2003. Class imbalance, and cost sensitivity: why under-sampling beats over-sampling. In Workshop on learning from imbalanced datasets II, volume 11, pages 1–8.

Mark Everingham, SM Eslami, Luc Van Gool, Christopher KI Williams, John Winn, and Andrew Zisserman. 2015. The pascal visual object classes challenge: A retrospective. International journal of computer vision, 111(1):98–136.

Hao Guo and Song Wang. 2021. Long-tailed multi-label visual recognition by collaborative training on uniform and re-balanced samplings. In Proceedings of the IEEE/CVF Conference on Computer Vision and Pattern Recognition, pages 15089–15098.

Zixian Guo, Bowen Dong, Zhilong Ji, Jinfeng Bai, Yiwen Guo, and Wangmeng Zuo. 2023. Texts as images in prompt tuning for multi-label image recognition. In Proceedings of the IEEE/CVF Conference on Computer Vision and Pattern Recognition, pages 2808–2817.

Kaiming He, Xiangyu Zhang, Shaoqing Ren, and Jian Sun. 2016. Deep residual learning for image recognition. In Proceedings of the IEEE conference on computer vision and pattern recognition, pages 770–778.

Chen Huang, Yining Li, Chen Change Loy, and Xiaoou Tang. 2016. Learning deep representation for imbalanced classification. In Proceedings of the IEEE conference on computer vision and pattern recognition, pages 5375–5384.

Xinyu Huang, Youcai Zhang, Ying Cheng, Weiwei Tian, Ruiwei Zhao, Rui Feng, Yuejie Zhang, Yaqian Li, Yandong Guo, and Xiaobo Zhang. 2022. Idea: Increasing text diversity via online multi-label recognition for vision-language pre-training. In Proceedings of the 30th ACM International Conference on Multimedia, pages 4573–4583.

Chao Jia, Yinfei Yang, Ye Xia, Yi-Ting Chen, Zarana Parekh, Hieu Pham, Quoc Le, Yun-Hsuan Sung, Zhen Li, and Tom Duerig. 2021. Scaling up visual and vision-language representation learning with noisy text supervision. In International Conference on Machine Learning, pages 4904–4916. PMLR.

Lie Ju, Zhen Yu, Lin Wang, Xin Zhao, Xin Wang, Paul Bonnington, and Zongyuan Ge. 2023. Hierarchical knowledge guided learning for real-world retinal disease recognition. IEEE Transactions on Medical Imaging.

Bingyi Kang, Yu Li, Sa Xie, Zehuan Yuan, and Jiashi Feng. 2020. Exploring balanced feature spaces for representation learning. In International Conference on Learning Representations.

Salman H Khan, Munawar Hayat, Mohammed Bennamoun, Ferdous A Sohel, and Roberto Togneri. 2017. Cost-sensitive learning of deep feature representations from imbalanced data. IEEE transactions on neural networks and learning systems, 29(8):3573–3587.

Tsung-Yi Lin, Priya Goyal, Ross Girshick, Kaiming He, and Piotr Dollár. 2017. Focal loss for dense object detection. In Proceedings of the IEEE international conference on computer vision, pages 2980–2988.

Tsung-Yi Lin, Michael Maire, Serge Belongie, James Hays, Pietro Perona, Deva Ramanan, Piotr Dollár, and C Lawrence Zitnick. 2014. Microsoft coco:

Common objects in context. In European conference on computer vision, pages 740–755. Springer.

Shilong Liu, Lei Zhang, Xiao Yang, Hang Su, and Jun Zhu. 2021. Query2label: A simple transformer way to multi-label classification. arXiv preprint arXiv:2107.10834.

Ziwei Liu, Zhongqi Miao, Xiaohang Zhan, Jiayun Wang, Boqing Gong, and Stella X Yu. 2019. Large-scale long-tailed recognition in an open world. In Proceedings of the IEEE/CVF Conference on Computer Vision and Pattern Recognition, pages 2537–2546.

Teli Ma, Shijie Geng, Mengmeng Wang, Jing Shao, Jiasen Lu, Hongsheng Li, Peng Gao, and Yu Qiao. 2021. A simple long-tailed recognition baseline via vision-language model. arXiv preprint arXiv:2111.14745.

Aditya Krishna Menon, Sadeep Jayasumana, Ankit Singh Rawat, Himanshu Jain, Andreas Veit, and Sanjiv Kumar. 2020. Long-tail learning via logit adjustment. arXiv preprint arXiv:2007.07314.

Wanli Ouyang, Xiaogang Wang, Cong Zhang, and Xiaokang Yang. 2016. Factors in finetuning deep model for object detection with long-tail distribution. In Proceedings of the IEEE conference on computer vision and pattern recognition, pages 864–873.

Alec Radford, Jong Wook Kim, Chris Hallacy, Aditya Ramesh, Gabriel Goh, Sandhini Agarwal, Girish Sastry, Amanda Askell, Pamela Mishkin, Jack Clark, et al. 2021. Learning transferable visual models from natural language supervision. In International Conference on Machine Learning, pages 8748–8763. PMLR.

Tal Ridnik, Emanuel Ben-Baruch, Nadav Zamir, Asaf Noy, Itamar Friedman, Matan Protter, and Lihi Zelnik-Manor. 2021. Asymmetric loss for multi-label classification. In Proceedings of the IEEE/CVF International Conference on Computer Vision, pages 82–91.

Tal Ridnik, Gilad Sharir, Avi Ben-Cohen, Emanuel Ben-Baruch, and Asaf Noy. 2023. Ml-decoder: Scalable and versatile classification head. In Proceedings of the IEEE/CVF Winter Conference on Applications of Computer Vision, pages 32–41.

Dvir Samuel and Gal Chechik. 2021. Distributional robustness loss for long-tail learning. In Proceedings of the IEEE/CVF International Conference on Computer Vision, pages 9495–9504.

Timo Schick and Hinrich Schütze. 2021. Exploiting cloze-questions for few-shot text classification and natural language inference. In Proceedings of the 16th Conference of the European Chapter of the Association for Computational Linguistics: Main Volume, pages 255–269.

Li Shen, Zhouchen Lin, and Qingming Huang. 2016. Relay backpropagation for effective learning of deep convolutional neural networks. In European conference on computer vision, pages 467–482. Springer.

Taylor Shin, Yasaman Razeghi, Robert L Logan IV, Eric Wallace, and Sameer Singh. 2020. Autoprompt: Eliciting knowledge from language models with automatically generated prompts. arXiv preprint arXiv:2010.15980.

Ximeng Sun, Ping Hu, and Kate Saenko. 2022. Dualcoop: Fast adaptation to multi-label recognition with limited annotations. arXiv preprint arXiv:2206.09541.

Jingru Tan, Changbao Wang, Buyu Li, Quanquan Li, Wanli Ouyang, Changqing Yin, and Junjie Yan. 2020. Equalization loss for long-tailed object recognition. In Proceedings of the IEEE/CVF conference on computer vision and pattern recognition, pages 11662–11671.

Changyao Tian, Wenhai Wang, Xizhou Zhu, Jifeng Dai, and Yu Qiao. 2022. Vl-ltr: Learning class-wise visual-linguistic representation for long-tailed visual recognition. In European Conference on Computer Vision, pages 73–91. Springer.

Grigorios Tsoumakas and Ioannis Katakis. 2007. Multi-label classification: An overview. International Journal of Data Warehousing and Mining (IJDWM), 3(3):1–13.

Jiang Wang, Yi Yang, Junhua Mao, Zhiheng Huang, Chang Huang, and Wei Xu. 2016. Cnn-rnn: A unified framework for multi-label image classification. In Proceedings of the IEEE conference on computer vision and pattern recognition, pages 2285–2294.

Peng Wang, An Yang, Rui Men, Junyang Lin, Shuai Bai, Zhikang Li, Jianxin Ma, Chang Zhou, Jingren Zhou, and Hongxia Yang. 2022. Unifying architectures, tasks, and modalities through a simple sequence-to-sequence learning framework. arXiv preprint arXiv:2202.03052.

Zhouxia Wang, Tianshui Chen, Guanbin Li, Ruijia Xu, and Liang Lin. 2017. Multi-label image recognition by recurrently discovering attentional regions. In Proceedings of the IEEE international conference on computer vision, pages 464–472.

Colin Wei, Jason Lee, Qiang Liu, and Tengyu Ma. 2018. On the margin theory of feedforward neural networks.

Tong Wu, Qingqiu Huang, Ziwei Liu, Yu Wang, and Dahua Lin. 2020. Distribution-balanced loss for multi-label classification in long-tailed datasets. In European Conference on Computer Vision, pages 162–178. Springer.

Peng Xia, Ze Chen, Juanxi Tian, Yangrui Gong, Ruibo Hou, Yue Xu, Zhenbang Wu, Zhiyuan Fan, Yiyang Zhou, Kangyu Zhu, et al. 2024a. Cares: A comprehensive benchmark of trustworthiness in medical vision language models. arXiv preprint arXiv:2406.06007.

Peng Xia, Ming Hu, Feilong Tang, Wenxue Li, Wenhao Zheng, Lie Ju, Peibo Duan, Huaxiu Yao, and Zongyuan Ge. 2024b. Generalizing to unseen domains in diabetic retinopathy with disentangled representations. arXiv preprint arXiv:2406.06384.

Peng Xia, Xingtong Yu, Ming Hu, Lie Ju, Zhiyong Wang, Peibo Duan, and Zongyuan Ge. 2023. Hg-clip: Exploring vision-language models with graph representations for hierarchical understanding. arXiv preprint arXiv:2311.14064.

Shichao Xu, Yikang Li, Jenhao Hsiao, Chiuman Ho, and Zhu Qi. 2022. A dual modality approach for (zero-shot) multi-label classification. arXiv preprint arXiv:2208.09562.

Yuan Yao, Ao Zhang, Zhengyan Zhang, Zhiyuan Liu, Tat-Seng Chua, and Maosong Sun. 2021. Cpt: Colorful prompt tuning for pre-trained vision-language models. arXiv preprint arXiv:2109.11797.

Jin Ye, Junjun He, Xiaojiang Peng, Wenhao Wu, and Yu Qiao. 2020. Attention-driven dynamic graph convolutional network for multi-label image recognition. In European conference on computer vision, pages 649–665. Springer.

Min-Ling Zhang and Zhi-Hua Zhou. 2007. Ml-knn: A lazy learning approach to multi-label learning. Pattern recognition, 40(7):2038–2048.

Min-Ling Zhang and Zhi-Hua Zhou. 2013. A review on multi-label learning algorithms. IEEE transactions on knowledge and data engineering, 26(8):1819–1837.

Yifan Zhang, Bryan Hooi, Lanqing Hong, and Jiashi Feng. 2021a. Test-agnostic long-tailed recognition by test-time aggregating diverse experts with self-supervision. arXiv preprint arXiv:2107.09249.

Yifan Zhang, Bingyi Kang, Bryan Hooi, Shuicheng Yan, and Jiashi Feng. 2021b. Deep long-tailed learning: A survey. arXiv preprint arXiv:2110.04596.

Boyan Zhou, Quan Cui, Xiu-Shen Wei, and Zhao-Min Chen. 2020. Bbn: Bilateral-branch network with cumulative learning for long-tailed visual recognition. In Proceedings of the IEEE/CVF conference on computer vision and pattern recognition, pages 9719–9728.

Kaiyang Zhou, Jingkang Yang, Chen Change Loy, and Ziwei Liu. 2022a. Conditional prompt learning for vision-language models. In Proceedings of the IEEE/CVF Conference on Computer Vision and Pattern Recognition, pages 16816–16825.

Kaiyang Zhou, Jingkang Yang, Chen Change Loy, and Ziwei Liu. 2022b. Learning to prompt for vision-language models. International Journal of Computer Vision, 130(9):2337–2348.

Linchao Zhu and Yi Yang. 2020. Inflated episodic memory with region self-attention for long-tailed visual recognition. In Proceedings of the IEEE/CVF Conference on Computer Vision and Pattern Recognition, pages 4344–4353.

Negative Object Presence Evaluation (NOPE) to Measure Object Hallucination in Vision-Language Models

Holy Lovenia[*,1,2] **Wenliang Dai**[†,1] **Samuel Cahyawijaya**[†,1] **Ziwei Ji**[1] **Pascale Fung**[1]
[1] The Hong Kong University of Science and Technology
[2] AI Singapore
holy@aisingapore.org, pascale@ust.hk

Abstract

Object hallucination poses a significant challenge in vision-language (VL) models, often leading to the generation of nonsensical or unfaithful responses with non-existent objects. However, the absence of a general measurement for evaluating object hallucination in VL models has hindered our understanding and ability to mitigate this issue. In this work, we present NOPE (Negative Object Presence Evaluation), a novel benchmark designed to assess object hallucination in VL models through visual question answering (VQA). We propose a cost-effective and scalable approach utilizing large language models to generate 29.5k synthetic negative pronoun (NegP) data of high quality for NOPE. We extensively investigate the performance of 10 state-of-the-art VL models in discerning the non-existence of objects in visual questions, where the ground truth answers are denoted as NegP (e.g., "none"). Additionally, we evaluate their standard performance on visual questions on 9 other VQA datasets. Through our experiments, we demonstrate that no VL model is immune to the vulnerability of object hallucination, as all models achieve accuracy below 10% on NegP. Furthermore, we uncover that lexically diverse visual questions, question types with large scopes, and scene-relevant objects capitalize the risk of object hallucination in VL models.

1 Introduction

In recent years, vision-language (VL) research has witnessed a proliferation of studies focusing on diverse methods, models, and learning strategies aimed at bridging the performance gap between human and model capabilities (Yang et al., 2021; Yi et al., 2018; Zhou et al., 2020; Ray et al., 2019; Gokhale et al., 2020; Dai et al., 2021, 2022; Ishii et al., 2021; Lovenia et al., 2022; Ji et al., 2022b; Lovenia et al., 2023). Furthermore, researchers have constructed more rigorous VL benchmarks to continually raise the performance standard (Antol et al., 2015; Sheng et al., 2021; Li et al., 2021b; Goyal et al., 2017; Marino et al., 2019). However, despite these efforts, VL models continue to grapple with the persistent issue of object hallucination, where generated responses unfaithfully contain objects non-existent in the input images (Ji et al., 2022a; Rohrbach et al., 2018; Dai et al., 2023b; Kayhan et al., 2021). As illustrated in Figure 1, the failure of the model to faithfully ground the visual input leads to the production of unfaithful answers. These instances of object hallucination not only result in incorrect responses but also shed light on fundamental issues within VL models, such as over-reliance on unimodal priors (Jing et al., 2020; Agrawal et al., 2018; Gupta et al., 2022; Niu et al., 2021a) and statistical bias (Agrawal et al., 2016; Goyal et al., 2017; Agarwal et al., 2020). These underlying problems impede the models' ability to comprehend the concept of non-existence.

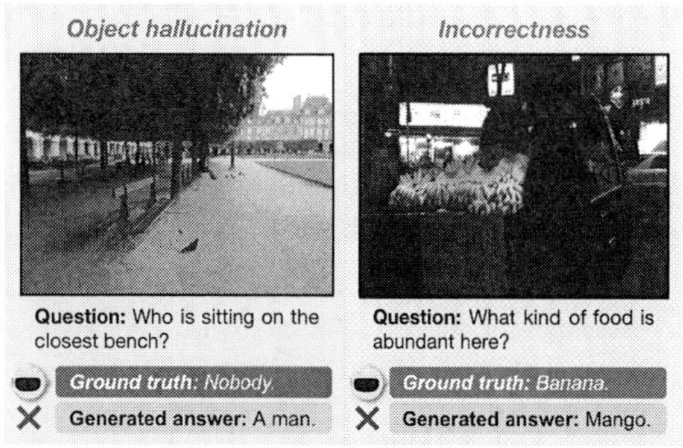

Figure 1: Example of object hallucination and incorrectness in VQA. The model hallucinates a non-existent man sitting on the closest bench in the left image, while in the right image, it simply answers inaccurately.

Despite the critical importance of addressing object hallucination in VL models, only a limited number of previous works have focused on mitigating this issue, primarily due to the challenges

[*] The majority of the work was done when the author was studying at HKUST.

[†] Joint second authors.

Proceedings of the 3rd Workshop on Advances in Language and Vision Research, pages 37–58
August 16, 2024 ©2024 Association for Computational Linguistics

posed by the existing evaluation method in terms of generalization and scalability. CHAIR (Rohrbach et al., 2018) has primarily concentrated on evaluating non-existent objects based on handcrafted parsing criteria as well as a predefined list of object categories and their synonyms in the context of image captioning tasks, typically utilizing 80 object categories from MSCOCO (Rohrbach et al., 2018; Biten et al., 2022; Yi et al., 2018). However, the applicability of CHAIR to other datasets requires the generation of a new object category list, which exhibits varying levels of granularity across different studies (Dai et al., 2023b; Biten et al., 2022).

In this paper, we present NOPE (**N**egative **O**bject **P**resence **E**valuation) to quantitatively assess object hallucination through VQA. We establish a clear distinction between object hallucination and incorrectness as follows: a) **object hallucination** refers to the phenomenon in VQA where a VL model's response includes a non-existent object, despite the ground truth answer being a negative indefinite pronoun (e.g., "none", "no one", "nobody", "nowhere", "neither") (Quirk et al., 1985) (NegP); and b) **incorrectness** occurs when a VL model fails to accurately respond to a question with a ground truth answer that is anything other than NegP, denoted as Others = $\mathbb{P}\setminus$NegP, where $\mathbb{P}$ represents the set of all phrases. By leveraging NegP, we evaluate object hallucination in NOPE, while Others allows us to assess normative correctness across diverse corpora. Our contributions are as follows:

1. By utilizing NOPE, we construct a VQA diagnostic benchmark to measure the object hallucination rate of VL models. Our experiment covers a balanced proportion of NegP and Others data with a total of ~30k and ~36k data in the dev and test sets, and includes 10 state-of-the-art VL baselines performances. We provide an in-depth analysis of the performances and limitations of the baselines.
2. We propose a novel automatic data generation pipeline to produce high-quality NegP VQA data from existing image captioning data by multi-turn prompting instruction-tuned large language models (LLMs). We verify and analyze our generated NegP data through automatic validation and human validation. Our **list-then-rewrite** method produces high-quality NegP VQA data with 92% validity.
3. Through extensive analysis in NOPE, we find that VL models tend to hallucinate more on data with higher lexical diversity, more scene-relevant objects, and larger answer scopes.

2 Related Work

2.1 Hallucination in Vision-Language

Only a few works study hallucination in vision-language, with the vast majority of them focusing on the task of image captioning. Rohrbach et al. (2018) propose CHAIR, an automatic evaluation metric to measure object hallucination in generated image captions, which is defined as a phenomenon where the models produce captions containing objects that do not exist in the input visual context. Rohrbach et al. (2018); Dai et al. (2023b); Sharma et al. (2018) also show that standard captioning metrics, e.g., CIDEr (Vedantam et al., 2015), METEOR (Banerjee and Lavie, 2005), SPICE (Niu et al., 2022), under-penalize object hallucination. These evaluations open up a way for efforts to mitigate hallucination in image captioning (Biten et al., 2022; Zhang et al., 2021; Xiao and Wang, 2021; Dai et al., 2023b). Concurrent to our work, Li et al. (2023b) propose POPE and frame the task of evaluating object hallucination as a binary-class VQA with only "yes/no" answer.

2.2 Question Generation for VQA Data

Most works rely on human annotators to generate visual questions with ensured quality: VQAv2.0 and VQAv1.0 (Goyal et al., 2017; Antol et al., 2015), Visual Genome (Krishna et al., 2016), Visual7W (Zhu et al., 2016), AdVQA (Sheng et al., 2021), Vizwiz (Gurari et al., 2018, 2019), TextVQA (Singh et al., 2019), R-VQA (Lu et al., 2018), VQA-Rephrasings (Shah et al., 2019), etc.

However, the cost of human annotation is expensive, thus encouraging the exploration of a more scalable option: automatic VQA data generation. Ren et al. (2015) present a simple question generation algorithm with a syntactic parser to convert image descriptions into QA forms. Johnson et al. (2017) use a functional program to generate synthetic images of objects as well as their relationships and relevant QA pairs using the ground-truth annotations. Kafle and Kanan (2017) populate multiple question templates with the image annotations (e.g., region descriptions, relationship graphs, bounding boxes) obtained from image captioning data to construct TDIUC. Changpinyo et al. (2022) annotate candidate answers by syntactically

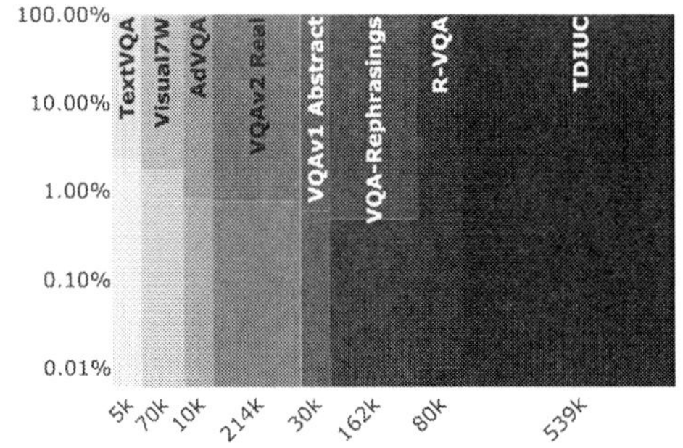

Figure 2: Only 0.4% of existing VQA corpora consist of NegP data. The rest 99.6% is Others.

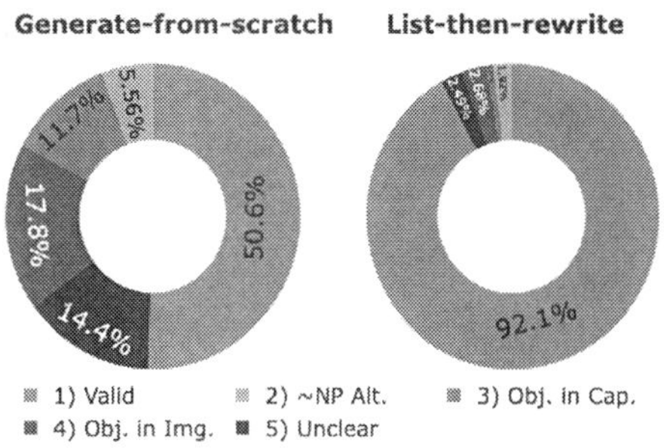

Figure 3: Human evaluation results of NegP questions by **generate-from-scratch** and **list-then-rewrite** according to the categories in §3.2.

parsing the captions, then derive questions from them. While prior studies focus on generating Others VQA data, we aim to generate NegP VQA data, which has never been done by past works.

3 NOPE to Overcome Limited NegP

As shown in Figure 2, there is only a minuscule amount of NegP data in the existing VQA datasets. In total, there are only ~0.4% of the existing VQA datasets are NegP, which are not sufficient to assess object hallucination in VL. For this reason, we create NOPE through a novel NegP data generation method that aims to produce questions whose ground truth answers point to the absence of appropriate existent objects. Such ground truth NegP answers are denoted as $A^{\text{NegP}} = \{"none", "nothing", "nowhere", "zero", "0", "no\ one", "nobody", "neither"\}$. We automatically generate synthetic NegP VQA data by leveraging the zero-shot prompting abilities of pretrained LLMs. To ensure the quality, we analyze the generated synthetic NegP VQA data through both automatic and manual human evaluation. The resulting NegP dataset is referred to as NOPE (**N**egative **O**bject **P**resence **E**valuation).

3.1 Prompting Methodology

We utilize an image captioning dataset $\mathcal{D}_{cap} = \{(v_i, c_i, l_i\}_{i=1}^{n}$, where v_i denotes a visual context, c_i denotes a textual caption, and l_i denotes the relevant image label annotations (i.e., names of objects in v_i). We rely on c_i to describe the objects and the relationship between objects depicted in v_i. We explore two prompting methods with varying degrees of flexibility to generate NegP questions from image captions: **generate-from-scratch** and **list-then-rewrite**. For clarity, we include all prompt templates with the examples in Appendix A and the automatic validation methods to ensure the validity of the generated questions in Appendix C.

Generate-from-scratch In this method, we prompt an LLM to generate a question q_i given three different variables: 1) an interrogative word $w_i \in \{"what", "where", "how\ many", "who", "which"\}$ to assert the question type needed for q_i, 2) a ground truth NegP answer $a_i \in A^{\text{NegP}}$ that matches w_i, and 3) an image caption c_i.

List-then-rewrite LLMs can infer conversational contexts and follow instructions over multiple turns (Nijkamp et al., 2023; Volum et al., 2022; Bang et al., 2023). Leveraging this multi-turn capability of LLMs, we frame our question generation task into two steps. (1) For object listing, given an image caption c_i and the relevant object annotations l_i, we prompt an LLM to list m objects $o_i = \{o_{i,j}\}_{j=1}^{m}$ that are "closely related"[1] but not mentioned. (2) For question rewriting, the LLM has to paraphrase a provided reference question, which is sourced from a diverse pool of human-generated question templates with an object placeholder in Appendix B. After obtaining m listed objects from (1), we pick m random question templates from the pool and replace the object placeholders with the listed objects o_i to construct the reference questions $r_i = \{r_{i,j}\}_{j=1}^{m}$. We prompt the LLM to paraphrase r_i to $q_i = \{q_{i,j}\}_{j=1}^{m}$ to increase the lexical variety of the rewritten questions q_i.

3.2 Human Evaluation Guidelines

We conduct a human evaluation to verify and analyze the quality of the generated questions obtained from §3.1, as well as measure the effectiveness

[1]We use "closely related" (hard) for brevity. However, this object-scene relevance can be switched to "loosely related" or "completely unrelated" in practice.

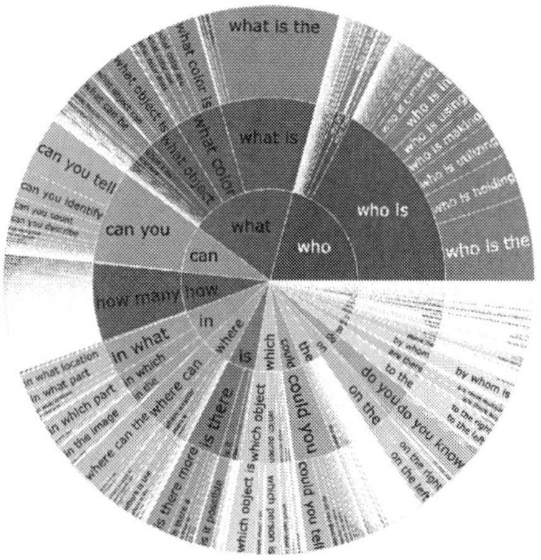

Figure 4: Distribution of NOPE's NegP questions by their starting phrases. The arc length is proportional to the number of questions containing the word.

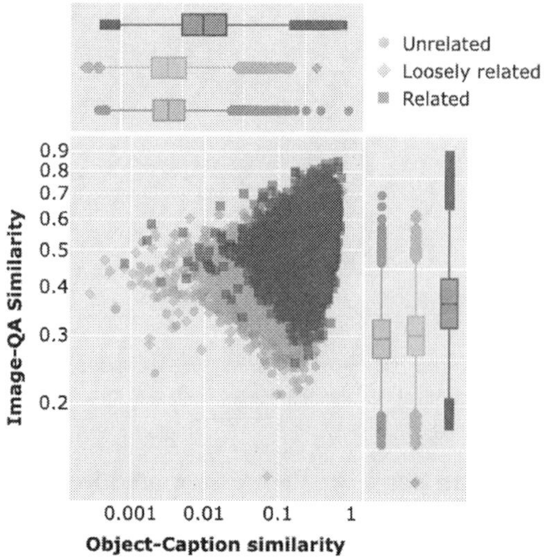

Figure 5: Object-scene relevance in the NOPE dataset. **Related** denotes "closely related" and **unrelated** denotes "completely unrelated" for brevity.

of the automatic validations performed. We employ three human annotators to perform the human evaluations. Detailed guidelines and examples are given prior to evaluation. We collect generated questions that are judged as valid and invalid by their automatic validation methods. Given a visual context, an image caption, a ground truth answer $\in A^{\text{NegP}}$, and a generated question, the annotators are asked to determine whether: 1) the question is valid, 2) the question has a possible Others answer alternative, 3) the question does not match the answer (according to both the image caption and the image), 4) the question does not match the answer (only according to the image), or 5) the question is unclear or confusing. The examples provided for each category can be seen in Appendix E.

3.3 Results and Quality Analysis

Using automatic validation approaches explained in §3.1 and implementation details in Appendix D, we compare the capabilities of various instruction-tuned LLMs in generating NegP VQA data. From the automatic validation results and analysis presented in Appendix F, we find that employing ChatGPT yields the highest-quality generated NegP questions by both **generate-from-scratch** and **list-then-rewrite** prompting methods, hence its use in the human evaluations. We conduct a human evaluation on randomly selected 150 generated questions from each method. For each sample, we ask 3 human experts to judge each generated question into one of the 5 options defined in §3.2.

Figure 3 shows the result of our human evaluation. For **generate-from-scratch**, only ±50% out of the subset that is judged as valid by the automatic validation is actually a valid and appropriate NegP question according to the human annotators, and the rest is judged as incorrect by human annotators. The **list-then-rewrite** prompting approach, on the other hand, displays a significantly better question-answer generation quality with ±92% of the generated questions denoted as valid by the human annotators. This fact demonstrates that existing LLMs still fail to perform complex tasks in an end-to-end manner, while decomposing the complex tasks into several subtasks and coupling them with simple rule-based approaches can significantly improve the LLMs' ability to perform the complex task effectively and efficiently.

A closer look at the questions generated by the **generate-from-scratch** method shows that while LLMs usually succeed in making questions in an end-to-end manner, 12% of the NegP generated questions include an existing object even though this information is sufficiently provided by the image caption. Moreover, 14% of the time, the generated questions also fail to include any objects and are overly generic, e.g., "What is not included in this image?", which aligns with the observations of (Jang et al., 2023; Hosseini et al., 2021; Ettinger, 2020; Kassner and Schütze, 2020) that LMs perform poorly on negation and struggles to understand that negation changes semantics. These facts show that LLMs cannot consistently perform this implicit task breakdown. From this human evaluation result, we can conjecture that the

NegP	dev	test
	14718	**17983**
NOPE (§3.4)	14718	14773
AdVQA	0	88
R-VQA	0	9
TDIUC	0	6
Visual7W	0	1276
VQAv1 Abstract Scenes	0	180
VQAv2 Balanced Real	0	1651

Others	dev	test
	14850	**18150**
AdVQA	1350	1650
R-VQA	2700	3300
TDIUC	1350	1650
TextVQA	1350	1650
Visual7W	2700	3300
VizWiz	1350	1650
VQA-Rephrasings	1350	1650
VQAv1 Abstract Scenes	1350	1650
VQAv2 Balanced Real	1350	1650

Table 1: The data statistics of NegP **(left)** and Others **(right)** subsets used in the evaluation.

generate-from-scratch prompting method is not reliable and fails to elicit the LLMs' understanding of complex tasks such as question generation. Using the **list-then-rewrite** method, we generate 29.5k NegP VQA data to build the NOPE dataset from OpenImagesV7 (Kuznetsova et al., 2020).

3.4 Dataset Statistics

NegP **Question Distribution** We cluster the generated questions into various types based on the starting n-grams in Figure 4. NOPE dataset exhibits a very broad lexical diversity of the generated questions, including variations in which the questions start with words other than the typical interrogative words (e.g., "what", "where", "how", etc.), such as "Could you tell...", "In what location...", "Do you know...", and more. This is vital to resist VL models' notorious brittleness against linguistic variations (Shah et al., 2019; Ray et al., 2019; Kervadec et al., 2021; Whitehead et al., 2020).

Object-Scene Relevance Based on the descriptor used in the object listing step in **list-then-rewrite**[1], the data in NOPE are divided into three categories. Figure 5 illustrates how these object-scene relevance descriptors of the generated NegP VQA data correspond to the relationship between the textual semantic similarity of the selected object and the image caption, as well as the image-text semantic similarity of the image and the QA pair. We compute the textual similarity using the Sentence-Transformer library[2] and the image-text similarity using CLIPScore (Hessel et al., 2021).

[2] https://www.sbert.net/docs/usage/semantic_textual_similarity.html

4 Experimental Settings

The object hallucination benchmark consists of the validation and test sets of 10 VQA corpora, including NOPE (§3.4) with balanced object-scene relevance proportions. It displays the comparison between incorrectness and object hallucination over various baselines, which serves as a foundation for assessing object hallucination in addition to the standard incorrectness in 10 VL models.

4.1 Datasets

Table 1 describes the data distribution of the dev and test sets of the benchmark. Each set respectively comprises ~30k and ~36k data, maintaining near-balanced proportions of NegP and Others data. To ensure the quality of the visual questions in the benchmark, we also analyze the lexical diversity and the fluency of the comprising datasets, which are useful to assert a robust evaluation using questions that are linguistically diverse and coherent. In Figure 6, we show that the datasets whose data construction utilizes automatic question generation, i.e., NOPE and TDIUC, have comparable lexical diversity and fluency to the other datasets, which entirely rely on question generation by human annotators.

For lexical diversity, we employ length-agnostic lexical diversity metrics, i.e., moving average type-token ratio (MATTR) (Covington and McFall, 2010), measure of textual lexical diversity (MTLD) (McCarthy, 2005), and hypergeometric distribution diversity (HDD) (McCarthy and Jarvis, 2007, 2010), and average them. We use LexicalRichness (Shen, 2021, 2022) v0.5.0[3] to calculate these metrics. We also employ a large pre-trained LM GPT-Neo (Black et al., 2021) with 2.7B param-

[3] https://pypi.org/project/lexicalrichness/

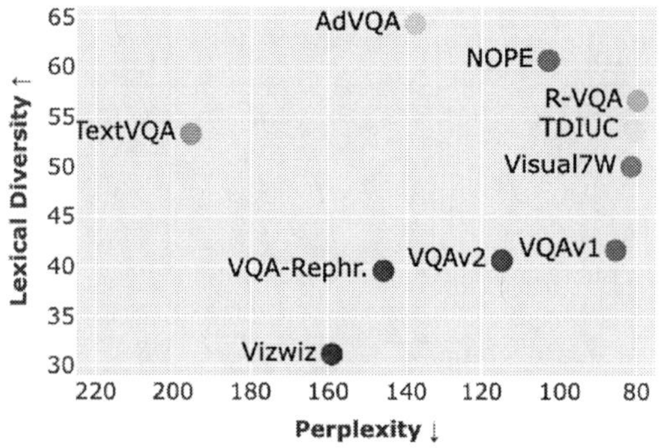

Figure 6: Question quality in the benchmark in terms of lexical diversity and fluency.

eters to compute the perplexity of the questions, which is often used as a measure of both lexical diversity (Lewis et al., 2017; Tevet and Berant, 2021) and fluency (Fan et al., 2018; Wang et al., 2019; Cahyawijaya et al., 2021; Anonymous, 2023).

4.2 Baselines

For the baselines in our benchmark, we employ various vision-language model architectures on the benchmark in both zero-shot & few-shot and fine-tuned fashion. For the fine-tuned setting, we utilize five models: 1) OFA (Wang et al., 2022b), which unifies architectures, tasks, and modalities by formulating a unified sequence-to-sequence abstraction via handcrafted instructions to achieve task agnosticism; 2) and 3) BLIP (Li et al., 2022), which incorporates two key contributions, i.e., multimodal mixture of encoder-decoder (MED) to operate as either a unimodal encoder, an image-grounded text encoder, or an image-grounded text decoder, and CapFilt as a new dataset bootstrapping method for learning from noisy image-text pairs; 4) ALBEF (Li et al., 2021a), which is trained using momentum distillation to improve learning from noisy web data; 5) GIT (Wang et al., 2022a), which employs an image encoder and a text decoder pre-trained using a language modeling objective to map the input image to its corresponding description.

For the zero-shot setting, we employ: 1) BLIP-2 (Li et al., 2023a), which utilizes a scalable multimodal pre-training method to enable any LLMs to ingest and understand images; 2) and 3) PromptCap (Hu et al., 2022), which is trained to generate captions that help downstream LMs answer visual questions; 4) InstructBLIP (Dai et al., 2023a), which is an instruction-tuned version of BLIP-2 on various tasks including VQA. We also employ 5) OpenFlamingo (Alayrac et al., 2022; Awadalla et al., 2023), which is an open-source version of a large pre-trained VL model specialized in few-shot prompting, in the two-shot setting. Table 2 provides the model and data sizes of the baselines and Appendix H lists the model variants.

	Model size	**# Pre-train images**
Zero-shot & Few-shot		
PromptCap$_{BASE}$	696M	34M
PromptCap	3B	34M
BLIP-2	3.8B	129M
OpenFlamingo	9B	~2.5B
VQA fine-tuned		
OFA	929M	34M
BLIP	385M	129M
BLIP$_{CapFilt-L}$	385M	129M
ALBEF	628M	14M
GIT$_{LARGE}$	347M	1.4B
InstructBLIP$_{FLAN_{XL}}$	3.8B	129M+

Table 2: VL baseline models in the benchmark.

4.3 Evaluation Settings

For both NegP and Others, we compute accuracy and METEOR (Banerjee and Lavie, 2005) to measure the performance of vision-language models on the benchmark. While accuracy measures the performance based on an exact match between the generated answer and the ground truth answer, METEOR caters to partial (i.e., unigram) matches by computing a score for this matching using a combination of unigram-precision, unigram-recall, and alignment between the unigrams in the generated answer and ground truth answer. Additionally, for NegP, we employ a rule-based accuracy, referred to as NegP accuracy, which focuses on determining whether the generated answer is a negative indefinite pronoun (i.e., $\in A^{\text{NegP}} = \{"none", "nothing", "nowhere", "zero", "0", "no\ one", "nobody", "neither"\}$) or not. All scores are computed per task and then the weighted averages according to each task size are retrieved.

5 Results

We present the results on the test set of the benchmark in Table 3. Examples of object hallucination are in Appendix I. While the VQA-finetuned baselines are slightly better at NegP and comparable to the zero-shot & few-shot baselines on Others, as in Figure 7, we observe that all zero-shot and VQA-finetuned baselines notably perform much worse on NegP tasks that Others with the averaged discrepancies of $\pm22\%$ and $\pm18\%$ accuracy,

	Others test (%)		NegP test (%)						
	Overall		Existing datasets		NOPE test (§3.4)		Overall		
	Acc.	METEOR	Acc.	METEOR	Acc.	METEOR	NegP Acc.	Acc.	METEOR
Zero-shot & few-shot									
PromptCap$_{BASE}$	30.18	21.45	2.87	3.05	0.21	0.29	0.95	0.68	0.78
PromptCap	<u>32.69</u>	22.66	3.61	2.20	0.42	0.56	1.67	0.99	0.85
BLIP-2	19.84	17.94	<u>4.39</u>	1.49	<u>2.11</u>	<u>1.22</u>	<u>5.25</u>	<u>2.51</u>	1.27
OpenFlamingo	14.29	**24.32**	0.09	<u>7.96</u>	0.00	0.08	0.02	0.02	<u>1.49</u>
VQA fine-tuned									
OFA	29.43	17.06	3.24	4.10	2.75	**9.11**	8.21	2.84	8.21
BLIP	23.27	12.07	5.95	5.12	1.60	3.63	6.48	2.38	3.90
BLIP$_{CapFilt-L}$	23.28	12.08	5.95	5.12	1.60	3.61	6.47	2.37	3.88
ALBEF	16.33	21.87	19.31	**26.31**	1.86	6.76	8.18	4.98	**10.25**
GIT$_{LARGE}$	**41.00**	21.75	**34.89**	20.43	4.00	5.90	**17.92**	**9.51**	8.49
InstructBLIP	40.62	<u>22.55</u>	21.40	13.50	**5.08**	5.19	17.69	7.99	6.67

Table 3: Weighted model performances on the test set of the benchmark. Errors made on Others VQA data represent incorrectness, while errors made on NegP VQA data represent object hallucination. **Bold** and <u>underline</u> denote the best performances overall and in the group, respectively.

respectively. This demonstrates that all baselines are more vulnerable and susceptible to object hallucination than standard incorrectness. In addition, less incorrectness does not entail less object hallucination. For instance, PromptCap$_{BASE}$, PromptCap, and BLIP have lower scores on NegP than ALBEF despite outperforming it on Others setting. It also means that existing evaluations that solely utilize Others cases cannot effectively capture the models' risk of object hallucination.

Another point that we observe is, GIT outperforms the other baselines on both NegP and Others data, as well as manages to surpass much bigger models (e.g., InstructBLIP and Flamingo), showing that GIT is more robust against both object hallucination and general incorrectness, despite being the smallest in size (Table 2) and having a simple architecture. This achievement could be attributed to its substantial number of pre-training images, which is an order of magnitude larger than those of the other baselines. This also aligns with (Hoffmann et al., 2022), in which for the same compute budget, a smaller model trained on more data outperforms a larger model trained on fewer data and achieves more optimal performance.

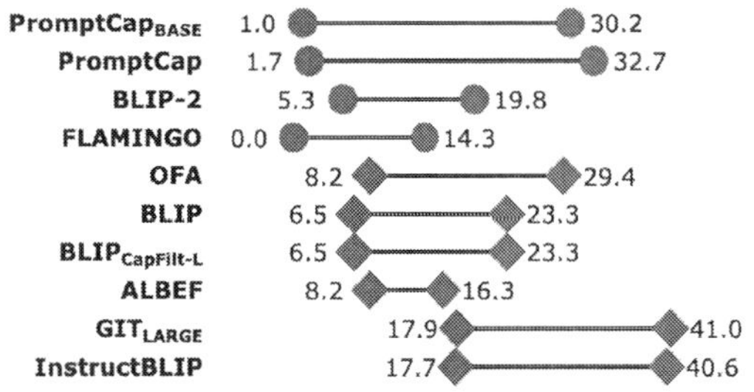

Figure 7: All baselines consistently score lower on NegP (%NegP Acc.) than Others (%Acc.).

6 Analysis and Discussions

6.1 Object hallucination and lexical diversity

Table 3 also show that NegP performance scores on existing datasets are significantly higher than on NOPE across the metrics, indicating that object hallucination is more likely to occur when the models attempt to solve the questions in NOPE. This is mainly due to the NOPE dataset having a relatively higher lexical diversity compared to the other NegP corpora, which are mostly composed of VQAv2 and Visual7W (see in Figure 6). This also aligns with the fact that NegP model performances have a strong negative Pearson correlation with the lexical diversity measures ($r = \{-0.8, -0.66, -0.65, -0.7\}$ for METEOR and HDD, MTLD, MATTR, perplexity) and proves that corpora with higher lexical diversity (e.g., NOPE) provide more challenging NegP VQA problems to assess object hallucination.

6.2 Object hallucination and language bias

As shown in Figure 9, among 5 NegP question types, all VQA-finetuned VL models fail on NegP questions about color (e.g., "What is the color of...?"), object (e.g., "What is the object

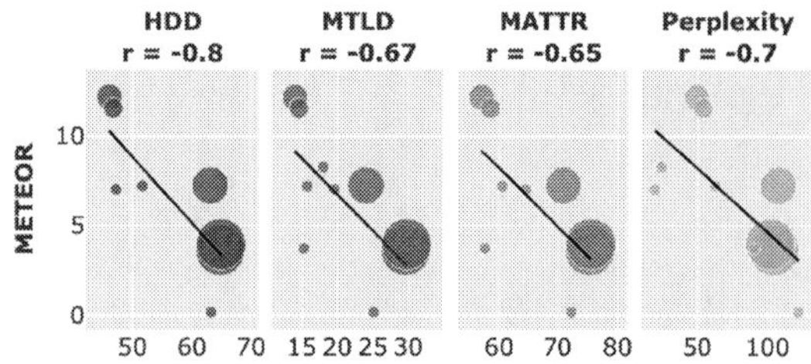

Figure 8: VL models are more prone to object hallucination on lexically diverse NegP VQA data. Dot size represents dataset size (§4.1).

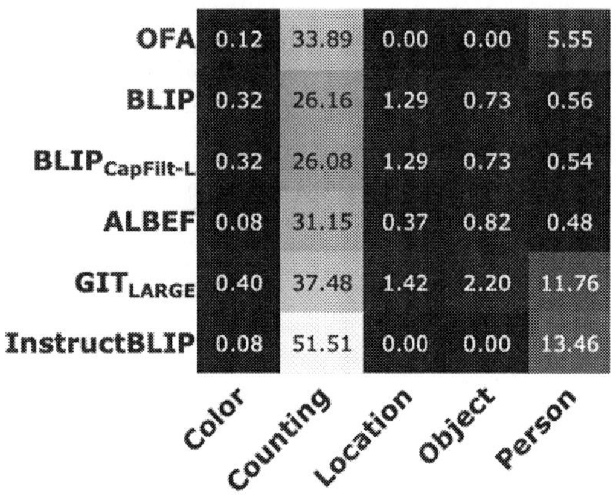

Figure 9: NegP performance of VQA fine-tuned baselines over different question types.

beside...?"), and location (e.g., "Where is...?"), while most VL models tend to hallucinate less on NegP questions about counting (e.g., "How many...?") and person (e.g., "Who is using...?"). A similar trend is observed for the zero-shot & few-shot baselines. We further inspect these two categories and find out that their answer scopes are of a smaller scope than the others in the training data. For instance, the answers to counting questions are often numbers ≤ 5, and the answers to the person questions are often the generic "man", "woman", "person", "people", and others which have fewer variations compared to object types, color names, or absolute and relative places. These facts suggest that existing VL models have a strong language bias (KV and Mittal, 2020; Niu et al., 2021b; Wu et al., 2022) toward certain question types, which result in acceptable NegP performances on those question types. Nevertheless, language bias does not solve object hallucination and even might make it worse, due to the VL models having weak visual grounding skills to verify the answer to the visual context, which might lead to errors on both NegP and Others questions.

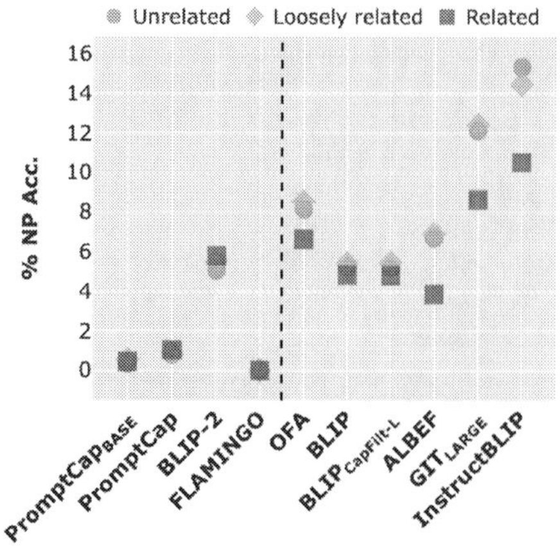

Figure 10: NegP performance of **(left)** zero-shot & few-shot and **(right)** VQA fine-tuned baselines per object-scene relevance.

6.3 Object hallucination and object-scene relevance

As shown in Figure 10, all VQA fine-tuned models perform lower when the object is closely related to the scene compared to when the object is loosely related or unrelated. This indicates that VL models have some degree of understanding NegP based on the relevance of the object in question with the scene. Although this helps VL models to understand about objects better in some cases, this also causes VL models to hallucinate more on objects that are relevant to the scene (Rohrbach et al., 2018; Kayhan et al., 2021; Dai et al., 2023b). On the other hand, the performance on loosely related or unrelated objects tend to be similar, which aligns with the similarity analysis provided in Figure 5. In contrast, for zero-shot & few-shot baselines, the differences between object-scene relevance are less apparent. However, in general, the NegP scores are also very low, except for BLIP-2, which suggests that most zero-shot models do not have an adequate understanding of NegP.

7 Conclusion

We have addressed the critical issue of object hallucination in VL models, which has been lacking a general measurement. We have introduced NOPE to assess object hallucination in VL models, investigating the discernment of objects' non-existence in visual questions by 10 state-of-the-art VL models, alongside their standard performances. Additionally, we have presented a cost-effective and scalable method for generating high-quality synthetic data with over 90% validity to overcome the severe underrepresentation of NegP cases. Through our comprehensive experiments, we have demonstrated that no VL model is exempt from object hallucination, highlighting their lack of understanding of negative object presence. Furthermore, we have identified lexical diversity, question type, and the relevance of the object to the visual scene as influential factors impacting VL models' susceptibility to object hallucination. These findings provide valuable insights into the assessment of object hallucination in VL, thereby paving the way for the future development of enhanced VL models.

8 Limitation and Future Work

Evaluation Metrics for Object Hallucination In this work, we show three metrics to measure object hallucination and incorrectness, i.e., the exact match accuracy, METEOR, and NegP accuracy. Nevertheless, in some cases, these metrics fail to capture some equivalent answer that has the same semantic meaning. For example, given an NegP question "Where is the spoon in the picture?" with the corresponding label "Nowhere", a system that answers with "There is no spoon in the picture" will get 0 scores on these three metrics, despite the answer is actually correct. We argue that the limitation of the existing metrics might hinder further research in alleviating object hallucination and we expect future works to focus on developing better metrics for measuring object hallucination.

Object Hallucination Outside of NegP Since object hallucination refers to an effect (i.e., generating non-existent objects) and not a cause, our measurement of object hallucination is limited to NegP cases, in which a VL model unfaithfully infers a supposedly non-existent object as existent in the visual context. For cases where a VL model provides an incorrect answer to Others VQA, the fine line between misclassification and object hallucination has not yet been defined.

Performances on Full Others Test Sets In order to observe the incorrectness of VL models on Others on various datasets, we compose a balanced set of ~15k data in our dev split and ~18k data in our test split from diverse VQA corpora. Obtaining the full performance on each of the source datasets requires re-running the baselines on the full test sets of each source dataset.

9 Ethics Statement

This research on object hallucination in vision-language models aims to improve the reliability and faithfulness of these models, which have significant applications in various fields such as healthcare and autonomous driving. We acknowledge the potential impact of our findings and commit to promoting responsible and ethical use of these models. We recognize that such models have the potential to perpetuate biases and stereotypes, and we have taken steps to mitigate this risk. For instance, we ensured that the synthetic data used in this study was generated in a manner that respects privacy and does not perpetuate biases or stereotypes. Furthermore, we recognize the importance of transparency and accountability in the development and use of these models. Therefore, we commit to sharing our findings and methodologies openly and making them accessible to the wider research community. We also acknowledge that these models can have unintended consequences and commit to ongoing monitoring and evaluation of their impact. Finally, we recognize that the development and use of these models must be guided by ethical principles that prioritize human well-being and social responsibility. We are committed to upholding these principles and contributing to the development of responsible and ethical practices in the field of vision-language modeling.

Acknowledgements

This work has been partially funded by PhD Fellowship Award, the Hong Kong University of Science and Technology; PF20-43679 Hong Kong PhD Fellowship Scheme, Research Grant Council, Hong Kong; and the National Research Foundation, Singapore under its AI Singapore Programme.

References

Vedika Agarwal, Rakshith Shetty, and Mario Fritz. 2020. Towards causal vqa: Revealing and reducing spurious correlations by invariant and covariant semantic editing. In *Proceedings of the IEEE/CVF Conference on Computer Vision and Pattern Recognition*, pages 9690–9698.

Aishwarya Agrawal, Dhruv Batra, and Devi Parikh. 2016. Analyzing the behavior of visual question answering models. In *Proceedings of the 2016 Conference on Empirical Methods in Natural Language Processing*, pages 1955–1960.

Aishwarya Agrawal, Dhruv Batra, Devi Parikh, and Aniruddha Kembhavi. 2018. Don't just assume; look and answer: Overcoming priors for visual question answering. In *Proceedings of the IEEE conference on computer vision and pattern recognition*, pages 4971–4980.

Jean-Baptiste Alayrac, Jeff Donahue, Pauline Luc, Antoine Miech, Iain Barr, Yana Hasson, Karel Lenc, Arthur Mensch, Katherine Millican, Malcolm Reynolds, et al. 2022. Flamingo: a visual language model for few-shot learning. *Advances in Neural Information Processing Systems*, 35:23716–23736.

Anonymous. 2023. Nusawrites: Constructing high-quality corpora for underrepresented and extremely low-resource languages. Anonymous preprint under review.

Stanislaw Antol, Aishwarya Agrawal, Jiasen Lu, Margaret Mitchell, Dhruv Batra, C Lawrence Zitnick, and Devi Parikh. 2015. Vqa: Visual question answering. In *Proceedings of the IEEE international conference on computer vision*, pages 2425–2433.

Anas Awadalla, Irena Gao, Joshua Gardner, Jack Hessel, Yusuf Hanafy, Wanrong Zhu, Kalyani Marathe, Yonatan Bitton, Samir Gadre, Jenia Jitsev, Simon Kornblith, Pang Wei Koh, Gabriel Ilharco, Mitchell Wortsman, and Ludwig Schmidt. 2023. Openflamingo.

Satanjeev Banerjee and Alon Lavie. 2005. Meteor: An automatic metric for mt evaluation with improved correlation with human judgments. In *Proceedings of the acl workshop on intrinsic and extrinsic evaluation measures for machine translation and/or summarization*, pages 65–72.

Yejin Bang, Samuel Cahyawijaya, Nayeon Lee, Wenliang Dai, Dan Su, Bryan Wilie, Holy Lovenia, Ziwei Ji, Tiezheng Yu, Willy Chung, et al. 2023. A multitask, multilingual, multimodal evaluation of chatgpt on reasoning, hallucination, and interactivity. *arXiv preprint arXiv:2302.04023*.

Ali Furkan Biten, Lluis Gomez, and Dimosthenis Karatzas. 2022. Let there be a clock on the beach: Reducing object hallucination in image captioning. In *Proceedings of the IEEE/CVF Winter Conference on Applications of Computer Vision*, pages 1381–1390.

Sid Black, Leo Gao, Phil Wang, Connor Leahy, and Stella Biderman. 2021. GPT-Neo: Large Scale Autoregressive Language Modeling with Mesh-Tensorflow.

Samuel Cahyawijaya, Genta Indra Winata, Bryan Wilie, Karissa Vincentio, Xiaohong Li, Adhiguna Kuncoro, Sebastian Ruder, Zhi Yuan Lim, Syafri Bahar, Masayu Khodra, Ayu Purwarianti, and Pascale Fung. 2021. IndoNLG: Benchmark and resources for evaluating Indonesian natural language generation. In *Proceedings of the 2021 Conference on Empirical Methods in Natural Language Processing*, pages 8875–8898, Online and Punta Cana, Dominican Republic. Association for Computational Linguistics.

Soravit Changpinyo, Doron Kukliansy, Idan Szpektor, Xi Chen, Nan Ding, and Radu Soricut. 2022. All you may need for vqa are image captions. In *Proceedings of the 2022 Conference of the North American Chapter of the Association for Computational Linguistics: Human Language Technologies*, pages 1947–1963.

Paul F Christiano, Jan Leike, Tom Brown, Miljan Martic, Shane Legg, and Dario Amodei. 2017. Deep reinforcement learning from human preferences. *Advances in neural information processing systems*, 30.

Hyung Won Chung, Le Hou, Shayne Longpre, Barret Zoph, Yi Tay, William Fedus, Eric Li, Xuezhi Wang, Mostafa Dehghani, Siddhartha Brahma, et al. 2022. Scaling instruction-finetuned language models. *arXiv preprint arXiv:2210.11416*.

Michael A. Covington and Joe D. McFall. 2010. Cutting the gordian knot: The moving-average type–token ratio (MATTR). *Journal of Quantitative Linguistics*, 17(2):94–100.

Wenliang Dai, Samuel Cahyawijaya, Zihan Liu, and Pascale Fung. 2021. Multimodal end-to-end sparse model for emotion recognition. In *Proceedings of the 2021 Conference of the North American Chapter of the Association for Computational Linguistics: Human Language Technologies*, pages 5305–5316, Online. Association for Computational Linguistics.

Wenliang Dai, Lu Hou, Lifeng Shang, Xin Jiang, Qun Liu, and Pascale Fung. 2022. Enabling multimodal generation on CLIP via vision-language knowledge distillation. In *Findings of the Association for Computational Linguistics: ACL 2022*, pages 2383–2395, Dublin, Ireland. Association for Computational Linguistics.

Wenliang Dai, Junnan Li, Dongxu Li, Anthony Meng Huat Tiong, Junqi Zhao, Weisheng Wang, Boyang Li, Pascale Fung, and Steven Hoi. 2023a. Instructblip: Towards general-purpose vision-language models with instruction tuning.

Wenliang Dai, Zihan Liu, Ziwei Ji, Dan Su, and Pascale Fung. 2023b. Plausible may not be faithful: Probing object hallucination in vision-language pre-training. pages 2136–2148.

Zhengxiao Du, Yujie Qian, Xiao Liu, Ming Ding, Jiezhong Qiu, Zhilin Yang, and Jie Tang. 2022. Glm: General language model pretraining with autoregressive blank infilling. In *Proceedings of the 60th Annual Meeting of the Association for Computational Linguistics (Volume 1: Long Papers)*, pages 320–335.

Allyson Ettinger. 2020. What bert is not: Lessons from a new suite of psycholinguistic diagnostics for language models. *Transactions of the Association for Computational Linguistics*, 8:34–48.

Angela Fan, Mike Lewis, and Yann Dauphin. 2018. Hierarchical neural story generation. In *Proceedings of the 56th Annual Meeting of the Association for Computational Linguistics (Volume 1: Long Papers)*, pages 889–898, Melbourne, Australia. Association for Computational Linguistics.

Tejas Gokhale, Pratyay Banerjee, Chitta Baral, and Yezhou Yang. 2020. Mutant: A training paradigm for out-of-distribution generalization in visual question answering. In *Proceedings of the 2020 Conference on Empirical Methods in Natural Language Processing (EMNLP)*, pages 878–892.

Yash Goyal, Tejas Khot, Douglas Summers-Stay, Dhruv Batra, and Devi Parikh. 2017. Making the v in vqa matter: Elevating the role of image understanding in visual question answering. In *Proceedings of the IEEE conference on computer vision and pattern recognition*, pages 6904–6913.

Vipul Gupta, Zhuowan Li, Adam Kortylewski, Chenyu Zhang, Yingwei Li, and Alan Yuille. 2022. Swapmix: Diagnosing and regularizing the over-reliance on visual context in visual question answering. In *Proceedings of the IEEE/CVF Conference on Computer Vision and Pattern Recognition*, pages 5078–5088.

Danna Gurari, Qing Li, Chi Lin, Yinan Zhao, Anhong Guo, Abigale Stangl, and Jeffrey P Bigham. 2019. Vizwiz-priv: A dataset for recognizing the presence and purpose of private visual information in images taken by blind people. In *Proceedings of the IEEE/CVF Conference on Computer Vision and Pattern Recognition*, pages 939–948.

Danna Gurari, Qing Li, Abigale J Stangl, Anhong Guo, Chi Lin, Kristen Grauman, Jiebo Luo, and Jeffrey P Bigham. 2018. Vizwiz grand challenge: Answering visual questions from blind people. In *Proceedings of the IEEE conference on computer vision and pattern recognition*, pages 3608–3617.

Jack Hessel, Ari Holtzman, Maxwell Forbes, Ronan Le Bras, and Yejin Choi. 2021. CLIPScore: A reference-free evaluation metric for image captioning. In *Proceedings of the 2021 Conference on Empirical Methods in Natural Language Processing*, pages 7514–7528, Online and Punta Cana, Dominican Republic. Association for Computational Linguistics.

Jordan Hoffmann, Sebastian Borgeaud, Arthur Mensch, Elena Buchatskaya, Trevor Cai, Eliza Rutherford, Diego de Las Casas, Lisa Anne Hendricks, Johannes Welbl, Aidan Clark, et al. 2022. Training compute-optimal large language models. *arXiv preprint arXiv:2203.15556*.

Arian Hosseini, Siva Reddy, Dzmitry Bahdanau, R Devon Hjelm, Alessandro Sordoni, and Aaron Courville. 2021. Understanding by understanding not: Modeling negation in language models. In *Proceedings of the 2021 Conference of the North American Chapter of the Association for Computational Linguistics: Human Language Technologies*, pages 1301–1312, Online. Association for Computational Linguistics.

Yushi* Hu, Hang* Hua, Zhengyuan Yang, Weijia Shi, Noah A Smith, and Jiebo Luo. 2022. Promptcap: Prompt-guided task-aware image captioning. *arXiv preprint arXiv:2211.09699*.

Etsuko Ishii, Genta Indra Winata, Samuel Cahyawijaya, Divesh Lala, Tatsuya Kawahara, and Pascale Fung. 2021. ERICA: An empathetic android companion for covid-19 quarantine. In *Proceedings of the 22nd Annual Meeting of the Special Interest Group on Discourse and Dialogue*, pages 257–260, Singapore and Online. Association for Computational Linguistics.

Srinivasan Iyer, Xi Victoria Lin, Ramakanth Pasunuru, Todor Mihaylov, Dániel Simig, Ping Yu, Kurt Shuster, Tianlu Wang, Qing Liu, Punit Singh Koura, et al. 2022. Opt-iml: Scaling language model instruction meta learning through the lens of generalization. *arXiv preprint arXiv:2212.12017*.

Joel Jang, Seonghyeon Ye, and Minjoon Seo. 2023. Can large language models truly understand prompts? a case study with negated prompts. In *Transfer Learning for Natural Language Processing Workshop*, pages 52–62. PMLR.

Ziwei Ji, Nayeon Lee, Rita Frieske, Tiezheng Yu, Dan Su, Yan Xu, Etsuko Ishii, Yejin Bang, Andrea Madotto, and Pascale Fung. 2022a. Survey of hallucination in natural language generation. *ACM Computing Surveys*.

Ziwei Ji, Yan Xu, I-Tsun Cheng, Samuel Cahyawijaya, Rita Frieske, Etsuko Ishii, Min Zeng, Andrea Madotto, and Pascale Fung. 2022b. VScript: Controllable script generation with visual presentation. In *Proceedings of the 2nd Conference of the Asia-Pacific Chapter of the Association for Computational Linguistics and the 12th International Joint Conference on Natural Language Processing: System Demonstrations*, pages 1–8, Taipei, Taiwan. Association for Computational Linguistics.

Chenchen Jing, Yuwei Wu, Xiaoxun Zhang, Yunde Jia, and Qi Wu. 2020. Overcoming language priors in vqa via decomposed linguistic representations. In *Proceedings of the AAAI conference on artificial intelligence*, volume 34, pages 11181–11188.

Justin Johnson, Bharath Hariharan, Laurens Van Der Maaten, Li Fei-Fei, C Lawrence Zitnick, and Ross Girshick. 2017. Clevr: A diagnostic dataset for compositional language and elementary visual reasoning. In *Proceedings of the IEEE conference on computer vision and pattern recognition*, pages 2901–2910.

Kushal Kafle and Christopher Kanan. 2017. An analysis of visual question answering algorithms. In *Proceedings of the IEEE international conference on computer vision*, pages 1965–1973.

Nora Kassner and Hinrich Schütze. 2020. Negated and misprimed probes for pretrained language models: Birds can talk, but cannot fly. In *Proceedings of the*

58th Annual Meeting of the Association for Computational Linguistics*, pages 7811–7818.

Osman Semih Kayhan, Bart Vredebregt, and Jan C. van Gemert. 2021. Hallucination in object detection — a study in visual part verification. In *2021 IEEE International Conference on Image Processing (ICIP)*, pages 2234–2238.

Corentin Kervadec, Grigory Antipov, Moez Baccouche, and Christian Wolf. 2021. Roses are red, violets are blue... but should vqa expect them to? In *Proceedings of the IEEE/CVF Conference on Computer Vision and Pattern Recognition (CVPR)*, pages 2776–2785.

Ranjay Krishna, Yuke Zhu, Oliver Groth, Justin Johnson, Kenji Hata, Joshua Kravitz, Stephanie Chen, Yannis Kalantidis, Li-Jia Li, David A Shamma, Michael Bernstein, and Li Fei-Fei. 2016. Visual genome: Connecting language and vision using crowdsourced dense image annotations.

Alina Kuznetsova, Hassan Rom, Neil Alldrin, Jasper Uijlings, Ivan Krasin, Jordi Pont-Tuset, Shahab Kamali, Stefan Popov, Matteo Malloci, Alexander Kolesnikov, et al. 2020. The open images dataset v4: Unified image classification, object detection, and visual relationship detection at scale. *International Journal of Computer Vision*, 128(7):1956–1981.

Gouthaman KV and Anurag Mittal. 2020. Reducing language biases in visual question answering with visually-grounded question encoder. In *Computer Vision – ECCV 2020*, pages 18–34, Cham. Springer International Publishing.

Mike Lewis, Denis Yarats, Yann Dauphin, Devi Parikh, and Dhruv Batra. 2017. Deal or no deal? end-to-end learning of negotiation dialogues. In *Proceedings of the 2017 Conference on Empirical Methods in Natural Language Processing*, pages 2443–2453, Copenhagen, Denmark. Association for Computational Linguistics.

Junnan Li, Dongxu Li, Silvio Savarese, and Steven Hoi. 2023a. Blip-2: Bootstrapping language-image pre-training with frozen image encoders and large language models. *ICML*.

Junnan Li, Dongxu Li, Caiming Xiong, and Steven Hoi. 2022. Blip: Bootstrapping language-image pre-training for unified vision-language understanding and generation. In *International Conference on Machine Learning*, pages 12888–12900. PMLR.

Junnan Li, Ramprasaath Selvaraju, Akhilesh Gotmare, Shafiq Joty, Caiming Xiong, and Steven Chu Hong Hoi. 2021a. Align before fuse: Vision and language representation learning with momentum distillation. *Advances in neural information processing systems*, 34:9694–9705.

Linjie Li, Jie Lei, Zhe Gan, and Jingjing Liu. 2021b. Adversarial vqa: A new benchmark for evaluating the robustness of vqa models. In *Proceedings of the IEEE/CVF International Conference on Computer Vision*, pages 2042–2051.

Yifan Li, Yifan Du, Kun Zhou, Jinpeng Wang, Wayne Xin Zhao, and Ji-Rong Wen. 2023b. Evaluating object hallucination in large vision-language models. *arXiv preprint arXiv:2305.10355*.

Holy Lovenia, Samuel Cahyawijaya, and Pascale Fung. 2023. Which one are you referring to? multimodal object identification in situated dialogue. In *Proceedings of the 17th Conference of the European Chapter of the Association for Computational Linguistics: Student Research Workshop*, pages 61–72, Dubrovnik, Croatia. Association for Computational Linguistics.

Holy Lovenia, Bryan Wilie, Romain Barraud, Samuel Cahyawijaya, Willy Chung, and Pascale Fung. 2022. Every picture tells a story: Image-grounded controllable stylistic story generation. In *Proceedings of the 6th Joint SIGHUM Workshop on Computational Linguistics for Cultural Heritage, Social Sciences, Humanities and Literature*, pages 40–52, Gyeongju, Republic of Korea. International Conference on Computational Linguistics.

Pan Lu, Lei Ji, Wei Zhang, Nan Duan, Ming Zhou, and Jianyong Wang. 2018. R-vqa: Learning visual relation facts with semantic attention for visual question answering. In *SIGKDD 2018*.

Kenneth Marino, Mohammad Rastegari, Ali Farhadi, and Roozbeh Mottaghi. 2019. Ok-vqa: A visual question answering benchmark requiring external knowledge. In *Proceedings of the IEEE/cvf conference on computer vision and pattern recognition*, pages 3195–3204.

Philip M. McCarthy. 2005. *An assessment of the range and usefulness of lexical diversity measures and the potential of the measure of textual, lexical diversity (MTLD)*. Ph.D. thesis, The University of Memphis.

Philip M McCarthy and Scott Jarvis. 2007. vocd: A theoretical and empirical evaluation. *Language Testing*, 24(4):459–488.

Philip M. McCarthy and Scott Jarvis. 2010. MTLD, vocd-d, and HD-d: A validation study of sophisticated approaches to lexical diversity assessment. *Behavior Research Methods*, 42(2):381–392.

Niklas Muennighoff, Thomas Wang, Lintang Sutawika, Adam Roberts, Stella Biderman, Teven Le Scao, M Saiful Bari, Sheng Shen, Zheng-Xin Yong, Hailey Schoelkopf, Xiangru Tang, Dragomir Radev, Alham Fikri Aji, Khalid Almubarak, Samuel Albanie, Zaid Alyafeai, Albert Webson, Edward Raff, and Colin Raffel. 2022. Crosslingual generalization through multitask finetuning.

Yixin Nie, Adina Williams, Emily Dinan, Mohit Bansal, Jason Weston, and Douwe Kiela. 2020. Adversarial NLI: A new benchmark for natural language understanding. In *Proceedings of the 58th Annual Meeting of the Association for Computational Linguistics*. Association for Computational Linguistics.

Erik Nijkamp, Bo Pang, Hiroaki Hayashi, Lifu Tu, Huan Wang, Yingbo Zhou, Silvio Savarese, and Caiming Xiong. 2023. Codegen: An open large language model for code with multi-turn program synthesis. In *The Eleventh International Conference on Learning Representations (ICLR)*.

Chuang Niu, Hongming Shan, and Ge Wang. 2022. Spice: Semantic pseudo-labeling for image clustering. *IEEE Transactions on Image Processing*, 31:7264–7278.

Yulei Niu, Kaihua Tang, Hanwang Zhang, Zhiwu Lu, Xian-Sheng Hua, and Ji-Rong Wen. 2021a. Counterfactual vqa: A cause-effect look at language bias. In *Proceedings of the IEEE/CVF Conference on Computer Vision and Pattern Recognition*, pages 12700–12710.

Yulei Niu, Kaihua Tang, Hanwang Zhang, Zhiwu Lu, Xian-Sheng Hua, and Ji-Rong Wen. 2021b. Counterfactual vqa: A cause-effect look at language bias. pages 12695–12705.

Randolph Quirk, Sidney Greenbaum, Geoffrey Leech, and Jan Svartoik. 1985. *A COMPREHENSIVE GRAMMAR OF THE ENGLISH LANGUAGE*. Longman, New York.

Alec Radford, Jong Wook Kim, Chris Hallacy, Aditya Ramesh, Gabriel Goh, Sandhini Agarwal, Girish Sastry, Amanda Askell, Pamela Mishkin, Jack Clark, et al. 2021. Learning transferable visual models from natural language supervision. In *International conference on machine learning*, pages 8748–8763. PMLR.

Colin Raffel, Noam Shazeer, Adam Roberts, Katherine Lee, Sharan Narang, Michael Matena, Yanqi Zhou, Wei Li, and Peter J. Liu. 2020. Exploring the limits of transfer learning with a unified text-to-text transformer. *Journal of Machine Learning Research*, 21(140):1–67.

Arijit Ray, Karan Sikka, Ajay Divakaran, Stefan Lee, and Giedrius Burachas. 2019. Sunny and dark outside?! improving answer consistency in vqa through entailed question generation. *arXiv preprint arXiv:1909.04696*.

Mengye Ren, Ryan Kiros, and Richard Zemel. 2015. Exploring models and data for image question answering. *Advances in neural information processing systems*, 28.

Anna Rohrbach, Lisa Anne Hendricks, Kaylee Burns, Trevor Darrell, and Kate Saenko. 2018. Object hallucination in image captioning. In *Proceedings of the 2018 Conference on Empirical Methods in Natural Language Processing*, pages 4035–4045.

Victor Sanh, Albert Webson, Colin Raffel, Stephen Bach, Lintang Sutawika, Zaid Alyafeai, Antoine Chaffin, Arnaud Stiegler, Arun Raja, Manan Dey, et al. 2022. Multitask prompted training enables zero-shot task generalization. In *International Conference on Learning Representations*.

Teven Le Scao, Angela Fan, Christopher Akiki, Ellie Pavlick, Suzana Ilić, Daniel Hesslow, Roman Castagné, Alexandra Sasha Luccioni, François Yvon, Matthias Gallé, et al. 2022. Bloom: A 176b-parameter open-access multilingual language model. *arXiv preprint arXiv:2211.05100*.

Meet Shah, Xinlei Chen, Marcus Rohrbach, and Devi Parikh. 2019. Cycle-consistency for robust visual question answering. In *Proceedings of the IEEE/CVF Conference on Computer Vision and Pattern Recognition*, pages 6649–6658.

Piyush Sharma, Nan Ding, Sebastian Goodman, and Radu Soricut. 2018. Conceptual captions: A cleaned, hypernymed, image alt-text dataset for automatic image captioning. In *Proceedings of the 56th Annual Meeting of the Association for Computational Linguistics (Volume 1: Long Papers)*, pages 2556–2565.

Lucas Shen. 2021. Measuring political media slant using text data.

Lucas Shen. 2022. LexicalRichness: A small module to compute textual lexical richness.

Sasha Sheng, Amanpreet Singh, Vedanuj Goswami, Jose Magana, Tristan Thrush, Wojciech Galuba, Devi Parikh, and Douwe Kiela. 2021. Human-adversarial visual question answering. *Advances in Neural Information Processing Systems*, 34:20346–20359.

Amanpreet Singh, Vivek Natarajan, Meet Shah, Yu Jiang, Xinlei Chen, Dhruv Batra, Devi Parikh, and Marcus Rohrbach. 2019. Towards vqa models that can read. In *Proceedings of the IEEE/CVF Conference on Computer Vision and Pattern Recognition (CVPR)*.

Nisan Stiennon, Long Ouyang, Jeffrey Wu, Daniel Ziegler, Ryan Lowe, Chelsea Voss, Alec Radford, Dario Amodei, and Paul F Christiano. 2020. Learning to summarize with human feedback. *Advances in Neural Information Processing Systems*, 33:3008–3021.

Guy Tevet and Jonathan Berant. 2021. Evaluating the evaluation of diversity in natural language generation. In *Proceedings of the 16th Conference of the European Chapter of the Association for Computational Linguistics: Main Volume*, pages 326–346, Online. Association for Computational Linguistics.

Hugo Touvron, Thibaut Lavril, Gautier Izacard, Xavier Martinet, Marie-Anne Lachaux, Timothée Lacroix, Baptiste Rozière, Naman Goyal, Eric Hambro, Faisal Azhar, et al. 2023. Llama: Open and efficient foundation language models. *arXiv preprint arXiv:2302.13971*.

Ramakrishna Vedantam, C Lawrence Zitnick, and Devi Parikh. 2015. Cider: Consensus-based image description evaluation. In *Proceedings of the IEEE conference on computer vision and pattern recognition*, pages 4566–4575.

Ryan Volum, Sudha Rao, Michael Xu, Gabriel DesGarennes, Chris Brockett, Benjamin Van Durme, Olivia Deng, Akanksha Malhotra, and Bill Dolan. 2022. Craft an iron sword: Dynamically generating interactive game characters by prompting large language models tuned on code. In *Proceedings of the 3rd Wordplay: When Language Meets Games Workshop (Wordplay 2022)*, pages 25–43, Seattle, United States. Association for Computational Linguistics.

Jianfeng Wang, Zhengyuan Yang, Xiaowei Hu, Linjie Li, Kevin Lin, Zhe Gan, Zicheng Liu, Ce Liu, and Lijuan Wang. 2022a. Git: A generative image-to-text transformer for vision and language. *Transactions of Machine Learning Research.*

Peng Wang, An Yang, Rui Men, Junyang Lin, Shuai Bai, Zhikang Li, Jianxin Ma, Chang Zhou, Jingren Zhou, and Hongxia Yang. 2022b. Ofa: Unifying architectures, tasks, and modalities through a simple sequence-to-sequence learning framework. In *International Conference on Machine Learning*, pages 23318–23340. PMLR.

Qingyun Wang, Lifu Huang, Zhiying Jiang, Kevin Knight, Heng Ji, Mohit Bansal, and Yi Luan. 2019. PaperRobot: Incremental draft generation of scientific ideas. In *Proceedings of the 57th Annual Meeting of the Association for Computational Linguistics*, pages 1980–1991, Florence, Italy. Association for Computational Linguistics.

Yizhong Wang, Yeganeh Kordi, Swaroop Mishra, Alisa Liu, Noah A Smith, Daniel Khashabi, and Hannaneh Hajishirzi. 2022c. Self-instruct: Aligning language model with self generated instructions. *arXiv preprint arXiv:2212.10560.*

Jason Wei, Maarten Paul Bosma, Vincent Zhao, Kelvin Guu, Adams Wei Yu, Brian Lester, Nan Du, Andrew Mingbo Dai, and Quoc V. Le. 2022a. Finetuned language models are zero-shot learners. In *International Conference on Learning Representations (ICLR).*

Jason Wei, Xuezhi Wang, Dale Schuurmans, Maarten Bosma, Fei Xia, Ed H Chi, Quoc V Le, Denny Zhou, et al. 2022b. Chain-of-thought prompting elicits reasoning in large language models. In *Advances in Neural Information Processing Systems.*

Spencer Whitehead, Hui Wu, Yi Ren Fung, Heng Ji, Rogerio Feris, and Kate Saenko. 2020. Learning from lexical perturbations for consistent visual question answering. *arXiv preprint arXiv:2011.13406.*

Yike Wu, Yu Zhao, Shiwan Zhao, Ying Zhang, Xiaojie Yuan, Guoqing Zhao, and Ning Jiang. 2022. Overcoming language priors in visual question answering via distinguishing superficially similar instances. In *Proceedings of the 29th International Conference on Computational Linguistics*, pages 5721–5729, Gyeongju, Republic of Korea. International Committee on Computational Linguistics.

Yijun Xiao and William Yang Wang. 2021. On hallucination and predictive uncertainty in conditional language generation. In *Proceedings of the 16th Conference of the European Chapter of the Association for Computational Linguistics: Main Volume.*

Zhengyuan Yang, Yijuan Lu, Jianfeng Wang, Xi Yin, Dinei Florencio, Lijuan Wang, Cha Zhang, Lei Zhang, and Jiebo Luo. 2021. Tap: Text-aware pretraining for text-vqa and text-caption. In *Proceedings of the IEEE/CVF conference on computer vision and pattern recognition*, pages 8751–8761.

Kexin Yi, Jiajun Wu, Chuang Gan, Antonio Torralba, Pushmeet Kohli, and Josh Tenenbaum. 2018. Neural-symbolic vqa: Disentangling reasoning from vision and language understanding. *Advances in neural information processing systems*, 31.

Aohan Zeng, Xiao Liu, Zhengxiao Du, Zihan Wang, Hanyu Lai, Ming Ding, Zhuoyi Yang, Yifan Xu, Wendi Zheng, Xiao Xia, Weng Lam Tam, Zixuan Ma, Yufei Xue, Jidong Zhai, Wenguang Chen, Zhiyuan Liu, Peng Zhang, Yuxiao Dong, and Jie Tang. 2023. GLM-130b: An open bilingual pre-trained model. In *The Eleventh International Conference on Learning Representations (ICLR).*

Susan Zhang, Stephen Roller, Naman Goyal, Mikel Artetxe, Moya Chen, Shuohui Chen, Christopher Dewan, Mona Diab, Xian Li, Xi Victoria Lin, et al. 2022. Opt: Open pre-trained transformer language models. *arXiv preprint arXiv:2205.01068.*

Wenqiao Zhang, Haochen Shi, Siliang Tang, Jun Xiao, Qiang Yu, and Yueting Zhuang. 2021. Consensus graph representation learning for better grounded image captioning. In *Proceedings of the AAAI Conference on Artificial Intelligence*, volume 35, pages 3394–3402.

Luowei Zhou, Hamid Palangi, Lei Zhang, Houdong Hu, Jason Corso, and Jianfeng Gao. 2020. Unified vision-language pre-training for image captioning and vqa. In *Proceedings of the AAAI conference on artificial intelligence*, volume 34, pages 13041–13049.

Yuke Zhu, Oliver Groth, Michael Bernstein, and Li Fei-Fei. 2016. Visual7w: Grounded question answering in images. In *Proceedings of the IEEE conference on computer vision and pattern recognition*, pages 4995–5004.

A Prompt Templates

We provide the prompt templates and examples for the **generate-from-scratch** and **list-then-rewrite** methods in Table 4 and Table 5, respectively.

Template 1
Create a question beginning with "<INTERROGATIVE_WORD>" from this image caption: "<IMAGE_CAPTION>" with an answer of "<ANSWER>".
Example: Create a question beginning with "who" from this image caption: "This image consists of an airplane in the air. On which, we can see the text. In the background, there is sky." with an answer of "nobody".
Generated question: Who is in the airplane in this image?

Template 2
Turn the text "<IMAGE_CAPTION>" into a "<INTERROGATIVE_WORD>" question with an answer "<ANSWER>":
Example: Turn the text "This is an outside view. Here I can see the cars on the ground and there are two persons standing. In the background there is a tent, shelter and trees. At the top of the image there is the sky. At the bottom there is grass." into a "how many" question with an answer "none":
Generated question: How many buildings are visible in the outside view?

Template 3
Given an answer "<ANSWER>", generate an appropriate question starting with "<INTERROGATIVE_WORD>" from the text "<IMAGE_CAPTION>".
Example: Given an answer "nowhere", generate an appropriate question starting with "where" from the text "In this picture, we see a woman. She is staring at something and she might be posing for the photo. We see a nail is pierced on her face. She might be taking bath. In the background, we see a wall and a white color object which looks like a bathtub.".
Generated question: Where is the ideal location to put a nail on a person's face while they are taking a bath?

Template 4
Write a question that begins with "<INTERROGATIVE_WORD>" and is answered by "<ANSWER>" based on the text "<IMAGE_CAPTION>".
Example: Write a question that begins with "what" and is answered by "nothing" based on the text "In this image I can see food item in a cooking vessel, which is on the stove. In the background there are some objects.".
Generated question: What can you see in the background of the image?

Template 5
Rewrite the statement "<IMAGE_CAPTION>" as a question that starts with interrogative phrase "<INTERROGATIVE_WORD>" and has an answer of "<ANSWER>".
Example: Rewrite the statement "In the image I can see food item in the bowl. The background of the image is blurred." as a question that starts with interrogative phrase "which" and has an answer of "neither".
Generated question: Which part of the image is not blurred and which object is visible in the bowl?

Table 4: Prompt templates used in the **generate-from-scratch** (§3.1) and their corresponding examples.

Object Listing Template
Description:
"<IMAGE_CAPTION>"

List 10 tangible objects that are closely related to the description, but are not mentioned there. Also avoid these objects: <IMAGE_LABELS>.
Example:
Description:
"In this picture we can see some food products in the glass jars."

List 10 tangible objects that are closely related to the description, but are not mentioned there. Also avoid these objects: Vegetable.
Response:
1. Spices, 2. Canned fruits, 3. Nuts, 4. Sugar, 5. Coffee beans, 6. Honey, 7. Pasta, 8. Chocolates, 9. Tea leaves, 10. Jams and preserves

---

Question Rewriting Template
Question templates:
<REFERENCE_QUESTIONS_BASED_ON_FIRST_TURN_ANSWER>

Paraphrase each of these <NUMBER> questions while keeping the sentence as a question with a question mark.
Example:
Question templates:
1. Who is using the object above the spices?
2. What object is located under the canned fruits?
3. Who is holding the object on the right of the nuts?
4. What is the color of the sugar?
5. Who is using the coffee beans?
6. What object is located on the left of the honey?
7. What object is located on the left of the pasta?
8. What object is located on the left of the chocolates?
9. What is the color of the tea leaves?
10. Where is the jams and preserves located in the image?

Paraphrase each of these 10 questions while keeping the sentence as a question with a question mark.
Generated question:
1. Who is the user of the spices in the picture?
2. Which product can be found below the canned fruits?
3. Who is the individual holding the object to the right of the nuts?
4. Can you tell me the color of the sugar in the glass jars?
5. Who might be utilizing the coffee beans shown in the image?
6. What is the item on the right side of the honey?
7. What comes up on the left of the pasta in the photograph?
8. What is situated on the left of the chocolates in the picture?
9. What is the color of the tea leaves displayed in the glass jars?
10. Where exactly can the jams and preserves be found in this image?

Table 5: Prompt templates used in the **list-then-rewrite** (§3.1) and their corresponding examples.

B Reference Question Templates

Table 6 presents the pool of question templates used to automatically build the reference questions for the **list-then-rewrite** in §3.1.

No	Question template	NegP answer
1	What is the color of the <OBJECT>?	none / nothing
2	What object is located above / under / on the left of / on the right of the <OBJECT>?	none / nothing
3	Where is the <OBJECT> located in the image?	nowhere
4	How many <OBJECT> are there in the image?	zero / 0 / none
5	Who is holding / using the <OBJECT>?	no one / nobody
6	Who is holding / using the object above / under / on the left of / on the right of the <OBJECT>?	no one / nobody

Table 6: Question templates utilized to construct the reference questions for the question rewriting step in the **list-then-rewrite** prompting methodology in §3.1.

C Automatic Validation Methodologies of NegP VQA Data Generation

Generate-from-scratch To ensure the validity of q_i, we use a model fine-tuned on natural language inference (NLI) to determine whether a generated question q_i and answer a_i pair (i.e., hypothesis) logically entails its corresponding image caption c_i (i.e., premise). We also utilize a fine-tuned binary classifier to determine whether a generated question q_i and answer a_i pair fits a given visual context v_i. If the question q_i and answer a_i pair is true (entailment) or undetermined (neutral) given c_i as well as matches with v_i, then the generated question q_i is judged as valid by the automatic validation.

List-then-rewrite For the automatic validation of a listed object $o_{i,j}$, we extract lemmatized noun tokens from its corresponding image caption c_i and obtain the object names from l_i as the objects present in v_i. If $o_{i,j}$ does not match with any of the extracted objects, then $o_{i,j}$ is a valid non-existent object. For the automatic validation of a generated question $q_{i,j}$, if $q_{i,j}$ does not contradict its respective reference question $r_{i,j}$, then the generated question $q_{i,j}$ is considered valid.

D Implementation Details of NegP VQA Data Generation

We implement §3.1 with the following LLMs that employ: 1) multi-task prompted fine-tuning, i.e., **BLOOMZ** (Muennighoff et al., 2022) and **T0** (Sanh et al., 2022); 2) instruction meta-learning, i.e., **OPT-IML** (Iyer et al., 2022); 3) synthetic self-instruct, i.e., **Alpaca** (Wang et al., 2022c); 4) instruction (Wei et al., 2022a) and chain-of-thought fine-tuning (Wei et al., 2022b), i.e., **FLAN T5** and **FLAN Alpaca** (Chung et al., 2022); 5) multi-task instruction pre-training, i.e., **ChatGLM** (Zeng et al., 2023); 6) conversation-style instruction tuning and reinforcement learning with human feedback (RLHF) (Christiano et al., 2017; Stiennon et al., 2020), i.e., **ChatGPT (GPT-3.5)**. More details are presented in Table 7.

We utilize Open Images v7 as our image captioning dataset $\mathcal{D}_{cap}$ with respect to the provided splits. For automatic validation with NLI, we use the RoBERTa model fine-tuned on various NLI corpora that achieves the best performance on the Adversarial NLI benchmark (Nie et al., 2020).[4] For automatic validation with image-QA pair classification, we build a simple CLIP-based (Radford et al., 2021) binary classifier. We provide the details in Appendix D.1. For the **list-then-rewrite** method, we use $m = 10$.

D.1 Image-QA Pair Classification

To construct a model for our image-QA pair classification, we construct a balanced image-QA corpus using NegP and Others VQA data randomly selected from 9 existing VQA datasets, i.e., VQAv2

[4]https://huggingface.co/ynie/roberta-large-snli_mnli_fever_anli_R1_R2_R3-nli

No	Model	Size	References	Access
1	BLOOMZ (3B)	3B	(Muennighoff et al., 2022; Scao et al., 2022)	https://huggingface.co/bigscience/bloomz-3b
2	BLOOMZ (7.1B)	7.1B	(Muennighoff et al., 2022; Scao et al., 2022)	https://huggingface.co/bigscience/bloomz-7b1
3	T0	3B	(Sanh et al., 2022)	https://huggingface.co/bigscience/T0_3B
4	OPT-IML	1.3B	(Iyer et al., 2022; Zhang et al., 2022)	https://huggingface.co/facebook/opt-iml-max-1.3b
5	Alpaca	7B	(Wang et al., 2022c; Touvron et al., 2023)	https://huggingface.co/chavinlo/alpaca-native
6	FLAN T5 XL	3B	(Chung et al., 2022; Raffel et al., 2020)	https://huggingface.co/google/flan-t5-xl
7	FLAN T5 XXL	11B	(Chung et al., 2022; Raffel et al., 2020)	https://huggingface.co/google/flan-t5-xxl
8	FLAN Alpaca XL	3B	(Chung et al., 2022; Wang et al., 2022c)	https://huggingface.co/declare-lab/flan-alpaca-xl
9	ChatGLM	6B	(Zeng et al., 2023; Du et al., 2022)	https://huggingface.co/THUDM/chatglm-6b
10	ChatGPT	175B	-	https://platform.openai.com/docs/models/gpt-3-5

Table 7: Instruction-tuned LLMs used in Appendix D.

(Balanced Real) (Antol et al., 2015), AdVQA (Sheng et al., 2021), VizWiz (Gurari et al., 2018, 2019), TextVQA (Singh et al., 2019), R-VQA (Lu et al., 2018), Visual7W (Zhu et al., 2016), TDIUC (Kafle and Kanan, 2017), VQA-Rephrasings (Shah et al., 2019), and VQAv1 (Abstract Scenes) (Antol et al., 2015).

For the image-QA pairs from the NegP VQA data, we assign a binary label of 1 (valid), which means that the QAs correctly fit the corresponding images as valid pairs. For the Others VQA data, we replace the Others ground truth answers with NegP answers $\in A^{\text{NegP}}$ to make the invalid image-QA pairs (a binary label of 0). We split the corpus into 6k training, 2k validation, and 2k test set.

Using this corpus, we train a simple classifier with one hidden layer on top of a frozen CLIP (Radford et al., 2021). We leverage the image-text alignment learned by CLIP (Radford et al., 2021), which has been pre-trained on 400M image-text pairs using contrastive learning, to extract the image features of the images and the textual features of their question-answer counterparts. We simply concatenate both image and text features, then input them into the classifier. Our image-QA pair classifier yields an F1-score of 91.29% on the test set.

E Human Evaluation Category Examples

We provide the human evaluation categories (§3.2) in Figure 11.

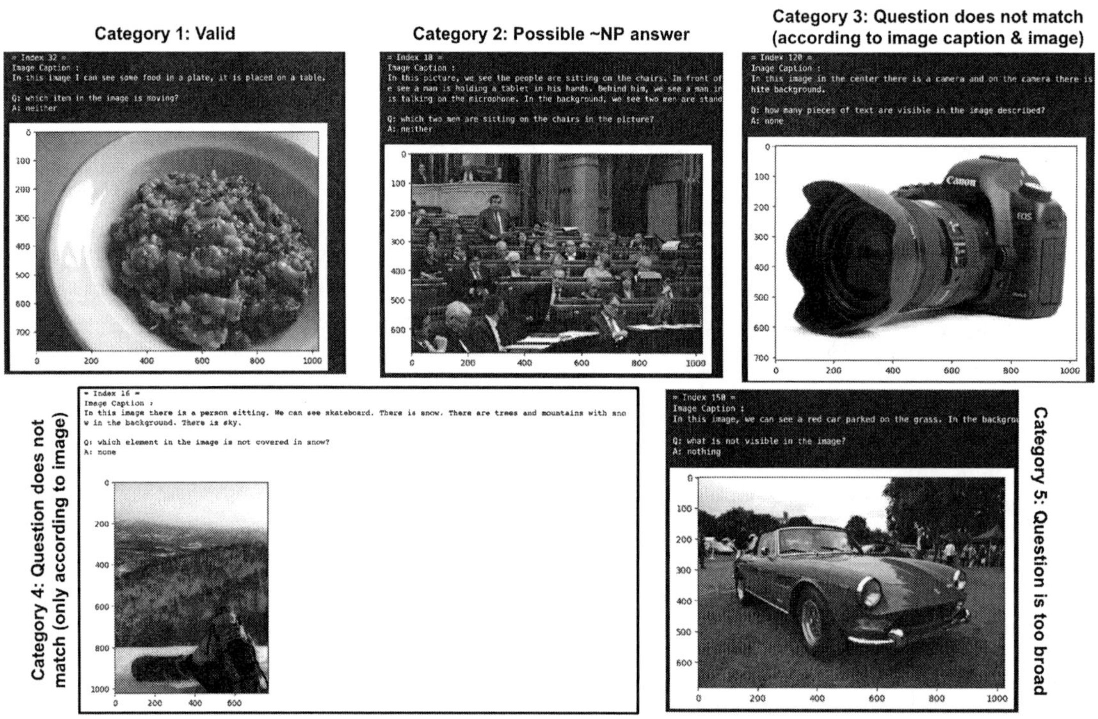

Figure 11: Examples of the human evaluation judgments for the **generate-from-scratch** prompting method in §3.2.

F Automatic Validation Results of NegP VQA Data Generation

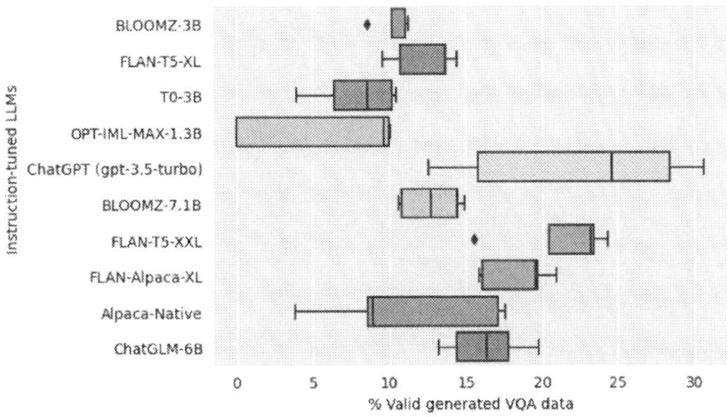

Figure 12: Automatic validation results on 1000 NegP questions generated using **generate-from-scratch** (§3.1) over five prompt templates.

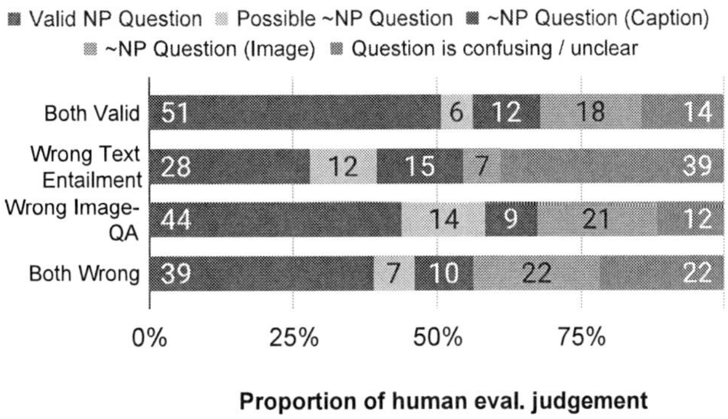

Figure 13: Human evaluation results on NegP questions generated by ChatGPT using **generate-from-scratch** (§3.1). The Y-axis denotes the verdict from the automatic validators, i.e., caption-QA and image-QA entailment models.

Generate-from-scratch Figure 12 shows the proportions of valid generated NegP VQA data using 10 instruction-tuned LLMs listed in Appendix D over five different prompt templates, where each model generates 1k questions per template. The prompt templates are provided in Appendix A. The result shows that only ~25% of the generated questions by the best-performing model, ChatGPT, are valid according to the automatic validation, while other models' valid generated questions range from 6%-23%. This indicates that the task of NegP question generation is more complex and difficult than the instructions used to fine-tune the LLMs.

Next, we conduct a human evaluation on randomly selected 240 generated questions (i.e., 60 for each category in §3.2) by ChatGPT, which is the best-performing model. We ask 3 human experts to judge each generated question and answer pair into one of the five options defined in §3.2. Figure 13 demonstrates the result of our human evaluation. The result shows that automatic validation judgments do not agree with the human judgments on a considerable amount of the data, even for simple valid/invalid classification, the automatic validation judgments misclassify 27%-50% of the subsets. From this result, we can conjecture that our automatic validation approach is not effective at verifying whether the generated NegP questions are valid or invalid and that the generate-from-scratch prompting method is not reliable and fails to elicit the LLMs' understanding of the task.

Instruction-tuned LLM	% Valid objects	% Valid objects & questions
FLAN T5 XL	11	10
FLAN T5 XXL	5	17
Alpaca	44	53
FLAN Alpaca XL	25	11
ChatGLM	84	44
ChatGPT	99	**98**

Table 8: Automatic validation results on 100 NegP questions generated using **list-then-rewrite** (§3.1).

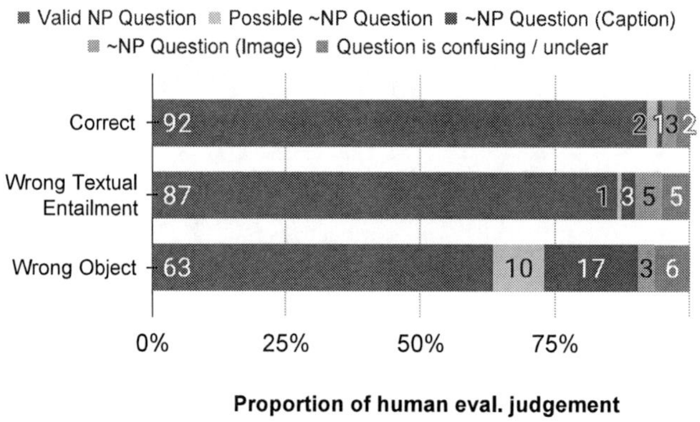

Figure 14: Human evaluation results on NegP questions generated by ChatGPT using **list-then-rewrite** (§3.1).

List-then-rewrite The automatic validation results on 100 generated questions (i.e., with the category proportion of 50, 35, and 15, respectively) by **list-then-rewrite** are provided in Table 8. The best-performing model, ChatGPT, yields 98% valid questions with a valid non-existent object according to the automatic validation judgments, which is a huge improvement compared to **generate-from-scratch**. Similarly, Alpaca and ChatGLM also experience the same increase in validity (albeit not as significant), while the FLAN family models deteriorate due to their inability to handle lists inside the instructions, thus forcing them to respond with only one object instead of 10 objects (§D).

Our human evaluation on 300 generated questions by ChatGPT (presented in Figure 14) also proves that, when we omit the question generation on the wrong object, we can achieve around 90% high-quality NegP questions generated by the **list-the-rewrite** method. However, this method would benefit from the establishment of a more suitable penalizing method to filter out the generated questions that are inconsistent with the image captions.

G Question Diversity of Existing VQA Datasets

We provide the illustrations of question diversity of existing VQA datasets: VQAv2 dataset (Antol et al., 2015) which utilizes a manual data generation method (presented in Figure 15a) and VQA-Rephrasings dataset (Shah et al., 2019) which utilizes an automatic data generation method (presented in Figure 15b).

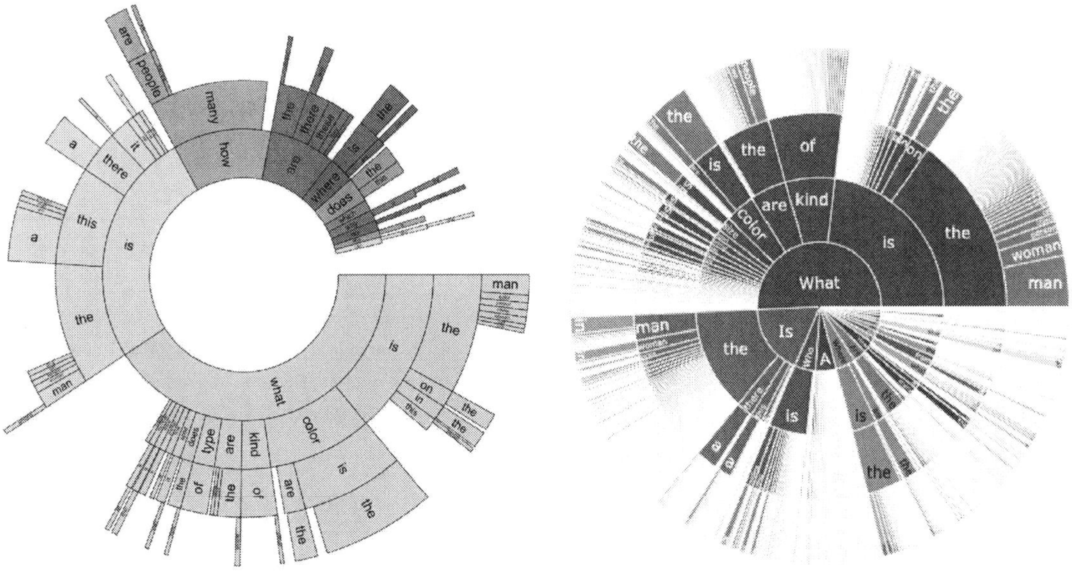

(a) VQAv2 dataset (Antol et al., 2015) (b) VQ^{2}A dataset (Changpinyo et al., 2022)

Figure 15: Question diversity of existing datasets. The figures are taken from the respective original papers.

H Baselines in NOPE Benchmark

The variant details of the baselines used in NOPE are presented in Table 9.

No	Model	References	Access
			Zero-shot & Few-shot
1	PromptCap$_{BASE}$	(Hu et al., 2022)	https://huggingface.co/tifa-benchmark/promptcap-coco-vqa, https://huggingface.co/allenai/unifiedqa-t5-base
2	PromptCap	(Hu et al., 2022)	https://huggingface.co/tifa-benchmark/promptcap-coco-vqa, https://huggingface.co/allenai/unifiedqa-t5-3b
3	BLIP-2	(Li et al., 2023a)	https://huggingface.co/Salesforce/blip2-opt-2.7b
4	OpenFlamingo	(Alayrac et al., 2022; Awadalla et al., 2023)	https://huggingface.co/OpenFlamingo/OpenFlamingo-9B
5	InstructBLIP	(Dai et al., 2023a)	https://huggingface.co/Salesforce/instructblip-flan-t5-xl
			VQA fine-tuned
1	OFA	(Wang et al., 2022b)	https://huggingface.co/OFA-Sys/ofa-huge-vqa
2	BLIP	(Li et al., 2022)	https://huggingface.co/Salesforce/blip-vqa-base
3	BLIP$_{CapFilt-L}$	(Li et al., 2022)	https://huggingface.co/Salesforce/blip-vqa-capfilt-large
4	ALBEF	(Li et al., 2021a)	https://github.com/salesforce/ALBEF#download#Finetuned-checkpoint-for-VQA
5	GIT$_{LARGE}$	(Wang et al., 2022a)	https://huggingface.co/microsoft/git-large-vqav2

Table 9: Variant details of the baselines in NOPE (§4.2).

I Examples of Object Hallucination in NOPE

We list the examples of object hallucination from the dev set of NOPE in Table 10.

ID	Object-scene relevance	Visual context	Question-answer	
390	Related	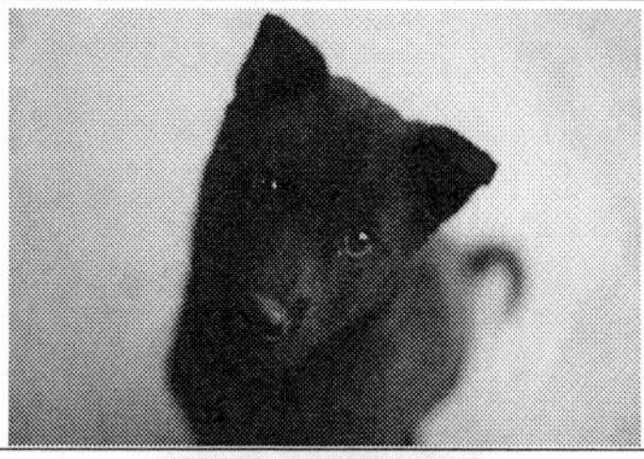	**Question**	can you point out the location of the dog collar in the image?
			GT answer	nowhere
			PromptCap	yes
			OpenFlamingo	The dog collar is located on the dog's neck.
			BLIP-2	yes, it is on the dog's collar
			OFA	no
			BLIP	no
			ALBEF	dog's neck
			GIT_{LARGE}	no
			InstructBLIP	no
822	Related		**Question**	how many menu cards have been captured in the image?
			GT answer	none
			PromptCap	1
			OpenFlamingo	10
			BLIP-2	none
			OFA	8
			BLIP	six
			ALBEF	2,3
			GIT_{LARGE}	0
			InstructBLIP	0
982	Related		**Question**	where can the clouds be spotted in the image?
			GT answer	nowhere
			PromptCap	in the sky
			OpenFlamingo	On the head of a goose.
			BLIP-2	the clouds are in the sky
			OFA	the sky
			BLIP	yes
			ALBEF	in the snow.
			GIT_{LARGE}	no
			InstructBLIP	sky
9165	Partially related		**Question**	who can you see using the fishing rod?
			GT answer	nobody
			PromptCap	a gray van
			OpenFlamingo	The owner of this Dodge B250 van.
			BLIP-2	the guy in the back of the van
			OFA	no 1
			BLIP	no idea
			ALBEF	man dancing
			GIT_{LARGE}	no
			InstructBLIP	no one
10135	Unrelated		**Question**	which color is the pillow in the image?
			GT answer	nothing
			PromptCap	blue
			OpenFlamingo	blue
			BLIP-2	blue
			OFA	black
			BLIP	red and white
			ALBEF	red black white
			GIT_{LARGE}	blue
			InstructBLIP	white

Table 10: Examples of object hallucination in the dev set of NOPE. The hallucinated answers are shown in **pink**.

How and where does CLIP process negation?

Vincent Quantmeyer[*]
Utrecht University
v.quantmeyer@gmail.com

Pablo Mosteiro
Utrecht University
p.mosteiro@uu.nl

Albert Gatt
Utrecht University
a.gatt@uu.nl

Abstract

Various benchmarks have been proposed to test linguistic understanding in pre-trained vision & language (VL) models. Here we build on the existence task from the VALSE benchmark (Parcalabescu et al., 2022) which we use to test models' understanding of negation, a particularly interesting issue for multimodal models. However, while such VL benchmarks are useful for measuring model performance, they do not reveal anything about the internal processes through which these models arrive at their outputs in such visio-linguistic tasks. We take inspiration from the growing literature on model interpretability to explain the behaviour of VL models on the understanding of negation. Specifically, we approach these questions through an in-depth analysis of the text encoder in CLIP (Radford et al., 2021), a highly influential VL model. We localise parts of the encoder that process negation and analyse the role of attention heads in this task. Our contributions are threefold. We demonstrate how methods from the language model interpretability literature (such as causal tracing) can be translated to multimodal models and tasks; we provide concrete insights into how CLIP processes negation on the VALSE existence task; and we highlight inherent limitations in the VALSE dataset as a benchmark for linguistic understanding.

1 Introduction

Research in vision & language (VL) modelling has produced various pre-trained models that are capable of jointly processing image and text information by learning multimodal representations (e.g., Li et al., 2019; Lu et al., 2019; Radford et al., 2021; Jia et al., 2021; Li et al., 2021). This makes them applicable to a host of downstream tasks, such as visual question answering, image caption generation or zero-shot image classification.

Various benchmarks have been proposed to test these models' understanding of different linguistic features, such as word order (Akula et al., 2020), verb meaning (Hendricks and Nematzadeh, 2021), and compositionality (Thrush et al., 2022). The VALSE benchmark (Parcalabescu et al., 2022) was introduced to test these models' ability to ground features such as existence, plurality, or spatial relations in images. An example of the existence piece is shown in Figure 1. Given an image, a model must choose between a correct caption and an incorrect foil, one of which contains a negation operator.

As such, this piece can be used to test a model's understanding of negation, a particularly interesting issue for multimodal models, which typically include a visual backbone pretrained on computer vision tasks such as object labelling. The models themselves are further pretrained on image-text pairs where there is likely to be a *positive* bias, since captions describing images will typically refer to what is depicted there. This raises the question whether VL models are capable of processing operators such as "no" in instances such as those in Figure 1. Indeed, negation remains a weakness of even the most state-of-the-art large language models (Truong et al., 2023)

In line with these intuitions, initial VALSE results reveal that models only achieve moderate performance in this (and other) linguistic categories.

[*]Work carried out as M.Sc. student at Utrecht University

Proceedings of the 3rd Workshop on Advances in Language and Vision Research, pages 59–72
August 16, 2024 ©2024 Association for Computational Linguistics

However, while VL benchmarks such as VALSE are useful for measuring current and future model performance, they do not reveal anything about the internal processes through which these models arrive at their outputs in such visio-linguistic tasks.

We aim to make use of the growing literature on model interpretability (Räuker et al., 2022) in order to explain the behaviour (and shortcomings) of VL models on the understanding of negation. To do this, we use the existence sub-task in VALSE, with some extensions, exploiting localisation techniques to quantify the roles that different model components play in this task. This yields the following research question: *Which components of VL models are responsible for the model's understanding of negation?* We address two issues that arise from this general question, namely (1) the extent to which processing of negation is localised vs. distributed; and (2) whether model performance on VALSE-like tasks involving negation can in part be explained by high-level dataset features.

Specifically, we approach these questions through an in-depth analysis of CLIP (Radford et al., 2021), a highly influential VL model. CLIP has a relatively simple design based exclusively on Transformers, which allows us to leverage interpretability techniques that target this architecture. Additionally, prior work by Parcalabescu and Frank (2023) shows that CLIP makes balanced use of text and image input and avoids so-called unimodal collapse (Madhyastha et al., 2018; Hessel and Lee, 2020; Frank et al., 2021), an important consideration for a study of multimodal model interpretability. Finally, CLIP remains central to developments in both vision (e.g. the CLIPSeg segmentation model; Lüddecke and Ecker, 2022) and VL tasks (e.g. CLIP is a component of several text-to-image and image-to-text models, including Mokady et al., 2021; Li et al., 2023; Ramesh et al., 2022; Rombach et al., 2022, among others).

In our analysis of negation, we focus on the CLIP text encoder. However, it is important to note that CLIP is pretrained with a multimodal contrastive objective, which has been shown to yield different representations compared to text-only encoders with comparable architecture but different training objectives (Wolfe and Caliskan, 2022). Thus, we take the insights into the text encoder's ability to process negation as reflecting on the success or otherwise of the contrastive, multimodal pretraining in such models.

The contributions of this work are threefold: firstly, we demonstrate how methods from the language model interpretability literature (e.g., causal tracing; Meng et al., 2023) can be translated to multimodal models and tasks; secondly, we provide concrete insights into how CLIP processes negation on the VALSE existence task; thirdly, we highlight inherent limitations in the VALSE dataset as a benchmark for linguistic understanding.

2 Related work

Vision-and-language models VL pretraining gained impetus from the development of multimodal, pretrained encoders inspired by BERT (Devlin et al., 2019). Bugliarello et al. (2021) provide a unified analysis of the varying VL BERT architectures.

With the introduction of CLIP (Radford et al., 2021), contrastive learning objectives have become prominent in VL models, with or without additional objectives that address multimodal fusion (Jia et al., 2021; Li et al., 2021; Singh et al., 2022a; Zeng et al., 2022). Models such as BLIP (Li et al., 2022) and FLAVA (Singh et al., 2022b) combine contrastive objectives with unimodal pretraining of vision and language encoders. Architectures such as Flamingo (Alayrac et al., 2022) and BLIP-2 (Li et al., 2023) reduce training cost by training relatively small networks to map between representations from pretrained image and language models.

In CLIP, an image encoder and a text encoder process their respective inputs completely separately from each other, i.e., without any multimodal cross-attention and project them into the same latent space. The goal of contrastive learning is to maximise similarity between matching image-text pairs, minimising the similarity between non-matching pairs. During inference, CLIP computes the similarity of an image and a text in the form of a scaled dot product between their embeddings. Contrastive objectives have been shown to yield better embedding representations (Wolfe and Caliskan, 2022) leading to improved performance on semantic evaluation tasks (Mu et al., 2018).

Vision-and-language benchmarks VL benchmarks focusing on specific linguistic phenomena play an important role in highlighting strengths and weaknesses in models' grounding capabilities. For example, a recent study combining several benchmarks (Bugliarello et al., 2023) showed that models still find certain linguistic phenomena challenging, and that grounding capabilities may be less related

Type	Image	Caption	Foil
Negation in foil		There are giraffes	There are no giraffes
Negation in caption		There are no people	There are people

Figure 1: Examples from VALSE existence (Parcalabescu et al., 2022). Caption and foil only differ in the presence or absence of the negator "no". The negator is either in the caption or the foil.

to model size, and more to other variables, including the fine-grained object recognition capabilities of the visual backbone (e.g. Zheng et al., 2022).

One class of benchmarks focuses on the robustness of models to syntactic permutations and/or their ability to reason compositionally when predicting whether visual inputs correspond to linguistic descriptions (e.g., Akula et al., 2020; Hendricks and Nematzadeh, 2021; Thrush et al., 2022; Ma et al., 2023; Yuksekgonul et al., 2023; Chen et al., 2023). Some of these benchmarks focus on specific linguistic phenomena, such as spatial relations (Liu et al., 2023; Kamath et al., 2023) or temporal relations (e.g. Kesen et al., 2024).

VALSE (Parcalabescu et al., 2022), on which we build the present study, prompts a model with an image along with both its correct caption and a foiled caption and tests a model's ability to distinguish the caption from foil. This extends the original foiling task introduced by Shekhar et al. (2017). VALSE is divided into six sub-tasks or 'pieces', corresponding to six different linguistic phenomena. In this paper, we focus exclusively on the existence piece; see Figure 1.

Model interpretability Räuker et al. (2022) define inner interpretability methods as those that help understand a model's internal structures and activations. One recurring strategy in such techniques is to analyse the effect of perturbations or ablations on the model's behaviour and output, whether this is applied to individual neurons (e.g. Zhou et al., 2018; Ghorbani and Zou, 2020) or to weights, with the goal of identifing modular subnetworks (Csordás et al., 2021).

The choice of a suitable level of granularity at which to apply ablation is largely dictated by the model's size and complexity. Interpretability methods for transformers often operate at the level of attention heads, MHA modules, MLPs, or full Transformer layers.[1] Meng et al. (2023) introduced the causal tracing methodology to localise factual associations in a model.

In Meng et al. (2023), this localisation step serves as the basis for subsequent model editing in the ROME method. However, follow-up work has suggested that the ability to edit knowledge in a particular layer does not imply that this knowledge is localised in this layer (Hase et al., 2023) and can also introduce unwanted side effects (Hoelscher-Obermaier et al., 2023). Given these uncertainties surrounding model editing techniques, the present study focuses on localisation only.

A final line of relevant interpretability literature focuses on attention patterns in large Transformer models, which reveal the role of specific attention heads in processing linguistic phenomena such as syntactic roles (Clark et al., 2019; Kovaleva et al., 2019; Vig and Belinkov, 2019). All of these studies converge on the finding that pre-trained Transformer language models allocate significant attention to tokens that do not carry inherent semantic meaning, such as the separator token in BERT or the start-of-sequence token in GPT-2.

[1]Goh et al. (2021) also produced neuron-level interpretations of CLIP's image encoder, albeit the ResNet and not the ViT variant.

	Correct	Ambiguous	Incorrect
	$d > 1$	$1 \geq d > -1$	$d \leq -1$
Caption	72	150	28
Foil	81	145	14

Table 1: Number of instances per segment in the VALSE existence dataset.

3 Methods

3.1 Definitions

A forward pass in CLIP of a single VALSE existence instance (Fig. 1) consists of a text caption, a text foil, and an image. This produces one similarity score for caption and image and one for caption and foil, denoted $S_{c,i}$ and $S_{f,i}$, respectively.

CLIP is said to correctly classify a caption-foil-image triple if $S_{c,i} > S_{f,i}$. We can quantify CLIP's classification performance using the difference between the two similarities. We denote this classification score $d = S_{c,i} - S_{f,i}$ and the absolute size of d can be seen as an indicator of CLIP's confidence in the classification.

3.2 Data

The VALSE existence benchmark consists of 505 image-caption-foil triples. The dataset is divided into instances where the negation is in the foil (249) and instances where the negation is in the caption (256). The presence or absence of a negation operator means that sometimes captions or foils can differ in token length. For our purposes, it is important that strings are of equal length; hence we insert the word *some* before the noun in non-negated sentences. See Appendix A.1 for full details.

CLIP only achieves a moderate accuracy of 0.686 on VALSE existence. To identify patterns of processing in the model that give rise to correct classification of negation it is necessary to analyse correctly and incorrectly classified instances separately. To do this consistently across different analyses, the dataset was divided into three segments (correct, ambiguous, incorrect) based on the classification score d. Table 1 shows the distribution of instances per segment.

3.3 Causal tracing

Here we outline our adaption of the causal tracing method from Meng et al. (2023) for the part of the dataset where the negation is in the foil. Figure 2 provides a visual summary of the method.

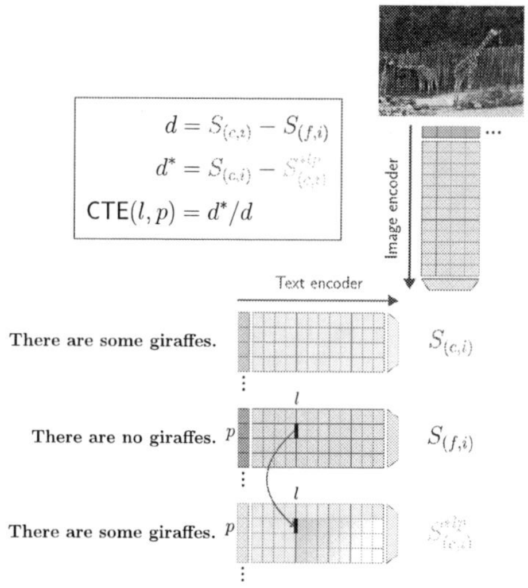

Figure 2: Illustration of the causal tracing methodology. The activation at a single position and layer from the negated forward pass are inserted into the corresponding layer and position of the non-negated forward pass. This shows what proportion of the original effect can be restored by this layer-position pair. Image and text are taken from VALSE existence (Parcalabescu et al., 2022).

A standard forward pass is carried out with caption, foil, and image, yielding the regular classification score $d = S_{c,i} - S_{f,i}$. Importantly, the activations from the forward pass at each layer and each position in the text encoder are recorded. In the subsequent modified forward pass only the (non-negated) caption is used in the forward pass alongside the image. During this forward pass, the text encoder's activation at a given layer and position is replaced by the activation from the foil's original forward pass at the corresponding layer and position. This is done individually for each combination of layer and position.

Intuitively, this achieves the following. The model processes the non-negated caption, but at a given layer and position it is made to behave as if it was processing the negated foil. If, and only if, a certain layer and position is specialised in processing negation, then substituting the activation from the negated forward pass into the non-negated one should affect the output in a visible way.

This intuition is quantified in the following way. For a given layer l and a position p the modified forward pass produces a similarity score $S^{*lp}_{c,i}$. This allows us to calculate a modified classification score

$$d^* = S_{c,i} - S^{*lp}_{c,i}$$

With this modified classification score we calculate

the causal tracing effect of layer l at position p

$$\text{CTE}(l,p) = d^*/d$$

This effect represents the proportion of the original classification score d that can be "restored" by layer l at position p.

To apply this method to cases where the negation is in the caption, one has to swap caption and foil such that, once again, the activations from the negated sentence (now the caption) are substituted into the forward pass of the non-negated sentence (now the foil). This means that we obtain a modified classification score, which is used to calculate the causal tracing effect in the same way.

$$d^* = S^{*lp}_{f,i} - S_{f,i}$$

This method yields a causal tracing effect for each layer and position for each VALSE existence triple. All captions in the dataset share the same beginning (SOT, There, is/are, a/some, subject) and ending set of tokens (., EOT). However, they differ in the number of tokens in between these two sets. Therefore, the CTE from all positions in between the beginning and end sets of tokens are averaged into one placeholder position called "further subject tokens". If there are no positions between the beginning and end sets, then a CTE of 0 is recorded at this position. Consequently, we can average CTEs across the dataset (or a segment thereof). To represent each instance according to its sequence length, the averaged effect at the "further subject tokens" position is weighted by the number of tokens that make up this position in each instance.

Lastly, we want to be able to describe the degree of localisation in particular layers. Localisation is strongest when one position in a layer, to the exclusion of all other positions, restores the full effect. Conversely, localisation is absent when each position restores the same proportion of the effect. Hence, we can quantify the degree of localisation in a layer l as the standard deviation of the causal tracing effects at each position in this layer, starting at the negator position.

3.4 Negator-selective attention in text encoder

The purpose of this analysis is to identify attention heads in CLIP's text encoder that selectively pay attention to negators. Since a regular forward pass consists of both caption and foil, this yields two attention maps per head in the text encoder. Each attention map is an array of size $P \times P$ where P is the number of positions in the input sequence, where the attention mask forces all elements to the right of the diagonal of this array to be 0.

The attention map is filtered to the column representing the position of the negator in the negated input sentence (or the quantifier in the corresponding non-negated sentence). To identify negator-selective attention, we subtract the values from the non-negated sentence from those from the negated sentence. Finally, the maximum of the resulting difference values is taken over all source positions and this represents the amount of negator-selective attention of a particular attention head on this particular dataset instance. This procedure can then be repeated over the whole dataset yielding an average negator-selective attention value a^N_{lh} for each attention head h in each layer l.

Instead of taking the maximum value over source positions, negator-selective attention can also be calculated for each source position. In heads with high negator-selective attention, this creates a more fine-grained picture of the negator-selective attention patterns involved.

To test the validity of the results from this analysis, it is further adapted to a subset of the CANNOT dataset (Anschütz et al., 2023), from which we use 554 negated sentences and create a positive counterpart for each. See Appendix A.2 for details.

4 Results

4.1 Causal tracing in text encoder

The left heatmap in Figure 3 shows the causal tracing effect per layer and position for the correct segment of the data with negation in the *foil*.

We are interested in the effect of components that lie in between the negator position in layer 0 (embeddings) and the last position in the final layer (encoder output), as these possibly mediate CLIP's correct processing of negation in the text input.[2] Figure 3 shows that this effect is limited to only a subset of positions and layers and seems to suggest a path through the model. In particular, in layers 0-3 the effect is practically limited to the negator position, suggesting that in these early layers the negation information is processed mainly at its original position. The effect at the negator position then drops sharply at layer 4 and further decreases until the final layer. This indicates that

[2]Since the encoder uses masked attention, positions prior to the negator position cannot be affected by the intervention and therefore do not show any effect.

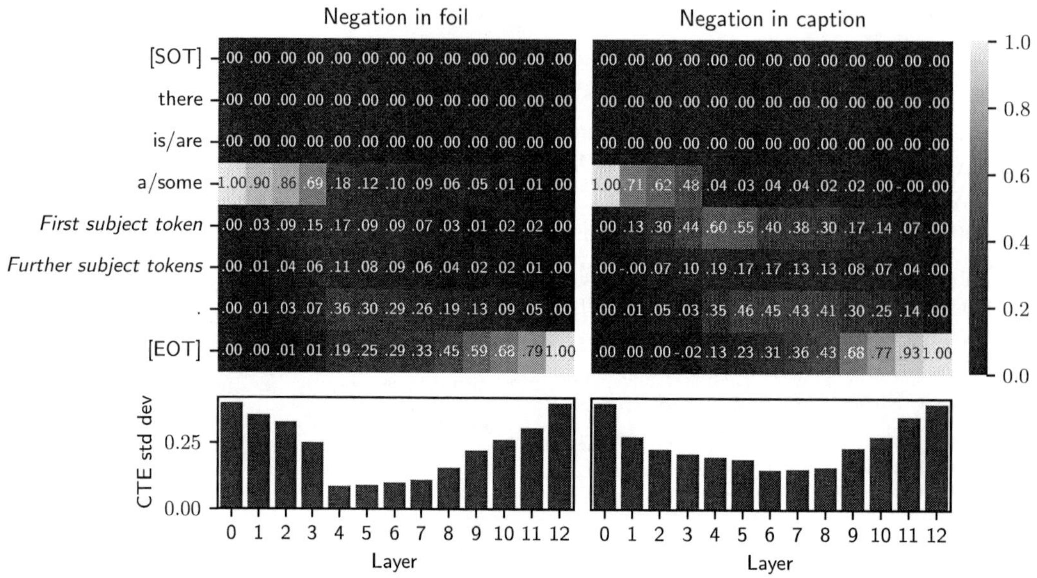

Figure 3: Causal tracing effect (CTE) of the correct segment, split by whether negation is in foil or caption. The heatmaps show the CTE of each layer-position pair in the text encoder. The bar charts show the standard deviation of all CTE in the corresponding layer as an overall measure of localisation. Layer 0 denotes the embedding layer.

the negator position only plays a pivotal role in the early layers and that the processing is in fact shifted to the second-to-last and last positions at layer 4. We will return to this in the analysis of attention patterns in Section 4.2. In the central layers 4-7 these two positions seem to play an equally important role, judging by their respective CTE, and from layer 8 onwards, the effect is concentrated in the last layer.

The bar charts in Figure 3 show the degree of localisation in each layer asmeasured by the standard deviation of the CTE. In line with the interpretation above, localisation is high in the early layers 0-3, then drops sharply in layer 4, remains low in the middle layers, and goes up again in the late layers 9-12.

The right part of Figure 3 shows the results from the same experiment on the correct segment of the data where the negation is in the *caption*. The general pattern of these results is comparable to the one described above. However, the first subject position already has a visible effect in the early layers, leading to reduced localisation. The effect of the first subject position becomes most pronounced in the middle layers which constitutes the most substantial difference between the two sets of results and in fact leads to greater localisation in the middle layers. In the late layers 9-12, the effect is once again concentrated in the last position.

4.2 Negator-selective attention in text encoder

Figure 4 shows the negator-selective attention of each attention head of each layer in CLIP's text encoder, divided by whether the negation is in foil or caption. As expected, the patterns in both parts of the dataset are practically identical, since this analysis is not affected by any visual input. As a general observation, only a small subset of heads display any negator-selective attention (8% of heads with $a_{lh}^{N} > 0.1$) and the majority of them are found in the early layers. The most negator-selective attention head is found in layer 4.

Note that these results are reported across all dataset segments (incorrect, ambiguous, correct), since the patterns do not meaningfully differ between them. This suggests that negator-selective attention cannot explain the difference in CLIP's classification performance on different instances of VALSE existence, since the same patterns are found in correctly and incorrectly classified cases. In fact, none of the attention heads that show negator-selective attention of at least 0.1 show a correlation between negator-selective attention and classification score (all $|r| < 0.2$).

Layer 4, where the most negator-selective attention is found, is the same layer, where the causal tracing results from Section 4.1 suggested that negation information is moved from its original position to later positions, in particular the second-to-last

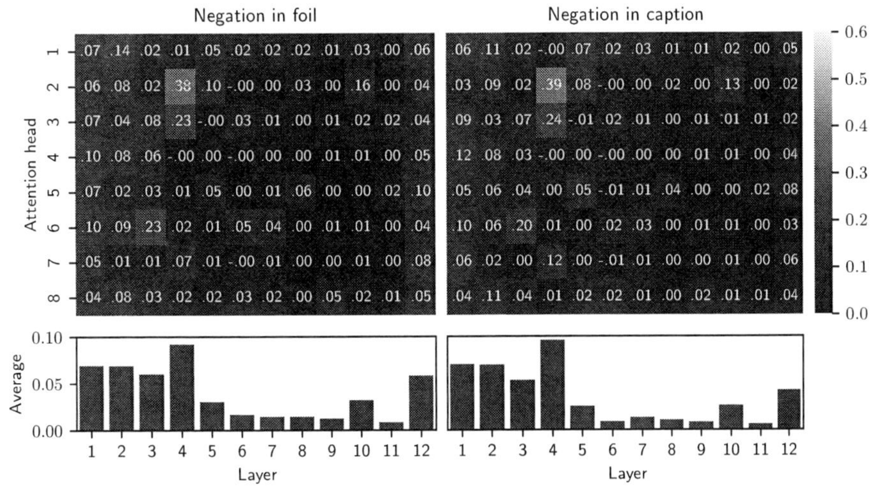

Figure 4: Negator-selective attention across all dataset segments, split by whether negation is in foil or caption. The heatmaps indicate the degree of negator-selective attention for each attention head and layer. The bar charts show the average of each layer as an overall measure of negator-selective attention.

one. We analyse the source of this negator-specific attention, i.e., which specific positions attend particularly to the negator position in the identified heads of interest. Figure 6 (Appendix A.3) confirms that the source of negator-selective attention in Head 2 is the second-to-last position. Furthermore, when the negation is in the caption, we find that additional negator-selective attention comes from the first subject position, which aligns with the greater role this position plays in this part of the dataset, as already suggested by the causal tracing results in Section 4.1. Thus, the causal tracing and negator-selective attention results form a coherent narrative.

We validate these observations using the CANNOT dataset. Here, we observe similar trends, with most negator-selective attention found in the early layers 1-4. See Appendix A.4 for details.

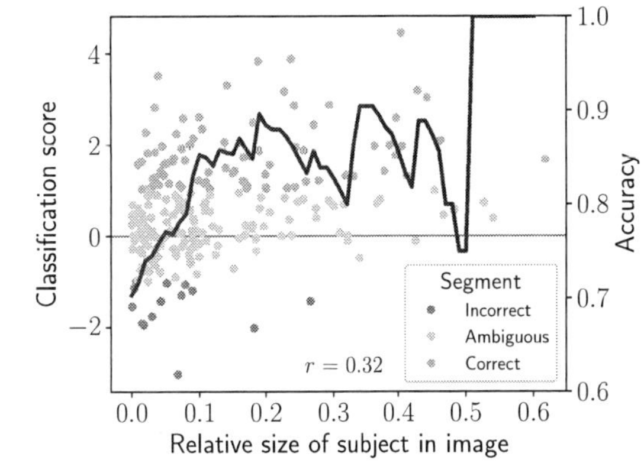

Figure 5: Relative size of image subject vs. CLIP's classification score. All instances where the subject from the caption is shown in the image. Colour indicates dataset segment. The blue line shows classification accuracy when imposing a minimum subject size threshold.

4.3 Dataset features

We investigate whether the similarity between a caption and a foil for a given VALSE instance is correlated with the instance's classification score. Full details are in Appendix A.5, especially Figure 8. We make two primary observations. First the classification score is weakly correlated with the similarity between caption and foil, especially for those instances when the negation is in the foil. Second, longer sequences exhibit greater foil-caption similarity, leading to lower scores.

To investigate the effect of the size of the caption's subject (e.g. 'giraffe' in Figure 1), we find its bounding box using CLIPSeg (Lüddecke and Ecker, 2022), and compare its relative size to the instance's classification score (Figure 5). The correlation of $r = 0.32$ shows that images with more prominent subjects tend to be classified more accurately. In fact, when imposing a subject size threshold of 0.1 (which removes 43% of instances), CLIP achieves an accuracy of 0.85. The accuracy as a function of the subject size threshold is shown by the line in Figure 5. Note, however, that the validity of these results decreases with higher thresholds, as the remaining sample size gets very small. Nonetheless, these results suggest that CLIP exhibits better existence classification results on instances with more salient subjects.

5 Discussion

The causal tracing results from Section 4.1 suggest relatively strong localisation in the early (1-3) and late (8-12) layers, meaning that negation is largely represented at singular positions in these layers.

In layer 4, the CTE at the negator position drops sharply, and this conincides with the finding of negator-selective attention heads in layer 4 which appear to shift negation information to later positions. The locations of these attention heads also overlap with those found on the CANNOT dataset, which provides initial evidence that the CLIP text encoder uses certain attention heads for specific syntactic functions.

In the middle layers localisation is generally lower with no single position restoring more than 60% of the original effect. This implies that representation of negation is distributed across positions and that the model relies on *combining* the representations at each position in order to make correct judgements about negations.

Furthermore, the first subject token position appears to play a unique role in cases with negation in the caption, which could be due to the asymmetry in the two tasks. When the negation is in the foil, the label's subject is shown in the image and, intuitively, once it is detected, a decision can be made and no further processing is necessary. Conversely, when the negation is in the caption, the entire image needs to be scanned to ensure that the label's caption is in fact absent from all parts of the image. This difference could be part of the reason why the first subject token position appears to play a role up until deeper layers of the network, when the negation is in the caption. The effects of the subject position in deeper layers could imply that the subject information is in fact more deeply processed and thus more strongly represented in the final text encoder's output which, in turn, could be conducive to the model's task of "searching" for the subject in the image's representation. However, these explanations are speculative and must not be accepted without further experiments.

Section 4.3 highlights that the label's length and the subject's size in the image show non-negligible correlations with respect to the classification score. This suggests that CLIP is better at the VALSE Existence task when labels are shorter and therefore produce less similar multimodal embeddings and when the subject in the image is sufficiently large.

Arguably, the more variance in classification score can be explained on the basis of such dataset variables, the less CLIP's benchmark score can be interpreted as an indicator of its linguistic understanding, thus calling into question the validity of the VALSE benchmark. However, none of the correlations found in the present study are particularly high and thus further analyses are needed to support this conclusion.

6 Limitations and future work

The degree of localisation found in CLIP's text encoder is hard to interpret without reference to other results. Future work could extend the present methodology to other tasks and potentially other models.

Our study is also limited to simple effects of individual layer/position pairs. An analysis of the *interaction* of certain layers or positions (e.g., by simultaneously patching activations in multiple places during causal tracing) might draw a more robust and conclusive picture of the inner processes that govern CLIP's understanding of negation.

More generally, localisation methods may not be suited for analysing model behaviour that is shown with only moderate reliability. Note that the methods used in the present study had originally been proposed and applied to language model capabilities that are shown reliably across a large corpus of data, e.g., indirect object identification (Wang et al., 2022), simple factual knowledge (Meng et al., 2023), or docstring completion (Heimersheim and Janiak, 2023). By contrast, CLIP does not reliably handle negation in a multimodal context (CLIP's accuracy is only 66.9%) and these results are based on a relatively small dataset ($n = 490$). In this case, methods like causal tracing do not intuitively lend themselves to *comparing* situations evincing a particular model behaviour to those where the behaviour is absent. That is because they focus on the degree to which an effect that represents a particular model behaviour can be restored or ablated, but the methodology breaks down when this effect isn't present in the first place.

Thus, whilst illuminating the role of various components in CLIP's processing of negation, we cannot provide strong insights into why this processing yields correct classifications only in a fraction of cases. Furthermore, since correct classification only occurs in a subset of instances of VALSE, which is moderately sized to begin with, the results described here require a larger and potentially more diverse dataset to obtain greater validity.

With respect to the validity of the underlying VALSE benchmark, it might be worthwhile to conduct a larger study on dataset features (e.g., image brightness, contrast, etc.) that correlate with benchmark performance. Comparisons with other VL benchmarks would further help putting these results into perspective. Such features that are predictive of benchmark performance limit the validity of linguistic benchmarks and highlight variables that should be controlled for in the creation of future benchmarks.

References

Arjun Akula, Spandana Gella, Yaser Al-Onaizan, Song-Chun Zhu, and Siva Reddy. 2020. Words Aren't Enough, Their Order Matters: On the Robustness of Grounding Visual Referring Expressions. In *Proceedings of the 58th Annual Meeting of the Association for Computational Linguistics*, pages 6555–6565, Online. Association for Computational Linguistics.

Jean-Baptiste Alayrac, Jeff Donahue, Pauline Luc, Antoine Miech, Iain Barr, Yana Hasson, Karel Lenc, Arthur Mensch, Katie Millican, Malcolm Reynolds, Roman Ring, Eliza Rutherford, Serkan Cabi, Tengda Han, Zhitao Gong, Sina Samangooei, Marianne Monteiro, Jacob Menick, Sebastian Borgeaud, Andrew Brock, Aida Nematzadeh, Sahand Sharifzadeh, Mikolaj Binkowski, Ricardo Barreira, Oriol Vinyals, Andrew Zisserman, and Karen Simonyan. 2022. Flamingo: A Visual Language Model for Few-Shot Learning. *Preprint*, arxiv:2204.14198.

Miriam Anschütz, Diego Miguel Lozano, and Georg Groh. 2023. This is not correct! Negation-aware Evaluation of Language Generation Systems. *Preprint*, arxiv:2307.13989.

Emanuele Bugliarello, Ryan Cotterell, Naoaki Okazaki, and Desmond Elliott. 2021. Multimodal Pretraining Unmasked: A Meta-Analysis and a Unified Framework of Vision-and-Language BERTs. *Preprint*, arxiv:2011.15124.

Emanuele Bugliarello, Laurent Sartran, Aishwarya Agrawal, Lisa Anne Hendricks, and Aida Nematzadeh. 2023. Measuring Progress in Fine-grained Vision-and-Language Understanding. *Preprint*, arxiv:2305.07558.

Xinyi Chen, Raquel Fernández, and Sandro Pezzelle. 2023. The BLA Benchmark: Investigating Basic Language Abilities of Pre-Trained Multimodal Models. In *Proceedings of the 2023 Conference on Empirical Methods in Natural Language Processing*, pages 5817–5830, Singapore. Association for Computational Linguistics.

Kevin Clark, Urvashi Khandelwal, Omer Levy, and Christopher D. Manning. 2019. What Does BERT Look at? An Analysis of BERT's Attention. In *Proceedings of the 2019 ACL Workshop BlackboxNLP: Analyzing and Interpreting Neural Networks for NLP*, pages 276–286, Florence, Italy. Association for Computational Linguistics.

Róbert Csordás, Sjoerd van Steenkiste, and Jürgen Schmidhuber. 2021. Are Neural Nets Modular? Inspecting Functional Modularity Through Differentiable Weight Masks. *Preprint*, arxiv:2010.02066.

Jacob Devlin, Ming-Wei Chang, Kenton Lee, and Kristina Toutanova. 2019. BERT: Pre-training of Deep Bidirectional Transformers for Language Understanding. *Preprint*, arxiv:1810.04805.

Stella Frank, Emanuele Bugliarello, and Desmond Elliott. 2021. Vision-and-Language or Vision-for-Language? On Cross-Modal Influence in Multimodal Transformers. In *Proceedings of the 2021 Conference on Empirical Methods in Natural Language Processing (EMNLP'21)*. ArXiv: 2109.04448.

Amirata Ghorbani and James Zou. 2020. Neuron Shapley: Discovering the Responsible Neurons. *Preprint*, arxiv:2002.09815.

Gabriel Goh, Nick Cammarata †, Chelsea Voss †, Shan Carter, Michael Petrov, Ludwig Schubert, Alec Radford, and Chris Olah. 2021. Multimodal Neurons in Artificial Neural Networks. *Distill*, 6(3):e30.

Peter Hase, Mohit Bansal, Been Kim, and Asma Ghandeharioun. 2023. Does Localization Inform Editing? Surprising Differences in Causality-Based Localization vs. Knowledge Editing in Language Models. *Preprint*, arxiv:2301.04213.

Stefan Heimersheim and Jett Janiak. 2023. A circuit for Python docstrings in a 4-layer attention-only transformer. *Alignment Forum*.

Lisa Anne Hendricks and Aida Nematzadeh. 2021. Probing Image-Language Transformers for Verb Understanding. *Preprint*, arxiv:2106.09141.

Jack Hessel and Lillian Lee. 2020. Does my multimodal model learn cross-modal interactions? It's harder to tell than you might think! In *Proceedings of the 2020 Conference on Empirical Methods in Natural Language Processing (EMNLP)*, pages 861–877, Online. Association for Computational Linguistics.

Jason Hoelscher-Obermaier, Julia Persson, Esben Kran, Ioannis Konstas, and Fazl Barez. 2023. Detecting Edit Failures In Large Language Models: An Improved Specificity Benchmark. *Preprint*, arxiv:2305.17553.

Matthew Honnibal, Ines Montani, Sofie Van Landeghem, and Adriane Boyd. 2020. *spaCy: Industrial-strength Natural Language Processing in Python*.

Chao Jia, Yinfei Yang, Ye Xia, Yi-Ting Chen, Zarana Parekh, Hieu Pham, Quoc V. Le, Yunhsuan Sung, Zhen Li, and Tom Duerig. 2021. Scaling Up Visual and Vision-Language Representation Learning With Noisy Text Supervision. *Preprint*, arxiv:2102.05918.

Amita Kamath, Jack Hessel, and Kai-Wei Chang. 2023. What's "up" with vision-language models? Investigating their struggle with spatial reasoning. *arXiv preprint*. ArXiv:2310.19785 [cs].

Ilker Kesen, Andrea Pedrotti, Mustafa Dogan, Michele Cafagna, Emre Can Acikgoz, Letitia Parcalabescu, Iacer Calixto, Anette Frank, Albert Gatt, Aykut Erdem, and Erkut Erdem. 2024. Vilma: A zero-shot benchmark for linguistic and temporal grounding in video-language models. In *Proceedings of the 12th International Conference on Learning Representations (ICLR)*, Vienna, Austria.

Olga Kovaleva, Alexey Romanov, Anna Rogers, and Anna Rumshisky. 2019. Revealing the Dark Secrets of BERT. In *Proceedings of the 2019 Conference on Empirical Methods in Natural Language Processing and the 9th International Joint Conference on Natural Language Processing (EMNLP-IJCNLP)*, pages 4365–4374, Hong Kong, China. Association for Computational Linguistics.

Junnan Li, Dongxu Li, Silvio Savarese, and Steven Hoi. 2023. BLIP-2: Bootstrapping Language-Image Pretraining with Frozen Image Encoders and Large Language Models. *Preprint*, arxiv:2301.12597.

Junnan Li, Dongxu Li, Caiming Xiong, and Steven Hoi. 2022. BLIP: Bootstrapping Language-Image Pretraining for Unified Vision-Language Understanding and Generation. *Preprint*, arxiv:2201.12086.

Junnan Li, Ramprasaath R. Selvaraju, Akhilesh Deepak Gotmare, Shafiq Joty, Caiming Xiong, and Steven Hoi. 2021. Align before Fuse: Vision and Language Representation Learning with Momentum Distillation. *Preprint*, arxiv:2107.07651.

Liunian Harold Li, Mark Yatskar, Da Yin, Cho-Jui Hsieh, and Kai-Wei Chang. 2019. VisualBERT: A Simple and Performant Baseline for Vision and Language. *Preprint*, arxiv:1908.03557.

Fangyu Liu, Guy Emerson, and Nigel Collier. 2023. Visual Spatial Reasoning. *Preprint*, arxiv:2205.00363.

Jiasen Lu, Dhruv Batra, Devi Parikh, and Stefan Lee. 2019. ViLBERT: Pretraining Task-Agnostic Visiolinguistic Representations for Vision-and-Language Tasks. *Preprint*, arxiv:1908.02265.

Timo Lüddecke and Alexander S. Ecker. 2022. Image Segmentation Using Text and Image Prompts. *Preprint*, arxiv:2112.10003.

Zixian Ma, Jerry Hong, Mustafa Omer Gul, Mona Gandhi, Irena Gao, and Ranjay Krishna. 2023. CREPE: Can Vision-Language Foundation Models Reason Compositionally? *Preprint*, arxiv:2212.07796.

Pranava Madhyastha, Josiah Wang, and Lucia Specia. 2018. Defoiling Foiled Image Captions. In *Proceedings of2018 Conference ofthe North American Chapter ofthe Association for Computational Linguistics: Human Language Technologies (NAACL-HLT'18)*, pages 433–438. ArXiv: 1805.06549.

Kevin Meng, David Bau, Alex Andonian, and Yonatan Belinkov. 2023. Locating and Editing Factual Associations in GPT. *Preprint*, arxiv:2202.05262.

Ron Mokady, Amir Hertz, and Amit H. Bermano. 2021. ClipCap: CLIP Prefix for Image Captioning. *Preprint*, arxiv:2111.09734.

Jiaqi Mu, Suma Bhat, and Pramod Viswanath. 2018. All-but-the-Top: Simple and Effective Postprocessing for Word Representations. *Preprint*, arxiv:1702.01417.

Letitia Parcalabescu, Michele Cafagna, Lilitta Muradjan, Anette Frank, Iacer Calixto, and Albert Gatt. 2022. VALSE: A Task-Independent Benchmark for Vision and Language Models Centered on Linguistic Phenomena. In *Proceedings of the 60th Annual Meeting of the Association for Computational Linguistics (Volume 1: Long Papers)*, pages 8253–8280, Dublin, Ireland. Association for Computational Linguistics.

Letitia Parcalabescu and Anette Frank. 2023. MM-SHAP: A Performance-agnostic Metric for Measuring Multimodal Contributions in Vision and Language Models & Tasks. *Preprint*, arxiv:2212.08158.

Alec Radford, Jong Wook Kim, Chris Hallacy, Aditya Ramesh, Gabriel Goh, Sandhini Agarwal, Girish Sastry, Amanda Askell, Pamela Mishkin, Jack Clark, Gretchen Krueger, and Ilya Sutskever. 2021. Learning Transferable Visual Models From Natural Language Supervision. *Preprint*, arxiv:2103.00020.

Aditya Ramesh, Prafulla Dhariwal, Alex Nichol, Casey Chu, and Mark Chen. 2022. Hierarchical Text-Conditional Image Generation with CLIP Latents. *Preprint*, arxiv:2204.06125.

Tilman Räuker, Anson Ho, Stephen Casper, and Dylan Hadfield-Menell. 2022. Toward Transparent AI: A Survey on Interpreting the Inner Structures of Deep Neural Networks. *Preprint*, arxiv:2207.13243.

Robin Rombach, Andreas Blattmann, Dominik Lorenz, Patrick Esser, and Björn Ommer. 2022. High-Resolution Image Synthesis with Latent Diffusion Models. *Preprint*, arxiv:2112.10752.

Ravi Shekhar, Sandro Pezzelle, Yauhen Klimovich, Aurélie Herbelot, Moin Nabi, Enver Sangineto, and Raffaella Bernardi. 2017. FOIL it! Find One mismatch between Image and Language caption. In *Proceedings of the 55th Annual Meeting of the Association for Computational Linguistics (Volume 1: Long Papers)*, pages 255–265, Vancouver, Canada. Association for Computational Linguistics.

Amanpreet Singh, Ronghang Hu, Vedanuj Goswami, Guillaume Couairon, Wojciech Galuba, Marcus Rohrbach, and Douwe Kiela. 2022a. FLAVA: A Foundational Language And Vision Alignment Model. *Preprint*, arxiv:2112.04482.

Amanpreet Singh, Ronghang Hu, Vedanuj Goswami, Guillaume Couairon, Wojciech Galuba, Marcus Rohrbach, and Douwe Kiela. 2022b. FLAVA: A Foundational Language And Vision Alignment Model. In *2022 IEEE/CVF Conference on Computer Vision and Pattern Recognition (CVPR)*, pages 15617–15629. ISSN: 2575-7075.

Tristan Thrush, Ryan Jiang, Max Bartolo, Amanpreet Singh, Adina Williams, Douwe Kiela, and Candace Ross. 2022. Winoground: Probing Vision and Language Models for Visio-Linguistic Compositionality. *Preprint*, arxiv:2204.03162.

Thinh Hung Truong, Timothy Baldwin, Karin Verspoor, and Trevor Cohn. 2023. Language models are not naysayers: An analysis of language models on negation benchmarks. *Preprint*, arxiv:2306.08189.

Jesse Vig and Yonatan Belinkov. 2019. Analyzing the Structure of Attention in a Transformer Language Model. In *Proceedings of the 2019 ACL Workshop BlackboxNLP: Analyzing and Interpreting Neural Networks for NLP*, pages 63–76, Florence, Italy. Association for Computational Linguistics.

Kevin Wang, Alexandre Variengien, Arthur Conmy, Buck Shlegeris, and Jacob Steinhardt. 2022. Interpretability in the Wild: A Circuit for Indirect Object Identification in GPT-2 small. *Preprint*, arxiv:2211.00593.

Robert Wolfe and Aylin Caliskan. 2022. Contrastive Visual Semantic Pretraining Magnifies the Semantics of Natural Language Representations. In *Proceedings of the 60th Annual Meeting of the Association for Computational Linguistics (Volume 1: Long Papers)*, pages 3050–3061, Dublin, Ireland. Association for Computational Linguistics.

Mert Yuksekgonul, Federico Bianchi, Pratyusha Kalluri, Dan Jurafsky, and James Zou. 2023. When and why vision-language models behave like bags-of-words, and what to do about it? *Preprint*, arxiv:2210.01936.

Yan Zeng, Xinsong Zhang, and Hang Li. 2022. Multi-Grained Vision Language Pre-Training: Aligning Texts with Visual Concepts. In *Proceedings of the 39th International Conference on Machine Learning*, pages 25994–26009. PMLR.

Kaizhi Zheng, Xiaotong Chen, Odest Chadwicke Jenkins, and Xin Wang. 2022. Vlmbench: A compositional benchmark for vision-and-language manipulation. *Advances in Neural Information Processing Systems*, 35:665 678.

Bolei Zhou, Yiyou Sun, David Bau, and Antonio Torralba. 2018. Revisiting the Importance of Individual Units in CNNs via Ablation. *Preprint*, arxiv:1806.02891.

A Appendix

A.1 Preprocessing of VALSE instances

Since caption and foil in the VALSE existence dataset differ only in the presence of the negator, they sometimes have a different number of tokens. Concretely, this is the case in "bare plural" sentences where there is no article or other qualifier in the non-negated sentence (e.g., "There are tennis players." vs "There are *no* tennis players."). Identifying differences in how CLIP processes negated vs. non-negated labels is a core facet of the present study and such comparisons are greatly facilitated if caption and foil have the same number of tokens. Therefore, labels were rephrased to achieve equal sequence length by inserting the qualifier "some" into the non-negated plural sentences right before the subject. For example, "There are tennis players" was rephrased to "There are *some* tennis players". 15 instances (0.03%) from the original dataset have labels that do not follow the simple "There is/are no [subject] ..." structure and therefore aren't amenable to the rephrasing rule described above. For reasons of simplicity, these were omitted from the rephrased dataset.

Importantly, rephrasing the dataset in this way only led to minor changes in CLIP's classification accuracy on this dataset (0.691 before, 0.686 after rephrasing). All analyses are based on the rephrased dataset, unless denoted otherwise.

A.2 CANNOT dataset

We use the CANNOT dataset to indpendently validate our analysis of negator-selective attention in the CLIP text encoder.

For the present purposes, the dataset is filtered to 554 negated sentences that contain the word "no" as the determiner of the sentence subject (e.g., "Medical organizations recommend *no* alcohol during pregnancy for this reason"), using a tokeniser from the spacy Python library (Honnibal et al., 2020).

For each of these sentences, a non-negated counterpart is then generated by replacing the word "no" with "some".

This yields a set of sentence pairs, comparable to the caption-foil pairs from VALSE existence, which thus allows us to apply the same methodology for negator-selective attention.

A.3 Negator-selective attention on VALSE

As discussed in Section 4.2, Figure 6 confirms that the source of negator-specific attention in Head 2 is the second-to-last position.

A.4 Negator-selective attention results on CANNOT

For validation purposes, Figure 7 shows negator-selective attention on a subset of the CANNOT dataset. Just like on the VALSE dataset, most negator-selective attention is found in the early layers 1-4. Head 2 in layer 4 once again shows particularly high negator-selective attention, albeit not the highest, which here is found in head 1 in layer 2. In summary, this provides converging evidence for the negator-selective attention results found in VALSE existence.

A.5 Dataset features

Figure 8 shows the cosine similarity of each instance's caption and foil in CLIP's multimodal embedding space against that instance's classification score, split by whether the negation is in the caption or foil.

When the negation is in the foil, similarity and score are weakly correlated ($r = -0.22$), whereas no correlation is found when the negation is in the caption ($r = 0.03$). The latter is however influenced by the presence of a set of outliers, all with the same caption "There are no people.". Removing them from this analysis yields a correlation of $r = -0.20$, comparable to the one found when the negation is in the foil.

Figure 8 also encodes sequence length, with longer sequences (darker colour) tending to exhibit greater caption-foil similarity. This is to be expected since caption and foil differ in exactly one position. If the total number of positions increases, then the relative size of this difference decreases, leading to greater similarity. These results suggest that CLIP's failure to correctly classify some VALSE Existence instances might be partly due to instances with longer captions and foils that are more similar in their representation and therefore more difficult to tell apart. However, filtering the dataset to instances with shorter sequences does not meaningfully improve CLIP's accuracy, suggesting that sequence length plays a minor role at best.

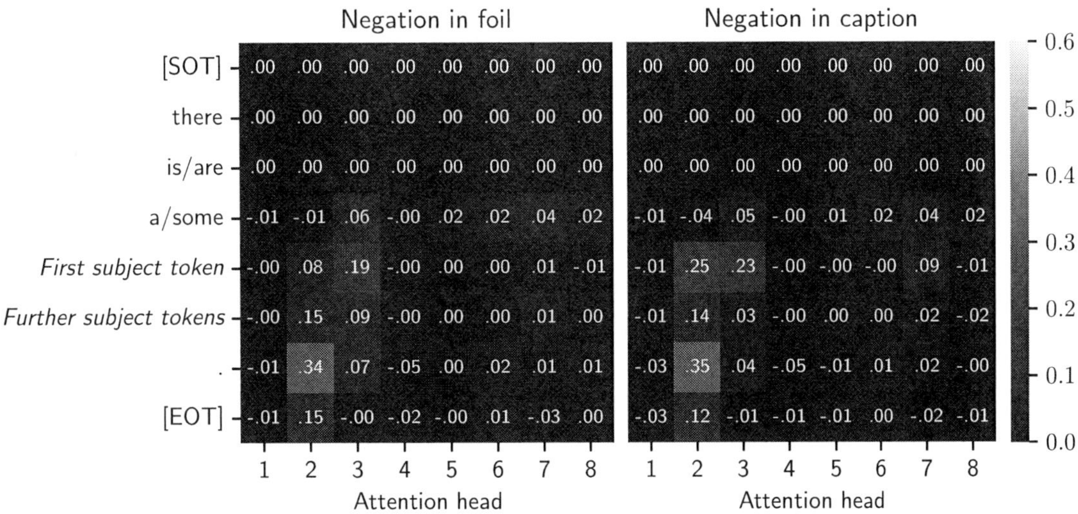

Figure 6: Source of negator-selective attention in layer 4 across all dataset segments, split by whether negation is in foil or caption. The heatmaps show the degree of negator-selective attention from each sequence position (y-axis) in each attention head (x-axis).

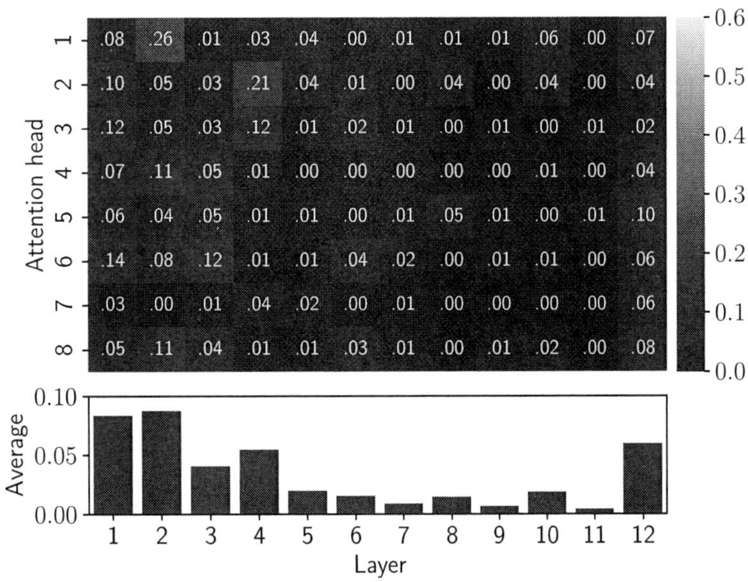

Figure 7: Negator-selective attention on the CANNOT dataset, to validate the results from Figure 4. The heatmaps indicate the degree of negator-selective attention for each attention head and layer. The bar charts show the average of each layer as an overall measure of negator-selective attention.

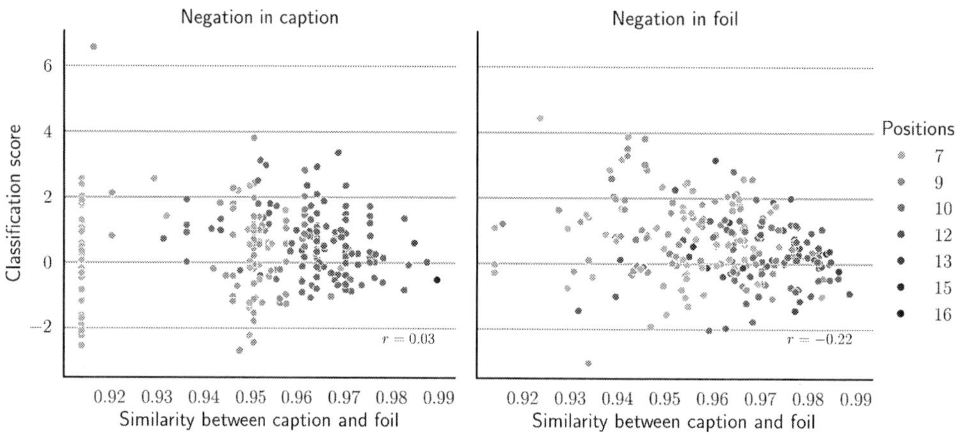

Figure 8: Cosine similarity of caption and foil in CLIP's multimodal embedding space vs. CLIP's classification score. Colour indicates dataset sequence length (i.e., number of tokens in sequence).

Enhancing Continual Learning in Visual Question Answering with Modality-Aware Feature Distillation

Malvina Nikandrou[1] Georgios Pantazopoulos[1,2] Ioannis Konstas[1,2] Alessandro Suglia[1,2]

[1]Heriot-Watt University; [2]Alana AI

{mn2002, gmp2000, i.konstas, a.suglia}@hw.ac.uk

Abstract

Continual learning focuses on incrementally training a model on a sequence of tasks with the aim of learning new tasks while minimizing performance drop on previous tasks. Existing approaches at the intersection of Continual Learning and Visual Question Answering (VQA) do not study how the multimodal nature of the input affects the learning dynamics of a model. In this paper, we demonstrate that each modality evolves at different rates across a continuum of tasks and that this behavior occurs in established encoder-only models as well as modern recipes for developing Vision & Language (VL) models. Motivated by this observation, we propose a modality-aware feature distillation (MAFED) approach which outperforms existing baselines across models of varying scale in three multimodal continual learning settings. Furthermore, we provide ablations showcasing that modality-aware distillation complements experience replay. Overall, our results emphasize the importance of addressing modality-specific dynamics to prevent forgetting in multimodal continual learning.

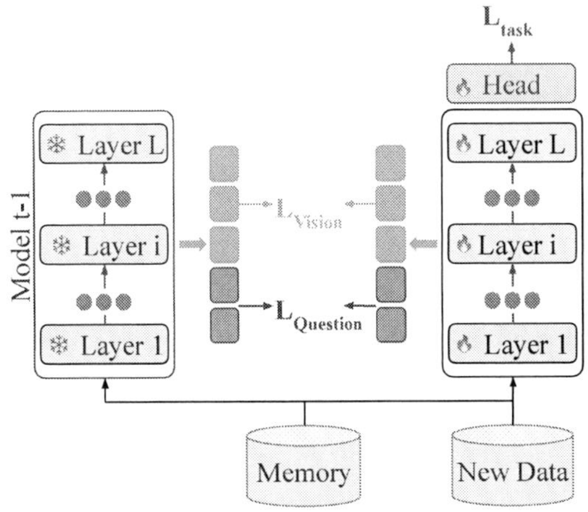

Figure 1: Overview of MAFED. Along with training on the data from the current task and a memory buffer, we apply feature distillation using the previous checkpoint as the teacher. The distillation losses applied to the representations from question and visual tokens are weighted separately to compensate for modality-specific training dynamics.

1 Introduction

Large Language Models (LLMs) (Touvron et al., 2023; Jiang et al., 2023) and Visual Language Models (VLMs) (Bai et al., 2023b; Liu et al., 2024), have achieved unprecedented performance and have become the go-to option for most NLP and Vision & Language (VL) tasks. However, once they have been trained, it is not straightforward how to update them to accommodate for novel concepts or concepts with reworked meanings. As a result, over time, the knowledge of these models may be obsolete or needs to be refined periodically to maintain their relevance. Consider two examples: 1) As of July 2023, Twitter has been re-branded to X with a new logo. 2) According to the Oxford English Dictionary (OED), as of March 2024, more than 1000 English words or phrases have been either been revised or included as novel entries[1]. In these cases, models trained with data from a preceding period will inevitably show performance deterioration (Lazaridou et al., 2021). Commercialized LLMs circumvent this limitation (OpenAI, 2022; Gemini Team et al., 2023; Anthropic, 2024) with statements regarding the knowledge cutoff of these models. On the other hand, humans continuously update their knowledge and acquire new skills over time. Continual learning is a paradigm that aims to simulate this behavior, focusing on models that learn incrementally from a sequence of tasks with minimal catastrophic forgetting (McCloskey and Cohen, 1989; Ratcliff, 1990).

Continual learning has started being explored more widely in VL settings (Greco et al., 2019; Srinivasan et al., 2022; Nikandrou et al., 2022;

[1]OED March 2024 update lists entries appearing for the first time, or entries with updated meanings.

Proceedings of the 3rd Workshop on Advances in Language and Vision Research, pages 73–85
August 16, 2024

Zhang et al., 2023; Lei et al., 2023; Cui et al., 2024). However, existing approaches do not explicitly account for the dissimilarities in the representation space of multimodal inputs and their effect on the learning dynamics, which we argue is necessary for effective continual learning of VL tasks. Previous work on the optimization dynamics of multimodal learning has demonstrated that different modalities are learned at different speeds (Wang et al., 2020; Wu et al., 2022). Using encoder and decoder-only VLMs, we empirically showcase a similar forgetting discrepancy (Section 4.1), which indicates that representations from each modality evolve at different rates across a sequence of tasks.

Motivated by this observation, we propose *MAFED*, a Modality-Aware FEature Distillation approach summarized in Figure 1. We explore different strategies for weighting the distillation losses derived from the tokens of each modality, using either fixed balanced weights or adaptive weights derived from the loss gradients computed with respect to the inputs. We combine both variants with experience replay and show promising results across all VLM families compared to established continual learning methods. Additionally, we conduct experiments with decoder-only VLMs ranging from 100M to 1B parameters, showing that although scale alleviates forgetting, certain settings remain challenging. Our ablations comparing experience replay and feature distillation approach showcase that these methods are complementary and yield greater performance when combined. Overall, our results emphasize the need to address modality-specific dynamics to effectively mitigate forgetting in multimodal continual learning.

2 Related Work

2.1 Continual Learning

Continual Learning Approaches Continual learning approaches can be categorized as regularization, replay, and architecture-based (Delange et al., 2021). Regularization-based approaches introduce auxiliary losses that aim to constrain the model weights (Kirkpatrick et al., 2017; Zenke et al., 2017; Aljundi et al., 2018), outputs (Li and Hoiem, 2018; Rebuffi et al., 2017), or internal representations (Hou et al., 2019). Replay-based approaches rely on storing (Chaudhry et al., 2019; Buzzega et al., 2020; Bagus and Gepperth, 2021) or generating samples (Van de Ven and Tolias, 2018; Sun et al., 2019) from past tasks so that they can be sampled along with new samples during training. Finally, architecture-based approaches introduce task-specific parameters, either by masking the model parameters (Yoon et al., 2020; Serrà et al., 2018) or adding new ones for each task (Fernando et al., 2017; Madotto et al., 2021).

Most recent work tends to combine techniques from multiple categories in order to maximize performance. Similarly, our work utilizes replay and regularization through feature distillation. Distillation has been used in various continual learning approaches. Some focus on knowledge distillation on the output level, using the logits (Li and Hoiem, 2018) or pseudo-labels from a past checkpoint (Wang et al., 2022; Karim et al., 2022). Other work applies distillation on the internal model representations (Dhar et al., 2019; Douillard et al., 2020; Kang et al., 2022). MAFED expands this line of work by introducing different weighting schemes to balance the distillation loss from visual and textual representations.

VL Continual Learning Previous work has studied varying instantiations of VL continual learning problems, including image captioning (Del Chiaro et al., 2020; Nguyen et al., 2019), compositional phrase generalization (Jin et al., 2020), and task-incremental learning (Srinivasan et al., 2022). Within VQA, prior work has investigated continual learning based on question types (Greco et al., 2019), across varying domains (Zhang et al., 2022; Lao et al., 2023), and from a compositionality perspective (Zhang et al., 2023). Lei et al. (2023); Nikandrou et al. (2022) further study how VQA models evolve in different settings, including novel visual scenes or different question types. However, these works have not investigated the effect of modality-aware methods with the exception of Qian et al. (2023) that focus on multimodal prompt learning for vision, text and fusion modules. In contrast, feature distillation does not assume separate modality-specific and multimodal parameters and can be applied to more varied VLM architectures.

2.2 VLMs

Progress in representation learning has led to models that achieve impressive performance across multimodal benchmarks (Goyal et al., 2017; Hudson and Manning, 2019; Li et al., 2023). Early approaches relied on complicated architectures (Tan and Bansal, 2019; Lu et al., 2019), and multiple learning objectives (Chen et al., 2020; Li et al.,

Figure 2: Illustration of tasks in each of the three continual learning settings for VQA. Each of these settings consists of five tasks. The first two settings are defined based on the visual categories. In Diverse Content, the objects present in each task are grouped randomly, while in Taxonomy Content, the objects are grouped based on their supercategory. Finally, in Question Types, the tasks are defined according to the type of the questions.

2021; Jia et al., 2021). More recently, given the rapid development of increasingly capable LLMs (Touvron et al., 2023; Jiang et al., 2023; Bai et al., 2023a), these approaches have been superseded by a new paradigm where representations from visual experts (Radford et al., 2021; Oquab et al., 2024) are treated as input tokens for the LLM. This shift has led the development of modern VLMs (Liu et al., 2024; Dai et al., 2024; Laurençon et al., 2024a) that are based on the same underlying principles with deviations regarding the choice of the experts, or how the patch tokens are integrated into the language model. Our experiments demonstrate the effectiveness of our approach in both encoder-only (Chen et al., 2020; Kim et al., 2021) as well as decoder-only models.

3 Preliminaries

3.1 Data

We leverage an existing evaluation suite for Continual Learning in VQA (Nikandrou et al., 2022) comprised of three settings based on the visual and the language input. In particular, each of these settings consists of five tasks and is designed to test the model's performance on learning varying concepts or question types. Figure 2 illustrates exemplary images and questions from different tasks in each of the settings. Below, we provide a brief summary for each of these settings.

Diverse Content corresponds to a real-world use case as well as a common standard procedure within continual learning (Lomonaco and Maltoni, 2017; Rebuffi et al., 2017; Zenke et al., 2017; Lin et al., 2021), where a model is trained on new sets of concepts progressively that do not necessarily comply to a taxonomy. Each task in this setting covers 10 distinct object categories from the COCO dateset (Lin et al., 2014).

Taxonomy Content In this setting, each task consists of questions regarding objects based on the same super-category. This setting contains questions from the following categories: Animals, Food, Interior, Sports, and Transport, and simulates a more progressive approach, where a model learns about a fixed (and similar) pool of concepts before being applied to a different domain. Importantly, we note that in both Diverse Content and Taxonomy Content, images containing objects shared between tasks are discarded to create clean task splits, preventing contamination between them. In total, there are 181K train, 45K validation, and 110K test samples for both settings.

Question Types The final setting resembles a scenario where the model learns to answer different categories of questions. In this setting, the model is tasked with learning from a sequence of five tasks: Count, Color, Scene-level, Subcategory, and Action recognition. Question Types have a total of 140K train, 35K validation, and 84K test samples.

3.2 Models

Throughout our experiments, we use two families of models, including encoder- and decoder-only pretrained models. Specifically, we use the encoder-only models, UNITER-base (Chen et al., 2020) and ViLT-base (Kim et al., 2021), that differ in terms of how the visual input is encoded. UNITER uses region features extracted from the Faster R-CNN

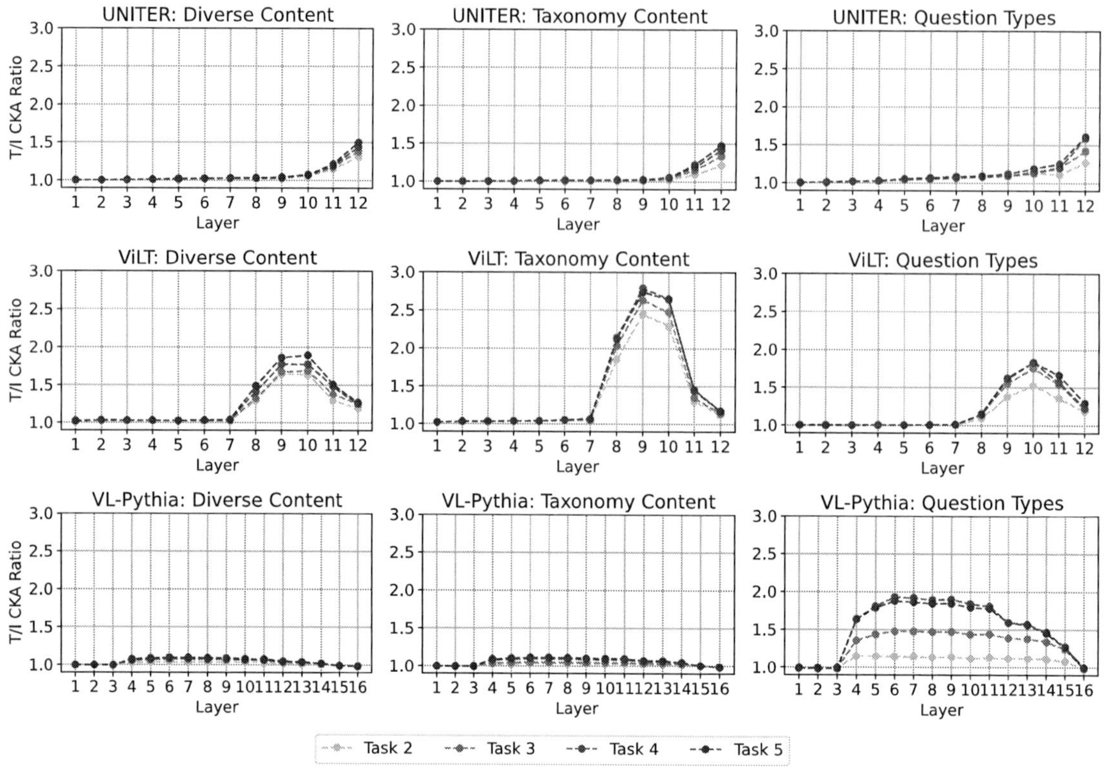

Figure 3: Ratio of text-to-image representation similarity across layers and tasks, for UNITER (first row), ViLT (second-row), and VL-Pythia (third-row). We consistently observe that in the earlier layers, the ratio is close to one, indicating that representations from both modalities change at a similar rate. However, in intermediate or deeper layers, text representations seem to retain larger similarities.

object detector (Anderson et al., 2018). On the other hand, ViLT is a patch-based model that does not use an additional vision encoder.

However, recent trends in the development of VLMs have moved towards decoder-only architectures that combine an expert vision encoder with an LLM using a connector module that learns a mapping between them (Liu et al., 2024). We employ a similar recipe to combine EVA02 (Fang et al., 2023) as the visual encoder and Pythia (Biderman et al., 2023) as our LLM. Regarding the connection module, we follow the LLaVA-1.5 (Liu et al., 2023) approach with a two-layer MLP that matches the dimensionality of the visual and the language embeddings. We refer to this model as VL-Pythia.

We refrain from using other existing VLMs for two reasons. First, we aim to match the parameters and pretraining data between the encoder-only and the generative models. Pythia models provide a collection of checkpoints covering a wide range of sizes that have been pretrained following a state-of-art transformer recipe (Su et al., 2024; Dao et al., 2022). For a controlled comparison with encoder-only models, we train VL-Pythia using the same data used to train UNITER and ViLT (see Appendix A.1 for additional details regarding the pretraining of the model). In particular, we use the checkpoints with 160M, 410M, and 1B parameters. The smaller model is on par with the encoder-only ones, while the larger models allow us to explore the role of model capacity. Secondly, existing VLMs (Liu et al., 2024; Dai et al., 2024; Bai et al., 2023a; Laurençon et al., 2024a,b) are typically instruction-tuned on datasets that include VQA-v2 (Goyal et al., 2017) on which the continual learning settings are based. This overlap is undesirable since we want to prevent any form of data contamination between tasks.

During continual learning, we keep the vision encoders of UNITER and VL-Pythia frozen. In encoder-only models, VQA is treated as a classification task. The classification (CLS) token is passed to a classification head that gets expanded with the new answers from each task. On the contrary, VL-Pythia is fine-tuned to generate answers autoregressively. In our experiments, we follow a greedy decoding strategy during inference.

4 Method

4.1 Motivation

In this work, we argue that modality-specific learning dynamics, and more specifically, the different speeds at which each modality is learned (Wu et al., 2022) or forgotten, should be accounted for in multimodal continual learning settings. We demonstrate this behavior by measuring the similarities of the question Q and image V representations from sequential model checkpoints using Centered Kernel Alignment (CKA) (Kornblith et al., 2019). In particular, we extract text Q_t and image V_t representations for data of the first task after training on the first $t = 1$ and each subsequent task $t = 2 \cdots T$, and we compute the CKA similarity across time. Finally, we visualize the ratio R_t of the text over image similarities:

$$R_t = \frac{CKA(Q_1, Q_t)}{CKA(V_1, V_t)} \quad \forall t = 2 \cdots T \tag{1}$$

Figure 3 shows the Text-to-Image CKA ratio per layer. We observe that there are differences in how the modalities evolve within the models and across settings. First, we note that the ratio is greater or equal to one in all cases, meaning that visual tokens exhibit decreasing similarity throughout the learning process. In UNITER, the ratio remains close to one for earlier layers and increases only for the last three layers. ViLT and Pythia exhibit a different trend, where the ratio peaks for intermediate layers. As a result, we hypothesize that incorporating the variability of each modality in a regularization technique can benefit continual learning strategies. Due to parameter sharing between the two modalities, we materialize this in a modality-aware feature distillation strategy, which we elaborate on below.

4.2 Modality-Aware Feature Distillation

Feature Distillation (FD) is an established continual learning technique (Hou et al., 2019; Douillard et al., 2020; Kang et al., 2022) that adds a regularization loss term to prevent the drift of model representations. Given two model checkpoints f_{t-1} and f_t from consecutive tasks, we extract representations H from an intermediate layer and compute the feature distillation loss l_i using the representations of each token h_i:

$$\mathrm{L}_{\mathrm{FD}} = \frac{1}{N}\sum_{i=1}^{N} l_i = \frac{1}{N}\sum_{i=1}^{N} \parallel h_{i,t} - h_{i,t-1} \parallel_2^2 \tag{2}$$

Assuming an example has Q text tokens and V visual tokens, we can rewrite Equation (2) in terms of the average loss contributed by the language and the vision tokens, $\mathrm{L}_{\mathrm{FD,Q}}$ and $\mathrm{L}_{\mathrm{FD,V}}$ respectively:

$$\mathrm{L}_{\mathrm{FD,weighted}} = \alpha \cdot \mathrm{L}_{\mathrm{FD,Q}} + (1 - \alpha) \cdot \mathrm{L}_{\mathrm{FD,V}} \tag{3}$$

In the simplest case, α is proportional to the number of tokens available from each input modality. In practice, this might be suboptimal since it depends on the input tokenization strategy. In fact, across the examined settings, the average tokenized inputs have approximately 9 question tokens and 33 or 199 visual tokens for region and patch-based image features, respectively. Consequently, visual tokens will dominate the distillation loss of Equation (3) potentially leading to inferior performance.

Therefore, we experiment with two modifications: i) MAFED-B which balances the losses from each modality by fixing α to 0.5, and ii) MAFED-A which uses an adaptive weighting approach based on modality importance inspired by Kang et al. (2022). Modality importances I_Q and I_V are estimated using the gradient of the VQA classification loss[2], with respect to the intermediate model representations H_m from each modality m. I_Q and I_V are updated at the beginning of each training task using the available memory data M_t as follows:

$$I_m = \mathbb{E}_{(x,y)\sim M_t}\left[\parallel \nabla_{H_m} L_{cls}(f_t(x), y) \parallel_F^2\right] \tag{4}$$

where $\parallel \cdot \parallel$ corresponds to the Frobenius norm. Finally, the weight α is computed by normalizing the importance of the question tokens:

$$\alpha = \frac{I_Q}{I_Q + I_V} \tag{5}$$

We apply feature distillation to all layers except the last since only the representation of CLS token in encoder-only and the final question token in decoder-only models is propagated to the model output's head. Furthermore, in Section 4.1, we showcased that the representations of deeper layers are affected more during continual learning. Therefore, we introduce a discount factor w_d that is used to weigh the contribution of the loss from each layer proportionally to its distance d from the model's head:

$$w_d = \frac{\gamma^d}{\sum_{d=0}^{D} \gamma^d} \tag{6}$$

[2]Or the language model head in the case of Pythia.

Model	Method	Diverse Content Accuracy	Diverse Content SBWT	Taxonomy Content Accuracy	Taxonomy Content SBWT	Question Types Accuracy	Question Types SBWT
UNITER	FT*	64.59 ± 0.56	-1.93 ± 0.39	63.65 ± 0.63	-3.89 ± 0.53	48.81 ± 5.56	-22.43 ± 7.02
	EWC*	66.26 ± 0.55	-0.67 ± 0.29	**67.70** ± 0.29	-0.62 ± 0.19	66.77 ± 3.54	-2.62 ± 2.28
	ER*	66.47 ± 0.51	-0.29 ± 0.18	66.76 ± 0.16	-1.22 ± 0.10	69.01 ± 0.76	-1.42 ± 0.31
	FD	66.67 ± 0.38	-0.17 ± 0.19	66.94 ± 0.23	-0.68 ± 0.17	69.53 ± 0.12	-1.22 ± 0.51
	MAFED-B	**66.77** ± 0.24	**-0.12** ± 0.17	67.05 ± 0.23	**-0.57** ± 0.08	**69.58** ± 0.55	-1.17 ± 0.31
	MAFED-A	66.52 ± 0.26	-0.23 ± 0.12	66.84 ± 0.25	-0.70 ± 0.45	69.34 ± 0.43	**-0.94** ± 0.48
	Multitask*	69.76 ± 0.18	-	70.08 ± 0.18	-	72.54 ± 0.15	-
ViLT	FT*	61.07 ± 0.41	-2.80 ± 0.41	61.25 ± 0.50	-4.09 ± 0.50	36.95 ± 11.09	-32.86 ± 11.09
	EWC*	61.80 ± 0.96	-1.14 ± 0.96	63.69 ± 0.46	-0.92 ± 0.46	60.25 ± 2.86	-8.19 ± 2.86
	ER*	64.22 ± 0.10	-0.25 ± 0.10	63.52 ± 0.20	-1.46 ± 0.20	65.61 ± 0.76	-2.86 ± 0.76
	FD	64.57 ± 0.57	-0.51 ± 0.12	64.24 ± 0.73	-1.07 ± 0.46	67.70 ± 0.54	-1.98 ± 0.70
	MAFED-B	64.78 ± 0.55	-0.34 ± 0.27	64.51 ± 0.36	-1.02 ± 0.17	**67.76** ± 0.27	**-1.85** ± 0.61
	MAFED-A	**65.00** ± 0.41	**-0.28** ± 0.19	**64.63** ± 0.37	**-0.89** ± 0.21	67.67 ± 0.46	-2.01 ± 0.84
	Multitask*	67.51 ± 1.94	-	67.84 ± 3.92	-	72.41 ± 3.75	-

Table 1: UNITER and ViLT average accuracy and semantic backward transfer over five task orders. * results reported in (Nikandrou et al., 2022).

where $\gamma \in (0, 1]$ is a hyperparameter such that lower γ values assign more weight to deeper layers, and $\gamma = 1$ weighs the losses from all layers equally. Unless stated otherwise, we combine feature distillation with replay since it requires no computational overhead and helps mitigate the miscalibration of the output layer, which can negatively impact performance on past tasks (Wu et al., 2019).

5 Experiments

5.1 Baselines

We compare our methods against naive *Fine Tuning* (FT), where a model is trained sequentially on each task. Our continual learning baselines include *Elastic Weight Consolidation* (EWC) (Kirkpatrick et al., 2017) and *Experience Replay* (ER) (Chaudhry et al., 2019), which have been shown to perform competitively. Finally, we report the upper bound performance of *Multitask* learning, where the model is trained on all tasks simultaneously. Note that this is the de facto standard for instruction-tuning in VLMs (Dai et al., 2024; Liu et al., 2023).

5.2 Evaluation Metrics

We measure the performance of a model using three metrics. First, we report the macro-average accuracy at the end of a training sequence, $\text{A} = \frac{1}{T}\sum_{i=1}^{T} A_{T,i}$, where $A_{T,i}$ depicts the performance of the model on the data from task i after training on final task T. Additionally, we report the Semantic Backward Transfer (SBWT) (Nikandrou et al., 2022), which captures the impact of catastrophic forgetting, weighted by the semantic similarity of the prediction and the target:

$$\text{SBWT} = \frac{1}{T-1}\sum_{i=1}^{T-1} S_{T,i} \tag{7}$$

where $S_{T,i}$ is the average weighted accuracy difference for task i.

5.3 Implementation Details

We train all models using the Adam optimizer (Kingma and Ba, 2014) and a learning rate schedule that follows linear decay after a warmup for 10% of the training steps. The maximum learning rate is optimized through grid search separately for each setting based on the performance of the fine-tuning method. For UNITER and ViLT, we set the number of epochs per task to 60 with a patience of 5. We found that VL-Pythia models reach their peak accuracy for fewer updates, possibly because they do not use a randomly initialized classification head. As a result, we set the maximum number of epochs to 15. For all replay and feature distillation runs, we keep a memory of 1000 randomly selected samples per task, ensuring that the same samples are stored across methods for the same task order. Further details about the selected hyperparameters are listed in Appendix A.2.

5.4 Results

5.4.1 Encoder-only Models

Table 1 reports the results across the three settings using the encoder-only models UNITER and ViLT. Adding the feature distillation loss improves upon the ER baseline in all settings. Although the benefits with UNITER are moderate, as ER already achieves low forgetting, when using ViLT,

Setting	Method	VL-Pythia 160M Accuracy	VL-Pythia 160M SBWT	VL-Pythia 410M Accuracy	VL-Pythia 410M SBWT	VL-Pythia 1B Accuracy	VL-Pythia 1B SBWT
Question Types	FT	25.98 ± 8.23	-31.35 ± 7.27	63.20 ± 2.10	-7.22 ± 1.98	65.52 ± 5.60	-6.16 ± 5.42
	EWC	41.55 ± 8.31	-8.58 ± 6.96	66.83 ± 2.45	-3.85 ± 2.48	66.78 ± 2.98	-5.30 ± 2.93
	ER	53.56 ± 0.72	-5.20 ± 1.06	70.25 ± 1.00	-0.52 ± 0.67	69.66 ± 3.34	-2.27 ± 1.88
	FD	56.19 ± 1.59	-3.04 ± 1.21	70.76 ± 0.50	-0.22 ± 0.25	71.85 ± 1.07	-0.62 ± 0.54
	MAFED-B	57.53 ± 0.76	-2.83 ± 0.42	70.82 ± 0.38	-0.17 ± 0.10	72.19 ± 1.40	-0.55 ± 0.80
	MAFED-A	**57.65** ± 0.24	**-2.46** ± 0.29	**71.06** ± 0.30	**-0.19** ± 0.28	**72.69** ± 0.12	**-0.10** ± 0.07
	Multitask	65.65 ± 0.14	-	71.96 ± 0.15	-	73.44 ± 0.18	-

Table 2: Performance of different VL-Pythia model sizes across three task orders.

FD offers substantial accuracy gains of up to 2.6 in Question Types. Comparing the feature distillation variants, modality-aware weighting (MAFED-A or MAFED-B) consistently boosts performance. For UNITER and ViLT in Question Types, equally balancing the modality losses with MAFED-B shows the best performance. In the image-based settings with ViLT, adaptive weighting performs better. Given the similarity ratios shown in Figure 3, these results suggest that MAFED-B is more effective when the relative change of text and vision representation is small, while MAFED-A is more appropriate in cases of larger discrepancies.

5.4.2 Scaling to larger decoder-only VLMs

Setting	Accuracy	BWT
Diverse Content	70.11	1.58
Taxonomy Content	69.03	0.44
Question Types	66.01	-9.70

Table 3: Average accuracy and backward transfer for finetuning VL-Pythia 1B across settings. We report the accuracy of three task orders on the validation set.

As decoder-only architectures have become more widely used, we also experiment with three model sizes of VL-Pythia (160M, 410M, 1B parameters). In our initial results shown in Table 3, we find that larger models exhibit no forgetting in the image-based settings of Diverse and Taxonomy Content. As a result, we focus on more challenging Question Types setting.

Table 2 provides the results for different continual learning strategies using the VL-Pythia variants. We observe that scaling leads to higher final accuracy and less catastrophic forgetting similar to previous work (Mirzadeh et al., 2022; Ramasesh et al., 2022). Nevertheless, even the largest explored model has a gap of almost 8% between naive finetuning and multitask learning. Compared to experience replay, we find that the benefit of EWC diminishes for larger models. As in encoder-only models, the inclusion of feature distillation further improves performance, and modality-aware weighting of the distillation losses is beneficial in all cases. For VL-Pythia, MAFED-A leads to the best performance, improving the accuracy on average by +2.6 compared to ER and +0.87 compared to FD. As mentioned in Section 5.4.1, we hypothesize that adaptive modality weighting can be particularly effective where the text and visual representations change more unequally. Overall, our results indicate that stabilizing the representations from vision and language tokens separately can improve multimodal continual learning.

6 Analysis

6.1 Distillation without Replay

Method	Accuracy	SBWT
FT	62.77	-5.27
ER	66.18	-3.42
FD	72.05	-1.00
w/o Replay	63.53	-4.87
MAFED-B	72.91	-0.16
w/o Replay	67.66	-3.67
MAFED-A	72.56	-0.24
w/o Replay	64.14	-4.09

Table 4: Ablation of feature distillation methods without replay using VL-Pythia (1B) on Question Types.

In the previous section, we applied feature distillation in conjunction with experience replay. Table 4 shows the performance when applying feature distillation with and without experience replay on VL-Pythia (1B) for one task order on the Question Types setting. Feature distillation improves the model performance, while standalone modality-aware methods are competitive with experience replay. The combination of the two approaches yields the greatest performance with no additional cost over standalone feature distillation. Both methods require maintaining a memory of past samples that are passed through the current model. Therefore, applying replay puts no additional overhead on training time and memory.

6.2 Distillation Layer Ablation

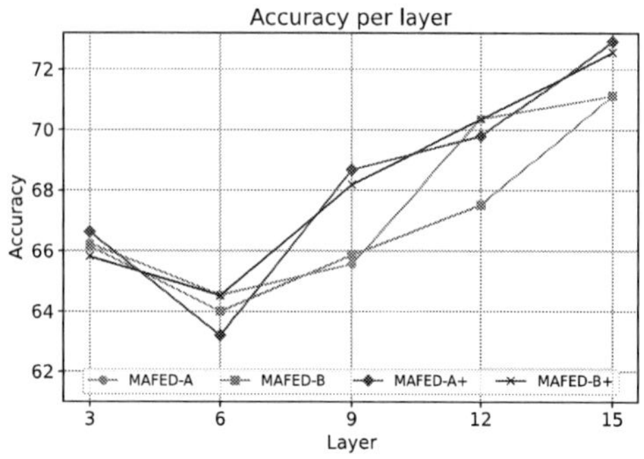

Figure 4: Ablation of feature distillation from a single or cumulative (+) model layers.

Next, we explore the effectiveness of applying modality-aware feature distillation from a single layer, as well as a subset of layers. Figure 4 illustrates the performance of VL-Pythia (1B) after applying MAFED-B and MAFED-A every three layers. As expected, applying both methods on a deeper layer of the model but also distilling from all previous layers yields greater performance. However, the performance of all four variants does not increase monotonically with the layer depth. More specifically, we observe that distilling from layer 6 leads to performance degradation. This behavior correlates with the results in Figure 3, where the per-modality similarities diverge the most at layer 6 and gradually align throughout the deeper layers of the model.

6.3 Modality Weights in MAFED-A

Figure 5 shows the weight α placed on the distillation loss of the language tokens using the MAFED-A method. In all models, MAFED-A assigns more weight to language tokens. Interestingly, we observe that in encoder-only models, the language weight progressively increases up to layer 8 and then drops. On the other hand, in VL-Pythia (1B), more than 90% of the weight is assigned to language tokens for all layers. We hypothesize that this is because the model is causal, and the last token before the answer is a text token.

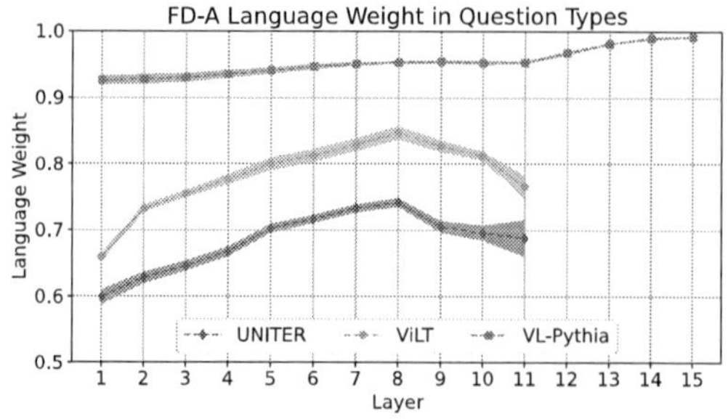

Figure 5: Language weight during MAFED-A. Note that language tokens in the encoder family (UNITER and ViLT) are weighted similarly across the layers of the models. For the causal VL-Pythia model, the language tokens have higher weights.

7 Conclusion

In this paper, we argued that applying approaches that were developed with unimodal models in mind is suboptimal for continual learning in VQA since this ignores modality-specific learning dynamics. We empirically showcased that the visual and the textual representations evolve at different rates – a phenomenon that occurs in both encoder-only and decoder-only VLMs. Given this observation, we proposed two modality-aware feature distillation approaches that equally weigh the distillation loss from each modality or adaptively estimate the importance of a modality based on the gradients with respect to the inputs. We believe this is a promising direction towards closing the gap with multitask training in multimodal continual learning.

7.1 Limitations & Future Work

Despite the promising results, our method has certain limitations. First, distillation is more computationally expensive than replay, as it requires accessing the representations from the previous model. However, compared to established distillation methods, MAFED-B improves performance with no overhead, while MAFED-A requires computing importance weights, which are only updated between tasks. Furthermore, our work does not investigate the potential effectiveness of architecture-based approaches, which could offer greater control over the learning of each modality through novel parameter-isolation approaches. Finally, we show that larger models exhibit less or even no forgetting depending on the setting. Future work should explore whether increasing the model size or the VL pretraining data (Ostapenko et al., 2022) can further decrease forgetting in VQA settings.

Acknowledgements

This work was supported by the Edinburgh International Data Facility (EIDF) and the Data-Driven Innovation Programme at the University of Edinburgh.

References

Rahaf Aljundi, Francesca Babiloni, Mohamed Elhoseiny, Marcus Rohrbach, and Tinne Tuytelaars. 2018. Memory aware synapses: Learning what (not) to forget. In *Proceedings of the European Conference on Computer Vision (ECCV)*, pages 139–154.

Peter Anderson, Xiaodong He, Chris Buehler, Damien Teney, Mark Johnson, Stephen Gould, and Lei Zhang. 2018. Bottom-up and top-down attention for image captioning and visual question answering. In *Proceedings of the IEEE Conference on Computer Vision and Pattern Recognition (CVPR)*.

Anthropic. 2024. Introducing the next generation of claude.

Benedikt Bagus and Alexander Gepperth. 2021. An investigation of replay-based approaches for continual learning. In *2021 International Joint Conference on Neural Networks (IJCNN)*, pages 1–9. IEEE.

Jinze Bai, Shuai Bai, Yunfei Chu, Zeyu Cui, Kai Dang, Xiaodong Deng, Yang Fan, Wenbin Ge, Yu Han, Fei Huang, et al. 2023a. Qwen technical report. *arXiv preprint arXiv:2309.16609*.

Jinze Bai, Shuai Bai, Shusheng Yang, Shijie Wang, Sinan Tan, Peng Wang, Junyang Lin, Chang Zhou, and Jingren Zhou. 2023b. Qwen-vl: A frontier large vision-language model with versatile abilities. *arXiv preprint arXiv:2308.12966*.

Stella Biderman, Hailey Schoelkopf, Quentin Gregory Anthony, Herbie Bradley, Kyle O'Brien, Eric Hallahan, Mohammad Aflah Khan, Shivanshu Purohit, USVSN Sai Prashanth, Edward Raff, et al. 2023. Pythia: A suite for analyzing large language models across training and scaling. In *International Conference on Machine Learning*, pages 2397–2430. PMLR.

Pietro Buzzega, Matteo Boschini, Angelo Porrello, Davide Abati, and Simone Calderara. 2020. Dark experience for general continual learning: a strong, simple baseline. In *NeurIPS*.

Arslan Chaudhry, Marcus Rohrbach, Mohamed Elhoseiny, Thalaiyasingam Ajanthan, Puneet Kumar Dokania, Philip H. S. Torr, and Marc'Aurelio Ranzato. 2019. Continual learning with tiny episodic memories. *CoRR*, abs/1902.10486.

Yen-Chun Chen, Linjie Li, Licheng Yu, Ahmed El Kholy, Faisal Ahmed, Zhe Gan, Yu Cheng, and Jingjing Liu. 2020. Uniter: Universal image-text representation learning. In *Computer Vision – ECCV 2020*, pages 104–120, Cham. Springer International Publishing.

Zhenyu Cui, Yuxin Peng, Xun Wang, Manyu Zhu, and Jiahuan Zhou. 2024. Continual vision-language retrieval via dynamic knowledge rectification. In *Proceedings of the AAAI Conference on Artificial Intelligence*, volume 38, pages 11704–11712.

Wenliang Dai, Junnan Li, Dongxu Li, Anthony Meng Huat Tiong, Junqi Zhao, Weisheng Wang, Boyang Li, Pascale N Fung, and Steven Hoi. 2024. Instructblip: Towards general-purpose vision-language models with instruction tuning. *Advances in Neural Information Processing Systems*, 36.

Tri Dao, Dan Fu, Stefano Ermon, Atri Rudra, and Christopher Ré. 2022. Flashattention: Fast and memory-efficient exact attention with io-awareness. *Advances in Neural Information Processing Systems*, 35:16344–16359.

Riccardo Del Chiaro, Bartł omiej Twardowski, Andrew Bagdanov, and Joost van de Weijer. 2020. Ratt: Recurrent attention to transient tasks for continual image captioning. In *Advances in Neural Information Processing Systems*, volume 33, pages 16736–16748. Curran Associates, Inc.

Matthias Delange, Rahaf Aljundi, Marc Masana, Sarah Parisot, Xu Jia, Ales Leonardis, Greg Slabaugh, and Tinne Tuytelaars. 2021. A continual learning survey: Defying forgetting in classification tasks. *IEEE Transactions on Pattern Analysis and Machine Intelligence*, pages 1–1.

Prithviraj Dhar, Rajat Vikram Singh, Kuan-Chuan Peng, Ziyan Wu, and Rama Chellappa. 2019. Learning without memorizing. In *Conference on Computer Vision and Pattern Recognition*.

Arthur Douillard, Matthieu Cord, Charles Ollion, Thomas Robert, and Eduardo Valle. 2020. Podnet: Pooled outputs distillation for small-tasks incremental learning. In *Computer Vision–ECCV 2020: 16th European Conference, Glasgow, UK, August 23–28, 2020, Proceedings, Part XX 16*, pages 86–102. Springer.

Yuxin Fang, Quan Sun, Xinggang Wang, Tiejun Huang, Xinlong Wang, and Yue Cao. 2023. Eva-02: A visual representation for neon genesis. *arXiv preprint arXiv:2303.11331*.

Chrisantha Fernando, Dylan Banarse, Charles Blundell, Yori Zwols, David Ha, Andrei A. Rusu, Alexander Pritzel, and Daan Wierstra. 2017. Pathnet: Evolution channels gradient descent in super neural networks. *CoRR*, abs/1701.08734.

Gemini Team, Rohan Anil, Sebastian Borgeaud, Yonghui Wu, Jean-Baptiste Alayrac, Jiahui Yu, Radu Soricut, Johan Schalkwyk, Andrew M. Dai, Anja Hauth, Katie Millican, David Silver, Slav Petrov,

Melvin Johnson, Ioannis Antonoglou, Julian Schrittwieser, Amelia Glaese, Jilin Chen, Emily Pitler, Timothy Lillicrap, Angeliki Lazaridou, Orhan Firat, James Molloy, Michael Isard, Paul R. Barham, Tom Hennigan, Benjamin Lee, Fabio Viola, Malcolm Reynolds, Yuanzhong Xu, Ryan Doherty, Eli Collins, Clemens Meyer, Eliza Rutherford, Erica Moreira, Kareem Ayoub, Megha Goel, et al. 2023. Gemini: A Family of Highly Capable Multimodal Models. *Preprint*, arxiv:2312.11805.

Yash Goyal, Tejas Khot, Douglas Summers-Stay, Dhruv Batra, and Devi Parikh. 2017. Making the v in vqa matter: Elevating the role of image understanding in visual question answering. In *Proceedings of the IEEE Conference on Computer Vision and Pattern Recognition (CVPR)*.

Claudio Greco, Barbara Plank, Raquel Fernández, and Raffaella Bernardi. 2019. Psycholinguistics meets continual learning: Measuring catastrophic forgetting in visual question answering. In *Proceedings of the 57th Annual Meeting of the Association for Computational Linguistics*, pages 3601–3605, Florence, Italy. Association for Computational Linguistics.

Saihui Hou, Xinyu Pan, Chen Change Loy, Zilei Wang, and Dahua Lin. 2019. Learning a unified classifier incrementally via rebalancing. In *The IEEE Conference on Computer Vision and Pattern Recognition (CVPR)*.

Drew A Hudson and Christopher D Manning. 2019. Gqa: A new dataset for real-world visual reasoning and compositional question answering. In *Proceedings of the IEEE/CVF conference on computer vision and pattern recognition*, pages 6700–6709.

Chao Jia, Yinfei Yang, Ye Xia, Yi-Ting Chen, Zarana Parekh, Hieu Pham, Quoc Le, Yun-Hsuan Sung, Zhen Li, and Tom Duerig. 2021. Scaling up visual and vision-language representation learning with noisy text supervision. In *International conference on machine learning*, pages 4904–4916. PMLR.

Albert Q Jiang, Alexandre Sablayrolles, Arthur Mensch, Chris Bamford, Devendra Singh Chaplot, Diego de las Casas, Florian Bressand, Gianna Lengyel, Guillaume Lample, Lucile Saulnier, et al. 2023. Mistral 7b. *arXiv preprint arXiv:2310.06825*.

Xisen Jin, Junyi Du, Arka Sadhu, Ram Nevatia, and Xiang Ren. 2020. Visually grounded continual learning of compositional phrases. In *Proceedings of the 2020 Conference on Empirical Methods in Natural Language Processing (EMNLP)*, pages 2018–2029, Online. Association for Computational Linguistics.

Minsoo Kang, Jaeyoo Park, and Bohyung Han. 2022. Class-incremental learning by knowledge distillation with adaptive feature consolidation. In *2022 IEEE/CVF Conference on Computer Vision and Pattern Recognition (CVPR)*, pages 16050–16059. IEEE.

Siddharth Karamcheti, Suraj Nair, Ashwin Balakrishna, Percy Liang, Thomas Kollar, and Dorsa Sadigh. 2024. Prismatic vlms: Investigating the design space of visually-conditioned language models. *arXiv preprint arXiv:2402.07865*.

Nazmul Karim, Umar Khalid, Ashkan Esmaeili, and Nazanin Rahnavard. 2022. Cnll: A semi-supervised approach for continual noisy label learning. In *Proceedings of the IEEE/CVF Conference on Computer Vision and Pattern Recognition (CVPR) Workshops*, pages 3878–3888.

Wonjae Kim, Bokyung Son, and Ildoo Kim. 2021. Vilt: Vision-and-language transformer without convolution or region supervision. In *Proceedings of the 38th International Conference on Machine Learning*, volume 139 of *Proceedings of Machine Learning Research*, pages 5583–5594. PMLR.

Diederik P Kingma and Jimmy Ba. 2014. Adam: A method for stochastic optimization. *arXiv preprint arXiv:1412.6980*.

James Kirkpatrick, Razvan Pascanu, Neil Rabinowitz, Joel Veness, Guillaume Desjardins, Andrei A Rusu, Kieran Milan, John Quan, Tiago Ramalho, Agnieszka Grabska-Barwinska, et al. 2017. Overcoming catastrophic forgetting in neural networks. *Proceedings of the national academy of sciences*, 114(13):3521–3526.

Simon Kornblith, Mohammad Norouzi, Honglak Lee, and Geoffrey Hinton. 2019. Similarity of neural network representations revisited. In *Proceedings of the 36th International Conference on Machine Learning*, volume 97 of *Proceedings of Machine Learning Research*, pages 3519–3529. PMLR.

Ranjay Krishna, Yuke Zhu, Oliver Groth, Justin Johnson, Kenji Hata, Joshua Kravitz, Stephanie Chen, Yannis Kalantidis, Li-Jia Li, David A Shamma, et al. 2017. Visual genome: Connecting language and vision using crowdsourced dense image annotations. *International journal of computer vision*, 123:32–73.

Mingrui Lao, Nan Pu, Yu Liu, Zhun Zhong, Erwin M. Bakker, Nicu Sebe, and Michael S. Lew. 2023. Multi-domain lifelong visual question answering via self-critical distillation. In *Proceedings of the 31st ACM International Conference on Multimedia*, MM '23, page 4747–4758, New York, NY, USA. Association for Computing Machinery.

Hugo Laurençon, Lucile Saulnier, Léo Tronchon, Stas Bekman, Amanpreet Singh, Anton Lozhkov, Thomas Wang, Siddharth Karamcheti, Alexander Rush, Douwe Kiela, et al. 2024a. Obelics: An open web-scale filtered dataset of interleaved image-text documents. *Advances in Neural Information Processing Systems*, 36.

Hugo Laurençon, Léo Tronchon, Matthieu Cord, and Victor Sanh. 2024b. What matters when building vision-language models? *arXiv preprint arXiv:2405.02246*.

Angeliki Lazaridou, Adhiguna Kuncoro, Elena Gribovskaya, Devang Agrawal, Adam Liska, Tayfun Terzi, Mai Gimenez, Cyprien de Masson d'Autume, Tomáš Kočiský, Sebastian Ruder, Dani Yogatama, Kris Cao, Susannah Young, and Phil Blunsom. 2021. Mind the gap: Assessing temporal generalization in neural language models. In *Advances in Neural Information Processing Systems*.

Stan Weixian Lei, Difei Gao, Jay Zhangjie Wu, Yuxuan Wang, Wei Liu, Mengmi Zhang, and Mike Zheng Shou. 2023. Symbolic replay: Scene graph as prompt for continual learning on vqa task. In *Proceedings of the AAAI Conference on Artificial Intelligence*, volume 37, pages 1250–1259.

Junnan Li, Ramprasaath Selvaraju, Akhilesh Gotmare, Shafiq Joty, Caiming Xiong, and Steven Chu Hong Hoi. 2021. Align before fuse: Vision and language representation learning with momentum distillation. *Advances in neural information processing systems*, 34:9694–9705.

Yifan Li, Yifan Du, Kun Zhou, Jinpeng Wang, Xin Zhao, and Ji-Rong Wen. 2023. Evaluating object hallucination in large vision-language models. In *The 2023 Conference on Empirical Methods in Natural Language Processing*.

Zhizhong Li and Derek Hoiem. 2018. Learning without forgetting. *IEEE Transactions on Pattern Analysis and Machine Intelligence*, 40(12):2935–2947.

Tsung-Yi Lin, Michael Maire, Serge Belongie, James Hays, Pietro Perona, Deva Ramanan, Piotr Dollár, and C. Lawrence Zitnick. 2014. Microsoft coco: Common objects in context. In *Computer Vision – ECCV 2014*, pages 740–755, Cham. Springer International Publishing.

Zhiqiu Lin, Jia Shi, Deepak Pathak, and Deva Ramanan. 2021. The CLEAR benchmark: Continual LEArning on real-world imagery. In *Thirty-fifth Conference on Neural Information Processing Systems Datasets and Benchmarks Track (Round 2)*.

Haotian Liu, Chunyuan Li, Yuheng Li, and Yong Jae Lee. 2023. Improved baselines with visual instruction tuning. *arXiv preprint arXiv:2310.03744*.

Haotian Liu, Chunyuan Li, Qingyang Wu, and Yong Jae Lee. 2024. Visual instruction tuning. *Advances in neural information processing systems*, 36.

Vincenzo Lomonaco and Davide Maltoni. 2017. Core50: a new dataset and benchmark for continuous object recognition. In *Proceedings of the 1st Annual Conference on Robot Learning*, volume 78 of *Proceedings of Machine Learning Research*, pages 17–26. PMLR.

Jiasen Lu, Dhruv Batra, Devi Parikh, and Stefan Lee. 2019. Vilbert: Pretraining task-agnostic visiolinguistic representations for vision-and-language tasks. *arXiv preprint arXiv:1908.02265*.

Andrea Madotto, Zhaojiang Lin, Zhenpeng Zhou, Seungwhan Moon, Paul Crook, Bing Liu, Zhou Yu, Eunjoon Cho, Pascale Fung, and Zhiguang Wang. 2021. Continual learning in task-oriented dialogue systems. In *Proceedings of the 2021 Conference on Empirical Methods in Natural Language Processing*, pages 7452–7467, Online and Punta Cana, Dominican Republic. Association for Computational Linguistics.

Michael McCloskey and Neal J Cohen. 1989. Catastrophic interference in connectionist networks: The sequential learning problem. In *Psychology of learning and motivation*, volume 24, pages 109–165. Elsevier.

Seyed Iman Mirzadeh, Arslan Chaudhry, Dong Yin, Huiyi Hu, Razvan Pascanu, Dilan Gorur, and Mehrdad Farajtabar. 2022. Wide neural networks forget less catastrophically. In *International conference on machine learning*, pages 15699–15717. PMLR.

Giang Nguyen, Tae Joon Jun, Trung Tran, Tolcha Yalew, and Daeyoung Kim. 2019. Contcap: A scalable framework for continual image captioning. *arXiv preprint arXiv:1909.08745*.

Mavina Nikandrou, Lu Yu, Alessandro Suglia, Ioannis Konstas, and Verena Rieser. 2022. Task formulation matters when learning continually: A case study in visual question answering. *arXiv preprint arXiv:2210.00044*.

OpenAI. 2022. Introducing ChatGPT.

Maxime Oquab, Timothée Darcet, Théo Moutakanni, Huy V. Vo, Marc Szafraniec, Vasil Khalidov, Pierre Fernandez, Daniel HAZIZA, Francisco Massa, Alaaeldin El-Nouby, Mido Assran, Nicolas Ballas, Wojciech Galuba, Russell Howes, Po-Yao Huang, Shang-Wen Li, Ishan Misra, Michael Rabbat, Vasu Sharma, Gabriel Synnaeve, Hu Xu, Herve Jegou, Julien Mairal, Patrick Labatut, Armand Joulin, and Piotr Bojanowski. 2024. DINOv2: Learning robust visual features without supervision. *Transactions on Machine Learning Research*.

Vicente Ordonez, Girish Kulkarni, and Tamara Berg. 2011. Im2text: Describing images using 1 million captioned photographs. In *Advances in Neural Information Processing Systems*, volume 24. Curran Associates, Inc.

Oleksiy Ostapenko, Timothee Lesort, Pau Rodríguez, Md Rifat Arefin, Arthur Douillard, Irina Rish, and Laurent Charlin. 2022. Continual learning with foundation models: An empirical study of latent replay. In *Conference on lifelong learning agents*, pages 60–91. PMLR.

Zi Qian, Xin Wang, Xuguang Duan, Pengda Qin, Yuhong Li, and Wenwu Zhu. 2023. Decouple before interact: Multi-modal prompt learning for continual visual question answering. In *Proceedings of the IEEE/CVF International Conference on Computer Vision*, pages 2953–2962.

Alec Radford, Jong Wook Kim, Chris Hallacy, Aditya Ramesh, Gabriel Goh, Sandhini Agarwal, Girish Sastry, Amanda Askell, Pamela Mishkin, Jack Clark, et al. 2021. Learning transferable visual models from natural language supervision. In *International conference on machine learning*, pages 8748–8763. PMLR.

Vinay Venkatesh Ramasesh, Aitor Lewkowycz, and Ethan Dyer. 2022. Effect of scale on catastrophic forgetting in neural networks. In *International Conference on Learning Representations*.

Roger Ratcliff. 1990. Connectionist models of recognition memory: constraints imposed by learning and forgetting functions. *Psychological review*, 97(2):285.

Sylvestre-Alvise Rebuffi, Alexander Kolesnikov, Georg Sperl, and Christoph H Lampert. 2017. icarl: Incremental classifier and representation learning. In *Proceedings of the IEEE conference on Computer Vision and Pattern Recognition*, pages 2001–2010.

Joan Serrà, Didac Suris, Marius Miron, and Alexandros Karatzoglou. 2018. Overcoming catastrophic forgetting with hard attention to the task. In *ICML*, pages 4555–4564.

Piyush Sharma, Nan Ding, Sebastian Goodman, and Radu Soricut. 2018. Conceptual captions: A cleaned, hypernymed, image alt-text dataset for automatic image captioning. In *Proceedings of the 56th Annual Meeting of the Association for Computational Linguistics (Volume 1: Long Papers)*, pages 2556–2565.

Tejas Srinivasan, Ting-Yun Chang, Leticia Pinto Alva, Georgios Chochlakis, Mohammad Rostami, and Jesse Thomason. 2022. Climb: A continual learning benchmark for vision-and-language tasks. In *Advances in Neural Information Processing Systems*, volume 35, pages 29440–29453. Curran Associates, Inc.

Jianlin Su, Murtadha Ahmed, Yu Lu, Shengfeng Pan, Wen Bo, and Yunfeng Liu. 2024. Roformer: Enhanced transformer with rotary position embedding. *Neurocomputing*, 568:127063.

Fan-Keng Sun, Cheng-Hao Ho, and Hung yi Lee. 2019. Lamol: Language modeling for lifelong language learning. In *International Conference on Learning Representations*.

Hao Tan and Mohit Bansal. 2019. Lxmert: Learning cross-modality encoder representations from transformers. *arXiv preprint arXiv:1908.07490*.

Hugo Touvron, Louis Martin, Kevin Stone, Peter Albert, Amjad Almahairi, Yasmine Babaei, Nikolay Bashlykov, Soumya Batra, Prajjwal Bhargava, Shruti Bhosale, et al. 2023. Llama 2: Open foundation and fine-tuned chat models. *arXiv preprint arXiv:2307.09288*.

Gido M Van de Ven and Andreas S Tolias. 2018. Generative replay with feedback connections as a general strategy for continual learning. *arXiv preprint arXiv:1809.10635*.

Weiyao Wang, Du Tran, and Matt Feiszli. 2020. What makes training multi-modal classification networks hard? In *Proceedings of the IEEE/CVF conference on computer vision and pattern recognition*, pages 12695–12705.

Zhen Wang, Liu Liu, Yiqun Duan, and Dacheng Tao. 2022. Continual learning through retrieval and imagination. In *Proceedings of the AAAI Conference on Artificial Intelligence*, volume 36, pages 8594–8602.

Nan Wu, Stanislaw Jastrzebski, Kyunghyun Cho, and Krzysztof J Geras. 2022. Characterizing and overcoming the greedy nature of learning in multi-modal deep neural networks. In *International Conference on Machine Learning*, pages 24043–24055. PMLR.

Yue Wu, Yinpeng Chen, Lijuan Wang, Yuancheng Ye, Zicheng Liu, Yandong Guo, and Yun Fu. 2019. Large scale incremental learning. In *Conference on Computer Vision and Pattern Recognition*.

Jaehong Yoon, Saehoon Kim, Eunho Yang, and Sung Ju Hwang. 2020. Scalable and order-robust continual learning with additive parameter decomposition. In *International Conference on Learning Representations*.

Friedemann Zenke, Ben Poole, and Surya Ganguli. 2017. Continual learning through synaptic intelligence. In *International Conference on Machine Learning*, pages 3987–3995. PMLR.

Xi Zhang, Feifei Zhang, and Changsheng Xu. 2023. Vqacl: A novel visual question answering continual learning setting. In *Proceedings of the IEEE/CVF Conference on Computer Vision and Pattern Recognition*, pages 19102–19112.

Yao Zhang, Haokun Chen, Ahmed Frikha, Yezi Yang, Denis Krompass, Gengyuan Zhang, Jindong Gu, and Volker Tresp. 2022. Cl-crossvqa: A continual learning benchmark for cross-domain visual question answering. *arXiv preprint arXiv:2211.10567*.

A Experiments

A.1 Pretraining VL-Pythia

We pretrain all VL-Pythia models following the LLaVA-1.5 recipe (Liu et al., 2023). The only difference is that we skip the first stage for multimodal alignment as recent work (Karamcheti et al., 2024) has shown that the two-stage training can be redundant and the same performance can achieved when omitting the first stage of training. Throughout VL pretraining, the vision encoder remains frozen, while the LLM and connector parameters are trained using the Adam optimizer (Kingma and Ba, 2014) with a batch size of 256 and a learning rate of 1e-3. For all models, we used the same data to train UNITER and ViLT - COCO (Lin et al., 2014), SBU captions (Ordonez et al., 2011), Visual Genome captions (Krishna et al., 2017) and Conceptual Captions 3M (Sharma et al., 2018). We perform one epoch of pretraining and keep the final checkpoint.

A.2 Hyperparameters

Model	Setting	Batch Size	LR	EWC λ	FD γ
UNITER	Diverse Content	1024	8e-5	500	0.8
	Taxonomy Content	1024	5e-5	500	0.8
	Question Types	512	5e-5	20K	0.6
ViLT	Diverse Content	1024	1e-5	500	1
	Taxonomy Content	1024	1e-5	700	1
	Question Types	512	8e-5	10K	0.5
VL-Pythia	Diverse Content	128	5e-5	-	0.5
	Taxonomy Content	128	5e-5	-	0.5
	Question Types	128	5e-5	10K	0.5

Table 5: Selected hyperparameters.

We tune the hyperparameters using grid search based on the validation accuracy of a single task order. For VL-Pythia variants, we use the same hyperparameters for all model sizes, as we find them to perform reasonably well. For UNITER and ViLT, we keep the batch size, learning rate (LR), and EWC loss weight λ reported in prior work (Nikandrou et al., 2022). For the remaining values, we perform the following grid search: lr $\in \{1e-5, 5.e-5, 8e-5, 1e-4\}$, EWC $\lambda \in \{500, 1K, 5K, 10K\}$, FD discount factor $\gamma \in [0.3, 1.0]$ with a step of 0.1.

English-to-Japanese Multimodal Machine Translation Based on Image-Text Matching of Lecture Videos

Ayu Teramen Takumi Ohtsuka Risa Kondo Tomoyuki Kajiwara Takashi Ninomiya
Graduate School of Science and Engineering, Ehime University, Japan
{teramen@ai., ohtsuka@ai., kondo@ai., kajiwara@, ninomiya@}cs.ehime-u.ac.jp

Abstract

We work on a multimodal machine translation of the audio contained in English lecture videos to generate Japanese subtitles. Image-guided multimodal machine translation is promising for error correction in speech recognition and for text disambiguation. In our situation, lecture videos provide a variety of images. Images of presentation materials can complement information not available from audio and may help improve translation quality. However, images of speakers or audiences would not directly affect the translation quality. We construct a multimodal parallel corpus with automatic speech recognition text and multiple images for a transcribed parallel corpus of lecture videos, and propose a method to select the most relevant ones from the multiple images with the speech text for improving the performance of image-guided multimodal machine translation. Experimental results on translating automatic speech recognition or transcribed English text into Japanese show the effectiveness of our method to select a relevant image.

1 Introduction

Multimodal machine translation (Sulubacak et al., 2020) is a machine translation (MT) approach that combines information from modalities other than text, such as audio and images. Since images provide visual information that is not included in audio or text, it is expected to improve translation quality by correcting errors in automatic speech recognition (ASR) or by complementing information in ambiguous text.

This study tackles the task of translating English audio or subtitles from lecture videos into Japanese. In such situations, since useful information can be obtained from the images in the presentation materials, image-guided MT can improve translation quality over text-only MT. However, some of the images derived from lecture videos are not directly related to the subtitle text, such as the image shown on the left in Figure 1, which shows only the speaker. No improvement in translation quality can be expected from such images.

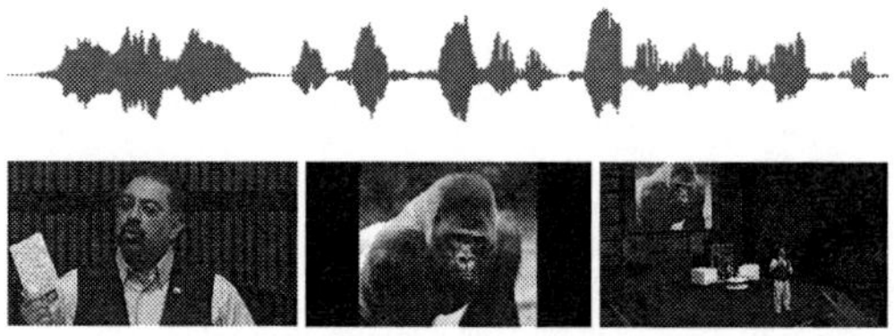

ASR text (English)	when you do that here's what I can promise you're going to be the 800-pound gorilla in the forest
Transcribed text (English)	So when you do that, here's what I can promise: You're going to be the 800 pound gorilla in the forest.
Translation (Japanese)	手書きの手紙の力によって、森にいる体重 300 キ ロの ゴリラのような存在になれるでしょう。

Figure 1: An example of our multimodal parallel corpus. Our corpus includes five sets of images, audio in English, ASR sentences in English, transcribed sentences in English, and reference translations in Japanese. Three images are included, corresponding to the beginning, middle, and end of the audio.

To improve the performance of image-guided MT, we propose a method to select the image most relevant to the text among multiple images that correspond in time to the subtitle text. Additionally, to evaluate our method, we construct a multimodal parallel corpus, TAIL[1] (English-to-Japanese **T**ranslation Corpus with **A**udio and **I**mages from **L**ecture Videos), consisting of English subtitles of lecture videos and their Japanese translations. Experimental results on translating ASR or transcribed English text into Japanese subtitles show the effectiveness of our method to select a relevant image.

[1] https://github.com/EhimeNLP/TAIL

Proceedings of the 3rd Workshop on Advances in Language and Vision Research, pages 86–91
August 16, 2024 ©2024 Association for Computational Linguistics

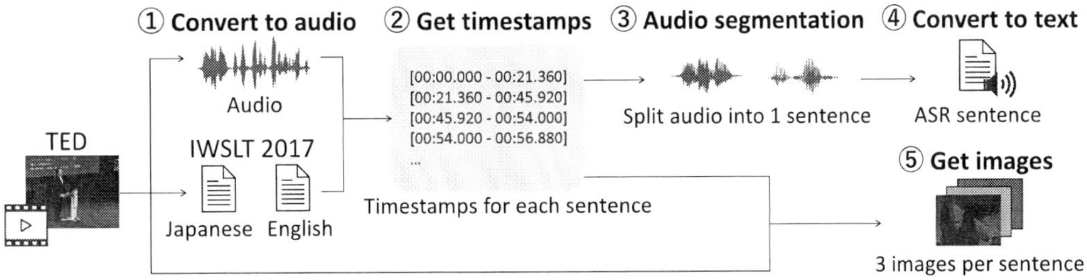

Figure 2: Overview of our corpus construction.

2 Related Work

2.1 Multimodal Parallel Corpus

Previous studies of multimodal MT have often involved adding some one modality to the text, such as MT from speech (Di Gangi et al., 2019; Wang et al., 2020; Salesky et al., 2021) or image-guided MT (Elliott et al., 2016; Parida et al., 2019; Thapliyal et al., 2022). Furthermore, we can expect further improvement in translation quality by combining three modalities of text, audio, and images. Previous studies combining the three modalities include video-guided MT, such as How-2 (Sanabria et al., 2018) and QED (Abdelali et al., 2014). However, these are limited in scope because How-2 only covers English-Portuguese language pairs and QED only covers education domain. To cover English-Japanese lecture subtitles, we need to expand the multimodal parallel corpus.

2.2 Image-guided Machine Translation

Image-guided MT (Specia et al., 2016) improves translation quality by complementing textual ambiguity with visual information derived from images. Early studies (Caglayan et al., 2016; Libovický and Helcl, 2017; Calixto and Liu, 2017) combined CNN-based visual representations with textual representations in RNN-based encoder-decoder models. In the modern approach (Li et al., 2022a), both vision and language inputs are encoded by the Transformer (Vaswani et al., 2017; Dosovitskiy et al., 2021), integrated by selective attention, and fed to the Transformer decoder. The image-guided machine translation model, based on the powerful Vision Transformer (Dosovitskiy et al., 2021), achieves higher translation quality with images that are more relevant to the text (Yuasa et al., 2023). Therefore, in situations where multiple images are available, translation quality can be improved by selecting images that are more relevant to the text.

2.3 Vision and Language Pre-training

In image-text matching, CLIP (Radford et al., 2021) and BLIP (Li et al., 2022b), trained by multimodal contrastive learning, have achieved state-of-the-art performance. Especially, BLIP is trained in a multi-task learning manner of image-text matching and image caption generation as well as contrastive learning, which allows a single model to perform both understanding and generating on vision and language tasks.

3 TAIL Corpus

For English-to-Japanese multimodal MT of lecture subtitles, we construct a corpus consisting of five sets of images, audio in English, ASR sentences in English, transcribed sentences in English, and reference translations in Japanese for lecture videos from TED.[2] Since an English-Japanese parallel corpus consisting of transcribed sentences for TED lecture videos has been released in the IWSLT2017 competition (Cettolo et al., 2017), we annotate it with images, audio, and ASR sentences, as shown in Figure 2.

3.1 Audio Annotation

First, we annotate both audio and ASR sentences in English on top of the IWSLT2017 En-Ja corpus.

Audio Acquisition We downloaded the lecture videos in MP4 format from the URLs provided in the metadata of the IWSLT2017 En-Ja corpus. These videos are converted to audio in FLAC format with `ffmpeg` converter.[3] (Step 1 in Figure 2)

Forced Alignment For each lecture video, the transcribed English sentences from the IWSLT2017 En-Ja corpus and the audio from Step 1 are aligned by aeneas toolkit.[4] Here, both

[2] https://www.ted.com
[3] https://ffmpeg.org
[4] https://github.com/readbeyond/aeneas

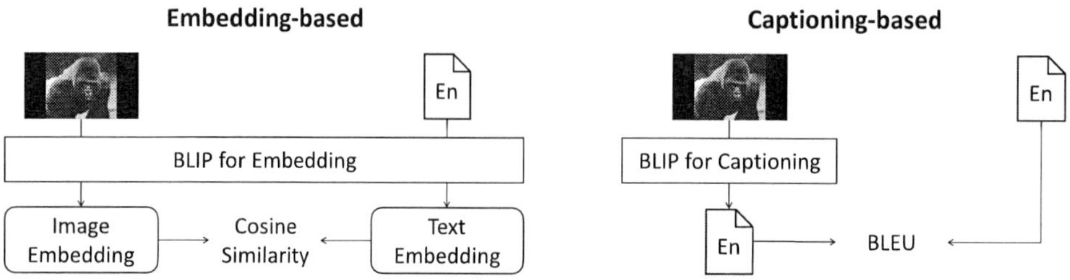

Figure 3: Overview of the proposed method of image-text matching.

start and end timestamps are recorded for each sentence (Step 2 in Figure 2), and the audio is segmented by `ffmpeg` (Step 3 in Figure 2).

Automatic Speech Recognition The audio, which was segmented into sentences in Step 3, is converted into text using `Google Speech Recognition`.[5] (Step 4 in Figure 2)

3.2 Image Annotation

In this section, we further annotate images on top of our corpus to construct five sets. Since some scenes in TED videos do not represent the content of the lecture, such as scenes showing only the speaker, we collect multiple images for each sentence. Specifically, we use three images corresponding to the beginning, middle, and end of the timestamp of each sentence. Three images per sentence were extracted using `OpenCV` library[6] with video and timestamps for each lecture video.

3.3 Parallel Corpus Filtering

The IWSLT2017 En-Ja corpus originally released 223k sentence pairs, but only 212k sentence pairs allowed us to access the videos from the URLs. To reduce noise in the corpus due to errors in timestamping and alignment, we automatically filter our parallel corpus. We filter out noisy sentence pairs by both sentence length difference and word error rate (WER) between automatically recognized (ASR) and manually transcribed (REF) English sentences. We keep $0.8 \leq$ len(ASR)/len(REF) ≤ 1.2 cases with small sentence length differences. Where len$(\cdot)$ is the number of words in the sentence. It also keeps WER(ASR, REF) ≤ 0.5 cases with small WER. In the WER calculation, text was lowercased and symbols were removed as a preprocessing step. This left 102k sentence pairs.

We further exclude pairs where all images are unrelated to the text, which is not beneficial to the image-guided MT. We compute the cosine similarity between the text and each of the three images assigned to it, and employ the 70,000 sentence pairs in descending order of their maximum value for our experiment. Here, BLIP-based multimodal embeddings (Li et al., 2022b) are used for similarity calculations, as in the next section.

4 Image-guided Machine Translation

In this study, as shown in Figure 1, we are given an English sentence that has been automatically recognized or manually transcribed from a lecture subtitle as well as three images that correspond in time to the text. The image-guided machine translation that we are working on is the task of inputting one image selected from among three images along with its English text and translating it into Japanese subtitles.

To select the image related to a given English sentence, we estimate the semantic similarity between vision and language. Both of the following two proposed methods are based on BLIP (Li et al., 2022b), a pre-trained multimodal model.

- **Embedding-based method:** Encode each given text and image with BLIP and then rank multiple images by the cosine similarity between their embeddings.

- **Captioning-based method:** Generate an English caption with BLIP from a given image and rank multiple images by the BLEU (Papineni et al., 2002) between the input text and the caption. (Right side of Figure 3)

5 Evaluation

5.1 Setting

Model Our multimodal MT model employed the Selective Attention model[7] (Li et al., 2022a).

[5] https://github.com/Uberi/speech_recognition
[6] https://opencv.org
[7] https://github.com/libeineu/fairseq_mmt

This model is a 4-layer, 128-dimensional Transformer (Vaswani et al., 2017) combined with image features from the Vision Transformer (vit_tiny_patch16_384) (Dosovitskiy et al., 2021). RAdam (Liu et al., 2020) was used for optimization and trained with a batch size of $4,096$ tokens and a learning rate of $1e-4$. Training was terminated when the cross-entropy loss in the validation dataset was not updated 10 times.

Data The TAIL corpus described in Section 3 was used for our experiments. We used 70,000 sentence pairs for training, 2,669 for validation, and 2,371 for evaluation. As a preprocessing, MosesTokenizer[8] (Koehn et al., 2007) and MeCab[9] (IPADIC) (Kudo et al., 2004) were used for word segmentation for English and Japanese, respectively. Subsequently, a subword segmentation with a vocabulary size of $16,000$ was performed by fastBPE[10] (Sennrich et al., 2016).

Comparison We evaluate the effectiveness of our image-text matching for image-guided MT by comparing it to the following three baseline models. Each model is trained three times with changing random seed, and the averaged BLEU (Papineni et al., 2002) is reported.

- **w/o Image baseline:** Text-only MT model. We discuss the effectiveness of the image-guided MT in comparison to this baseline.
- **w/ Random Image baseline:** An image-guided MT model that uses a randomly selected image from the entire dataset. We discuss the effectiveness of the use of related images in comparison to this baseline.
- **w/ Related Image baseline:** An image-guided MT model that uses a randomly selected image from a set of three images that correspond in time to given sentence. We discuss the effectiveness of the use of the most related images in comparison to this baseline.

5.2 Results

Automatic Evaluation Experimental results are shown in the BLEU columns of Table 1. Note that the ASR column is the translation quality for automatically recognized English sentences, while the IWSLT column is for manually transcribed English sentences. Compared to the baseline model without images, the other image-guided MT models achieved significantly higher translation quality. This suggests the effectiveness of complementing MT of lecture subtitles with images.

	BLEU		Accuracy
	ASR	IWSLT	IWSLT
w/o Image	3.94	4.73	-
w/ Random Image	7.04	8.98	-
w/ Related Image	7.07	8.97	0.495
Embedding-based	**7.30**	**9.48**	**0.785**
Captioning-based	6.96	8.90	0.410

Table 1: Performance of English-Japanese Translation.

Two baselines of image-guided MT (w/ Random Image and w/ Related Image) achieved comparable translation quality. This suggests that simply using images that correspond in time to the input text does not necessarily result in high performance. In contrast, our embedding-based method of selecting images to match text achieved the best performance for both ASR and IWSLT text.

Human Evaluation The Accuracy column in Table 1 shows the human evaluation of the accuracy of image selection for randomly sampled 200 texts. Note that these samples do not include cases where all images are related to or unrelated to the text. As with translation quality, our embedding-based method achieved the best performance. These results reveal a strong correlation between the performance of image-text matching and translation quality. It is suggested that multimodal MT performance can be improved by selecting images that are well related to the text.

6 Conclusion

In this study, we constructed a multimodal parallel corpus of images, audio in English, ASR sentences in English, transcribed sentences in English, and reference translations in Japanese of approximately 75k sentence pairs to generate cross-lingual subtitles from lecture videos. Experimental results reveal that our embedding-based image-text matching method contributes to improved performance of image-guided machine translation. Our future work includes further improvement of translation quality by combining multiple images.

[8] https://github.com/moses-smt/mosesdecoder
[9] https://taku910.github.io/mecab/
[10] https://github.com/glample/fastBPE

Acknowledgments

These research results were obtained from the commissioned research (No.22501) by National Institute of Information and Communications Technology (NICT), Japan.

References

Ahmed Abdelali, Francisco Guzman, Hassan Sajjad, and Stephan Vogel. 2014. The AMARA Corpus: Building Parallel Language Resources for the Educational Domain. In *Proceedings of the Ninth International Conference on Language Resources and Evaluation*, pages 1856–1862.

Ozan Caglayan, Walid Aransa, Yaxing Wang, Marc Masana, Mercedes García-Martínez, Fethi Bougares, Loïc Barrault, and Joost van de Weijer. 2016. Does Multimodality Help Human and Machine for Translation and Image Captioning? In *Proceedings of the First Conference on Machine Translation*, pages 627–633.

Iacer Calixto and Qun Liu. 2017. Incorporating Global Visual Features into Attention-based Neural Machine Translation. In *Proceedings of the 2017 Conference on Empirical Methods in Natural Language Processing*, pages 992–1003.

Mauro Cettolo, Marcello Federico, Luisa Bentivogli, Jan Niehues, Sebastian Stüker, Katsuhito Sudoh, Koichiro Yoshino, and Christian Federmann. 2017. Overview of the IWSLT 2017 Evaluation Campaign. In *Proceedings of the 14th International Conference on Spoken Language Translation*, pages 2–14.

Mattia A. Di Gangi, Roldano Cattoni, Luisa Bentivogli, Matteo Negri, and Marco Turchi. 2019. MuST-C: a Multilingual Speech Translation Corpus. In *Proceedings of the 2019 Conference of the North American Chapter of the Association for Computational Linguistics: Human Language Technologies*, pages 2012–2017.

Alexey Dosovitskiy, Lucas Beyer, Alexander Kolesnikov, Dirk Weissenborn, Xiaohua Zhai, Thomas Unterthiner, Mostafa Dehghani, Matthias Minderer, Georg Heigold, Sylvain Gelly, Jakob Uszkoreit, and Neil Houlsby. 2021. An Image is Worth 16x16 Words: Transformers for Image Recognition at Scale. In *Proceedings of the Ninth International Conference on Learning Representations*.

Desmond Elliott, Stella Frank, Khalil Sima'an, and Lucia Specia. 2016. Multi30K: Multilingual English-German Image Descriptions. In *Proceedings of the 5th Workshop on Vision and Language*, pages 70–74.

Philipp Koehn, Hieu Hoang, Alexandra Birch, Chris Callison-Burch, Marcello Federico, Nicola Bertoldi, Brooke Cowan, Wade Shen, Christine Moran, Richard Zens, Chris Dyer, Ondřej Bojar, Alexandra Constantin, and Evan Herbst. 2007. Moses: Open Source Toolkit for Statistical Machine Translation. In *Proceedings of the 45th Annual Meeting of the Association for Computational Linguistics*, pages 177–180.

Taku Kudo, Kaoru Yamamoto, and Yuji Matsumoto. 2004. Applying Conditional Random Fields to Japanese Morphological Analysis. In *Proceedings of the 2004 Conference on Empirical Methods in Natural Language Processing*, pages 230–237.

Bei Li, Chuanhao Lv, Zefan Zhou, Tao Zhou, Tong Xiao, Anxiang Ma, and JingBo Zhu. 2022a. On Vision Features in Multimodal Machine Translation. In *Proceedings of the 60th Annual Meeting of the Association for Computational Linguistics*, pages 6327–6337.

Junnan Li, Dongxu Li, Caiming Xiong, and Steven Hoi. 2022b. BLIP: Bootstrapping Language-Image Pre-training for Unified Vision-Language Understanding and Generation. In *Proceedings of the 39th International Conference on Machine Learning*, pages 12888–12900.

Jindřich Libovický and Jindřich Helcl. 2017. Attention Strategies for Multi-Source Sequence-to-Sequence Learning. In *Proceedings of the 55th Annual Meeting of the Association for Computational Linguistics*, pages 196–202.

Liyuan Liu, Haoming Jiang, Pengcheng He, Weizhu Chen, Xiaodong Liu, Jianfeng Gao, and Jiawei Han. 2020. On the Variance of the Adaptive Learning Rate and Beyond. In *Proceedings of the Eighth International Conference on Learning Representations*.

Kishore Papineni, Salim Roukos, Todd Ward, and Wei-Jing Zhu. 2002. Bleu: a Method for Automatic Evaluation of Machine Translation. In *Proceedings of the 40th Annual Meeting of the Association for Computational Linguistics*, pages 311–318.

Shantipriya Parida, Ondrej Bojar, and Satya Ranjan Dash. 2019. Hindi Visual Genome: A Dataset for Multimodal English-to-Hindi Machine Translation. *Computación y Sistemas*, 23(4):1499–1505.

Alec Radford, Jong Wook Kim, Chris Hallacy, Aditya Ramesh, Gabriel Goh, Sandhini Agarwal, Girish Sastry, Amanda Askell, Pamela Mishkin, Jack Clark, Gretchen Krueger, and Ilya Sutskever. 2021. Learning Transferable Visual Models From Natural Language Supervision. In *Proceedings of the 38th International Conference on Machine Learning*, pages 8748–8763.

Elizabeth Salesky, Matthew Wiesner, Jacob Bremerman, Roldano Cattoni, Matteo Negri, Marco Turchi, Douglas W. Oard, and Matt Post. 2021. The Multilingual TEDx Corpus for Speech Recognition and Translation. In *Proceedings of the 22nd Annual Conference of the International Speech Communication Association*, pages 3655–3659.

Ramon Sanabria, Ozan Caglayan, Shruti Palaskar, Desmond Elliott, Loïc Barrault, Lucia Specia, and Florian Metze. 2018. How2: A Large-scale Dataset for Multimodal Language Understanding. In *Proceedings of the 32nd Conference on Neural Information Processing Systems*.

Rico Sennrich, Barry Haddow, and Alexandra Birch. 2016. Neural Machine Translation of Rare Words with Subword Units. In *Proceedings of the 54th Annual Meeting of the Association for Computational Linguistics*, pages 1715–1725.

Lucia Specia, Stella Frank, Khalil Sima'an, and Desmond Elliott. 2016. A Shared Task on Multimodal Machine Translation and Crosslingual Image Description. In *Proceedings of the First Conference on Machine Translation*, pages 543–553.

Umut Sulubacak, Ozan Caglayan, Stig-Arne Grönroos, Aku Rouhe, Desmond Elliott, Lucia Specia, and Jörg Tiedemann. 2020. Multimodal Machine Translation through Visuals and Speech. *Machine Translation*, 34:97–147.

Ashish V. Thapliyal, Jordi Pont Tuset, Xi Chen, and Radu Soricut. 2022. Crossmodal-3600: A Massively Multilingual Multimodal Evaluation Dataset. In *Proceedings of the 2022 Conference on Empirical Methods in Natural Language Processing*, pages 715–729.

Ashish Vaswani, Noam Shazeer, Niki Parmar, Jakob Uszkoreit, Llion Jones, Aidan N Gomez, Łukasz Kaiser, and Illia Polosukhin. 2017. Attention is All you Need. In *Proceedings of the 31st Conference on Neural Information Processing Systems*, pages 5998–6008.

Changhan Wang, Juan Pino, Anne Wu, and Jiatao Gu. 2020. CoVoST: A Diverse Multilingual Speech–To-Text Translation Corpus. In *Proceedings of The 12th Language Resources and Evaluation Conference*, pages 4197–4203.

Ryoya Yuasa, Akihiro Tamura, Tomoyuki Kajiwara, Takashi Ninomiya, and Tsuneo Kato. 2023. Multimodal Neural Machine Translation Using Synthetic Images Transformed by Latent Diffusion Model. In *Proceedings of the 61st Annual Meeting of the Association for Computational Linguistics: Student Research Workshop*, pages 76–82.

VideoCoT: A Video Chain-of-Thought Dataset with Active Annotation Tool

Yan Wang[1], Yawen Zeng[2*], Jingsheng Zheng[1], Xiaofen Xing[1], Jin Xu[1,3], Xiangmin Xu[1]
[1]South China University of Technology, Guangzhou, China
[2]ByteDance, Beijing, China
[3]Pazhou Lab, Guangzhou, China
ftwyan@mail.scut.edu.cn

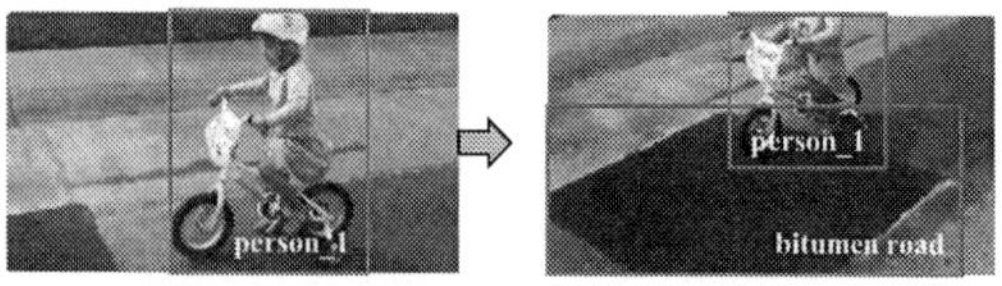

Video: 3IAUsdx5C8_000004_000014

(a) Spatio-temporal changes in video.

Question: Why does [person_1] have to stop?

A: Because it is controlled by [person_1].
B: Because [person_1] can't eat anymore.
C: [person_1] ran into a newly - spread bitumen road.
D: Because [person_1] has to use the machine to do the exercise.
E: Because [person_1] is hurdler.

(b) Significant differences among options.

Question: Why does [person_1] have to stop?
A: Because it is controlled by [person_1].
B: Because [person_1] can't eat anymore.
C: [person_1] ran into a newly - spread bitumen road.
D: Because [person_1] has to use the machine to do the exercise.
E: Because [person_1] is hurdler.

(a) Significant differences among options.

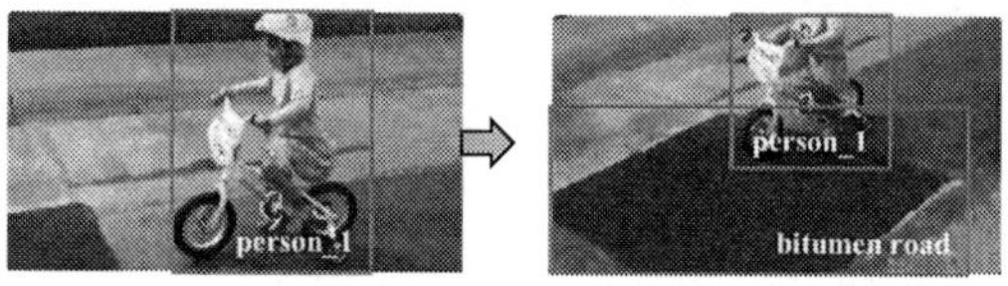

Video: 3IAUsdx5C8_000004_000014

(b) Spatio-temporal changes in video.

Figure 1: The case analysis of video question answering.

human labeling can be reduced and the quality of the dataset can be guaranteed. With the help of the automatic annotation tool, we strive to contribute three datasets, namely VideoCoT, TopicQA, TopicCoT. Furthermore, we propose a simple but effective benchmark based on the collected datasets, which exploits CoT to maximize the complex reasoning capabilities of MLLMs. Extensive experiments demonstrate the effectiveness our solution.

1 Introduction

With the emergence of ChatGPT[1], large language models (LLMs) have experienced unprecedented growth and have gradually expanded into the multimodal domain. Pioneers have explored multiple feasible paths around multimodal large models (MLLMs), such as training MLLMs from scratch (e.g. Kosmos-1 (Huang et al., 2023)), or bridging LLMs and vision modules (e.g. BLIP-2 (Li et al., 2023b)). Moreover, prompt engineering, chain-of-thought (CoT), and instruction tuning for multimodal LLMs are also flourishing. However, the majority of current research focuses on images, with video research (Deng et al., 2022; Zeng et al., 2022) remaining underdeveloped. For instance, Alayrac et al. (2022) employs a video understanding model to extract features, which are then inputted, while Ye et al. (2023) utilizes multiple frames of the video as input. Similarly, few researchers have devoted attention to sub-fields such as video prompt engineering (Li et al., 2023a; Zeng, 2022), and video instruction fine-tuning (Zhang et al., 2023b). We attribute this phenomenon to the fact that MLLMs are less mature than LLMs that solely rely on natural language input, and there are still numerous issues to be explored.

To advance the development of MLLMs for videos, our primary interest lies in CoT in videos. Video CoT has multiple benefits as follows: 1) Towards OpenQA in video. Currently, the VideoQA dataset widely adopts the form of multiple-choice questions, but there are significant differences between the answer options (Kamalloo et al., 2023). As illustrated in Fig.1(a), the options between A-E are significantly different, especially the descriptions of eating and being a hurdler are completely irrelevant to the video. This fact lead to models

*Corresponding author.
[1]https://openai.com/blog/chatgpt

Dataset	Rationale	Language	#Videos	#Q	Video Source	Annotation	QA Task
MSVD-QA (Chen and Dolan, 2011)	✗	English	1.9K	50K	Web Videos	Auto	OE
MovieQA (Tapaswi et al., 2016)	✗	English	6.7K	6.4K	Movies	Manual	MC
MSRVTT-QA (Xu et al., 2017)	✗	English	10K	243K	Web Videos	Auto	OE
TVQA (Lei et al., 2019)	✗	English	21K	152K	TV	Manual	MC
ActivityNet-QA (Yu et al., 2019)	✗	English	5.8K	58K	Web Videos	Manual	OE
NExT-QA (Xiao et al., 2021)	✗	English	5.4K	52K	YFCC-100M	Manual	MC,OE
Causal-VidQA (Li et al., 2022)	✗	English	26K	107K	Kinetics-700	Manual	MC
FIBER (Castro et al., 2022)	✗	English	28K	2K	VaTEX	Manual	OE
VideoCoT (Ours)	✓	English, Chinese	11K	22K	Kinetics-700	Auto, Manual	MC, OE
TopicQA (Ours)	✗	English, Chinese	11K	22K	Kinetics-700	Auto, Manual	MC, OE
TopicCoT (Ours)	✓	English, Chinese	11K	22K	Kinetics-700	Auto, Manual	MC, OE

Table 1: Comparision between our collected datasets (i.e. VideoCoT, TopicQA and TopicCoT) and other existing datasets. Among them, MC in the "QA Task" column means multiple-choice, while OE represents open-ended question answering.

finding shortcuts to the dataset pattern. 2) Enhance understanding. Videos contain more temporal and spatial changes than images, and CoT can help capture the complex semantics of these changes (Zeng et al., 2021). As shown in Fig.1(b), the key to solving the question, that is, the girl changes from moving to stopping (temporal) and the appearance of the bitumen road (spatial), is to develop with the video. 3) Improving the reasoning ability of MLLMs. A more logical CoT can enhance the reasoning ability of MLLMs when used for training.

Although video CoT shows great potential, creating a video CoT dataset is a non-trivial task. The process of fully annotating CoTs by humans is both tedious and expensive, which is why we aim to develop an automatic pipeline for generating CoTs. Intuitively, one widely adopted strategy is to use off-the-shelf MLLMs or LLMs as assistants for reasoning. However, there are several challenges that need to be addressed. Firstly, MLLMs do not possess strong reasoning abilities and cannot directly generate reliable CoTs. Secondly, while LLMs have reasoning capabilities, they cannot use images as input for CoT generation. Lastly, machine-generated data is often unreliable due to ethical doubts and hallucination issues (Liu et al., 2023; Qin et al., 2023), which require human correction for quality control.

Therefore, in this paper, we develop an automatic annotation tool that combines machine and human experts, under the active learning paradigm (Zhang et al., 2023a). As shown in Fig.2, active learning is a strategy that involves interaction between the model and human experts, where the model actively seeks the opinions and standards of experts when encountering difficult samples (Zhai et al., 2022). In this way, the workload of human labeling can be reduced and the quality of the dataset can be guaranteed in the process(Wu et al., 2024; Lu et al., 2021). Specifically, we will train a prompt generator to guide LLMs to generate complex CoT based on video information. Meanwhile, we will formulate a quality score to evaluate the generated CoT sentences from multiple aspects. Among them, low-quality sentences will be modified by human experts, and the modified CoT will be used to train the prompt generator to guide LLMs to generate more reasonable CoT(Guo et al., 2022; Liu et al., 2022).

With the help of the aforementioned automatic annotation tools under the active learning paradigm, we strive to contribute three videoCoT datasets, namely **VideoCoT, TopicQA, TopicCoT**. Among them, VideoCoT is designed to supplement CoT between question and answer from existing datasets. Furthermore, we leverage the topic items in the dataset to construct TopicQA, which enables MLLMs to learn the relevant relationship between videos and topics, and TopicCoT, which facilitates reasoning about the topic relevance. Furthermore, we apply these datasets to propose a simple benchmark. Extensive experiments demonstrate the effectiveness of our datasets and solution. The main contributions are summarized as follows:

- To the best of our knowledge, this is the first work that introduces an automatic annotation tool under the active learning paradigm for complex CoT generation in the video domain.
- We have collected three dataset to fill the vacuum of Video CoT via our automatic annotation tool, namely VideoCoT, TopicQA, TopicCoT.
- We propose a simple but effective benchmark

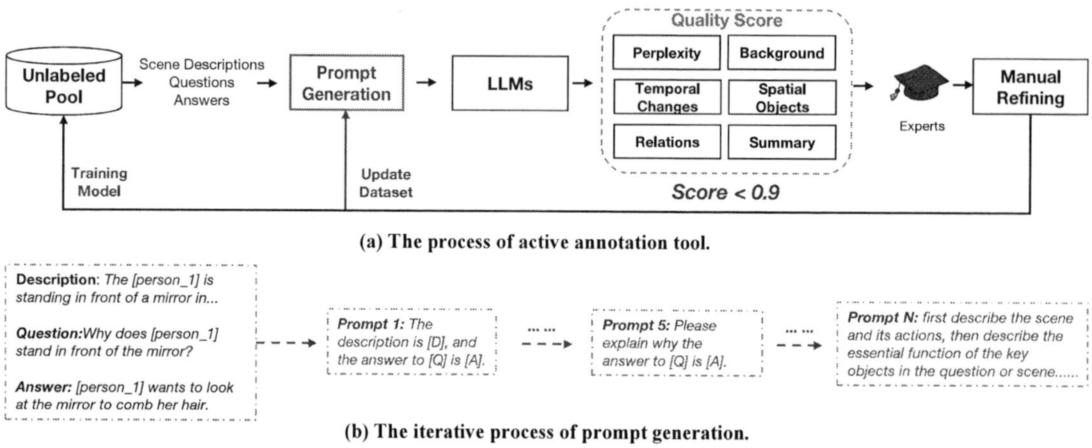

Figure 2: The process of automatic dataset construction for VideoCoT and TopicCoT.

based on the collected datasets, which exploits CoT to achieve better reasoning ability.

2 Related Work

2.1 Multimodal Large Models

As a result of the flourishing development of LLMs (Pan and Zeng, 2023), many frameworks and techniques have been extended, such as prompt engineering, chain-of-thought, and instruction tuning. In the field of multimedia, these hotspots are still the topic of discussion (Li et al., 2024). Subsequently, Zhu et al. (2023) proposed mini-GPT4, Li et al. (2023b) introduced blip2, and Ye et al. (2023) intruduced mPLUG-OWL. However, the majority of current research focuses on images, with video research remaining underdeveloped. To fill the academic vacuum, we propose an automatic annotation tool under the active learning paradigm, and further collect three datasets based on it. In this way, the complex reasoning ability of MLLMs is improved (Rajesh et al., 2023; Zeng et al., 2024).

2.2 Chain-of-Thought

Chain-of-Thought (CoT) has been proven to be an effective strategy to enhance reasoning, and its effectiveness has been widely demonstrated in the field of LLMs (Ma et al., 2023). In the field of multimedia, works such as ScienceQA (Lu et al., 2022) and VisualCoT (Rose et al., 2023) have also been proposed. Inspired by the above work, we try to extend the potential of CoT in the field of video understanding, which helps improve the reasoning ability of MLLMs.

3 Dataset Collection

Following Causal-VidQA (Li et al., 2022), we built three datasets around videos based on Kinetics-700, namely VideoCoT, TopicQA, and TopicCoT. In this section, we will introduce the process of active annotation tool, on which both VideoCoT and TopicCoT are collected.

3.1 Active Annotation Tool

Fig.2 illustrates the pipeline of our automatic dataset construction approach, which implements the prompt generation for LLMs under the active learning paradigm to generate the logical CoT processes. Active learning is an interrogation method between the model and human experts (Zhang et al., 2023a), which reduces the annotation workload and guarantees the quality of the dataset.

Specifically, the automated process is divided into three steps, namely prompt generation, automatic scoring, and expert refinement. Among them, prompt generation aims to generate suitable prompt to guide LLMs to generate comprehensive and reasonable CoT, while automatic scoring checks the quality of machine-generated CoT from multiple quality dimensions. Among them, the low-quality CoT will be refined and modified by experts, which is also used to train the prompt generator to improve the quality of CoT generation.

3.1.1 Prompt Generation

We try to drive the off-the-shelf LLMs (i.e. GPT-4) to generate some high-quality CoT data for us, but unfortunately, the logic of the generated sentences obtained by the fixed template (i.e. prompt) is incomplete and incoherent. Therefore, we introduce a prompt generator to maximize the potential of guiding LLMs and ultimately reduce manual labor.

Specifically, we borrow a summarization model (Rao et al., 2021) capable of handling long sentences as the prompt generator, which will be trained in interaction with human experts. In the initial stage, it is fed a long video description, a question and a answer, and finally outputs a short summary. Obviously, such a prompt is difficult to guide LLMs to get a reasonable CoT between the question and the answer, so it needs to learn from human modified sentences. We will present the scoring mechanism and human refinement in the next subsection.

After multiple rounds of iterations, the generator will flexibly deal with different videos to generate corresponding prompts. Thereafter, since MLLMs do not yet have good reasoning capabilities (which is what we hope to do), we still implement generation based on LLMs (i.e. GPT-4). Finally, after manual inspection with less labor, a reasonable CoT can be obtained, as shown in the Fig.3.

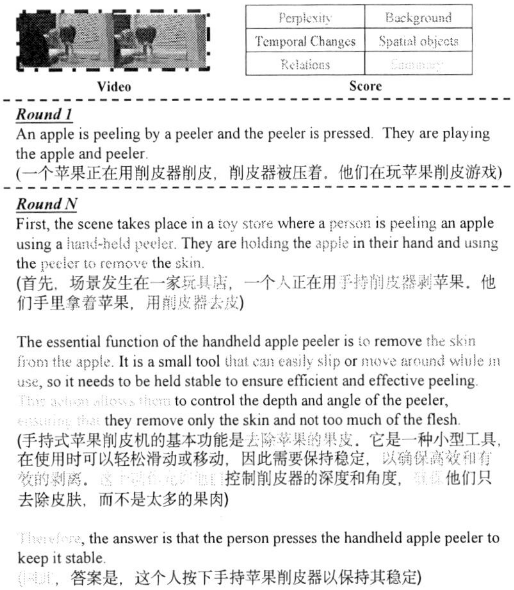

Figure 3: After multiple rounds of training, the quality score of the generated CoT is improved from 0.07 to 0.97.

3.1.2 Automatic Scoring

In order for a quality-required CoT to be generated, we believe that a high-quality CoT $\mathcal{C}_{vCoT}$[2] should have both: 1) the generated sentences are fluent, 2) a comprehensive understanding of objects and relations, 3) and reasonable reasoning between the question and the answer. To achieve this, we design a scoring function $\mathcal{S}_{vCoT}$ that automatically evaluates from six dimensions, i.e., perplexity $\mathcal{S}_{ppl}$, background $\mathcal{S}_{bac}$, temporal changes $\mathcal{S}_{tem}$, spatial objects $\mathcal{S}_{spa}$, relations $\mathcal{S}_{rel}$, summary $\mathcal{S}_{sum}$.

$$\mathcal{S}_{vCoT} = \mathcal{S}_{ppl} + \mathcal{S}_{bac} + \mathcal{S}_{tem} + \mathcal{S}_{spa} + \mathcal{S}_{rel} + \mathcal{S}_{sum}. \tag{1}$$

Among them, the "perplexity" evaluates the fluency of generated CoT, and its reciprocal is used as part of the quality score (Basu et al., 2021). This score is closer to 1 when the CoT sentence $\mathcal{C}_{vCoT}$ is more fluent.

$$\mathcal{S}_{ppl} = \frac{1}{PPL(\mathcal{C}_{vCoT})}. \tag{2}$$

The "background" $\mathcal{S}_{bac}$ indicates whether the generated CoT describes the video scene or not. We collect some keywords to evaluate this, i.e., when a sentence of CoT has words such as *background*, *video scene*, etc., it is considered to meet the quality requirement.

$$\mathcal{S}_{bac} = \begin{cases} 1 & \text{if the video scene is described in } \mathcal{C}_{vCoT} \\ 0 & \text{otherwise} \end{cases} \tag{3}$$

The "spatial objects" $\mathcal{S}_{spa}$ and "temporal changes" $\mathcal{S}_{tem}$ represent how many objects and actions are included in the generated CoT, respectively. The objects and actions (extracted by GRiT(Wu et al., 2022)) that should be included are taken as the evaluation criteria, i.e. the more objects and actions are included in $\mathcal{C}_{vCoT}$, the higher the score $\mathcal{S}_{spa}$ and $\mathcal{S}_{tem}$. Conversely, if irrelevant objects or actions appear in the sentence $\mathcal{C}_{vCoT}$ (most likely hallucinations), the score will be negative.

$$\mathcal{S}_{spa} = \frac{\text{pos}_o(\mathcal{C}_{vCoT}) - \text{neg}_o(\mathcal{C}_{vCoT})}{\text{ground\_truth}(\mathcal{C}_{vCoT})}, \tag{4}$$

$$\mathcal{S}_{tem} = \frac{\text{pos}_a(\mathcal{C}_{vCoT}) - \text{neg}_a(\mathcal{C}_{vCoT})}{\text{ground\_truth}(\mathcal{C}_{vCoT})}, \tag{5}$$

where pos_o and pos_a indicate the number of objects and actions present in the CoT, where pos indicates real presence in the video, and neg indicates hallucinated objects or actions.

The "relations" $\mathcal{S}_{rel}$ represents whether the generated CoT has the analysis of spatio-temporal relationship among objects, and the connection with video scene. And the "summary" $\mathcal{S}_{sum}$ evaluates whether a summary is included in the generated $\mathcal{C}_{vCoT}$ (i.e., the answer is output via step-by-step

[2] C_v represents "video", while C_{vCoT} represents VideoCoT, which serves to differentiate it from TopicCoT C_{tCoT}.

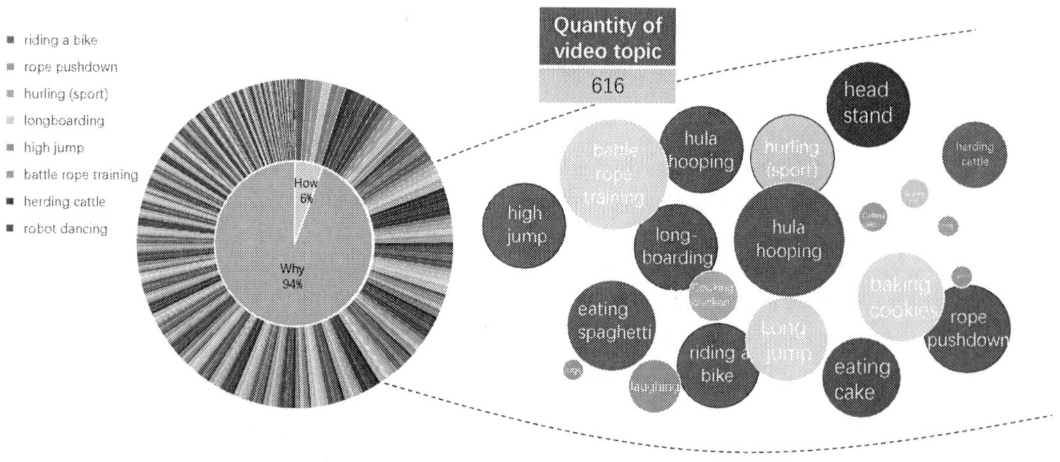

Figure 4: The topic and question distribution for VideoCoT and TopicCoT.

reasoning).

$$\mathcal{S}_{rel} = \begin{cases} 1 & \text{if the analysis is included in } \mathcal{C}_{vCoT} \\ 0 & \text{otherwise} \end{cases} \quad (6)$$

$$\mathcal{S}_{sum} = \begin{cases} 1 & \text{if the summary is included in } \mathcal{C}_{vCoT} \\ 0 & \text{otherwise} \end{cases} \quad (7)$$

All the above scores belong to the interval from 0 to 1, which is convenient for us to do further normalization. The automatic score S serves as a “rough indicator" to identify the worst sample and help us optimize prompt generator. In particular, since $\mathcal{S}_{spa}$ and $\mathcal{S}_{tem}$ are more important for this task, we set the balance parameters in Eqn.1 as $(0.1, 0.1, 0.3, 0.3, 0.1, 0.1)$. Furthermore, to control the quality of CoT, when the normalized score is lower than 0.9, it will be sent to human experts for refinement.

3.1.3 Expert Refinement

We enlisted ten human experts with backgrounds in artificial intelligence to participate in the annotation process. To ensure consistency in the labeling results across different experts, a 5-rounds pre-annotation training was conducted prior to official annotation. Specifically, each expert was required to label a small number of samples to gain an understanding of the annotation rules, which were standardized to ensure consistency among all participants.

For the generated CoT whose quality score is less than the threshold (i.e. 0.9), they will be modified by human experts. As much as possible, experts are asked to make sentences include scene descriptions in video, spatio-temporal relationships, and logical reasoning between the question and answer. Meanwhile, the refined samples will return to the dataset pool and participate in training of prompt generation until the quality of all annotations meets our requirements. Through this interactive active learning paradigm, the high-quality CoT are semi-automatically constructed.

3.2 Automatic Datatset Construction

With the help of the aforementioned annotation tool under the active learning paradigm, we strive to contribute three datasets, namely VideoCoT, TopicQA, TopicCoT.

3.2.1 VideoCoT

VideoCoT is designed to supplement CoT between question and answer from existing datasets, CausalVidQA. Based on the settings, we collect $11,182$ samples containing CoT, as shown in Table 1.

3.2.2 TopicQA

Further, we leverage the topic items in the Kinetics-700 dataset to construct TopicQA, which enables MLLMs to learn the relevant relationship between videos and topics. In this dataset, we take “is the video relevant to the topic” as the question and “yes” or “no” as the answer.

3.2.3 TopicCoT

TopicCoT, similar to the construction process of VideoCoT, which contains step-by-step reasoning between questions and answers in TpoicQA. Specifically, TopicCoT $\mathcal{C}_{tCoT}$ is still based on our automatic annotation tool, but the scoring function is different, which is defined as follows:

$$\mathcal{S}_{tCoT} = \mathcal{S}_{ppl} + \mathcal{S}_{tem} + \mathcal{S}_{spa} + \mathcal{S}_{con} + \mathcal{S}_{sum}. \quad (8)$$

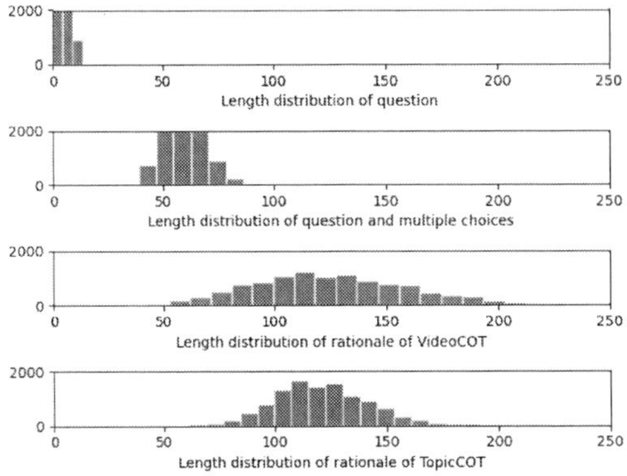

Figure 5: The length distribution of our dataset, where the y-axis represents the number of samples whose length is the x-axis value.

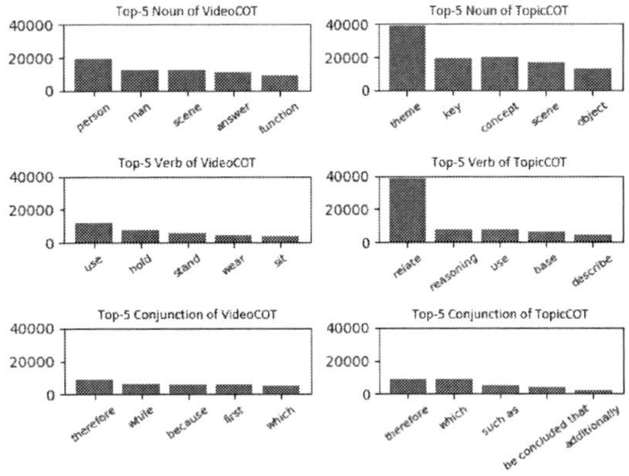

Figure 6: The top words of our dataset, where the y-axis represents the frequency of word count.

where $\mathcal{S}_{con}$ represents the concept of the topic, and the others are consistent with Eqn.1. Moreover, the balance parameters are set to $(0.1, 0.2, 0.2, 0.4, 0.1)$ for normalization. Then, when this score $\mathcal{S}_{tCoT}$ is less than 0.9, it will be sent to humans for modification.

3.3 Dataset Analysis

3.3.1 Property Quality

The statistical analysis of textual description in our VideoCoT and TopicCoT dataset is shown in Fig.5. Based on statistical results, the original dataset, which includes both questions and multiple choices, has an average length of approximately 50 words. In contrast, the rationale length of our VideoCoT and TopicCoT is distributed between 100 and 150 words.

3.3.2 Diversity Quality

To assess the diversity of sentences in the VideoCoT and TopicCoT datasets, we conduct a word frequency analysis of nouns, verbs, and conjunctions, which represent descriptive, temporal, and logical aspects, respectively. Fig.6 illustrates the top 5 frequency of each category in the rationale of the two datasets. **1) Noun**: We observe that the high-frequency nouns in VideoCoT mostly refer to specific objects, such as "person" and "man", as well as key words in the reasoning process, such as "scene", "answer" and "function". In contrast, the top nouns in TopicCoT mainly involve "topic" and "concept", indicating that detailed descriptions revolve around the topic and object concepts of the video. **2) Verb**: The main verbs in VideoCoT describe specific human activities, focusing on the temporal aspect of the video. In TopicCoT, the high-frequency verbs are mostly reasoning verbs, focusing on the association between the question and the topic of the video. **3) Conjunction**: The conjunction with the highest frequency in both datasets is "therefore", which indicates the logical and summary aspects of the rationale.

3.3.3 Visualization Quality

To verify the rationality of the human experts' operation, we also check some cases as shown in the Fig.3. There are two languages present in our dataset, namely English and Chinese. The initial generated by LLMs was of low quality, which hindered the establishment of relationships. However, after undergoing multiple round of interaction between human and model, the score of generated CoT increased from 0.07 to 0.97 points, indicating a significant improvement in the quality of the output.

4 Proposed Method

The overall training framework is depicted with an illustration in Fig.7. For the task of video question answering (Zhong et al., 2022), multiple choice (MC) is more popular, but the differences between the options are too significant, and it is easy for the model to find shortcuts. Therefore, we are committed to achieving a free-form open-ended (OE) with logic rationale (Lu et al., 2022).

4.1 Training strategy of original dataset

The input of MC strategy is defined as $X = (X_Q, X_{MC}, X_V)$, where X_Q represents the question, X_{MC} represents answer options, and X_V represents the image.

Following the work of (Kamalloo et al., 2023), who trains the model using fixed long sentence

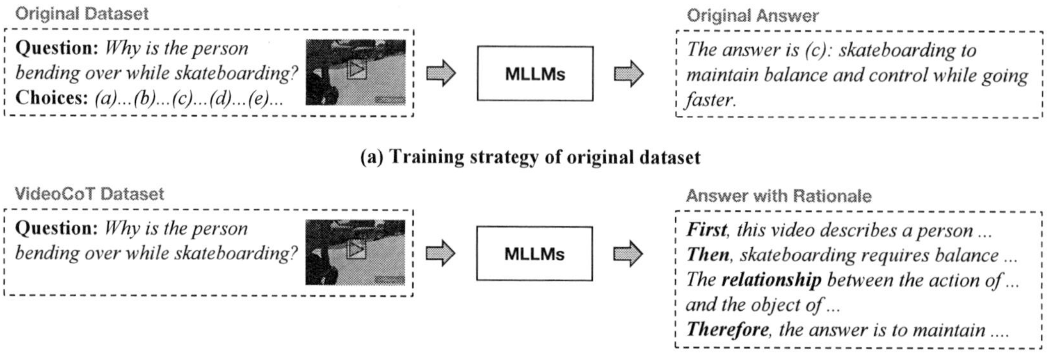

(a) Training strategy of original dataset

(b) Training strategy of our VideoCoT

Figure 7: Comparison of training strategies on the original dataset and our datasets.

templates with correct options for filling in the blanks, the probability of generating an answer can be formulated as follows:

$$p(Y|X_Q, X_{MC}, X_V) \tag{9}$$

$$=\sum_{t=1}^{m} \log p(y_t|y_{<t}, X_Q, X_{MC}, X_V), \tag{10}$$

where $Y=(y_1, y_2, \ldots, y_m)$ represents the target tokens.

4.2 Training strategy of VideoCoT

Similarly, the input of OE strategy is defined as $X=(X_Q, X_V)$.

In this way, the input X will be removed the answer options X_{MC}, while the target answer Y will be redefined as the rationale $R=(r_1, r_2, \ldots, r_n)$.

Formally, the probability of generating rationale can be formulated as follows:

$$p(R|X_Q, X_V)=\sum_{t=1}^{n} \log p(r_t|r_{<t}, X_Q, X_V). \tag{11}$$

Through this training strategy of CoT, more prior knowledge of MLLMs can be invoked, and finally answer questions through logical reasoning.

5 Experiments

5.1 Experimental Settings

5.1.1 Datasets

Our datasets are split into 3 non-overlapping subsets, where 0.6, 0.2 and 0.2 are used for training, validation and testing.

5.1.2 Evaluation Protocol

We adopt accuracy as our evaluation metric, which is utilized to measure whether the answers generated by models are correct. Notably, in the multi-choice setting, the accuracy Acc_{MC} can be directly compared with ground-truth. In the case of open-ended QA, we adopt two metrics, 1) Acc_{OE}(keywords): whether the "summary" sentence hits the keywords in the ground-truth answer. Specifically, keywords and their synonyms are acquired by giving some few-shot template and QA pair to GPT4. We then calculate the correct proportion of keywords for each question as its score. 2) Acc_{OE}(GPT-4): regard GPT-4[3] as a referee to evaluate semantic relevance.

5.1.3 Baselines

We select the following models as our baselines: mPLUG-Owl (Ye et al., 2023), VisualGLM (Du et al., 2022), mini-GPT4 (Zhu et al., 2023).

5.2 Overall Performance Comparison

To verify the effectiveness of our datasets, we train several MLLMs with the original dataset and our datasets respectively[4]. Among them, for the evaluation of OE task, we adopt two kinds of metrics, namely a hard metric (based on keywords) and a soft metric (based on GPT-4).

The experimental results are presented in Table 2, and the following observations can be made: 1) In comparison to the multi-choice setup, both models exhibit improved performance in open-ended QA accuracy. Upon analyzing the multi-choice outputs, it is evident that the models often provide justifications for each individual option rather than selecting a single response to address the given question. 2) The superiority of both VideoCoT trained MLLMs over the original method is evident in the improvements observed across both keyword

[3] `https://openai.com/product/gpt-4`

[4] TopicQA is an ordinary QA dataset, which will not be adopted to discuss the impact of CoT on reasoning ability, but it can still be a traditional QA dataset.

Model	Acc_{MC}	VideoCoT		TopicCoT	VideoCoT & TopicCoT
		Acc_{OE}(GPT-4)	Acc_{OE}(keywords)	Acc_{OE}(GPT-4)	Acc_{OE}(GPT-4)
mPLUG-Owl	31.51%	48.32%	52.66%	40.12%	–
VisualGLM	13.81%	45.32%	46.78%	23.34%	–
mini-GPT4	29.05%	43.58%	51.21%	19.21%	–
mPLUG-Owl (trained)	–	77.42% (+29.1)	81.24% (+28.58)	89.76% (+49.64)	90.18%
VisualGLM (trained)	–	69.91% (+24.59)	70.71% (+23.93)	78.96% (+55.62)	79.24%
mini-GPT4 (trained)	–	64.14% (+20.56)	75.20% (+23.99)	82.55% (+63.34)	82.85%

Table 2: Overall performance comparison among various methods on our VideoCoT and TopicCoT.

and GPT-4 metrics. This highlights the significant impact of employing a chain of thoughts within the generation model's creative process. 3) We also observe that the accuracy of keywords on all models surpasses the accuracy of GPT-4, which is due to the former metric being more relaxed than the latter. 4) Additionally, we conduct an experiment utilizing a hybrid training dataset comprising both VideoCoT and TopicCoT. The subsequent evaluation of models take place on the testing of VideoCoT. Remarkably, when contrasted with models solely trained on VideoCoT, the GPT-4 metric exhibited a noteworthy improvement through hybrid training. This improvement surpassed the performance of all models that are only trained on VideoCoT. This outcome serves as a compelling indicator that hybrid training fosters a reciprocal influence, allowing models to acquire the capacity for incremental and reasoned thinking.

5.3 Reasoning Ability Visualization

The visualization is shown in Fig.8, the mPLUG-Owl possesses the capability to depict the content of the image and execute the basic task of question and answer. However, its performance is unsatisfactory when confronted with more complex questions that necessitate reasoning. Conversely, upon being trained on our datasets, it acquires the ability to identify objects in the image (e.g. "a group of people"), discern the fundamental functions of objects or events (e.g. "the essential fuction of"), and finally integrate objects and relationships to engage in reasoning (e.g. "because they might participating in a fitness event").

Question: *Why is the person running?*
Answer: *The person wants to keep fit.*

mPLUG-Owl:
The person is running on a treadmill in the gym...

mPLUG-Owl trained on VideoCoT:
First, a group of people is standing in front of an exercise machine and running on the track.
Then, the essential function of the exercise machine is to provide resistance for the legs during exercise. This can help improve muscle strength and endurance.
Therefore, the answer to why someone is running on the track is because they might participating in a fitness event...

Figure 8: The visualization case of generated answers.

6 Conclusions

In this work, we strive to explore the collection of CoT datasets on videos to bootstrap OpenQA on videos and improve the inference ability of MLLMs. To reduce the cost of manual annotation, we develop an automatic annotation tool that combines machine and human experts, under the active learning paradigm. With the help of this annotation tool, we contribute three videoCoT datasets, namely VideoCoT, TopicQA, TopicCoT. Experimental results show that our datasets achieve superior effectiveness, diversity and explainability.

Acknowledgements

This work is supported in part by the National Natural Science Foundation of China (62372187), in part by the National Key Research and Development Program of China (2022YFC3601005) and in part by the Guangdong Provincial Key Laboratory of Human Digital Twin (2022B1212010004).

Limitations

In regards to the active annotation tool, using our tool on additional datasets can enhance the visual reasoning abilities of more models. However, funding constraints limited the invitation of annotation experts. Nonetheless, we are committed to expanding the impact of this paper in future research. Moreover, our training resources currently restrict the application of our dataset to significantly more larger models.

References

Jean-Baptiste Alayrac, Jeff Donahue, Pauline Luc, Antoine Miech, Iain Barr, Yana Hasson, Karel Lenc, Arthur Mensch, Katie Millican, Malcolm Reynolds, Roman Ring, Eliza Rutherford, Serkan Cabi, Tengda Han, Zhitao Gong, Sina Samangooei, Marianne Monteiro, Jacob Menick, Sebastian Borgeaud, Andrew Brock, Aida Nematzadeh, Sahand Sharifzadeh, Mikolaj Binkowski, Ricardo Barreira, Oriol Vinyals, Andrew Zisserman, and Karen Simonyan. 2022. Flamingo: a visual language model for few-shot learning. *Preprint*, arXiv:2204.14198.

Sourya Basu, Govardana Sachitanandam Ramachandran, Nitish Shirish Keskar, and Lav R. Varshney. 2021. Mirostat: A neural text decoding algorithm that directly controls perplexity. *Preprint*, arXiv:2007.14966.

Santiago Castro, Ruoyao Wang, Pingxuan Huang, Ian Stewart, Oana Ignat, Nan Liu, Jonathan C. Stroud, and Rada Mihalcea. 2022. Fiber: Fill-in-the-blanks as a challenging video understanding evaluation framework. *Preprint*, arXiv:2104.04182.

David L. Chen and William B. Dolan. 2011. Collecting highly parallel data for paraphrase evaluation. In *ACL*, Portland, OR.

Chaorui Deng, Qi Wu, Qingyao Wu, Fuyuan Hu, Fan Lyu, and Mingkui Tan. 2022. Visual grounding via accumulated attention. *IEEE Transactions on Pattern Analysis and Machine Intelligence*, 44(3):1670–1684.

Zhengxiao Du, Yujie Qian, Xiao Liu, Ming Ding, Jiezhong Qiu, Zhilin Yang, and Jie Tang. 2022. Glm: General language model pretraining with autoregressive blank infilling. In *Proceedings of the 60th Annual Meeting of the Association for Computational Linguistics (Volume 1: Long Papers)*, pages 320–335.

Yong Guo, Yin Zheng, Mingkui Tan, Qi Chen, Zhipeng Li, Jian Chen, Peilin Zhao, and Junzhou Huang. 2022. Towards accurate and compact architectures via neural architecture transformer. *IEEE Transactions on Pattern Analysis and Machine Intelligence*, 44(10):6501–6516.

Shaohan Huang, Li Dong, Wenhui Wang, Yaru Hao, Saksham Singhal, Shuming Ma, Tengchao Lv, Lei Cui, Owais Khan Mohammed, Barun Patra, Qiang Liu, Kriti Aggarwal, Zewen Chi, Johan Bjorck, Vishrav Chaudhary, Subhojit Som, Xia Song, and Furu Wei. 2023. Language is not all you need: Aligning perception with language models. *Preprint*, arXiv:2302.14045.

Ehsan Kamalloo, Nouha Dziri, Charles L. A. Clarke, and Davood Rafiei. 2023. Evaluating open-domain question answering in the era of large language models. *Preprint*, arXiv:2305.06984.

Jie Lei, Licheng Yu, Mohit Bansal, and Tamara L. Berg. 2019. Tvqa: Localized, compositional video question answering. *Preprint*, arXiv:1809.01696.

Jiangtong Li, Li Niu, and Liqing Zhang. 2022. From representation to reasoning: Towards both evidence and commonsense reasoning for video question-answering. In *CVPR*.

Juncheng Li, Kaihang Pan, Zhiqi Ge, Minghe Gao, Hanwang Zhang, Wei Ji, Wenqiao Zhang, Tat-Seng Chua, Siliang Tang, and Yueting Zhuang. 2023a. Empowering vision-language models to follow interleaved vision-language instructions. *Preprint*, arXiv:2308.04152.

Junnan Li, Dongxu Li, Silvio Savarese, and Steven Hoi. 2023b. Blip-2: Bootstrapping language-image pre-training with frozen image encoders and large language models. *Preprint*, arXiv:2301.12597.

KunChang Li, Yinan He, Yi Wang, Yizhuo Li, Wenhai Wang, Ping Luo, Yali Wang, Limin Wang, and Yu Qiao. 2024. Videochat: Chat-centric video understanding. *Preprint*, arXiv:2305.06355.

Jing Liu, Bohan Zhuang, Zhuangwei Zhuang, Yong Guo, Junzhou Huang, Jinhui Zhu, and Mingkui Tan. 2022. Discrimination-aware network pruning for deep model compression. *IEEE Transactions on Pattern Analysis and Machine Intelligence*, 44(8):4035–4051.

Xiao Liu, Hanyu Lai, Hao Yu, Yifan Xu, Aohan Zeng, Zhengxiao Du, Peng Zhang, Yuxiao Dong, and Jie Tang. 2023. Webglm: Towards an efficient web-enhanced question answering system with human preferences. *Preprint*, arXiv:2306.07906.

Pan Lu, Swaroop Mishra, Tony Xia, Liang Qiu, Kai-Wei Chang, Song-Chun Zhu, Oyvind Tafjord, Peter Clark, and Ashwin Kalyan. 2022. Learn to explain: Multimodal reasoning via thought chains for science question answering. *Preprint*, arXiv:2209.09513.

Yaojie Lu, Hongyu Lin, Jin Xu, Xianpei Han, Jialong Tang, Annan Li, Le Sun, Meng Liao, and Shaoyi Chen. 2021. Text2event: Controllable sequence-to-structure generation for end-to-end event extraction. *Preprint*, arXiv:2106.09232.

Yuhan Ma, Haiqi Jiang, and Chenyou Fan. 2023. Sci-cot: Leveraging large language models for enhanced knowledge distillation in small models for scientific qa. *Preprint*, arXiv:2308.04679.

Keyu Pan and Yawen Zeng. 2023. Do llms possess a personality? making the mbti test an amazing evaluation for large language models. *Preprint*, arXiv:2307.16180.

Yujia Qin, Zihan Cai, Dian Jin, Lan Yan, Shihao Liang, Kunlun Zhu, Yankai Lin, Xu Han, Ning Ding, Huadong Wang, Ruobing Xie, Fanchao Qi, Zhiyuan Liu, Maosong Sun, and Jie Zhou. 2023. Webcpm: Interactive web search for chinese long-form question answering. *Preprint*, arXiv:2305.06849.

Kousik Rajesh, Mrigank Raman, Mohammed Asad Karim, and Pranit Chawla. 2023. Bridging the gap: Exploring the capabilities of bridge-architectures for complex visual reasoning tasks. *Preprint*, arXiv:2307.16395.

Roshan Rao, Joshua Meier, Tom Sercu, Sergey Ovchinnikov, and Alexander Rives. 2021. Transformer protein language models are unsupervised structure learners. In *ICLR*. OpenReview.net.

Daniel Rose, Vaishnavi Himakunthala, Andy Ouyang, Ryan He, Alex Mei, Yujie Lu, Michael Saxon, Chinmay Sonar, Diba Mirza, and William Yang Wang. 2023. Visual chain of thought: Bridging logical gaps with multimodal infillings. *Preprint*, arXiv:2305.02317.

Makarand Tapaswi, Yukun Zhu, Rainer Stiefelhagen, Antonio Torralba, Raquel Urtasun, and Sanja Fidler. 2016. Movieqa: Understanding stories in movies through question-answering. *Preprint*, arXiv:1512.02902.

Danyang Wu, Zhenkun Yang, Jitao Lu, Jin Xu, Xiangmin Xu, and Feiping Nie. 2024. Ebmgc-gnf: Efficient balanced multi-view graph clustering via good neighbor fusion. *IEEE Transactions on Pattern Analysis and Machine Intelligence*, pages 1–15.

Jialian Wu, Jianfeng Wang, Zhengyuan Yang, Zhe Gan, Zicheng Liu, Junsong Yuan, and Lijuan Wang. 2022. Grit: A generative region-to-text transformer for object understanding. *Preprint*, arXiv:2212.00280.

Junbin Xiao, Xindi Shang, Angela Yao, and Tat-Seng Chua. 2021. Next-qa:next phase of question-answering to explaining temporal actions. *Preprint*, arXiv:2105.08276.

Dejing Xu, Zhou Zhao, Jun Xiao, Fei Wu, Hanwang Zhang, Xiangnan He, and Yueting Zhuang. 2017. Video question answering via gradually refined attention over appearance and motion. In *ACM MM*, MM '17, page 1645–1653, New York, NY, USA. Association for Computing Machinery.

Qinghao Ye, Haiyang Xu, Guohai Xu, Jiabo Ye, Ming Yan, Yiyang Zhou, Junyang Wang, Anwen Hu, Pengcheng Shi, Yaya Shi, Chenliang Li, Yuanhong Xu, Hehong Chen, Junfeng Tian, Qian Qi, Ji Zhang, and Fei Huang. 2023. mplug-owl: Modularization empowers large language models with multimodality. *Preprint*, arXiv:2304.14178.

Zhou Yu, Dejing Xu, Jun Yu, Ting Yu, Zhou Zhao, Yueting Zhuang, and Dacheng Tao. 2019. Activitynet-qa: A dataset for understanding complex web videos via question answering. *Preprint*, arXiv:1906.02467.

Runhao Zeng, Wenbing Huang, Mingkui Tan, Yu Rong, Peilin Zhao, Junzhou Huang, and Chuang Gan. 2022. Graph convolutional module for temporal action localization in videos. *IEEE Transactions on Pattern Analysis and Machine Intelligence*, 44(10):6209–6223.

Yawen Zeng. 2022. Point prompt tuning for temporally language grounding. In *SIGIR*, pages 2003–2007.

Yawen Zeng, Da Cao, Xiaochi Wei, Meng Liu, Zhou Zhao, and Zheng Qin. 2021. Multi-modal relational graph for cross-modal video moment retrieval. In *CVPR*, pages 2215–2224. Computer Vision Foundation / IEEE.

Yawen Zeng, Yiru Wang, Dongliang Liao, Gongfu Li, Jin Xu, Hong Man, Bo Liu, and Xiangmin Xu. 2024. Contrastive topic-enhanced network for video captioning. *Expert Systems with Applications*, 237:121601.

Yajing Zhai, Yawen Zeng, Da Cao, and Shaofei Lu. 2022. Trireid: Towards multi-modal person reidentification via descriptive fusion model. In *ICMR*, pages 63–71. ACM.

Zhisong Zhang, Emma Strubell, and Eduard Hovy. 2023a. A survey of active learning for natural language processing. *Preprint*, arXiv:2210.10109.

Zhuosheng Zhang, Aston Zhang, Mu Li, Hai Zhao, George Karypis, and Alex Smola. 2023b. Multimodal chain-of-thought reasoning in language models. *Preprint*, arXiv:2302.00923.

Yaoyao Zhong, Junbin Xiao, Wei Ji, Yicong Li, Weihong Deng, and Tat-Seng Chua. 2022. Video question answering: Datasets, algorithms and challenges. *Preprint*, arXiv:2203.01225.

Deyao Zhu, Jun Chen, Xiaoqian Shen, Xiang Li, and Mohamed Elhoseiny. 2023. Minigpt-4: Enhancing vision-language understanding with advanced large language models. *Preprint*, arXiv:2304.10592.

Enhancing Conceptual Understanding in Multimodal Contrastive Learning through Hard Negative Samples

Philipp J. Rösch[1], **Norbert Oswald**[1], **Michaela Geierhos**[1], and **Jindřich Libovický**[2]
[1]Bundeswehr University Munich, Germany
[2]Faculty of Mathematics and Physics, Charles University, Czech Republic
{philipp.roesch,norbert.oswald,michaela.geierhos}@unibw.de
libovicky@ufal.mff.cuni.cz

Abstract

Current vision-language models leveraging contrastive learning often face limitations in developing fine-grained conceptual understanding. This is due to random negative samples during pretraining, causing almost exclusively very dissimilar concepts to be compared in the loss function. Consequently, the models struggle with fine-grained semantic differences. To address this problem, we introduce a novel pretraining method incorporating synthetic hard negative text examples. The hard negatives replace terms corresponding to visual concepts, leading to a more fine-grained visual and textual concept alignment. Further, we introduce InpaintCOCO, a new challenging dataset for assessing the fine-grained alignment of colors, objects, and sizes in vision-language models. We created the dataset using generative inpainting from COCO images by changing the visual concepts so that the images no longer match their original captions. Our results show significant improvements in fine-grained concept understanding across various vision-language datasets, including our InpaintCOCO dataset.

1 Introduction

Recent advancements in vision-language (VL) modeling have demonstrated the effectiveness of contrastive learning in various multimodal tasks (Radford et al., 2021; Jia et al., 2021; Yao et al., 2021). However, this training method does not provide sufficient training signals for several important visual concepts (Zhao et al., 2023). We attributed it to the objective function's use of random and, therefore, too dissimilar negative samples, which prevents the model from learning fine-grained semantic representations of the concepts.

Therefore, we propose a novel approach to address the issue of poorly represented concepts in contrastive learning. We introduce a mechanism to incorporate hard negative samples into the contrastive learning loss. Specifically, we generate synthetic hard negative samples by substituting keywords in the captions of original image-text pairs, disrupting the alignment between the image content and its description.

This paper presents three key contributions:

(i) We present a novel method for using hard negative samples in the contrastive learning objective, allowing the model to focus on refining its understanding of concepts.

(ii) By introducing hard negative samples in the language component, we compel the model to learn proper visual and language alignment. Our approach improves multimodal performance, although it operates exclusively on the language side of the model.

(iii) To evaluate the model from the visual perspective, we create a challenge set with over 1,260 adversarial examples by using generative image inpainting. This dataset serves as a comprehensive benchmark, allowing us to assess the model's ability to validate its conceptual understanding. This is because the image was created in a standardized setting in which only a small part was changed.

In this work, we conduct extensive evaluations of four basic concepts – color, object, location, and size. These concepts were selected as examples to demonstrate the effectiveness and robustness of our proposed approach in capturing nuanced semantic relations, but it is important to note that the choice of concepts is flexible and can be tailored to specific applications. Furthermore, our methodology is easy to construct, requiring only minimal domain expertise and the simple usage of regular expressions. This study shows that simple tweaks in contrastive learning can significantly enhance multimodal understanding and model performance.

Proceedings of the 3rd Workshop on Advances in Language and Vision Research, pages 102–115
August 16, 2024 ©2024 Association for Computational Linguistics

I_1 	T_1^{pos}	T_2^{neg}	T_3^{neg}	T_1^{hn}
	a white cat sits under a black open umbrella.	a person standing on a loading platform next to a train.	a man leans near the door of a creatively painted tour bus.	a **brown** cat sits under a black open umbrella.

Figure 1: Classical contrastive learning approaches use (I_1, T_1^{pos}) as positive pairs in combination with negative samples like T_2^{neg} and T_3^{neg} to learn an image-text alignment. A bag of words (e.g., nouns) is often sufficient to extract the correct text that matches a given image, resulting in only broad concepts learned. We also use hard negatives like T_1^{hn} so that fine-grained semantic concepts are learned for visual and textual alignment.

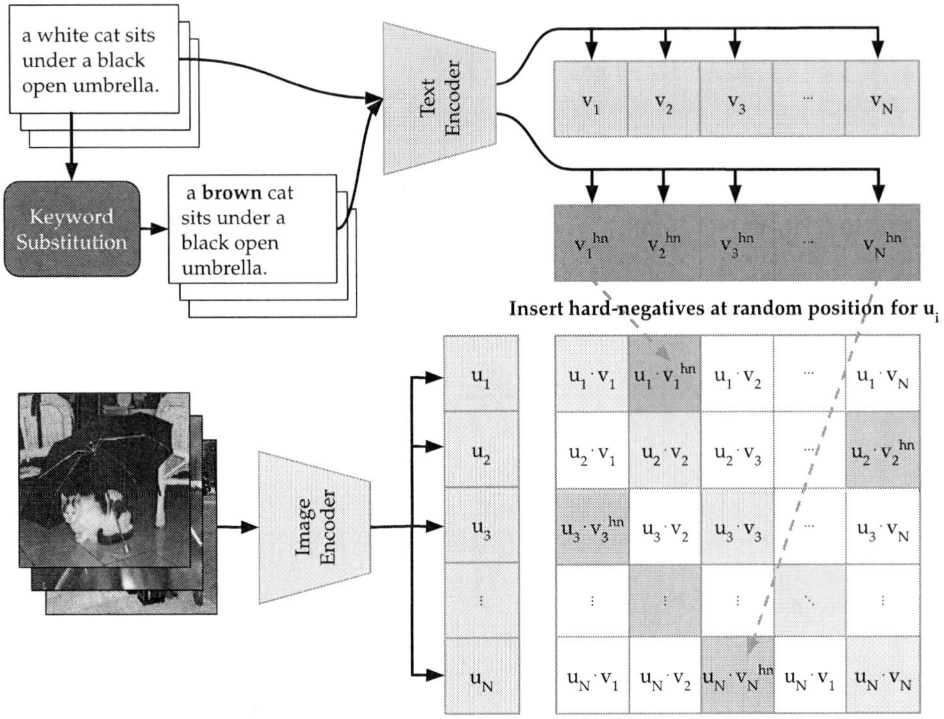

Figure 2: Hard negative contrastive learning: Keyword substitution produces hard negative text samples, which are then randomly injected for each image u_i, replacing a simple negative sample in InfoNCE loss.

2 Vision-Language Representation Learning

Contrastive Learning. The objective of contrastive representation learning is to learn representations that are close to each other for similar samples and distant from each other for dissimilar samples. While many objectives originally addressed a single modality (Chopra et al., 2005; Schroff et al., 2015; Sohn, 2016; Oord et al., 2018), the idea can also be extended to multimodal training as well.

A successful example of multimodal learning is CLIP (Radford et al., 2021). CLIP is a Transformer-based model that consists of an image encoder and a text encoder, which are trained simultaneously. The objective is to maximize the cosine similarity of the image and text embeddings from the correct image-text pairs and to minimize the similarity between the incorrect pairs. A batch of N training samples (i.e., matching image-text pairs) results in a similarity matrix for each image-text combination. The main diagonal indicates the correct pair matches; the remaining entries correspond to negative entries. The symmetric cross-entropy loss is applied on $N \times N$ similarity scores.

This heuristical construction of negative samples has several issues. Negative captions can still match the given image in some cases, especially if the text is short and lacks details. Additionally, the negative pairs are often very dissimilar, which causes the model to decide only on coarse-grained features.

We illustrate this in Figure 1 with text-image

pair I_1 and T_1^{pos}. The original learning process only uses negative text samples, such as T_2^{neg} and T_3^{neg}. Here, it is sufficient that the model can assign or negate objects from texts (i.e., nouns) to the objects in the image. The fact that no "person" and no "door" are present in image I_1 is sufficient for the model to discard these image descriptions. As a result, fine-grained concepts like object-color alignment, size, or spatial details ("cat under umbrella") are not necessary for reaching low loss. In this example, the model can rely solely on the presence and absence of specific objects. In this scenario, the caption can be seen as a bag of words without linguistic structure.

We address this problem by creating new hard negative data samples to learn more fine-grained concepts. See § 3 for details.

Related work. Several approaches incorporate hard negative samples in multimodal learning.

Radenovic et al. (2023) use importance sampling (based on Robinson et al., 2021), which up-samples hard negative samples and down-samples or ignores simple negatives. Yet, they reweight the simple negative samples per batch only but do not create new, challenging samples requiring fine-grained understanding.

Rösch and Libovický (2022) propose keyword permutation to create hard negative samples to learn spatial concepts. They added a spatial understanding classifier as an auxiliary pretraining objective and evaluated the models on visual question answering (VQA). Their model is based on LXMERT (Tan and Bansal, 2019) and not on a contrastive learning approach like CLIP.

Doveh et al. (2023) generate hard negatives using a rule-based procedure where they replace keywords. Moreover, they implement an approach where they randomly parse parts of speech and fill the mask using a BERT encoder with a plausible but wrong word. Unlike us, they do not incorporate hard negatives into the similarity matrix but use an auxiliary loss summed with the original contrastive loss. They use four distinct loss functions in total, introducing an additional layer of complexity to the overall procedure. In contrast, our approach uses the original loss function, with minimal modifications limited to the text inputs.

3 Contrastive Learning with Hard Negatives

We present a novel contrastive learning approach using sampled negative pairs and artificially generated textual hard negatives.

Instead of training with one positive sample and several weak negative samples, we create a scenario where models also minimize the similarity to hard negative *textual* samples. This forces the model to learn fine-grained concepts during training.

We use keyword substitutions for different concepts to break the correct meaning of an image caption. See Figure 1 for an example of the concept *color*. As a result, the new caption still lists, e.g., correct objects (e.g., "cat" and "umbrella") and actions (e.g., "cat sits") from the image but is no longer correct. We call this a "hard negative sample". Using these samples during training, we ensure that fine-grained concepts are learned. The idea to inject hard negative samples in contrastive learning is highlighted in Figure 2.

3.1 Creating Hard Negative Text Samples

For various concepts, we replace specific keywords using a *regex*-based tool. For example, we replace "white cat" with "brown cat" or "cat" with "dog". We create substitution heuristics for four different concepts, namely *colors*, *objects*, *size*, *location*:

- For *color*, any of the 9 most occurring color names in COCO can be replaced by any other color name.
- For *objects*, any of 80 object names can be replaced by any other. The 80 words originate from COCO object categories.
- For *location* keywords we use 12 one-to-one substitution relations.
- For *size* keywords we use 11 one-to-one substitution relations.

The full list of heuristics is shown in Table 3 in the Appendix. The created samples are used for training and evaluation in § 5.1 and § 5.3.

The keywords were selected based on dataset statistics. For specific applications, a domain expert may have to select other terms (e.g. specific colors in the fashion industry).

3.2 Training Details

In our experiments, we use CLIP's image and text encoder from the ViT-B/32 model,[1] which has 87 million and 63 million parameters respectively.

[1] https://huggingface.co/openai/clip-vit-base-patch32

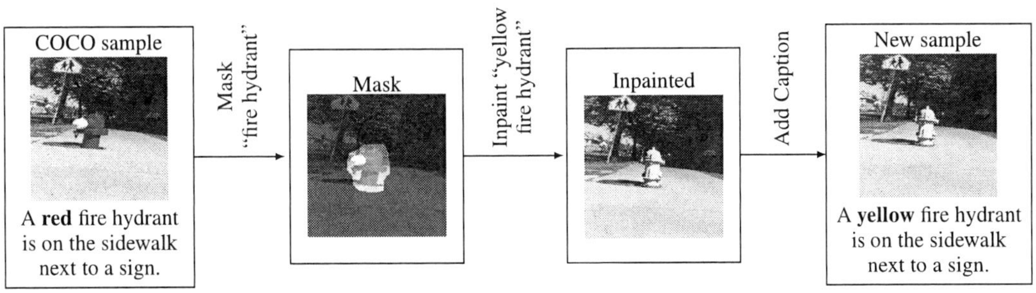

Figure 3: Create hard negative image samples using open vocabulary segmentation for the masking prompt and text-to-image generation for the inpainting prompt. Additionally, a new correct caption is created manually. The InpaintCOCO dataset was created for concepts *object*, *color*, and *size*.

And hence, is a relatively small model compared with current multimodal GenAI models. Our code is modular, and any image and text encoder from `transformers` (Wolf et al., 2020) can be used in the framework.

We train all models using a batch size of 64. For concepts with multiple negative examples (i.e., *color*, *object*), we train models with 1, 2, and 3 hard negatives. This results in a proportion of hard negatives of 1.5%, 3%, and 4.5%, respectively. We only use one hard negative for the other concepts.

In all experiments, we use Adam optimizer (Kingma and Ba, 2014) with a weight decay of 0.1. We run evaluations with different learning rates (5×10^{-7}, 1×10^{-6}, 5×10^{-6}, 1×10^{-5}, 5×10^{-5}) and finally use 5×10^{-6}, since it leads to the best trade-off results for evaluation displayed in Figure 4. We do not use a learning rate scheduler since weights are already aligned. (This is not the case if encoders that were not trained simultaneously are used.) Checkpoints are saved every 10% of the data, and we train for 3 epochs.

The training time for all models was less than two hours on an Nvidia V100. Utilizing FP16 training, the GPU memory consumption remained below 12 GB.

3.3 Training Data

CLIP is pretrained on 400 million image-text pairs from web sources, and we continue the model pretraining. We use the COCO image captioning dataset (Lin et al., 2015), which has 591 thousand image-text pairs (2017 train version). For each concept, we filtered out samples where at least one keyword was present so that a keyword substitution could be applied. For evaluation, we use the validation set of COCO 2017. The respective dataset sizes are shown in the Appendix in Table 5.

4 InpaintCOCO: Challenge Set from the Visual Perspective

Many multimodal tasks, such as VL Retrieval and Visual Question Answering, present results in terms of overall performance. Unfortunately, this approach overlooks more nuanced concepts, leaving us unaware of which specific concepts contribute to the success of current models and which are ignored. More recent benchmarks attempt to assess particular aspects of vision-language models in response to this limitation. Some existing datasets focus on linguistic concepts utilizing one image paired with multiple captions; others adopt a visual or cross-modal perspective. In this study, we are particularly interested in fine-grained visual concept understanding, which we believe is not covered in existing benchmarks in sufficient isolation. Therefore, we create the InpaintCOCO dataset with image pairs with minimum differences that lead to changes in the captions.

Related Work. Benchmarks such as ARO (Yuksekgonul et al., 2023) or VL-CheckList (Zhao et al., 2022) evaluate models from the language perspective. ARO examines understanding of attributes and relations without using specific concepts such as color or size. VL-CheckList[2] is a dataset that investigates concrete concepts such as location, size, material, color, and relations.

On the other side, SVO (Hendricks and Nematzadeh, 2021) is a dataset that allows analysis from the visual perspective (2 images with 1 caption). Here, relations that deal with verbs are examined. To our knowledge, the only dataset that deals with fine-grained comprehension from a cross-model perspective is Winoground (Thrush et al., 2022). The dataset consists of two image-

[2]Parts of the dataset are not available anymore.

text pairs that are very similar to each other. This benchmark probes object relations that do not refer to specific concepts. The images show similar concepts but are very dissimilar in overall appearance. For samples of the two latter datasets, see Figure 5 in the Appendix. Both datasets contain real-world images that are in some ways similar in terms of objects, but the scenes still differ significantly. Therefore, it is difficult to tell which image differences cause the model predictions.

We overcome this limitation by creating InpaintCOCO, the first dataset with only minor changes in the *visual* components, so that concept comprehension can be analyzed in a more standardized setting.

Dataset Creation. The dataset creation process can be viewed a complement to textual hard-negative samples (§ 3) in the visual domain. Unlike keyword substitutions, this cannot be done automatically with sufficient accuracy. Even though image segmentation and generative inpainting tools reach impressive results, they still require human supervision to produce high-quality images. Creating a high-quality test set, therefore, requires annotation work.

To generate hard negative image samples, we need to change individual details in the image so that the textual image description no longer fits. The procedure is illustrated in Figure 3.

The annotation proceeds as follows: The annotators are provided with an image and decide if they want to edit it. If yes, they input the prompt for the object that should be replaced. Using the open vocabulary segmentation model CLIPSeg[3] (Lüddecke and Ecker, 2022) we obtain a mask for our object of interest (i.e., "fire hydrant"). Then, the annotator inputs a prompt for Stable Diffusion v2 Inpainting[4] (Rombach et al., 2022) (e.g. with the prompt "yellow fire hydrant"), which shows three candidate images. The annotators can try new prompts or skip the current image if the result is insufficient. Finally, the annotator enters a new caption that matches the edited image. See Appendix A for all details. The images and captions come from the COCO 2017 validation data. We only use images that contain the desired concept and where licenses allow adaptations.

We provide 452 images for the concept *object*, 465 for *color*, and 343 for *size*. In contrast to the training process, objects in images are only replaced with objects from the same COCO super category, i.e., "cat" with another animal or "chair" for another piece of furniture. Since *location* would require erasing at one spot and implanting objects at another in a nontrivial way (especially regarding depth), we discard this one concept in the newly created dataset. The dataset will be available upon publishing via the HuggingFace hub.

5 Experiments

We run several experiments to evaluate the proposed method. We compare the original OpenAI model (**Orig.**), with continued pretraining CLIP model using the classical contrastive learning approach (**Clas.**) and our method with 1 up to 3 hard negative values per batch (**HN1**, **HN2**, **HN3**). We measure both how well concepts are learned and whether the general image retrieval capability of the model changes on the COCO dataset (§ 5.1). Additionally, we evaluate the method using our InpaintCOCO challenge set (§ 5.2), and several other datasets (§ 5.3).

5.1 Fine-grained vs. Coarse Understanding

Fine-grained Concept Understanding. Here, we are interested in whether models have learned detailed concept knowledge. We pose the evaluation as a ranking problem with one image on one side and n different texts on the other side. Besides the correct text (containing the correct keyword), we generate all possible $n-1$ negative examples using the same procedure as in § 3.1 and rank the texts with the model. We evaluate the ranking using the top-1 accuracy. See Table 4 in the Appendix for some examples.

General Image Retrieval. We evaluate the general capabilities of our models using the COCO dataset. We want the general retrieval capability to remain high even though we train our models with a focus on one concept. We report text-to-image retrieval Recall@5 on the whole COCO validation set.

Results. Results are shown in Figure 4 (and exact results per epoch are displayed in Table 7 in the Appendix). The performance of the original OpenAI CLIP is shown with a black dot and constantly reaches the worst results. Continued pretraining on COCO massively increases the general retrieval

[3]https://huggingface.co/CIDAS/clipseg-rd64-refined

[4]https://huggingface.co/stabilityai/stable-diffusion-2-inpainting

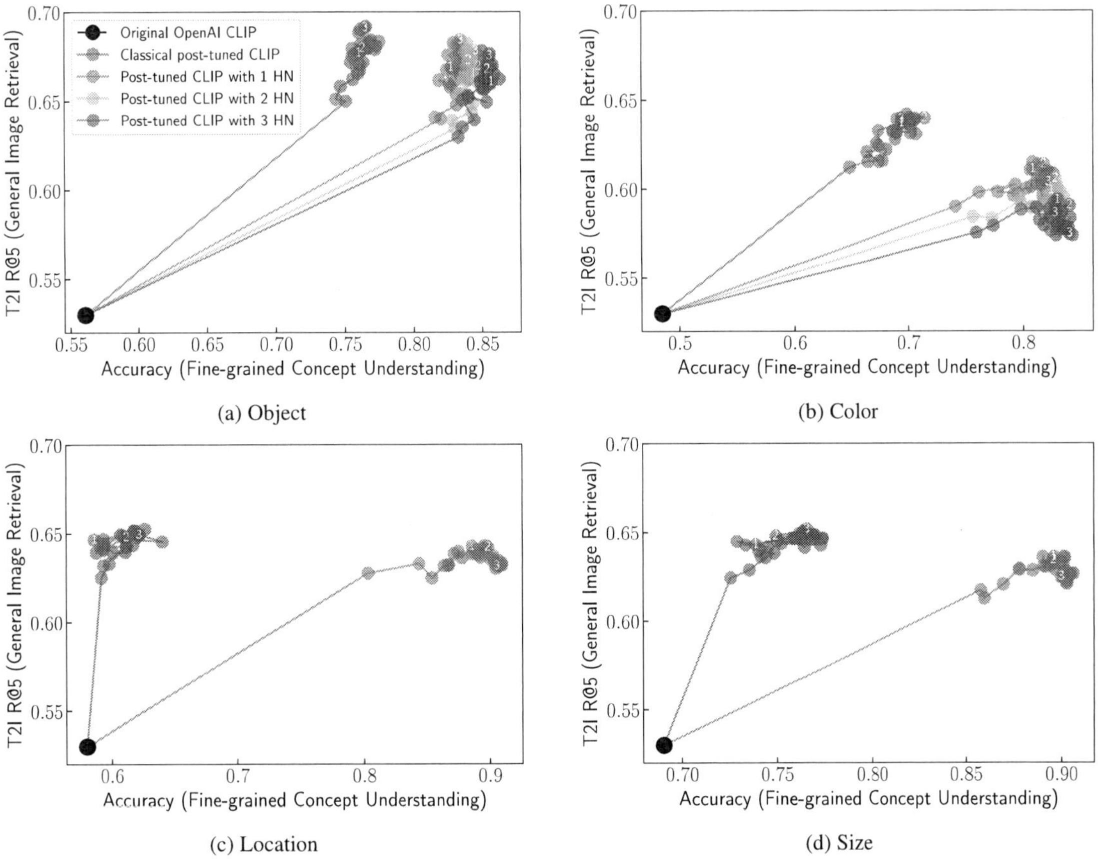

Figure 4: Fine-grained Concept Understanding vs. General Image Retrieval: Results for four different concepts trained on corresponding dataset subsets. Checkpoints are evaluated after every 10% of the data (circles); checkpoints at epoch ends are marked with the respective numbers. The results are also in a table form in Table 7 in the Appendix.

performance for all concepts, showing the successful domain adaptation regarding this dataset. It also improves the concept understanding for all concepts except for *location*. We are especially interested in the trade-off between general retrieval and concept understanding for the different types of further pretrained models. The following values are based on model checkpoints at the end of the epoch.

For ***objects***, we observe a performance increase regarding the fine-grained comprehension from 0.56 for the original OpenAI CLIP models to 0.76 when further pretraining on COCO. Using the hard negatives approach, performance increases by 7 to 10 percentage points, depending on the hard negative proportion and training duration. Here, the general retrieval performance only drops by 1 to 2 percentage points in relation to the classical approach.

We observe a similar pattern can be seen for the concept ***color***. Understanding of the concept improved by 11 to 15 percentage points compared to the original training process. On the other hand, the general comprehension pattern loses 3 to 4 percentage points with HN1 and slightly more with hard negative values. In this case, one hard example seems sufficient to learn concepts.

A single hard negative sample per batch is enough to enhance spatial understanding (***location***). Here, concept comprehension improves by 29 or 30 percentage points (depending on the duration of training) to around 90%. Both the original CLIP model and the further pretrained model only achieved around 60%. The general understanding decreases by 1 percentage point only or by 2 percentage points with long training. A substantial improvement in location comprehension is achieved with negligible loss in overall understanding

We observe a similar pattern for the ***size*** concept. Further pretraining on COCO improves concept understanding by 5 to 8 percentage points to around 75%. On the other hand, if the new

Epoch	Orig.	Clas.	HN1	HN2	HN3
1	0.78	0.85	0.88	0.88	0.88
2	0.78	0.84	0.86	0.88	0.88
3	0.78	0.87	0.88	0.89	0.90

(a) Object

Epoch	Orig.	Clas.	HN1	HN2	HN3
1	0.62	0.83	0.89	0.89	0.89
2	0.62	0.83	0.90	0.90	0.91
3	0.62	0.83	0.90	0.91	0.92

(b) Color

Epoch	Orig.	Clas.	HN1
1	0.26	0.27	0.55
2	0.26	0.28	0.57
3	0.26	0.30	0.60

(c) Size

Table 1: Accuracy for fine-grained understanding from the visual perspective following Equation (1) for InpaintCOCO dataset.

learning concept is used, the result is 90%, which corresponds to an additional improvement of 15 percentage points. Depending on training time, the general image retrieval capabilities lose no or only 3 percentage points. As with location, an almost continuous improvement can be observed.

Across all concepts, hard negative contrastive learning can significantly increase concept understanding. This also applies to settings with just one hard example. It is shown that with a small adjustment in the objective, the models can learn a much more complex understanding of image and text. Meanwhile, the general ability to represent images and texts is hardly affected.

5.2 Challenge Set Results

The ranking-based evaluation in the previous section only assessed the model capabilities from the language perspective in a very similar setup to how the model was trained. This section assesses the model from the vision perspective using our InpaintCOCO challenge set.

We consider an image pair from the InpaintCOCO dataset correctly classified if the correct images would be more likely to be retrieved based on the original caption and the newly created caption. This leads to the formula,

$$\begin{aligned} \mathrm{sim}(i_{\mathrm{COCO}}, t_{\mathrm{COCO}}) > \mathrm{sim}(i_{\mathrm{inp}}, t_{\mathrm{COCO}}) \quad \wedge \\ \mathrm{sim}(i_{\mathrm{inp}}, t_{\mathrm{inp}}) > \mathrm{sim}(i_{\mathrm{COCO}}, t_{\mathrm{inp}}) \end{aligned} \tag{1}$$

with image i and text t, originating from the original COCO and InpaintCOCO dataset. The corresponding results for each concept are displayed in Table 1.

The results show that continued pretraining improves understanding of all three concepts (object, color, size). The improvements between the original OpenAI CLIP model and the further pretrained model are 6 to 9 percentage points for the object and 21 for the color concept. The improvements are less distinct for size, with a 1 to 4 percentage point gain, which aligns with the textual comprehension results displayed in Figure 4d.

For the ***object*** concept, hard negative training brought a 7 to 10 percentage point improvement for the textual viewpoint (see Table 7). For the evaluation from the visual perspective, improvements are 2 to 4 percentage points. This relatively smaller improvement is likely because each object could be replaced with the 79 other object names during training. Still in this evaluation, a replacement was only executed within the COCO super-category (5 to 10 object names per super-category). The differences in performance between the three models using hard negative training is ≤ 2 percentage points.

The evaluation of the ***color*** concept shows an improvement of 6 to 9 percentage points for the visual perspective. From the textual perspective (Table 7), the improvement was at over 11 percentage points. As before, using more hard negative samples during training does not further improve the performance systematically (≤ 2 percentage point).

For the ***size*** concept, we see a big improvement for both perspectives when using hard negative models. From the visual perspective, there is an improvement of over 28 percentage points (Table 1c), and from the textual perspective, 13 to 16 percentage points.

The results show that training for just one epoch is sufficient for learning the concepts *object*, *color*, and *size*, and further training does not continue improving the results systematically. Additionally, using a single hard negative is sufficient to improve understanding of the concepts.

Dataset	Concept	Count	Orig.	Clas.	HN1	HN2	HN3
Flickr30k	object	30,926	.48	.66	.75	.77	.79
	color	45,003	.50	.64	.72	.73	.74
	location	20,097	.62	.64	.89		
	size	14,853	.75	.79	.92		
SBU	object	200,310	.33	.41	.48	.49	.50
	color	162,652	.51	.54	.61	.62	.62
	location	159,673	.61	.60	.79		
	size	47,069	.63	.65	.73		
Fashion200K	object	3,628	.24	.25	.35	.38	.39
	color	141,413	.68	.68	.69	.69	.70
NASA Earth Instagram	color	132	.43	.48	.55	.55	.58
Old Book Illustrations	object	124	.27	.35	.38	.35	.31
	location	95	.61	.50	.77		
	size	82	.61	.63	.79		

Table 2: Fine-grained concept understanding results (accuracy) for a diverse selection of datasets where the sample size is larger 50. Evaluated on dataset subsets where corresponding keywords are present.

5.3 Evaluations on other Datasets

We further investigate the performance of our model using more VL datasets. First, we evaluate the models using general VL datasets. The investigated concepts occur with different frequencies, and for high-quality results, it is important that these concepts are understood to increase the overall performance. Therefore, we further investigate fine-grained concept understanding on the Flickr30k (Young et al., 2014) and SBU Captioned Photo (Ordonez et al., 2011) datasets.

Fine-grained concept understanding is also important in specific domains. For example, in fashion, a correct assignment of garments and colors is important, not the mere presence of colors in the image. For this analysis, we evaluated our models on the very specific datasets Fashion200K (Han et al., 2017), NASA Earth Instagram,[5] and Old Book Illustrations.[6] These datasets are very heterogeneous in their appearance.

All models achieve good results except the *color* concept on the Fashion200k dataset and *object* concept on Old Book Illustrations. For the former, this is because images usually show garments with a distinct color. Yet, there is little background noise or noise from irrelevant items, which can confuse the color alignment of the model in this dataset. The latter shows old-fashioned drawings with objects very dissimilar to those in the COCO dataset. Our approach to learn concepts works very well for the remaining evaluations.

[5]https://huggingface.co/datasets/nkasmanoff/nasa_earth_instagram

[6]https://huggingface.co/datasets/gigant/oldbookillustrations

6 Conclusion

We introduce a robust method for enhancing fine-grained concept understanding with minimal impact on general retrieval capabilities using hard negative sampling in contrastive learning. We show that various concepts can be learned efficiently with minor text input adjustments. Moreover, improvements in concept understanding are observable after continued pretraining on only 10% of our data. Furthermore, one hard negative sample per image in a batch of 64 proves sufficient to incorporate the concept of interest into the model.

We comprehensively evaluate our method on several datasets, including our new challenge set. Our method outperforms classical contrastive learning on all investigated concepts. Existing datasets often focus on linguistic perturbations or use dissimilar images, precluding a structured evaluation of permuted visual concepts in isolation. To address this gap, InpaintCOCO represents the first dataset adjusting minor image parts in a controlled setting, facilitating cross-model fine-grained understanding. This ensures that the model's output is influenced only by one object and not the rest of the scene.

The results show that fine-grained concept understanding also generalizes to images of different styles when using InpaintCOCO and domain-specific datasets. Our method is data-efficient and requires only a little domain knowledge to design the hard negatives. This makes it particularly suitable for domain adaptation in image retrieval, as well as for developing new CLIP-based models, e.g., for object detection (Minderer et al., 2023).

Acknowledgements

The authors gratefully acknowledge the compute time granted by Monacum One at Bundeswehr University Munich. The work at CUNI, including annotation payments, was supported by Charles University project PRIMUS/23/SCI/023.

Limitations and Risks

Our research introduces a novel method for training CLIP aimed at incorporating concepts and representations that are challenging to learn using current approaches. In our experiments, we only used one specific CLIP model; however, we believe there is no reason why the method should not work or work systematically differently for smaller or larger CLIP models.

We conducted training with the well-studied COCO captioning dataset, which is standard in multimodal research. The proposed method is expected to show consistent performance also using other multimodal training datasets. Notably, evaluations on out-of-domain datasets, where the model was not trained, emphasize the robustness of our approach. One essential prerequisite for our methodology to work is the presence of keywords of interest in the training corpus and language and domain knowledge to decide how the keywords should be replaced. The keyword substitution will be more difficult in languages with more complex morphology than in English. Experiments involved using four concepts with a carefully chosen set of keywords. Depending on domain-specific tasks, other keywords might be of interest (e.g., a large list of garments for the fashion domain).

COCO is a dataset with image-text pairs where the captions are proper sentences, displaying a specific level of detail, and are carefully created by annotators. The images in the COCO dataset come from Flickr from 2014; therefore, they reflect the Flickr user structure at that time, i.e., the images mostly show the Western world and/or other countries from the Western perspective. The captions are in English. Thus, the model we developed does not generalize well beyond the Western world. However, we believe that is the limitation of the dataset, and the presented method itself is dataset agnostic.

The primary application goal of the models we worked with is to make image collections better accessible. Similar to other work on this VL modeling that enables better image understanding at scale, there is a risk of using technology based on the models for activities such as large-scale video surveillance.

References

S. Chopra, R. Hadsell, and Y. LeCun. 2005. Learning a similarity metric discriminatively, with application to face verification. In *2005 IEEE Computer Society Conference on Computer Vision and Pattern Recognition (CVPR)*, volume 1, pages 539–546 vol. 1.

Sivan Doveh, Assaf Arbelle, Sivan Harary, Rameswar Panda, Roei Herzig, Eli Schwartz, Donghyun Kim, Raja Giryes, Rogerio Feris, Shimon Ullman, and Leonid Karlinsky. 2023. Teaching structured vision&language concepts to vision&language models. *arXiv preprint arXiv:2211.11733*.

Xintong Han, Zuxuan Wu, Phoenix X Huang, Xiao Zhang, Menglong Zhu, Yuan Li, Yang Zhao, and Larry S Davis. 2017. Automatic spatially-aware fashion concept discovery. In *Proceedings of the IEEE/CVF International Conference on Computer Vision (ICCV)*.

Lisa Anne Hendricks and Aida Nematzadeh. 2021. Probing image-language transformers for verb understanding. In *Findings of the Association for Computational Linguistics: ACL-IJCNLP 2021*, pages 3635–3644, Online. Association for Computational Linguistics.

Chao Jia, Yinfei Yang, Ye Xia, Yi-Ting Chen, Zarana Parekh, Hieu Pham, Quoc Le, Yun-Hsuan Sung, Zhen Li, and Tom Duerig. 2021. Scaling up visual and vision-language representation learning with noisy text supervision. In *International conference on machine learning*, pages 4904–4916. PMLR.

Diederik P Kingma and Jimmy Ba. 2014. Adam: A method for stochastic optimization. *arXiv preprint arXiv:1412.6980*.

Tsung-Yi Lin, Michael Maire, Serge Belongie, Lubomir Bourdev, Ross Girshick, James Hays, Pietro Perona, Deva Ramanan, C. Lawrence Zitnick, and Piotr Dollár. 2015. Microsoft coco: Common objects in context. *arXiv preprint arXiv:1405.0312*.

Timo Lüddecke and Alexander Ecker. 2022. Image segmentation using text and image prompts. In *Proceedings of the IEEE/CVF Conference on Computer Vision and Pattern Recognition (CVPR)*, pages 7086–7096.

Matthias Minderer, Alexey Gritsenko, and Neil Houlsby. 2023. Scaling open-vocabulary object detection. *Preprint*, arXiv:2306.09683.

Aaron van den Oord, Yazhe Li, and Oriol Vinyals. 2018. Representation learning with contrastive predictive coding. *arXiv preprint arXiv:1807.03748*.

Vicente Ordonez, Girish Kulkarni, and Tamara Berg. 2011. Im2text: Describing images using 1 million captioned photographs. In *Advances in Neural Information Processing Systems*, volume 24. Curran Associates, Inc.

Filip Radenovic, Abhimanyu Dubey, Abhishek Kadian, Todor Mihaylov, Simon Vandenhende, Yash Patel, Yi Wen, Vignesh Ramanathan, and Dhruv Mahajan. 2023. Filtering, distillation, and hard negatives for vision-language pre-training. *arXiv preprint arXiv:2301.02280*.

Alec Radford, Jong Wook Kim, Chris Hallacy, Aditya Ramesh, Gabriel Goh, Sandhini Agarwal, Girish Sastry, Amanda Askell, Pamela Mishkin, Jack Clark, Gretchen Krueger, and Ilya Sutskever. 2021. Learning transferable visual models from natural language supervision. *arXiv preprint arXiv:2103.00020*.

Joshua Robinson, Ching-Yao Chuang, Suvrit Sra, and Stefanie Jegelka. 2021. Contrastive learning with hard negative samples. *arXiv preprint arXiv:2010.04592*.

Robin Rombach, Andreas Blattmann, Dominik Lorenz, Patrick Esser, and Björn Ommer. 2022. High-resolution image synthesis with latent diffusion models. In *Proceedings of the IEEE/CVF Conference on Computer Vision and Pattern Recognition (CVPR)*, pages 10684–10695.

Philipp J. Rösch and Jindřich Libovický. 2022. Probing the role of positional information in vision-language models. In *Findings of the Association for Computational Linguistics: NAACL 2022*, pages 1031–1041, Seattle, United States. Association for Computational Linguistics.

Florian Schroff, Dmitry Kalenichenko, and James Philbin. 2015. Facenet: A unified embedding for face recognition and clustering. In *2015 IEEE Conference on Computer Vision and Pattern Recognition (CVPR)*. IEEE.

Christoph Schuhmann, Romain Beaumont, Richard Vencu, Cade W Gordon, Ross Wightman, Mehdi Cherti, Theo Coombes, Aarush Katta, Clayton Mullis, Mitchell Wortsman, Patrick Schramowski, Srivatsa R Kundurthy, Katherine Crowson, Ludwig Schmidt, Robert Kaczmarczyk, and Jenia Jitsev. 2022. LAION-5b: An open large-scale dataset for training next generation image-text models. In *Thirty-sixth Conference on Neural Information Processing Systems Datasets and Benchmarks Track*.

Piyush Sharma, Nan Ding, Sebastian Goodman, and Radu Soricut. 2018. Conceptual captions: A cleaned, hypernymed, image alt-text dataset for automatic image captioning. In *Proceedings of the 56th Annual Meeting of the Association for Computational Linguistics (Volume 1: Long Papers)*, pages 2556–2565, Melbourne, Australia. Association for Computational Linguistics.

Kihyuk Sohn. 2016. Improved deep metric learning with multi-class n-pair loss objective. In *Advances in Neural Information Processing Systems*, volume 29.

Hao Tan and Mohit Bansal. 2019. LXMERT: Learning cross-modality encoder representations from transformers. In *Proceedings of the 2019 Conference on Empirical Methods in Natural Language Processing and the 9th International Joint Conference on Natural Language Processing (EMNLP-IJCNLP)*, pages 5100–5111, Hong Kong, China. Association for Computational Linguistics.

Tristan Thrush, Ryan Jiang, Max Bartolo, Amanpreet Singh, Adina Williams, Douwe Kiela, and Candace Ross. 2022. Winoground: Probing vision and language models for visio-linguistic compositionality. In *Proceedings of the IEEE/CVF Conference on Computer Vision and Pattern Recognition*, pages 5238–5248.

Thomas Wolf, Lysandre Debut, Victor Sanh, Julien Chaumond, Clement Delangue, Anthony Moi, Pierric Cistac, Tim Rault, Rémi Louf, Morgan Funtowicz, Joe Davison, Sam Shleifer, Patrick von Platen, Clara Ma, Yacine Jernite, Julien Plu, Canwen Xu, Teven Le Scao, Sylvain Gugger, Mariama Drame, Quentin Lhoest, and Alexander M. Rush. 2020. Transformers: State-of-the-art natural language processing. In *Proceedings of the 2020 Conference on Empirical Methods in Natural Language Processing: System Demonstrations*, pages 38–45, Online. Association for Computational Linguistics.

Lewei Yao, Runhui Huang, Lu Hou, Guansong Lu, Minzhe Niu, Hang Xu, Xiaodan Liang, Zhenguo Li, Xin Jiang, and Chunjing Xu. 2021. Filip: Fine-grained interactive language-image pre-training. *arXiv preprint arXiv:2111.07783*.

Peter Young, Alice Lai, Micah Hodosh, and Julia Hockenmaier. 2014. From image descriptions to visual denotations: New similarity metrics for semantic inference over event descriptions. *Transactions of the Association for Computational Linguistics*, 2:67–78.

Mert Yuksekgonul, Federico Bianchi, Pratyusha Kalluri, Dan Jurafsky, and James Zou. 2023. When and why vision-language models behave like bags-of-words, and what to do about it? In *The Eleventh International Conference on Learning Representations*.

Tiancheng Zhao, Tianqi Zhang, Mingwei Zhu, Haozhan Shen, Kyusong Lee, Xiaopeng Lu, and Jianwei Yin. 2022. An explainable toolbox for evaluating pre-trained vision-language models. In *Proceedings of the 2022 Conference on Empirical Methods in Natural Language Processing: System Demonstrations*, pages 30–37, Abu Dhabi, UAE. Association for Computational Linguistics.

Tiancheng Zhao, Tianqi Zhang, Mingwei Zhu, Haozhan Shen, Kyusong Lee, Xiaopeng Lu, and Jianwei Yin. 2023. Vl-checklist: Evaluating pre-trained vision-language models with objects, attributes and relations. *arXiv preprint arXiv:2207.00221*.

A Appendix

Creating Hard Negative Samples In Table 3, we specify all used substitution keywords for the concepts *object*, *color*, *location*, and *size*.

Table 4 lists text samples for the fine-grained concept understanding task, which is used in § 5.1 for each concept.

Concept	Keywords
object	[person, bicycle, car, motorbike, aeroplane, bus, train, truck, boat, traffic light, fire hydrant, stop sign, parking meter, bench, bird, cat, dog, horse, sheep, cow, elephant, bear, zebra, giraffe, backpack, umbrella, handbag, tie, suitcase, frisbee, skis, snowboard, sports ball, kite, baseball bat, baseball glove, skateboard, surfboard, tennis racket, bottle, wine glass, cup, fork, knife, spoon, bowl, banana, apple, sandwich, orange, broccoli, carrot, hot dog, pizza, donut, cake, chair, sofa, potted plant, bed, dining table, toilet, tv monitor, laptop, mouse, remote, keyboard, cell phone, microwave, oven, toaster, sink, refrigerator, book, clock, vase, scissors, teddy bear, hair drier, toothbrush]
color	[blue, red, green, yellow, black, white, brown, gray, orange]
location	left ↔ right, above ↔ below, under ↔ over, foreground ↔ background, in front of ↔ behind, back ↔ front
size	large ↔ small, little ↔ big, tall ↔ short, long → short, thin ↔ fat, huge ↔ tiny, giant → tiny

Table 3: All keywords that can be replaced for the four concepts. That are 80 for *object*, 9 for *color*, 12 for *location* and 11 for *size*. In lists, each word can be replaced by any other word. "↔" and "→" denote words that can be replaced in both and one direction, respectively.

✗ A small yellow person on a branch of a tree.
✗ A small yellow bicycle on a branch of a tree.
✗ ...
✓ A small yellow **bird** on a branch of a tree.
✗ A small yellow cat on a branch of a tree.
✗ ...

(a) Object (for all 80 object names)

✗ a blue cat sits under a black open umbrella.
✗ a red cat sits under a black open umbrella.
✗ a green cat sits under a black open umbrella.
✗ a yellow cat sits under a black open umbrella.
✗ a black cat sits under a black open umbrella.
✓ a **white** cat sits under a black open umbrella.
✗ a brown cat sits under a black open umbrella.
✗ a gray cat sits under a black open umbrella.
✗ a orange cat sits under a black open umbrella.

(b) Color

✓ a white cat sits **under** a black open umbrella.
✗ a white cat sits over a black open umbrella.

(c) Location

✓ A **small** yellow bird on a branch of a tree.
✗ A large yellow bird on a branch of a tree.

(d) Size

Table 4: Exemplary image descriptions that are used as text samples in the fine-grained concept understanding task (see § 5.1) for the example images displayed in Figure 1 or Figure 3.

Concept	Further pretraining dataset size	Evaluation dataset size
object	305,056	12,907
color	92,006	3,907
location	58,156	2,527
size	60,626	2,601

Table 5: COCO dataset size for all concepts used for further pretraining CLIP and evaluation.

COCO training and evaluation data. Table 5 shows the size of the training datasets and fine-grained concept understanding evaluation datasets. The images predominantly depict scenes from the USA and Western countries, and all captions are exclusively in English.

There are many large-scale VL datasets available to pretrain or further pretrain models (e.g., Conceptual Caption (Sharma et al., 2018) or LAION-5B (Schuhmann et al., 2022) with 3.3 million and 5 billion image-text pairs respectively). Yet, results in Figure 4 indicate that training on a small-sized COCO dataset (even for just one epoch) is sufficient to learn the concepts of interest.

Fine-grained VL Benchmarks. In Table 6, we list different benchmark datasets for fine-grained understanding in VL. Some image-text samples for ARO and Winoground are displayed in Figure 5 since these datasets provide two images per sample – similar to InpaintCOCO. However, unlike InpaintCOCO, the visual representations are very different regarding the scenes presented in these datasets.

Challenge Set Creation. Undergraduate student workers created the challenge set. They were provided with an interactive Python environment with which they interacted via various prompts and inputs. The description of the task and the problem of the research question was made available to them (see Figure 6). In addition to a detailed written explanation of how the tool works, they were also

Dataset	Size	Perspective	Samples	Tasks
ARO	77k	Linguistic	1 image ↔ 2 texts	Attributes, Relations, Order understanding
VL-CheckList	410k	Linguistic	1 image ↔ 2 texts	Attributes, Relations, Object understanding
SVO-Probs	48k	Visual	2 images ↔ 1 text	Relations (Verb Understanding)
Winoground	400	Cross-modal	2 images ↔ 2 texts	Relations
InpaintCOCO	1,260	Cross-modal	2 images ↔ 2 texts	Attributes, Object understanding

Table 6: Datasets for fine-grained understanding in VL.

Figure 5: Samples from visual and cross-model datasets.

given "best practices," which were created by one student and reviewed by the authors.

For color, any other *color* and for *size*, the opposite statement can be chosen. Yet, within *objects*, the students were asked to replace with objects from the same COCO super-category (to ensure that no "plain" needs to be inpainted in an indoor scene). There are 12 super categories for the 80 object names: person, vehicle, outdoor, animal, accessory, sports, kitchen, food, furniture, electronic, appliance, and indoor.

The workflow comprises these steps:

1. A random COCO (2017 validation) image is shown with all its captions containing a concept keyword.
2. The annotator enters a masking prompt for the segmentation task based on the object of interest (e.g., "fire hydrant" in Figure 3). They can also enlarge the mask within the x and y dimensions by passing additional parameters. This is useful if a larger object is to be inserted into the image. Several attempts can be made until the mask meets the requirements. Only then the next step is carried out.
3. Then, the annotator enters an inpainting prompt (the image generation takes roughly 1 minute). They are provided with three different inpainted images. They proceed if at least one high-quality image has been generated.
4. The best image is chosen from the three proposals.
5. Based on the selection before, they rate the pictures as "very good" or "okay".
6. Finally, a new, correct caption is added based on one of the original COCO captions.

A subset of students had pre-existing roles within the university, while others were purposefully recruited for the designated task. The compensation for student assistants adhered to the legally stipulated wages in their respective countries, amounting to CZK 300.00 per hour in the Czech Republic and EUR 12.00 per hour in Germany.

Challenge Set Details. Our InpaintCOCO challenge set is based on the famous COCO dataset. All captions follow "Creative Commons Attribution 4.0 License" and hence can be changed. Images originate from Flickr, and have diverse licenses ("Attribution License", "Attribution-NonCommercial-ShareAlike License", "Attribution-NonCommercial License", "Attribution-ShareAlike License") which all allow scientific usage and modification (like inpaining).

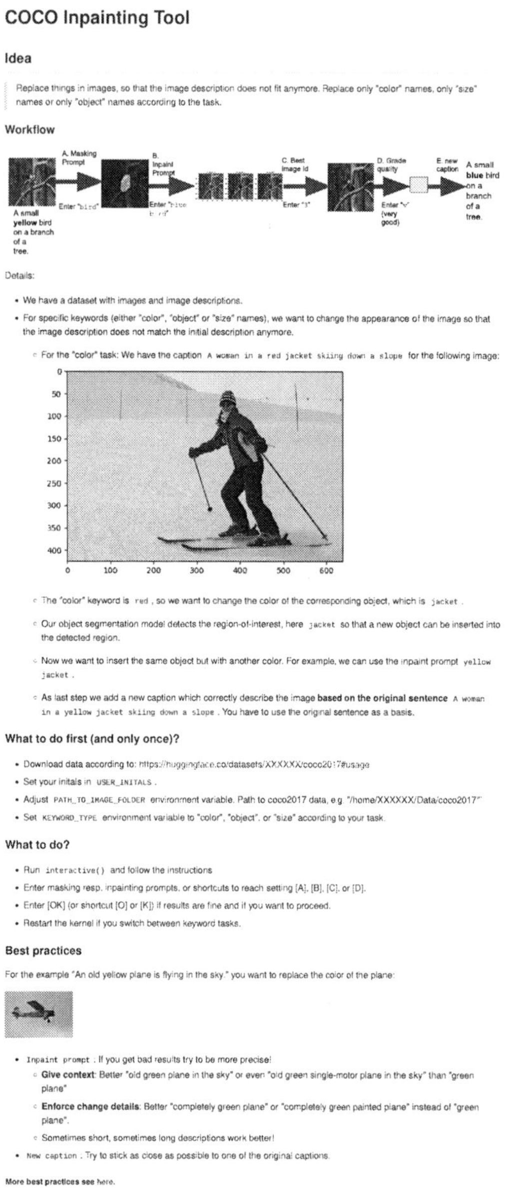

COCO Inpainting Tool

Idea

> Replace things in images, so that the image description does not fit anymore. Replace only "color" names, only "size" names or only "object" names according to the task.

Workflow

Details:

- We have a dataset with images and image descriptions.
- For specific keywords (either "color", "object" or "size" names), we want to change the appearance of the image so that the image description does not match the initial description anymore.
  - For the "color" task: We have the caption `A woman in a red jacket skiing down a slope` for the following image:

  - The "color" keyword is `red`, so we want to change the color of the corresponding object, which is `jacket`.
  - Our object segmentation model detects the region-of-interest, here `jacket` so that a new object can be inserted into the detected region.
  - Now we want to insert the same object but with another color. For example, we can use the inpaint prompt `yellow jacket`.
  - As last step we add a new caption which correctly describe the image **based on the original sentence** `A woman in a yellow jacket skiing down a slope`. You have to use the original sentence as a basis.

What to do first (and only once)?

- Download data according to: https://huggingface.co/datasets/XXXXXX/coco2017#usage
- Set your initals in `USER_INITALS`.
- Adjust `PATH_TO_IMAGE_FOLDER` environment variable. Path to coco2017 data, e.g. "/home/XXXXXX/Data/coco2017"
- Set `KEYWORD_TYPE` environment variable to "color", "object", or "size" according to your task.

What to do?

- Run `interactive()` and follow the instructions
- Enter masking resp. inpainting prompts, or shortcuts to reach setting [A], [B], [C], or [D].
- Enter [OK] (or shortcut [O] or [K]) if results are fine and if you want to proceed.
- Restart the kernel if you switch between keyword tasks.

Best practices

For the example "An old yellow plane is flying in the sky." you want to replace the color of the plane:

- `Inpaint prompt`: If you get bad results try to be more precise!
  - **Give context**: Better "old green plane in the sky" or even "old green single-motor plane in the sky" than "green plane"
  - **Enforce change details**: Better "completely green plane" or "completely green painted plane" instead of "green plane".
  - Sometimes short, sometimes long descriptions work better!
- `New caption`: Try to stick as close as possible to one of the original captions.

More best practices see here.

Figure 6: Instructions of inpainting tool provided to student workers.

Individual licenses are listed in each sample of the dataset.

Experiment Results. For numeric results from Figure 4 see Table 7. In this Table fine-grained concept understanding results (Accuracy) and COCO text-to-image retrieval results (T2I R@5) are presented. "Orig.", "Clas.", "HN1", "HN2", and "HN3" indicate the original OpenAI CLIP model, the classical further pretrained model, and models trained with 1, 2, or 3 hard negative samples.

A **bird** is standing on top of a car.	A **cat** is standing on top of a car.

(a) Object

A couple of **white** bathroom sinks sitting next to a toilet.	A couple of **black** bathroom sinks sitting next to a toilet.

(b) Color

A living room with white furniture and a **small** wooden table.	A living room with white furniture and a **huge** wooden table.

(c) Size

Figure 7: InpaintCOCO samples for all concepts.

Concept	Epoch	Accuracy Orig.	Clas.	HN1	HN2	HN3	T2I R@5 Orig.	Clas.	HN1	HN2	HN3
object	1	.56	.76	.83	.84	.86	.53	.68	.67	.67	.66
	2	.56	.76	.84	.85	.85	.53	.68	.67	.67	.67
	3	.56	.76	.83	.85	.86	.53	.69	.68	.68	.68
color	1	.48	.69	.81	.82	.83	.53	.64	.61	.60	.59
	2	.48	.71	.82	.83	.84	.53	.64	.61	.61	.59
	3	.48	.69	.82	.83	.84	.53	.64	.60	.59	.57
location	1	.58	.59	.89			.53	.65	.64		
	2	.58	.61	.90			.53	.65	.64		
	3	.58	.62	.91			.53	.65	.63		
size	1	.69	.74	.90			.53	.64	.64		
	2	.69	.75	.90			.53	.65	.63		
	3	.69	.77	.90			.53	.65	.62		

Table 7: Accuracy of fine-grained concept understanding (evaluated on dataset subsets) and COCO text-to-image Recall@5 for general image retrieval (evaluated on whole dataset) for models trained on respectively concepts. Checkpoints for epochs 1 to 3.

Vision Language Models for Spreadsheet Understanding: Challenges and Opportunities

Shiyu Xia*†, Junyu Xiong*†, Haoyu Dong‡, Jianbo Zhao†, Yuzhang Tian†, Mengyu Zhou, Yeye He, Shi Han, Dongmei Zhang
Microsoft Corporation

Abstract

This paper explores capabilities of Vision Language Models on spreadsheet comprehension. We propose three self-supervised challenges with corresponding evaluation metrics to comprehensively evaluate VLMs on Optical Character Recognition (OCR), spatial perception, and visual format recognition. Additionally, we utilize the spreadsheet table detection task to assess the overall performance of VLMs by integrating these challenges. To probe VLMs more finely, we propose three spreadsheet-to-image settings: column width adjustment, style change, and address augmentation.

We propose variants of prompts to address the above tasks in different settings. Notably, to leverage the strengths of VLMs in understanding text rather than two-dimensional positioning, we propose to decode cell values on the four boundaries of the table in spreadsheet boundary detection. Our findings reveal that VLMs demonstrate promising OCR capabilities but produce unsatisfactory results due to cell omission and misalignment, and they notably exhibit insufficient spatial and format recognition skills, motivating future work to enhance VLMs' spreadsheet data comprehension capabilities using our methods to generate extensive spreadsheet-image pairs in various settings.

1 Introduction

Spreadsheets are widely-used for data management and analysis (Birch et al., 2018; Wu et al., 2023). However, they are designed to be "human-friendly, not "machine-friendly" 1. Cells are arranged on the grid and illustrated by various visual formats like borders, colors, and bold fonts. Unlike machines, humans naturally leverage these visual cues to understand the layouts and structures of spreadsheets, such as the location of the table (e.g., "A2:N32") using borders, the headers (e.g., "A2:N3") using bold fonts, and aggregated rows and columns (e.g., rows 17, 19, and 20) using fill colors.

While LLMs have shown promising performance in serializing spreadsheets as text sequences (Chen et al., 2024; Li et al., 2024), representing spreadsheets in this manner loses critical visual signals. With the recent surge in Vision Language Models (VLMs) (Laurençon et al., 2024), we propose studying the capability of language models to leverage visual signals for spreadsheet understanding. Fortunately, a spreadsheet can be straightforwardly processed using third-party tools like Interop and converted into an image. This motivates us to construct spreadsheet-image pairwise data for self-supervised tasks. To this end, we propose three self-supervised tasks to comprehensively examine critical abilities of VLMs separately: Optical Character Recognition (OCR) of cells, two-dimensional spatial position perception, and visual format recognition. Finally, we use spreadsheet table detection (Dong et al., 2019), a fundamental and enabling task in Microsoft Excel and Google Sheets, to jointly examine the effectiveness of VLMs, as this task combines the challenges of all three self-supervised tasks.

Specifically, as shown in Figure. 1, spreadsheet images present the following challenges: 1) The rows and columns are very compact, even overlapping, which makes the OCR task difficult. Specifically, VLMs sometimes struggle to split multiple cells and mistakenly treat them as a single cell. 2) The absence of explicit cell addresses and clear boundaries between rows and columns makes it difficult to perceive spatial locations. 3) Spreadsheets often contain a variety of formats, making it hard to recognize all formats precisely at the pixel level. To address these issues, we propose three different spreadsheet-to-image settings to probe the VLMs' performance: column width adjustment,

* Equal contribution.
† Work during internship at Microsoft.
‡ Corresponding author.

Proceedings of the 3rd Workshop on Advances in Language and Vision Research, pages 116–128
August 16, 2024 ©2024 Association for Computational Linguistics

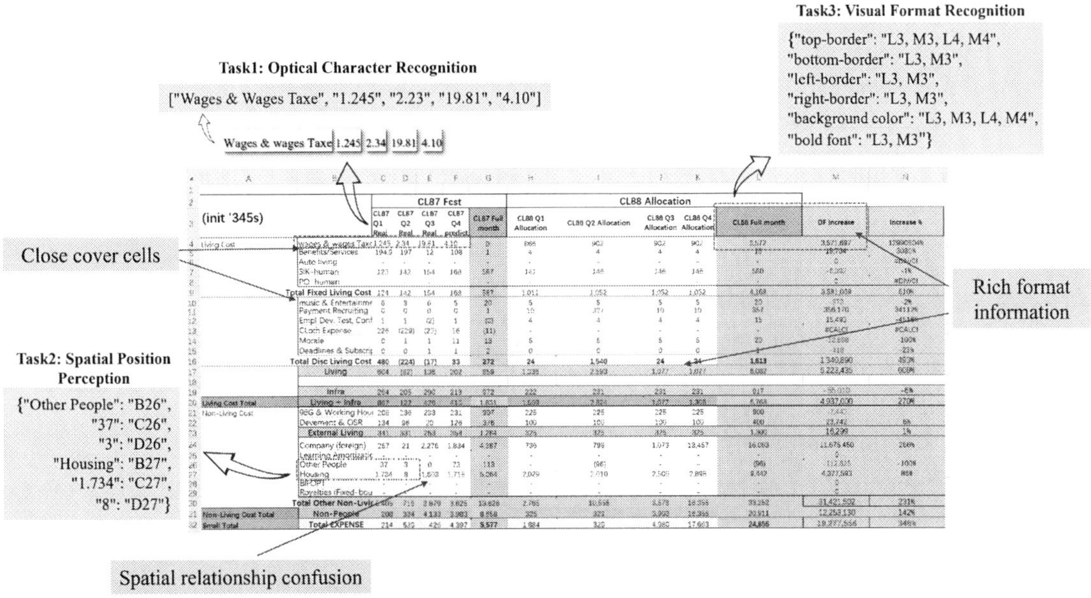

Figure 1: A sample spreadsheet showing various challenging points in spreadsheet understanding task.

style change, and address augmentation respectively, as shown in Figure. 2.

We explore variants of prompts to address the above tasks in different settings. Notably, to leverage the strengths of VLMs in understanding text rather than two-dimensional positioning, we propose to decode cell values on the four boundaries of the table rather than decoding regions like "A2:E5" directly in the task of spreadsheet boundary detection. By analyzing the experiment results, we draw the following conclusions: Firstly, VLMs possess strong OCR capabilities, yet they often encounter issues of cell omission and prediction misalignment when dealing with spreadsheet images. Secondly, VLMs lack robust spatial perception in images because they need to infer the number of rows and columns implicitly on a large two-dimensional cell grid rather than reading it directly. It is highly noteworthy that their performance on recognizing visual formats on a cell grid is far from satisfactory; they are far from human-level in comprehending spreadsheet formats. Lastly, in the task of spreadsheet table detection, VLMs do not perform as well as the existing CNN-based TableSense (Dong et al., 2019), which is well-trained using a human-labeled dataset, indicating that there is still a long way to go in understanding spreadsheet images for VLMs.

2 Related Work

2.1 Table Representation

The advent of Large Language Models (LLMs) has significantly spotlighted the task of processing structured data (Jiang et al., 2023; Tang et al., 2023; Guo et al., 2023), particularly tabular data. In the quest to effectively communicate tabular data to LLMs, researchers have devised numerous formats, including HTML, JSON, Markdown, and XML, to represent such data. Studies by Sui et al. (Sui et al., 2023a) and Singha et al. (Singha et al., 2023) have underscored the efficacy of using Markdown and HTML for tabular data representation. However, these methods do not apply to spreadsheets since they have a single table assumption with an explicit region. Moreover, they do not leverage visual formats. (Deng et al., 2024) explored the usage of LLMs to evaluate representations of tables in image form, and Singh et al. (Singh et al., 2023) examined the capability of GPT-4 with vision(GPT-4V) (Achiam et al., 2023) on structured data, but they also focus on table-based input but not spreadsheet input that can include multiple tables and scattered notes. In contrast, there's a growing interest in exploring the vision perspective of spreadsheets to leverage the visual cues and take the whole spreadsheet rather than a single table as input. For instance, Dong et al. (Dong et al., 2019) uses CNN to capture spatial layouts of spreadsheet. However, our research diverges by focusing on exploring LLMs' ability to understand spreadsheet images. (Huang et al., 2023) proposed to model table boundaries as language sequences and use sequence decoder for table recognition.

2.2 Table-Related Tasks

Previous research has extensively explored tasks related to tables, encompassing table QA, table fact-checking, table-to-text, table manipulation, and table interpretation, etc (Pasupat and Liang, 2015; Novikova et al., 2017; Chen et al., 2020; Sui et al., 2023b; Li et al., 2023; Zhang et al., 2023). However, many of these tasks primarily revolve around understanding tables at the textual level. In reality, tables are often embedded within documents, images, and web pages, necessitating the exploration of related tasks such as table header detection, table structure recognition, and table recognition.

In recent studies, Fang et al. (Fang et al., 2012) identified tables within PDF documents using existing table extraction tools and employed machine learning algorithms to construct classifiers for identifying and categorizing table headers. Nassar et al. (Nassar et al.) introduced a novel table unit object detection decoder based on Transformer architecture to comprehend table structures. Ly et al. (Ly and Takasu, 2023) decomposed the table recognition task into two subtasks: table structure recognition and cell content recognition. They proposed an end-to-end multi-task learning model to address these subtasks.

However, our current study focuses more on the understanding of spreadsheet images by VLMs. This involves investigating the OCR capabilities of VLMs, their aptitude in capturing formatting information, their perception of spatial positioning, and their efficacy in detecting tables from spreadsheets (Dong et al., 2019).

3 Preliminary

3.1 Probing tasks

We design the following three probing tasks to evaluate the performance of VLMs on spreadsheet understanding.

Optical Character Recognition (OCR): A spreadsheet is a two-dimensional cell grid that differs from plain text. In OCR tasks for text, the output simply sequences the characters. However, OCR for spreadsheets not only involves recognizing characters but also requires organizing them in units of distinct cells as shown in Task1 of Figure. 1.

Understanding spatial position: The ability of VLMs to perceive the spatial position of images has been a long-standing challenge. Unlike ordinary images, spreadsheet images employ a precise two-dimensional coordinate system, where misalignment of rows and columns severely disrupts the understanding of information. Each cell's address corresponds to exact row and column coordinates, however, the images don't explicitly indicate the coordinate positions, so we define the top row in the image as the first row and the leftmost column as the first column. Consequently, the address of the cell located at the intersection of the first row and first column is defined as "1,1". Cell numbers increase from left to right and from top to bottom. As shown in Task2 of Figure. 1, the address for "Other People" is "B26." But for spreadsheet images without given coordinate positions, it should be recognized as "26,2".

Understanding visual format information: Spreadsheets contain rich formatting details that enhance comprehension and processing. If VLMs could "read" format information in images, it would perceive the images much like human do. Although spreadsheets contains a variety of format, we primarily focus on top border, bottom border, left border, right border, bold font, and fill color as shown in Task3 of Figure. 1.

3.2 Spreadsheet Table Detection Task

Spreadsheet table detection (Dong et al., 2019), involves identifying all tables within a given spreadsheet and determining their respective ranges. The spreadsheet will feature a visually rich design containing several tables scattered throughout, each potentially featuring a unique structure. Variability in the layout and structure of multiple tables contains rich visual information greatly complicating the task by obscuring table boundaries. Spreadsheet table detection is a horizontal and enabling task benefiting various intelligent features in spreadsheet softwares. Therefore, We employ this critical task in our work to assess the extent to how visual information influences the ability of VLMs to comprehend spreadsheets.

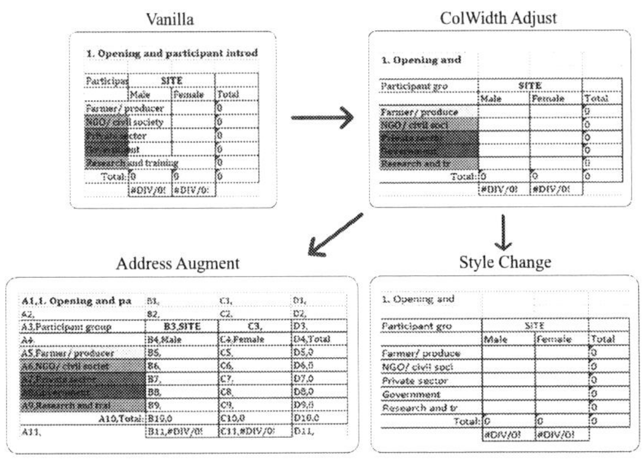

Figure 2: Illustration of spreadsheet-to-image settings.

Prompt: The image I provide is a spreadsheet. Please output the value of each cell in order from left to right and top to bottom. That is, the first cell value of the current row should follow the last cell value of the previous row. If the cell value is empty, please ignore it. Please return strictly in the following format (do not output anything else):
["Cell-1", "Cell-2", ...]
Note that the data such as "Cell-1" above are replaced with real cell values.
Here's the image:
<image>

Figure 3: The prompt of OCR task.

4 Methodology

4.1 Dataset Construction

In order to study the spreadsheet understanding capabilities of VLMs such as GPT-4V and Gemini (Team et al., 2023), we convert the spreadsheet dataset (Dong et al., 2019) into images using the Microsoft Office Interop Excel library [1] without any human labeling efforts. Then we can simply reverse the dataset to get image-spreadsheet pairs.

Next, to probe the differences for VLMs to understand image spreadsheets under various image settings, we propose three processing methods on the input spreadsheet shown as Figure. 2. They are column width adjustment, style change, and address augment, respectively.

Column Width Adjustment: Since the column width effect the maximum number of characters displayed in each cell, if the column width is too small, the content between multiple cells will be very compact, making it difficult for the model (or even humans) to distinguish it. If the column width is too large, space will be wasted. Therefore, we come up with a setting that adjusts the column width based on the text length, but if the text length is too long, we limit it to the first 15 characters.

Style Change: Spreadsheet style attributes mainly include background color and various font properties such as bold, italic, fill color, and size. These styling elements serve specific functions, for instance, background color often groups similar data, while font color and bolding emphasize important details. These styles provide distinct visual cues within the spreadsheet. To minimize the influence of these stylistic elements on the understanding of VLMs, it's necessary to standardize these attributes: removing background colors and bold formatting from each cell, setting font color to black, and using a consistent font type and size, such as Calibri at 12pt, etc.

Address Augment: In spreadsheets, cell contents typically serve the sole purpose of storing data. However, a comprehensive understanding of the spreadsheet requires grasping the spatial relationships and format correspondences between cells. Existing VLMs may struggle to robustly capture these precise spatial relationships. To address this, we propose a new setting that incorporates cell address information alongside the cell content. That is, we explicitly concatenate the cell address (e.g., "A1") with its value (e.g., "day"), using a comma to separate them. This results in a fashion like "A1, day."

4.2 Optical Character Recognition

We instruct the VLM to sequentially decode the text of each cell in the spreadsheet image, moving from top to bottom and left to right, while omitting cells that contain null values. Figure. 3 provides a prompt example.

Evaluation Method: We adopt two kinds of evaluation method, Strict and longest common substring (LCS). As shown in Figure. 4, the LCS argorithm is uesd to find the longest common subsequence between the predicted sequence and the ground truth sequence. It helps to effectively alleviate the problem of poor performance caused by missing some cells in the output and can test the OCR ability of the VLMs to the greatest extent.

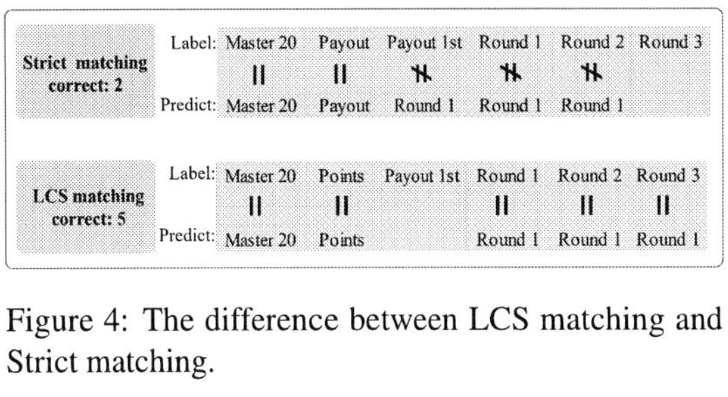

Figure 4: The difference between LCS matching and Strict matching.

[1] https://github.com/microsoft/Windows-Packaging-Samples/tree/master/OfficeInterop/Excel.Interop

Prompt: Given an input that consists of an image containing the spreadsheet and a list which elements are cell values in that spreadsheet. Please output the address where it appears in the spreadsheet for each cell value in the list in the order in the list. Specifically:
1. The cell values contained in the list are arranged in order from top to bottom and from left to right. If the cell value is empty, it does not appear in the list.
2. Cells are referenced by the column and row indices. The address of the first cell in the upper left corner of the spreadsheet is "1,1". The number of columns increases from left to right, and the number of rows increases from top to bottom.
3. The output should be strictly in the following JSON format(Don't output anything else).

```
{
  "Cell-1":["Address-1"],
  "Cell-2":["Address-2"],
  "Cell-3":["Address-3"],
  ...
}
```

Note that the above data such as "Address-1" is replaced with the real "row number, column number", and the data such as "Cell-1" is replaced with the real cell value.
Here are the image and the list:
<image> <values list>

Figure 5: The prompt for vanilla experiment of spatial position perception task.

Prompt: I have provided an image of a spreadsheet. The first cell in the upper left corner of the spreadsheet is addressed as "1,1", representing the first row and first column. The column numbers increase from left to right, and the row numbers increase from top to bottom. Each cell can have one of six formats: "top-border" indicates if the cell has a top border; "bottom-border" if it has a bottom border; "left-border" if it has a left border; "right-border" if it has a right border; "bold font" if the font in the cell is bold; and "background color" denotes if the cell is filled with a color, with white indicating no fill. Your task is to output the addresses of all cells with each format, arranged from left to right and top to bottom. The output should strictly adhere to the following JSON format (please do not output anything else):

```
{
  "top-border": ["Address-1", "Address-2", ...],
  "bottom-border": ["Address-1", "Address-2", ...],
  "left-border": ["Address-1", "Address-2", ...],
  "right-border": ["Address-1", "Address-2", ...],
  "font bold": ["Address-1", "Address-2", ...],
  "background color": ["Address-1", "Address-2", ...]
}
```

In this structure, 'Address' refers to the cell address, such as '1,2', '2,4', etc.
Here is the image:
<image>

Figure 6: The prompt for vanilla experiment of visual format recognition task.

4.3 Spatial Position Perception

We prompt the VLMs to recognize the spatial positions of specified cells ensuring that each cell value and its address correspond uniquely. Figure. 5 provides a prompt for vanilla experiment, other prompts see Appendix A.

Specifically, we input a spreadsheet image along with a list of randomly shuffled cell values into the VLMs. Then, we prompt the VLMs to output the address corresponding to each value. It is important to note that for the vanilla, colwidth adjust, and style change experiments, the input image does not contain cell addresses. Therefore, the addresses output by the VLMs should be composed of the row and column indices of the cell, in the form "2,3". In contrast, the address augment experiment outputs addresses in the form "C2".

4.4 Visual Format Recognition

We have defined six specific cell formats: top border, bottom border, left border, right border, bold font, and fill color. For each format, we instruct the VLMs to identify and output the addresses of all cells that exhibit the specified format. Figure. 6 provides a prompt for vanilla experiment, other prompts see Appendix A.

This experiment is similar to the spatial position perception experiment. The addresses output by the vanilla and colwidth adjust experiments should be composed of the row and column indices of the cell in the form "1,2", while the address augment experiment outputs addresses in the form "B1".

4.5 Spreadsheet Table Detection

We instruct VLMs to detect all table ranges from spreadsheet images. Figure. 7 provides a prompt for vanilla experiment, other prompts see Appendix A.

By convention, contiguous cell ranges are represented by the addresses of the upper left and lower right cells, separated by ":", and cells are referenced by their column and row indices, e.g., "A4:D120". However, when presenting a spreadsheet as an image input to the VLMs, the image may lack the ability to deduce the cell addresses. To address this challenge, we propose a novel approach where the VLMs directly decode the contents of the four boundaries of the table. Subsequently, these decoded contents are mapped to a conventional addresses using our proposed method as introduced in the follow paragraph.

Specifically, except for the address augment experiment, which can directly output a range in the form "A4:D120," the other experiments output the result by decoding the four boundaries.

Mapping Algorithm: Consider a spreadsheet S comprising m rows and n columns, where each cell is represented by $c_{i,j}$, with i and j denoting its row and column index, respectively, within the spreadsheet.

$$S = \begin{bmatrix} c_{1,1} & c_{1,2} & \cdots & c_{1,n} \\ c_{2,1} & c_{2,2} & \cdots & c_{2,n} \\ \vdots & \vdots & \ddots & \vdots \\ c_{m,1} & c_{m,2} & \cdots & c_{m,n} \end{bmatrix} \quad (1)$$

By allowing the model to decode the four boundaries of all tables, we obtain the model's prediction result denoted as $Predict = [T_1, T_2, ...]$. Among them, T_i means the predicted four boundaries of the i-th table, that is,

$$T_i = \left\{ \begin{array}{l} B_t : [c_1, c_2, \ldots, c_t], \\ B_b : [c_1, c_2, \ldots, c_b], \\ B_l : [c_1, c_2, \ldots, c_l], \\ B_r : [c_1, c_2, \ldots, c_r] \end{array} \right\} \quad (2)$$

Among them, B_t, B_b, B_l and B_r represent the contents of *top_border*, *bottom_border*, *left_border* and *right_border* respectively. For top_border and bottom_border, we can map it to the most likely row index in the spreadsheet through algorithm 1. For left_border and right_border, we only need to transpose them and do the same. Finally, after we obtain the row/column index corresponding to each predicted border, we process it into a region such as "A1:D9".

Algorithm 1: Map the content of a specific row to the corresponding row index.

Input : The border content B predicted by the model and the contents S of the spreadsheet.
Initialize the origin confidence $Conf$ to 0.8.;
Initial the result index res to -1.;
for $i = 1$ **to** $|S|$ **do**
    if $|S[i]| \geq |B|$ **then**
        $tList \leftarrow S[i]$;
        $sList \leftarrow B$;
    end
    else
        $tList \leftarrow B$;
        $sList \leftarrow S[i]$;
    end
    $sCnt \leftarrow |sList|$;
    $tCnt \leftarrow |tList|$;
    for $j = 1$ **to** $tCnt$ **do**
        if $j + shortCnt > tCnt$ **then**
            Break;
        end
        $cConf \leftarrow \frac{\sum_{k=1}^{sCnt}(sList[k]==tList[k])}{\text{sCnt}}$;
        if $cConf \geq Conf$ **then**
            $res \leftarrow i$;
            $Conf \leftarrow cConf$;
        end
    end
end
Output : the result index res.

5 Experiment Setting

We conducted experiments using GPT-4V (*2024-02-15 preview*) (Achiam et al., 2023) and Gemini (*1.5-pro lateset until 2024-05-16*) (Team et al., 2023). To ensure consistent experimental parameters, we set the generation temperature for both GPT-4V and Gemini-pro to 0.7, top_p to 0.95, and max_output_token to 4096.

Due to GPT-4V's input image restrictions—specifically, that the image file size must be less than 4MB and the resolution must

Prompt: The picture I provide is a spreadsheet. I need your help to find all the tables in the spreadsheet and return the boundaries of each table. Specifically, for each table boundary, find: (1) the top-most-row, (2) the bottom-most-row, (3) the left-most-column and (4) the right-most-column. Please output the results according to the following rules.
1. Please strictly follow the format to return each cell value on the table boundaries for each table. The cell values must be output accurately and in order (just output the values shown on the picture);
2. The values of the vertex cell in the upper left corner of the table should appear on both the top-most row and left-most column, and the value of the vertex cell in the lower right corner of the table appear on both the right-most column and bottom-most-row;
3. If some cell values are empty, do not output these cells;
4. Keep in mind that tables don't contain titles and comments, but may contain header rows (head or left), which help you find the correct table.
If you have two tables in an Excel spreadsheet, the output format should be as follows (don't output anything else):

```
[
  {
    "top-most-row": ["cell-1", "cell-2", ...],
    "bottom-most-row": ["cell-1", "cell-2", ...],
    "left-most-column": ["cell-1", "cell-2", ...],
    "right-most-column": ["cell-1", "cell-2", ...]
  },
  {
    "top-most-row": ["cell-1", "cell-2", ...],
    "bottom-most-row": ["cell-1", "cell-2", ...],
    "left-most-column": ["cell-1", "cell-2", ...],
    "right-most-column": ["cell-1", "cell-2", ...]
  }
]
```

Here's the input image:
<image>

Figure 7: Zero-shot prompt for vanilla images decoding four boundaries on spreadsheet table detection task.

be between 50×50 and $10,000 \times 10,000$ pixels—we filtered 76 images from the test dataset of TableSense (Dong et al., 2019) to meet these criteria. For each experiment, we evaluate the models using precision, recall, and F1, repeating each experiment three times and taking the average results.

6 Experiment Result

6.1 Performance of Optical Character Recognition

Table. 1 presents the OCR task results of GPT-4V and Gemini-pro, calculated using both Strict and LCS matching methods. From the table, we can observe:

1) Both GPT-4V and Gemini-pro are generally capable of accurately recognizing the content in spreadsheet images. Specifically, the best performance of GPT-4V and Gemini-pro can reach F1 scores of 79.59% and 81.85%, respectively, demonstrating their strong ability to recognize content in a two-dimensional grid.

2) For both GPT-4V and Gemini-pro, the performance of LCS matching far exceeds that of Strict matching, indicating that they tend to miss some cells or predict misalignments during performing OCR task, causing almost all predictions to be incorrect from the first missed cell in Strict matching. Specifically, GPT-4V's F1 scores under LCS matching are higher than Strict matching by 54.98%, 62.63%, and 52.98% and Gemini-pro's F1 scores under LCS matching are higher by 66.51%, 65.16%, and 66.9% for the three different inputs, respectively.

3) Preprocessing spreadsheets by adjusting column width significantly enhances the OCR capabilities of VLMs on spreadsheet images, but further preprocessing with style change does not improve

%		Strict match			LCS match		
		Precision	Recall	F1	Precision	Recall	F1
	Vanilla	14.78	12.68	13.65	74.32	63.74	68.63
GPT-4V	ColWidth Adjust	17.87	15.24	16.96	83.87	75.74	79.59
	Style Change	27.44	25.54	26.46	82.40	76.69	79.44
	Vanilla	9.26	8.08	8.63	80.61	70.39	75.14
Gemini-pro	ColWidth Adjust	16.13	13.03	14.42	89.03	71.94	79.58
	Style Change	16.40	13.74	14.95	89.80	75.20	81.85

Table 1: Precision, recall and F1 results of GPT-4V and Gemini-pro on OCR task. Among them, colwidth adjust is the processing operation of column width adjustment.

the OCR performance of VLMs. Specifically, adjusting column width can increase GPT-4V's F1 scores by 3.31% and 10.96% in the Strict match and LCS match methods, respectively, and increase Gemini-pro's F1 scores by 5.79% and 4.44% in the Strict match and LCS match methods, respectively.

4) Gemini-pro's OCR capability on spreadsheet images is slightly stronger than that of GPT-4V. Specifically, in the vanilla and style change experiments, Gemini-pro's F1 scores are 6.51% and 2.41% higher than those of GPT-4V, respectively.

Finally, we analyze the results of GPT4-V on a case in detail in Appendix B.1.

%		Precision	Recall	F1
	$\text{Vanilla}_{\text{number}}$	12.44	12.37	12.41
GPT-4V	$\text{ColWidth Adjust}_{\text{number}}$	13.45	13.35	13.39
	$\text{Style Change}_{\text{number}}$	12.16	12.14	12.15
	$\text{Address Augment}_{\text{address}}$	48.87	49.09	48.97
	$\text{Vanilla}_{\text{number}}$	16.72	18.00	17.33
Gemini-pro	$\text{ColWidth Adjust}_{\text{number}}$	14.29	15.40	14.82
	$\text{Style Change}_{\text{number}}$	16.75	18.13	17.41
	$\text{Address Augment}_{\text{address}}$	83.66	87.53	85.55

Table 2: Precision, recall and F1 results of GPT-4V and Gemini-pro on spatial position perception task.

%		Precision	Recall	F1
GPT-4V	$\text{Vanilla}_{\text{number}}$	24.97	11.69	15.79
	$\text{ColWidth Adjust}_{\text{number}}$	24.31	11.07	14.77
	$\text{Address Augment}_{\text{address}}$	28.88	13.28	17.83
Gemini-pro	$\text{Vanilla}_{\text{number}}$	35.27	13.28	17.53
	$\text{ColWidth Adjust}_{\text{number}}$	35.09	12.69	16.93
	$\text{Address Augment}_{\text{address}}$	41.93	16.78	22.19

Table 3: Precision, recall and F1 results of GPT-4V and Gemini-pro on visual format recognition task.

6.2 Performance of Spatial Position Perception

Table 2 shows the results of GPT-4V and Gemini-pro in performing spatial position perception tasks. Analyzing the results in Table 2, we first observe that GPT-4V and Gemini-pro perform poorly in the vanilla, colwidth adjust, and style change experiments. This underperformance is attributed to the three types of experiments demanding that the VLMs count the rows and columns in the spreadsheet. However, the boundaries of rows and columns in the spreadsheet are often unclear due to the lack of borders or the presence of line breaks that cause content overlap (e.g., "A5", "C3", etc. in Figure. 1).

Secondly, we noted that although preprocessing spreadsheets with address augment can significantly enhance the performance of both GPT-4V and Gemini-pro, since address augment allows VLMs to fully utilize their OCR capabilities, GPT-4V does not achieve the same level of OCR performance as Gemini-pro. This suggests that GPT-4V may not understand the task prompts as thoroughly as Gemini-pro.

In addition, we observe that in the four types of experiments, Gemini-pro outperform GPT-4V in F1 scores by 4.92%, 1.43%, 5.26%, and 36.58%, respectively, indicating that Gemini-pro has a stronger spatial position perception capability in spreadsheet image tasks.

Finally, we analyze the results of GPT4-V on a case in detail in Appendix B.2.

6.3 Performance of Visual Format Recognition

Table 3 presents the results of GPT-4V and Gemini-pro in testing their ability to recognition the visual

%		Zero-Shot			One-Shot			Trained		
		Precision	Recall	F1	Precision	Recall	F1	Precision	Recall	F1
GPT-4V	Vanilla$_{four}$	52.38	10.23	17.11	49.29	8.66	14.68	-	-	-
	ColWidth Adjust$_{four}$	49.43	17.49	25.79	48.72	15.10	23.05	-	-	-
	Address Augment$_{range}$	9.26	14.85	11.41	14.60	13.86	14.22	-	-	-
Gemini-pro	Vanilla$_{four}$	25.96	18.40	21.53	35.82	6.98	11.67	-	-	-
	ColWidth Adjust$_{four}$	26.66	22.40	24.33	26.93	7.03	11.15	-	-	-
	Address Augment$_{range}$	9.08	19.94	12.47	7.62	15.55	10.00	-	-	-
TableSense	Text Input	-	-	-	-	-	-	80.21	76.24	78.17

Table 4: Precision, recall and F1 results of GPT-4V, Gemini-pro and TableSense (Dong et al., 2019) on spreadsheet table detection task.

format information in spreadsheet images. The results indicate that the best F1 scores for GPT-4V and Gemini-pro across multiple experiments are only 17.83% and 22.19%, respectively. This demonstrates that their ability to comprehend format information in images is quite poor and that they cannot deeply understand images by combining format information as humans do. Therefore, this is an area where VLMs need improvement in the future. Additionally, in two types of experiments, Gemini-pro's F1 scores are higher than GPT-4V's by 1.74%, 2.16% and 4.36%, respectively, indicating that Gemini-pro again has a slight edge over GPT-4V in this aspect.

Then, we analyze the results of GPT4-V on a case in detail in Appendix B.3.

6.4 Performance of Spreadsheet Table Detection

The results of GPT-4V and Gemini-pro for the spreadsheet table detection task are shown in Table 4. Firstly, we can see that the F1 scores obtained by having the VLMs decode the four boundaries and then applying our proposed mapping algorithm are significantly higher than those obtained by directly outputting the address range (e.g., "A1:C10"). Specifically, GPT-4V's zero-shot performance is 5.7% and 14.38% higher, and Gemini-pro's is 9.06% and 11,86% higher,respectively, which can be attributed to their excellent OCR capabilities.

Secondly, both GPT-4V and Gemini-pro fall significantly short when compared to TableSense, with the closest F1 result still being 52.38% lower. However, it is worth noting that TableSense inputs inputs serialized text from the spreadsheet, whereas the VLMs we are exploring take images as input. This indicates that there is a long way to go in continuously improving VLMs to achieve results comparable to text input.

Moreover, we observed an anomalous result: the one-shot results of GPT-4V and Gemini-pro are generally worse than their zero-shot results. This might be due to the complex structure of spreadsheets, where providing an example can lead VLMs to favor outputs with structures similar to the example, resulting in misjudgments.

Finally, we analyze the results of GPT4-V on a case in detail in Appendix B.4.

7 Conclusion and Future Work

In this paper, we develop a suite of probing tasks aimed at evaluating the critical capabilities of VLMs in OCR, comprehension of formatting details, and recognition of spatial positioning within spreadsheet images. Our findings demonstrate that while VLMs possess strong OCR capabilities, they are prone to cell omission and prediction misalignment during OCR tasks on spreadsheet images. Furthermore, their spatial perception is insufficient, as they struggle to accurately determine the row and column numbers of cells in a two-dimensional spreadsheet grid. Surprisingly, VLMs cannot comprehend visual formats well like humans. Additionally, we introduce a spreadsheet table detection task designed to thoroughly assess the ability of VLMs to interpret spreadsheet images effectively. However, the performance of this task falls short of that achieved by existing SOTA method, indicating that processing and comprehending spreadsheets remains a significant challenge.

Future research could focus on handling larger spreadsheet images and segmenting these spreadsheets without compromising the integrity of their format and spatial relationships. Despite these challenges, the potential benefits of treating spreadsheets as images are substantial. In this paper, we have proposed methods that can massively generate spreadsheet-image pairs, and under our proposed settings, we can control various challenges. Utilizing these methods to generate large amounts of data, we train open-source large models to enhance their understanding of structured data on grids, further advancing the comprehensive capabilities of large models towards AGI.

References

Josh Achiam, Steven Adler, Sandhini Agarwal, Lama Ahmad, Ilge Akkaya, Florencia Leoni Aleman, Diogo Almeida, Janko Altenschmidt, Sam Altman, Shyamal Anadkat, et al. 2023. Gpt-4 technical report. *arXiv preprint arXiv:2303.08774*.

David Birch, David Lyford-Smith, and Yike Guo. 2018. The future of spreadsheets in the big data era. *arXiv preprint arXiv:1801.10231*.

Wenhu Chen, Hongmin Wang, Jianshu Chen, Yunkai Zhang, Hong Wang, Shiyang Li, Xiyou Zhou, and William Yang Wang. 2020. Tabfact: A large-scale dataset for table-based fact verification. *Preprint*, arXiv:1909.02164.

Yibin Chen, Yifu Yuan, Zeyu Zhang, Yan Zheng, Jinyi Liu, Fei Ni, and Jianye Hao. 2024. Sheetagent: A generalist agent for spreadsheet reasoning and manipulation via large language models. *arXiv preprint arXiv:2403.03636*.

Naihao Deng, Zhenjie Sun, Ruiqi He, Aman Sikka, Yulong Chen, Lin Ma, Yue Zhang, and Rada Mihalcea. 2024. Tables as images? exploring the strengths and limitations of llms on multimodal representations of tabular data. *arXiv preprint arXiv:2402.12424*.

Haoyu Dong, Shijie Liu, Shi Han, Zhouyu Fu, and Dongmei Zhang. 2019. Tablesense: Spreadsheet table detection with convolutional neural networks. In *Proceedings of the AAAI conference on artificial intelligence*, volume 33, pages 69–76.

Jing Fang, Prasenjit Mitra, Zhi Tang, and C Lee Giles. 2012. Table header detection and classification. In *Proceedings of the AAAI Conference on Artificial Intelligence*, volume 26, pages 599–605.

Jiayan Guo, Lun Du, and Hengyu Liu. 2023. Gpt4graph: Can large language models understand graph structured data? an empirical evaluation and benchmarking. *arXiv preprint arXiv:2305.15066*.

Yongshuai Huang, Ning Lu, Dapeng Chen, Yibo Li, Zecheng Xie, Shenggao Zhu, Liangcai Gao, and Wei Peng. 2023. Improving table structure recognition with visual-alignment sequential coordinate modeling. In *Proceedings of the IEEE/CVF Conference on Computer Vision and Pattern Recognition*, pages 11134–11143.

Jinhao Jiang, Kun Zhou, Zican Dong, Keming Ye, Wayne Xin Zhao, and Ji-Rong Wen. 2023. Structgpt: A general framework for large language model to reason over structured data. *arXiv preprint arXiv:2305.09645*.

Hugo Laurençon, Léo Tronchon, Matthieu Cord, and Victor Sanh. 2024. What matters when building vision-language models? *arXiv preprint arXiv:2405.02246*.

Hongxin Li, Jingran Su, Yuntao Chen, Qing Li, and ZHAO-XIANG ZHANG. 2024. Sheetcopilot: Bringing software productivity to the next level through large language models. *Advances in Neural Information Processing Systems*, 36.

Peng Li, Yeye He, Dror Yashar, Weiwei Cui, Song Ge, Haidong Zhang, Danielle Rifinski Fainman, Dongmei Zhang, and Surajit Chaudhuri. 2023. Table-gpt: Table-tuned gpt for diverse table tasks. *arXiv preprint arXiv:2310.09263*.

Nam Tuan Ly and Atsuhiro Takasu. 2023. An end-to-end multi-task learning model for image-based table recognition. *arXiv preprint arXiv:2303.08648*.

A Nassar, N Livathinos, M Lysak, and PWJ Staar. Tableformer: table structure understanding with transformers. corr abs/2203.01017 (2022).

Jekaterina Novikova, Ondřej Dušek, and Verena Rieser. 2017. The e2e dataset: New challenges for end-to-end generation. *Preprint*, arXiv:1706.09254.

Panupong Pasupat and Percy Liang. 2015. Compositional semantic parsing on semi-structured tables. *Preprint*, arXiv:1508.00305.

Mukul Singh, José Cambronero, Sumit Gulwani, Vu Le, and Gust Verbruggen. 2023. Assessing gpt4-v on structured reasoning tasks. *arXiv preprint arXiv:2312.11524*.

Ananya Singha, José Cambronero, Sumit Gulwani, Vu Le, and Chris Parnin. 2023. Tabular representation, noisy operators, and impacts on table structure understanding tasks in llms. *arXiv preprint arXiv:2310.10358*.

Yuan Sui, Mengyu Zhou, Mingjie Zhou, Shi Han, and Dongmei Zhang. 2023a. Gpt4table: Can large language models understand structured table data? a benchmark and empirical study. *arXiv preprint ArXiv:2305.13062*.

Yuan Sui, Jiaru Zou, Mengyu Zhou, Xinyi He, Lun Du, Shi Han, and Dongmei Zhang. 2023b. Tap4llm: Table provider on sampling, augmenting, and packing semi-structured data for large language model reasoning. *arXiv preprint arXiv:2312.09039*.

Xiangru Tang, Yiming Zong, Yilun Zhao, Arman Cohan, and Mark Gerstein. 2023. Struc-bench: Are large language models really good at generating complex structured data? *arXiv preprint arXiv:2309.08963*.

Gemini Team, Rohan Anil, Sebastian Borgeaud, Yonghui Wu, Jean-Baptiste Alayrac, Jiahui Yu, Radu Soricut, Johan Schalkwyk, Andrew M Dai, Anja Hauth, et al. 2023. Gemini: a family of highly capable multimodal models. *arXiv preprint arXiv:2312.11805*.

Xindong Wu, Hao Chen, Chenyang Bu, Shengwei Ji, Zan Zhang, and Victor S Sheng. 2023. Huss: A heuristic method for understanding the semantic structure of spreadsheets. *Data Intelligence*, 5(3):537–559.

Tianshu Zhang, Xiang Yue, Yifei Li, and Huan Sun. 2023. Tablellama: Towards open large generalist models for tables. *arXiv preprint arXiv:2311.09206*.

A Prompt Examples

Figure. 8 shows the prompt for address augment experiment in spatial position perception task; Figure. 9 shows the prompt for address augment experiment in visual format recognition task; Figure. 10 shows the prompt for spreadsheet table detection task under different experiment setting and output format.

Prompt: Given an input that consists of an image containing the spreadsheet and a list which elements are cell values in that spreadsheet. Please output the address where it appears in the spreadsheet for each cell value in the list in the order in the list. Specifically:
1. Each cell in the spreadsheet contains a cell address and its corresponding value, separated by a comma, for example, "A1,Year". The value may be empty, resulting in cell content like "A1,".
2. The cell values contained in the list are arranged in order from top to bottom and from left to right. If the cell value is empty, it does not appear in the list.
3. The output should be strictly in the following JSON format(Don't output anything else).
{
"Cell-1":["Address-1"],
"Cell-2":["Address-2"],
"Cell-3":["Address-3"],
...
}
Note that the above data such as "Address-1" is replaced with the real cell address and the data such as "Cell-1" is replaced with the real cell value.
Here are the image and the list:
<image> <values list>

Figure 8: The prompt for address augment experiments of spatial position perception task.

Prompt: The provided image depicts the spreadsheet where each cell contains a cell address and its corresponding value, separated by a comma, for example, "A1,Year". The value may be empty, resulting in cell content like "A1,". Each cell may have six formats. Specifically, the "top-border" indicates whether the cell has a top border, the "bottom-border" indicates whether the cell has a bottom border, the "left-border" indicates whether the cell has a left border, and the "right-border" indicates whether there is a right border, the "bold font" indicates whether the font in the cell is bold, and the "background color" indicates whether the cell is filled with the background color (white represents no filling). For each format, your task is to output the addresses of all cells with this format, arranged from left to right and top to bottom. The output should strictly adhere to the following JSON format(Don't output anything else):
{
"top-border": ["Address-1", "Address-2", ...],
"bottom-border": ["Address-1", "Address-2", ...],
"left-border": ["Address-1", "Address-2", ...],
"right-border": ["Address-1", "Address-2", ...],
"font bold": ["Address-1", "Address-2", ...],
"background color": ["Address-1", "Address-2", ...]
}
In this structure, "Address" represents the cell address.
Here's the image:
<image>

Figure 9: The prompt for address augment experiments of visual format recognition task.

Prompt: The image I provide is a spreadsheet. The address of the first cell in the upper left corner of the spreadsheet is "1,1", which is the first row and first column. The number of columns increases from left to right, and the number of rows increases from top to bottom. I need you to find the range of each table in the spreadsheet. For each table, find: (1) the number of top row, (2) the number of bottom row, (3) the number of leftmost column and (4) the number of rightmost column. Specifically:
1. There may be one or more tables in the spreadsheet, so all RANGE should be returned strictly in the list form, for example ["number_top, number_bottom, number_left, number_right",...] (don't output anything else).
2. Keep in mind that tables don't contain titles and comments, but may contain header rows (head or left), which help you find the correct table.
Here's the input image:
<image>

(a) The zero-shot prompt for outputting ranges in vanilla experiments.

Prompt: The provided image depicts the spreadsheet where each cell contains a cell address and its corresponding value, separated by a comma, for example, "A1,Year". The value may be empty, resulting in cell content like "A1,". I need you to find the range of each table in the spreadsheet and output addresses of the cells in the top-left and bottom-right corners separated by ":", like "Address-1: Address-2". Specifically:
1. There may be one or more tables in a spreadsheet, so you should output all the RANGE in list form: ["Address_1:Address_2", "Address_3:Address_4", ...], don't output anything else.
2. Keep in mind that tables don't contain notes, captions and comments, but may contain table headers and row headers, which help you find the correct table.
Here's the input image:
<image>

(b) The zero-shot prompt for outputting ranges in address augment experiments.

Prompt: The picture I provide is a spreadsheet. I need your help to find the number of tables in the spreadsheet and the boundaries of each table. Specifically, for each table boundary, find: (1) the top-most-row, (2) the bottom-most-row, (3) the left-most-column and (4) the right-most-column. Please output the results according to the following rules.
1. Please strictly follow the format to return the number of tables you find and each cell value on the table boundaries. The cell values must be output accurately and in order (just output the values shown on the picture);
2. If some cell values are empty, do not output these cells;
3. The values of the vertex cell in the upper left corner of the table should appear on both the top-most row and left-most column, and the value of the vertex cell in the lower right corner of the table appear on both the right-most column and bottom-most-row;
4. Keep in mind that tables don't contain titles and comments, but may contain header rows (head or left), which help you find the correct table.
If you have two tables in an Excel spreadsheet, the output format should be as follows (don't output anything else):
[
{
"top-most-row": ["cell-1", "cell-2", ...],
"bottom-most-row": ["cell-1", "cell-2", ...],
"left-most-column": ["cell-1", "cell-2", ...],
"right-most-column": ["cell-1", "cell-2", ...]
},
{
"top-most-row": ["cell-1", "cell-2", ...],
"bottom-most-row": ["cell-1", "cell-2", ...],
"left-most-column": ["cell-1", "cell-2", ...],
"right-most-column": ["cell-1", "cell-2", ...]
}
]
I have given two pictures containing the spreadsheet, the first is an example I gave, which will be introduced below; the second is the picture I need you to give answers according to the requirements above.
Example:
Input: The first image
Output:
[
{
"top-most-row": ["Industry Group", "Project Name", "Responsible Pa", "Project Type", "SS Exposure", "Assessment of R", "Updated", "Update/Comments"],
"bottom-most-row": ["Torradyne Group", "--", "Sold?", "1/8/2000"],
"left-most-column": ["Industry Group", "Coal", "Exploration / E", "Acquisition & D", "Oil Field Servi", "Pulp & Paper", "Steel", "Other"],
"right-most-column": ["Update/Comments"]
}
]
Input: The second image
Output:

(c) The one-shot prompt for decoding four boundaries in vanilla experiments

Prompt: The provided image depicts the spreadsheet where each cell contains a cell address and its corresponding value, separated by a comma, for example, "A1,Year". The value may be empty, resulting in cell content like "A1,". I need you to find the range of each table in the spreadsheet and output addresses of the cells in the top-left and bottom-right corners separated by ':', like "Address-1: Address-2". Specifically:
1. There may be one or more tables in a spreadsheet, so you should output all the RANGE in list form: ["Address_1:Address_2", "Address_3:Address_4", ...], don't output anything else.
2. Keep in mind that tables don't contain titles and comments, but may contain header rows (head or left), which help you find the correct table.
I have given two pictures containing the spreadsheet, the first is an example I gave, which will be introduced below; the second is the picture I need you to give answers according to the requirements above.
Example:
Input: The first image
Output:
["A3:H57"]
Input: The second image
Output:

(d) The one-shot prompt for outputting ranges in address augment experiments.

Figure 10: The prompt of spreadsheet table detection task.

B Case Study

B.1 A case of OCR task

In order to deeply explore the impact of different reconstructed spreadsheet images on GPT-4V's OCR capabilities, we will analyze the case shown in Figure. 12 in detail.

First, by comparing the results of Figure. 12a and Figure. 12b, we can clearly find that not adjusting the column width in the spreadsheet will cause the OCR capability of GPT-4V to drop significantly. This is due to the fact that the cell content in many spreadsheets will not be fully displayed when the column width is not adjusted, and there may be overlap or coverage between adjacent cells, as shown in Figure. 12a.

Secondly, by observing these three pictures, we will find that GPT-4V has insufficient positioning capabilities when performing OCR, resulting in some cells being missed or misplaced during the prediction process. For example, GPT-4V's prediction results for the three pictures in Figure. 12 ignore the first two lines of the spreadsheet, and in both Figure. 12b and Figure. 12c, GPT-4V predicts "Aronowitz, Alan" to "713-858-7795" After, but actually it should be in front.

B.2 A case of spatial position perception task

Figure. 11 presents a tangible example evaluating GPT-4V's proficiency in spatial position awareness within spreadsheet environments. Upon scrutiny, it's apparent that even in relatively straightforward scenarios, both vanilla and style change experi-

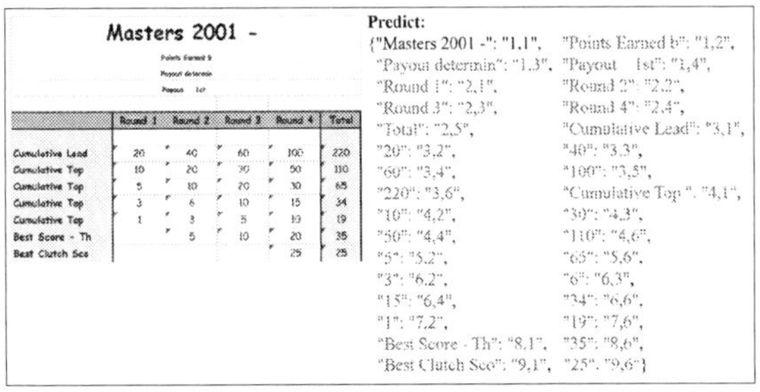

(a) Vanilla

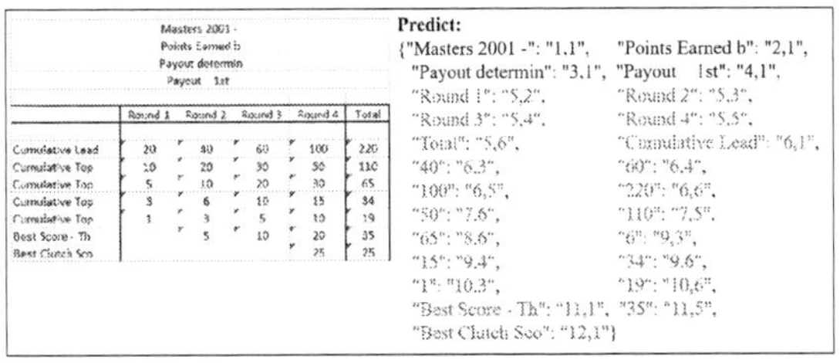

(b) Style Change

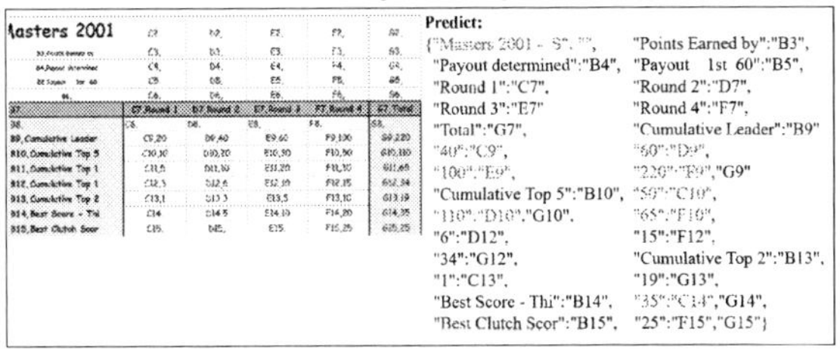

(c) Address Augment

Figure 11: An example of GPT-4V on spatial position perception task. The content marked in red indicates the LCS match error prediction

ments reveal GPT-4V's inadequate performance in accurately predicting position. While GPT-4V effectively forecasts column positions for most cells, it consistently struggles with row positions, consistently displaying an offset. This issue becomes more pronounced in the presence of empty rows, leading to inaccuracies in subsequent cell position predictions.

In contrast, the address augment experiment showcases a comparatively better performance by GPT-4V. This improvement can be attributed to its impressive OCR capabilities, allowing it to accurately identify and pair cell addresses with their corresponding values within a single cell.

B.3 A case of visual format recognition task

The case depicted in Figure. 14 presents the outcomes of GPT-4V's analysis under vanilla and address augment experiments. Examination of these results reveals GPT-4V's limited grasp of format information in both scenarios, indicating its potential inability to comprehend spreadsheet format details akin to humans, likely due to image encoding constraints. Upon meticulous scrutiny of GPT-4V's outputs, a discernible trend emerges: it tends to follow imaginary rules to identify locations featuring specific formats. For instance, under the vanilla experiment, GPT-4V consistently identifies the three-line area spanning from "1,1: 1,6", "2,1:2,6", and "6,1:6,6" for bottom borders. Similarly, under the address agument condition, it consistently outputs areas such as "A1:F1", "A5:F5", and "A7:F7" representing top borders.

B.4 A case of spreadsheet table detection task

In order to explore the performance of GPT-4V on the spreadsheet table detection task, We will analyze the case in detail.

First, by analyzing Figure. 14a, we can find that the reason why one-shot effect is worse than zero-shot effect is that the example we give always have inevitable biases, which will induce the VLMs to make wrong judgments, even worse than the VLMs' own judgment under zero-shot setting. Furthermore, VLMs have serious hallucination problems so in one-shot experiments settings, there is always a tendency to output example answers as part of the results.

Second, by comparing predictions in Figure. 14b, we can find that the GPT-4V makes an error to directly output the address of the table range, while GPT-4V correctly output the values on the four boundaries of the table. According to the previous experiment results, we learn that the VLMs has poor spatial perception of spreadsheet images, so it's hard for them to infer the address of table ranges accurately. In contrast, VLMs has quite strong OCR capabilities, which allow to decode the cell values on the table boundaries.

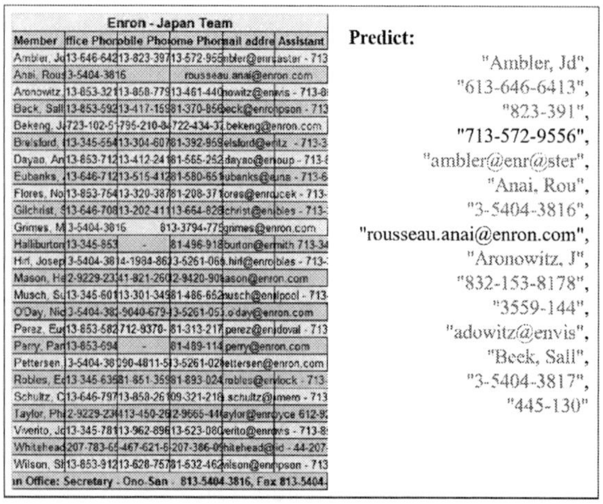

(a) Vanilla

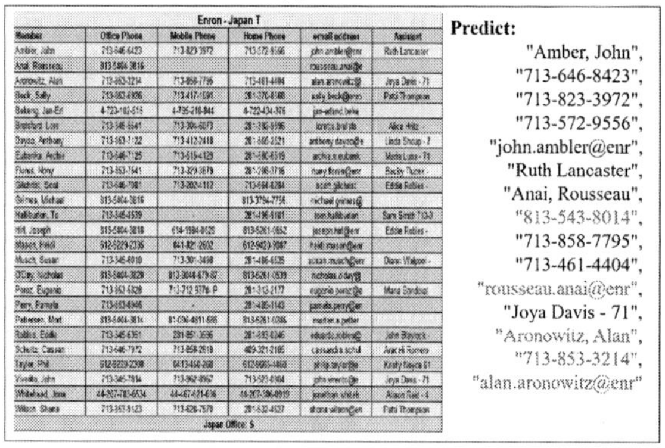

(b) ColWidth Adjust

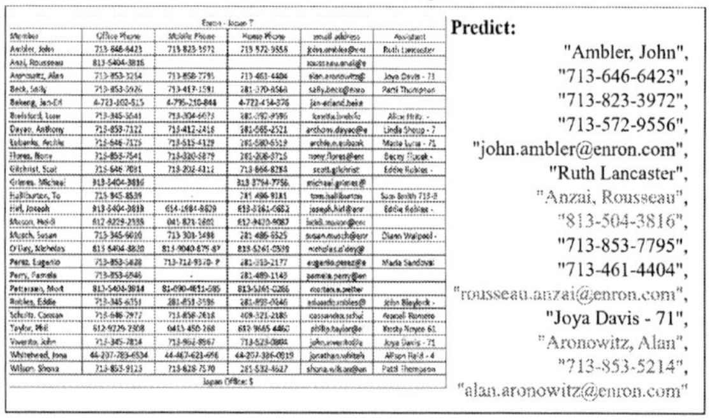

(c) Style Change

Figure 12: An example of GPT-4V on OCR task. Due to space limitations, only the contents of the first 15 cells are shown. The content marked in red indicates the LCS match error prediction.

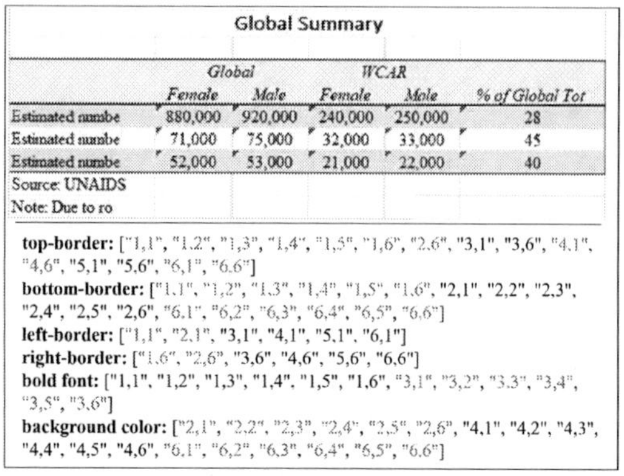

(a) Vanilla

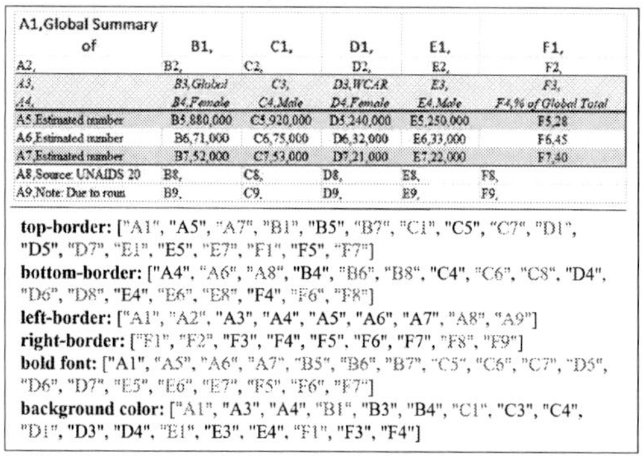

(b) Address Augment

Figure 13: An example of GPT-4V on visual format recognition task. The content marked in red indicates the wrong predictions.

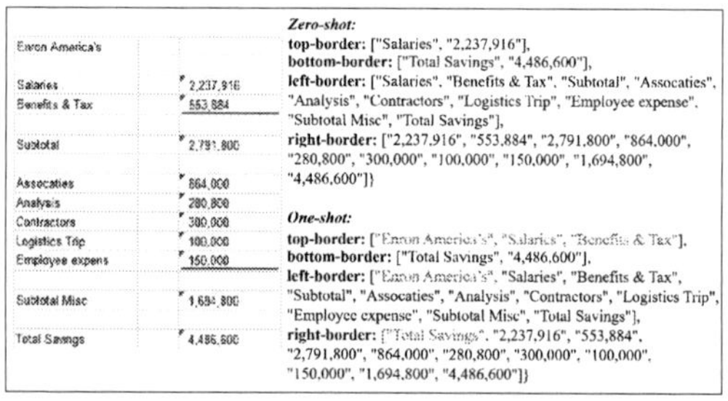

(a) zeroshot vs. oneshot

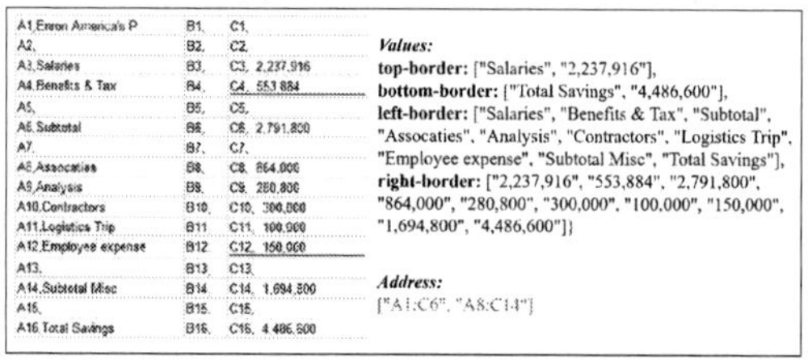

(b) four vs. range

Figure 14: An example of GPT-4V on spreadsheet table detection task. The red color represents the wrong predictions.

SlideAVSR: A Dataset of Paper Explanation Videos for Audio-Visual Speech Recognition

Hao Wang[1] **Shuhei Kurita**[2] **Shuichiro Shimizu**[3] **Daisuke Kawahara**[1,2,4]
[1] Waseda University [2] National Institute of Informatics (NII) [3] Kyoto University [4] LLMC, NII
conan1024hao@akane.waseda.jp skurita@nii.ac.jp
sshimizu@nlp.ist.i.kyoto-u.ac.jp dkw@waseda.jp

Abstract

Audio-visual speech recognition (AVSR) is a multimodal extension of automatic speech recognition (ASR), using video as a complement to audio. In AVSR, considerable efforts have been directed at datasets for facial features such as lip-readings, while they often fall short in evaluating the image comprehension capabilities in broader contexts. In this paper, we construct **SlideAVSR**, an AVSR dataset using scientific paper explanation videos. SlideAVSR provides a new benchmark where models transcribe speech utterances with texts on the slides on the presentation recordings. As technical terminologies that are frequent in paper explanations are notoriously challenging to transcribe without reference texts, our SlideAVSR dataset spotlights a new aspect of AVSR problems. As a simple yet effective baseline, we propose DocWhisper, an AVSR model that can refer to textual information from slides, and confirm its effectiveness on SlideAVSR.

1 Introduction

Research on multimodal models capable of handling multiple types of data, such as language, images, videos, and audio simultaneously, has garnered significant attention. An example is audio-visual speech recognition (AVSR), a multimodal extension of automatic speech recognition (ASR), using video as a complement to audio. Most previous studies in AVSR have been conducted with the aim of improving accuracy on lip reading datasets (Afouras et al., 2018a,b). While models built in these studies (Shi et al., 2022; Pan et al., 2022; Haliassos et al., 2023) demonstrate high performance on lip reading data, their applicability to other types of videos remains limited.

In this paper, we aim to evaluate the image comprehension capabilities of AVSR models across a broader spectrum of visual contents than facial features. To achieve this, we construct SlideAVSR, an AVSR dataset that contains various technical terms that are notoriously challenging to transcribe without referring to textual information on slides. Specifically, we collect scientific paper explanation videos from YouTube, apply data refinement procedures with several custom filters, and perform data partitioning considering the speakers' accents.

Furthermore, we propose DocWhisper, a simple yet effective AVSR baseline that can efficiently refer to the content of slides using optical character recognition (OCR). In experiments utilizing SlideAVSR, DocWhisper demonstrated a performance improvement of up to 14.3% compared to Whisper (Radford et al., 2022), which relies solely on audio input. Additionally, to address the long-tail problem in OCR results, we introduce FQ Ranker, which calculates word ranks based on the frequency of word occurrences, and we evaluate its effectiveness integrated with DocWhisper.

2 Related Work

Compared to the efforts that have been made on lip reading datasets (Chung et al., 2017; Chung and Zisserman, 2017a,b; Afouras et al., 2018a,b; Shillingford et al., 2019), AVSR datasets in other types of videos remain scarce. VisSpeech (Gabeur et al., 2022) is constructed from a subset of the instructional video dataset HowTo100M (Miech et al., 2019) where the visual stream and speech audio are semantically related. The audiovisual diarization benchmark in the Ego4D challenge (Jain et al., 2023) consists of 585 egocentric video clips. In terms of utilizing textual information extracted from videos, SlideSpeech (Wang et al., 2023) builds an AVSR dataset on online conference videos enriched with slides. However, the filtering process of SlideSpeech relies heavily on human annotators. In this work, we exclude videos and utterances that do not correspond to slides by utilizing a vision language model. This approach reduces annotation costs and enhances the purity and quality of our dataset within the slide domain.

In the context of extending Whisper to an AVSR model, Peng et al. (2023) employed CLIP (Radford et al., 2021) to transform the input visual stream into word sequences, which were then utilized as prompts for Whisper. They reported that this approach enhances the zero-shot performance on VisSpeech. In this study, we employ OCR to create prompts and implement fine-tuning to improve performance rather than using zero-shot prompting.

3 SlideAVSR: Dataset Construction

In this study, we construct SlideAVSR, an AVSR dataset based on scientific paper explanation videos incorporating various technical terms, making accurate transcription difficult without referring to the slides. Based on JTubeSpeech (Takamichi et al., 2021), a framework for building audio corpora from YouTube videos, we implement several custom filters to target videos, thereby applying high-precision data refinement. This section describes the construction flow of SlideAVSR. Figure 1 illustrates the flow.

3.1 Data Collection

Creating search queries. We first collect videos with search queries that are related to top conferences in the field of artificial intelligence. We create queries in the format {Conference} {Year} {Form}. The list of target conferences is provided in Appendix A. Considering the increased prevalence of online conferences since COVID-19, we focus on the years 2020 to 2023. The forms include "paper", "workshop", and "talk". An example search query is "ACL 2023 paper".

Obtaining videos with subtitles. Using the search queries, we retrieve video IDs with subtitles and download them.[1] To ensure data quality, only videos with manual subtitles are considered. Additionally, we set the following criteria:

- Duration between 5 and 20 minutes (videos that are too short or too long are less likely to be paper explanation videos).
- Video format: MP4, 720P, H264.
- Audio format: single-channel, 16bit, 16kHz.

A total of 636 videos were downloaded.

3.2 Filtering

We curate several filters to remove videos that are not paper explanations or do not include slides.

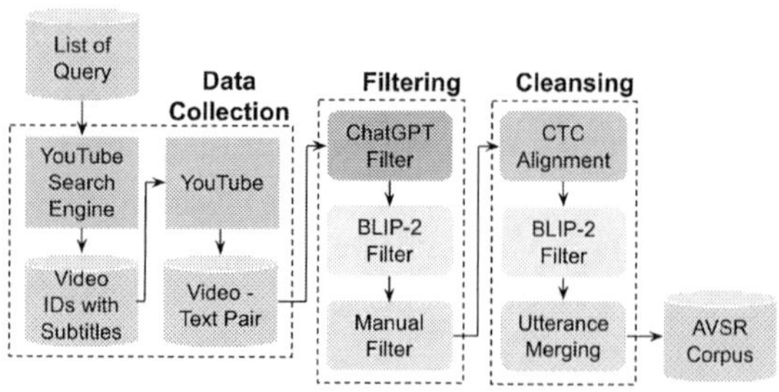

Figure 1: Construction flow of SlideAVSR.

ChatGPT filter. We provide the videos' description for ChatGPT[2] to confirm the following:

- This video is an explanation of a paper.
- The description is written in English.

We perform three times of generation, and if "Yes" is outputted at least once, we adopt the video; otherwise, we discard it. We show the details of the model and prompt in Appendix B. A total of 342 videos were excluded, leaving 294 videos for subsequent processes.

BLIP-2 filter for videos. We capture screenshots at the beginning, end, and three quartile points in the timeline for each video, and then present these screenshots to the vision language model BLIP-2 (Li et al., 2023) to verify the following:

- This image is a screenshot, not a photo.
- This image is a part of slides.

We perform generation for each screenshot, and if "Yes" is outputted at least once, we adopt the video; otherwise, we discard it. We show the details of the model and prompt in Appendix B. A total of 6 videos were excluded, leaving 288 videos for subsequent processes.

Manual filter. We conduct manual checks to remove inappropriate videos that are not excluded by the automatic filters, including:

- Videos rarely showing slides.
- Videos unrelated to paper explanations, such as conference openings.

A total of 38 videos were excluded, leaving 250 videos for subsequent processes.

3.3 Cleansing

We implement audio-subtitle alignment, exclude utterances that do not correspond to slides, and merge short utterances for data cleansing.

[1] https://github.com/yt-dlp/yt-dlp

[2] https://openai.com/product

CTC alignment. Due to the inaccuracy in the timing of subtitles, we implement audio-subtitle alignment and scoring using CTC segmentation (Kürzinger et al., 2020). We set the threshold to -7 and exclude utterances with lower scores. The details of the model are shown in Appendix B. Approximately 2.5% of utterances were excluded through this process.

BLIP-2 filter for utterances. We capture screenshots at the midpoint of each utterance, followed by filtering using BLIP-2. Three generations are conducted for each screenshot, and if "Yes" is outputted at least once, we adopt the utterance; otherwise, we discard it. The employed prompt is identical to the BLIP-2 filter in Section 3.2. Approximately 1.0% of utterances were excluded through this process.

Merging utterances. Subtitles created by video authors occasionally exhibit unnatural segmentation, resulting in exceedingly brief spans. Utilizing the audio segments obtained through CTC segmentation, we implement a merging process, combining two consecutive utterances into a single entity if the end time of the preceding utterance aligns with the start time of the subsequent one and their cumulative duration does not exceed 15 seconds. This procedure significantly enhanced Whisper's ASR performance by approximately 20%.

3.4 Data Partitioning

Previous studies (Meyer et al., 2020; Javed et al., 2023; DiChristofano et al., 2023) have suggested that the performance of ASR systems significantly varies depending on the speaker's accent[3]. Based on the hypothesis that visual information contributes to the recognition of challenging accents, we ask native English speakers to classify the speakers' accents in SlideAVSR and perform dataset partitioning. We partition the dataset into Train, Dev, and TestA, reserving a smaller yet significant TestB subset for South Asian English (SAE) accents. During partitioning, we have ensured that the same speaker did not belong to multiple partitions. Additionally, 5 videos with machine-generated audio were manually excluded by the annotators.

Through the construction flow, we produced an AVSR dataset of around 36 hours from 245 videos. We show the statistics of the dataset in Table 1.

[3]The term "accent" in this paper refers to comprehensive prosodic information, including accent, intonation, tone, etc.

	#videos	#speakers	#utterances	#hours
Train	195	172	15,803	29.26
Dev	20	20	1,515	3.08
TestA	15	15	1,034	2.21
TestB	15	13	1,111	1.90
Total	245	220	19,463	36.45

Table 1: Statistics of SlideAVSR.

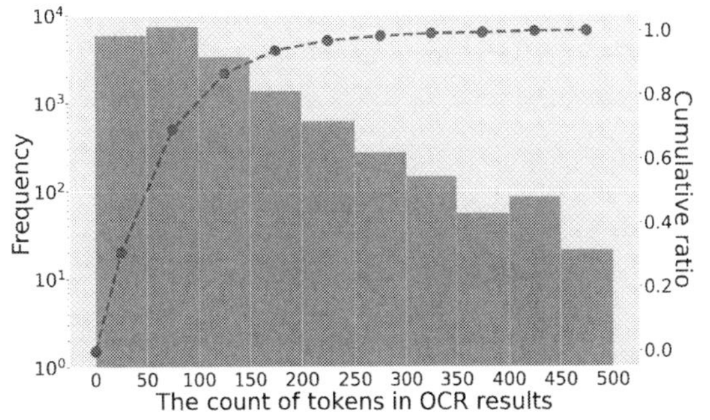

Figure 2: Frequency distribution of the number of words in OCR results. While samples with over 500 words are present, they are omitted for brevity.

4 Experiments

4.1 Approaches

DocWhisper processes the input video stream through an OCR module, extracting textual information into word sequences, which are then provided to Whisper as prompts for fine-tuning and inference. While Peng et al. (2023) employed prompts derived from CLIP in zero-shot learning, our preliminary experiments did not reveal a performance improvement in zero-shot learning on SlideAVSR. Given that Whisper's pretraining (Radford et al., 2022) did not use prompts, we speculate that Whisper loses robustness when it faces diverse prompts.

We show the frequency distribution of the number of words in OCR results in Figure 2. The distribution is long-tail, which means that only 70% of the samples can be covered even if we include 100 words in the prompts[4]. To address this issue, we propose FQ Ranker, which calculates word ranks based on the frequency of word occurrences. Given the demonstrated high correlation between word frequency and familiarity as shown in previous studies (Coltheart, 1981; Tanaka-Ishii, 2021), increasing the rank of less frequent and more challenging words is expected to enhance the information content of prompts.

[4]Whisper typically assigns a maximum length of 224 to prompts, making inputs with over 100 words challenging.

Type	Example
Technical term	`W Hyp: we select quantum ~~adhering~~ 2 and nxt as representative of pos protocols`
(41%)	`D Hyp: we select quantum ethereum 2 and nxt as representative of pos protocols`
Inflection	`W Hyp: manual ~~transcript~~ we call this setting supervised things we have paired data`
(28%)	`D Hyp: manual transcripts we call this setting supervised things we have paired data`
Mishearing	`W Hyp: we can also perform other tasks like ~~normal~~ view synthesis`
(24%)	`D Hyp: we can also perform other tasks like novel view synthesis`
Name	`W Hyp: this is a work done at ibm research with ~~gilmosecci chileo~~ and irina ~~rich~~`
(7%)	`D Hyp: this is a work done at ibm research with guillermo cecchi and irina rish`

Table 2: Error types and examples that are substitution errors in Whisper (W) but correct in DocWhisper (D).

Model	Modality	Fine-tune	K^a	TestA	TestB
Whisper	A	✗	0	8.23	11.18
		✓		8.07	11.25
DocWhisper	A + V	✓	25	7.35	10.82
+ FQ Ranker				7.42	10.59
DocWhisper	A + V	✓	50	7.08	10.43
+ FQ Ranker				7.26	10.35
DocWhisper	A + V	✓	75	7.02	10.04
+ FQ Ranker				7.26	10.29
DocWhisper	A + V	✓	100	**6.91**	**10.01**
+ FQ Ranker				7.04	10.22

[a]Indicating maximum word counts for prompts.

Table 3: Quantitative evaluation (WER) on SlideAVSR.

4.2 Implement Details

We used Whisper large-v3[5] as a base model and Word Error Rate (WER) for evaluation. In the case of DocWhisper, we captured screenshots at the midpoint of each utterance, fed them into the OCR module, and used the recognized text as the prompts to Whisper. In this case, multiple utterances might share the same slide. We use Google Cloud Vision API[6] for OCR. The prompts were presented to the model as word sequences, such as "word 1, word 2, ..., word n". FQ Ranker utilized word frequency counts obtained from the English Wikipedia and sorted the OCR results in ascending order based on word frequency. We conducted experiments with different maximum word counts for prompts ($K \in \{25, 50, 75, 100\}$) and with or without FQ Ranker. More implementation details are provided in Appendix C.

4.3 Results

We show the results of quantitative evaluations for Whisper and DocWhisper in Table 3. In both models, the scores of the TestB set, consisting of videos with SAE accents, were inferior to the scores of the TestA set, indicating that Whisper struggles with rare accents. With fine-tuning, Whisper demonstrated a 1.9% improvement on the TestA set. However, no notable improvement was observed for the TestB set. Despite the presence of videos with SAE accents in the training data, their limited quantity was deemed insufficient to address the challenges posed by difficult accents.

Compared to the fine-tuned Whisper, DocWhisper exhibited a maximum improvement of 14.3% on TestA and 11% on TestB. We gather that referring to textual information on slides can significantly improve speech recognition performance on SlideAVSR. We also found that as the maximum word count of prompts increased, the performance improved, indicating that maximizing information content contributes to performance enhancement.

FQ Ranker improved the scores on TestB when the maximum word count of prompts was set to 25; however, this advantage was reversed when the maximum word count exceeded 50. Details provided in Section 4.4 indicate that transcriptions corrected by DocWhisper do not exclusively consist of technical terms, which suggests the potential for misinterpretation even in words with high familiarity. We also speculate that sorting words based on word frequency disrupts the ordered contextual information, thus increasing the difficulty of Whisper's decoder, which is a language model, to refer to the textual information on the slides.

4.4 Analysis of Specific Examples

Among Whisper's errors (deletions, substitutions, and insertions), DocWhisper corrected substitution errors the most. To delve into the details, we collected 100 instances that are substitution errors in Whisper but correct in DocWhisper and categorized them into four groups: technical term, inflection, mishearing, and name. While the anticipated large proportion (41%) of technical terms was observed, noteworthy percentages were also found for inflection (28%) and mishearing (24%). Many words with high familiarity could result in lower ranks when sorting based on word frequency, potentially causing a decline in the performance of FQ Ranker. We show the error types and specific examples in Table 2 and more details in Appendix D.

[5]https://huggingface.co/openai/whisper-large-v3

[6]https://cloud.google.com/vision

5 Conclusion and Future Work

We constructed an AVSR dataset, SlideAVSR, by utilizing paper explanation videos. We proposed DocWhisper, which leverages OCR to refer to slide content. We verified the effectiveness of DocWhisper on SlideAVSR and conducted a detailed analysis. Additionally, we introduced FQ Ranker, which calculates word ranks based on word frequency, and evaluated its performance on DocWhisper.

In the future, we plan to continually refine OCR-based methods and aim to construct an end-to-end AVSR model that is not dependent on OCR. Furthermore, we intend to build a benchmark that allows a comprehensive evaluation of the image comprehension capabilities of AVSR models by incorporating diverse types of videos, such as sports commentary, gaming commentary, cooking videos, and more. Ultimately, we aim to construct a foundation model for AVSR that exhibits high performance across diverse video inputs.

Limitations

In comparison to mainstream AVSR datasets, SlideAVSR exhibits a notably limited number of videos and speakers. This may lead to data imbalance and create obstacles to the model's training process. In addition, due to our focused collection of scientific paper explanation videos related to artificial intelligence, imbalances may have emerged in terms of speaker nationality, age, and gender.

Compared to SlideSpeech (Wang et al., 2023), we introduced a vision-language model to filter videos and utterances that do not correspond to the slides, thereby reducing annotation costs and improving the quality of the dataset. However, our dataset construction process still relies on manual annotation. Fully automating this process will be a major challenge for the future.

In Section 3.4, we attempted to classify speakers' accents by collaborating with native English speakers. However, the task of assigning precise labels to every video was impeded by the complexity of distinguishing certain speakers' accents. As a result, we selectively picked out videos with South Asian English accents, leaving the remainder unlabeled. Ideally, each data split should exhibit a comparable distribution of accents, but this was unattainable due to the aforementioned challenges.

Ethical Considerations

In adherence to the terms of use and copyright policies governing the YouTube platform, we collected data exclusively from publicly available videos. We acknowledge the potential presence of sensitive information in our dataset, such as personal names and portraits. To prioritize privacy and responsible data sharing, we plan to release OCR results and public video URLs instead of raw video files. Furthermore, the release of our dataset will be strictly limited to research purposes.

References

Triantafyllos Afouras, Joon Son Chung, Andrew Senior, Oriol Vinyals, and Andrew Zisserman. 2018a. Deep audio-visual speech recognition. *IEEE Transactions on Pattern Analysis and Machine Intelligence*, 44(12):8717–8727.

Triantafyllos Afouras, Joon Son Chung, and Andrew Zisserman. 2018b. Lrs3-ted: a large-scale dataset for visual speech recognition.

Joon Son Chung, Andrew Senior, Oriol Vinyals, and Andrew Zisserman. 2017. Lip reading sentences in the wild. In *2017 IEEE Conference on Computer Vision and Pattern Recognition (CVPR)*, pages 3444–3453.

Joon Son Chung and Andrew Zisserman. 2017a. Lip reading in profile.

Joon Son Chung and Andrew Zisserman. 2017b. Lip reading in the wild. In *Computer Vision – ACCV 2016*, pages 87–103, Cham. Springer International Publishing.

Max Coltheart. 1981. The mrc psycholinguistic database. *The Quarterly Journal of Experimental Psychology Section A*, 33(4):497–505.

Alex DiChristofano, Henry Shuster, Shefali Chandra, and Neal Patwari. 2023. Global performance disparities between english-language accents in automatic speech recognition.

Valentin Gabeur, Paul Hongsuck Seo, Arsha Nagrani, Chen Sun, Karteek Alahari, and Cordelia Schmid. 2022. Avatar: Unconstrained audiovisual speech recognition.

Alexandros Haliassos, Pingchuan Ma, Rodrigo Mira, Stavros Petridis, and Maja Pantic. 2023. Jointly learning visual and auditory speech representations from raw data. In *The Eleventh International Conference on Learning Representations*.

Suyog Jain, Rohit Girdhar, Andrew Westbury, and et al. 2023. Ego4d challenge 2023. Https://ego4d-data.org/docs/challenge/.

Tahir Javed, Sakshi Joshi, Vignesh Nagarajan, Sai Sundaresan, Janki Nawale, Abhigyan Raman, Kaushal Bhogale, Pratyush Kumar, and Mitesh M. Khapra. 2023. Svarah: Evaluating english asr systems on indian accents.

Ludwig Kürzinger, Dominik Winkelbauer, Lujun Li, Tobias Watzel, and Gerhard Rigoll. 2020. Ctc-segmentation of large corpora for german end-to-end speech recognition. In *International Conference on Speech and Computer*, pages 267–278. Springer.

Junnan Li, Dongxu Li, Silvio Savarese, and Steven Hoi. 2023. BLIP-2: bootstrapping language-image pre-training with frozen image encoders and large language models. In *ICML*.

Ilya Loshchilov and Frank Hutter. 2019. Decoupled weight decay regularization.

Josh Meyer, Lindy Rauchenstein, Joshua D. Eisenberg, and Nicholas Howell. 2020. Artie bias corpus: An open dataset for detecting demographic bias in speech applications. In *Proceedings of the Twelfth Language Resources and Evaluation Conference*, pages 6462–6468, Marseille, France. European Language Resources Association.

Antoine Miech, Dimitri Zhukov, Jean-Baptiste Alayrac, Makarand Tapaswi, Ivan Laptev, and Josef Sivic. 2019. HowTo100M: Learning a Text-Video Embedding by Watching Hundred Million Narrated Video Clips. In *ICCV*.

Xichen Pan, Peiyu Chen, Yichen Gong, Helong Zhou, Xinbing Wang, and Zhouhan Lin. 2022. Leveraging unimodal self-supervised learning for multimodal audio-visual speech recognition. In *Proceedings of the 60th Annual Meeting of the Association for Computational Linguistics (Volume 1: Long Papers)*, pages 4491–4503, Dublin, Ireland. Association for Computational Linguistics.

Puyuan Peng, Brian Yan, Shinji Watanabe, and David Harwath. 2023. Prompting the hidden talent of web-scale speech models for zero-shot task generalization. In *Interspeech*.

Alec Radford, Jong Wook Kim, Chris Hallacy, Aditya Ramesh, Gabriel Goh, Sandhini Agarwal, Girish Sastry, Amanda Askell, Pamela Mishkin, Jack Clark, Gretchen Krueger, and Ilya Sutskever. 2021. Learning transferable visual models from natural language supervision.

Alec Radford, Jong Wook Kim, Tao Xu, Greg Brockman, Christine McLeavey, and Ilya Sutskever. 2022. Robust speech recognition via large-scale weak supervision.

Bowen Shi, Wei-Ning Hsu, Kushal Lakhotia, and Abdelrahman Mohamed. 2022. Learning audio-visual speech representation by masked multimodal cluster prediction. *arXiv preprint arXiv:2201.02184*.

Brendan Shillingford, Yannis Assael, Matthew W. Hoffman, Thomas Paine, Cían Hughes, Utsav Prabhu, Hank Liao, Hasim Sak, Kanishka Rao, Lorrayne Bennett, Marie Mulville, Misha Denil, Ben Coppin, Ben Laurie, Andrew Senior, and Nando de Freitas. 2019. Large-scale visual speech recognition. In *Proc. Interspeech 2019*, pages 4135–4139.

Shinnosuke Takamichi, Ludwig Kürzinger, Takaaki Saeki, Sayaka Shiota, and Shinji Watanabe. 2021. Jtubespeech: corpus of japanese speech collected from youtube for speech recognition and speaker verification.

Kumiko Tanaka-Ishii. 2021. *Statistical Universals of Language*. Springer Cham.

Haoxu Wang, Fan Yu, Xian Shi, Yuezhang Wang, Shiliang Zhang, and Ming Li. 2023. Slidespeech: A large-scale slide-enriched audio-visual corpus.

A The list of target conferences used in data collection

We show our target conferences in Table 4.

Topic	Conference
NLP	ACL, NAACL, EMNLP
CV	CVPR, ICCV, ECCV
Speech	INTERSPEECH, ICASSP
AI	AAAI, IJCAI
ML	ICLR, ICML, NeurIPS
Data Mining	KDD, WSDM, WWW
Database	SIGMOD, VLDB, ICDE
IR	SIGIR
HCI	CHI

Table 4: Target conferences.

B Models and prompts used in data filtering and cleansing

We introduce the details of the models and prompts employed in the ChatGPT filter, BLIP-2 filter, and CTC alignment as described in Section 3.2 and 3.3.

ChatGPT filter. We used gpt-3.5-turbo. The prompt we used is shown in Table 5.

Here is a description of a YouTube video:
{DESCRIPTION}
Using the description, check whether the video meets the following criteria.
- This video is a presentation video of a research paper.
- The description is written in English.
Attention, you can only answer 'Yes' or 'No' and you can only answer one time.

Table 5: Prompt for ChatGPT filter.

BLIP-2 filter. We used blip2-flan-t5-xl[7]. The prompt we used is shown in Table 6.

Question: This image is a screenshot of a video,
check whether the image meets the following criteria.
- It is a screen-sharing, not a photo shoot.
- It is a part of a slide for a research presentation.
Attention, you can only answer 'Yes' or 'No' and you can only answer one time.
Answer:

Table 6: Prompt for BLIP-2 filter.

CTC alignment. We used kamo-naoyuki_wsj[8] and ESPnet implemenations[9].

[7]https://huggingface.co/Salesforce/blip2-flan-t5-xl
[8]https://huggingface.co/espnet/kamo-naoyuki_wsj
[9]https://github.com/espnet/espnet

C Implement details

We fine-tuned both Whisper and DocWhisper using AdamW (Loshchilov and Hutter, 2019) with a learning rate of 2e-5, and we linearly warmed up the learning rate over 1,000 steps. The batch size was set to 16. Training was conducted for 10 epochs, and the checkpoint with the best performance on the Dev set was used for evaluation. Additionally, training was performed with three different seed values, and the average was computed. We performed text normalization[10] for evaluation. All experiments were conducted on a single NVIDIA A100 (40G) GPU.

D Specific examples

The corresponding screenshots to Table 2 are shown below, and the parts referred to in the correction are circled in red.

All the variations from the same lexical element, such as plural nouns, conjugated verbs, and third-person singular verbs, were classified as inflection. If the label and prediction are not from the same lexical element, we classified the error as technical terms, mishearing, and names, respectively.

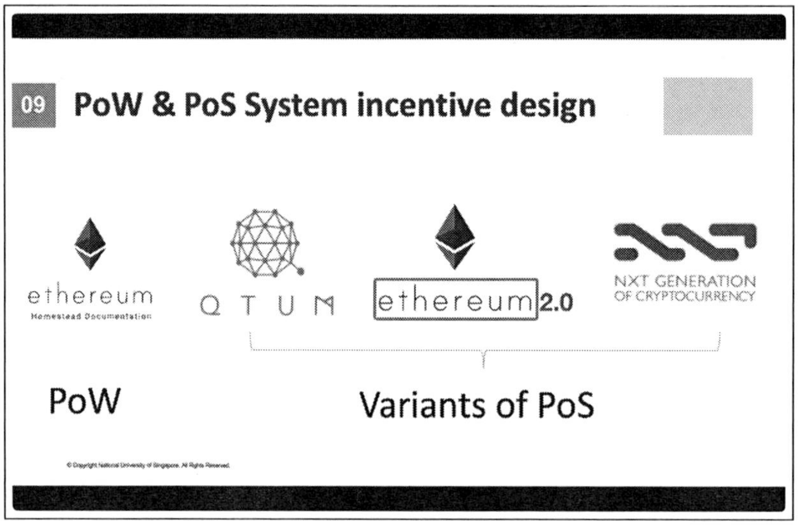

https://www.youtube.com/watch?v=eepUV9NJxFs

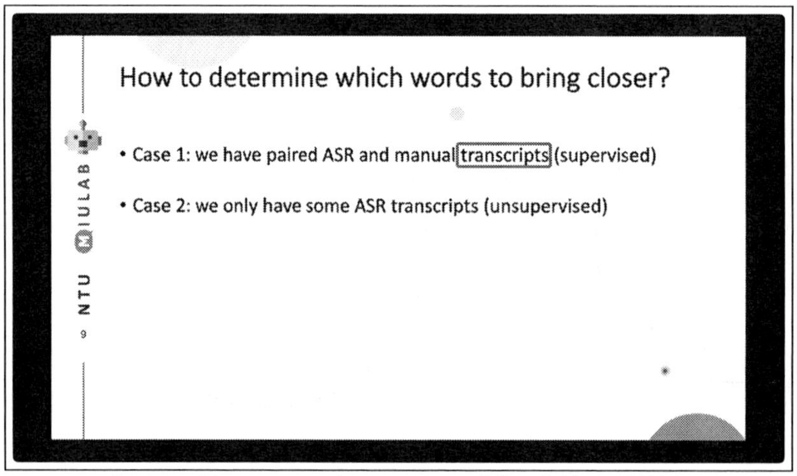

https://www.youtube.com/watch?v=dvUutyo72R4

[10] https://github.com/openai/whisper

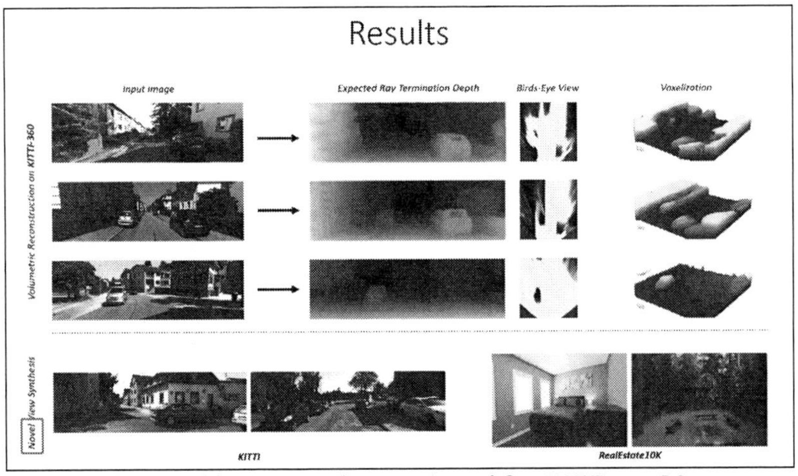

https://www.youtube.com/watch?v=0VGKPmomrR8

https://www.youtube.com/watch?v=CQBdQz1bmls

Causal and Temporal Inference in Visual Question Generation by Utilizing Pre-trained Models

Zhanghao Hu and **Frank Keller**
School of Informatics, University of Edinburgh, UK
huzh666295@gmail.com, keller@inf.ed.ac.uk

Abstract

Visual Question Generation is a task at the crossroads of visual and language learning, impacting broad domains like education, medicine, and social media. While existing pre-trained models excel in fact-based queries with image pairs, they fall short of capturing human-like inference, particularly in **understanding causal and temporal relationships** within videos. Additionally, the computational demands of prevalent pre-training methods pose challenges. In response, our study introduces a framework that leverages vision-text matching pre-trained models to guide language models in recognizing event-entity relationships within videos and generating inferential questions. Demonstrating efficacy on the NExT-QA dataset, which is designed for causal and temporal inference in visual question answering, our method successfully guides pre-trained language models in recognizing video content. We present methodologies for abstracting causal and temporal relationships between events and entities, pointing out the importance of consistent relationships among input frames during training and inference phases and suggesting an avenue for future exploration[1].

1 Introduction

Visual Question Generation (VQG) is an emerging task of multi-modal learning, integrating vision and language. Since its inception (Lin and Parikh, 2016), VQG has influenced diverse domains like education (Zhao et al., 2022), social media (Yeh et al., 2022), and human-computer interaction (Lee et al., 2018). Existing datasets primarily cater to factoid question answering, extracting direct answers from visual content (Yeh et al., 2022). However, factoid question answering lacks inherent depth in human thinking, exemplified by the disparity between a fact-based query like "Was anyone injured in the crash?" and a more insightful, causal question "Why do these drivers have accidents in the middle of intersections?" or a temporal question "What will the police do after the crash?"

This research addresses a critical gap in the VQG landscape: *the absence of studies exploring inference aligned with human thinking.* Moreover, unlike singular images, videos offer richer details of relationships between events and entities, prompting our focus on two fundamental types of reasoning—*causal inference and temporal inference.* Through this approach, we aim to introduce a new challenge of inferential question generation originating from videos and auxiliary text and advance the field of VQG.

Meanwhile, despite advancements in VQG, the computational demands (Radford et al., 2021) of pre-training models, particularly visual transformers (Dosovitskiy et al., 2020), pose challenges. Our work distinguishes itself by harnessing pre-trained vision-to-text matching models instead of embarking on resource-intensive model training from scratch. Inspired by prior successes (Mokady et al., 2021), our approach expedites question generation by leveraging the knowledge embedded in existing models, thereby enhancing the quality and efficiency of the process.

The contributions of this paper are as follows:

1. As far as we know, we are the first to explore the task of causal and temporal video question generation. We propose a framework (figure 1) and establish a baseline step by step by comparing video encoders, language model sizes, and stage fine-tuning strategies. Additionally, we propose an evaluation metric to enhance VQG grounding assessment.

2. Experiments on the NExT-QA dataset display the efficacy of our methods in combining vision and language. *We highlight the importance of consistent frame relationships during training and inference for deriving event-*

[1]The code is available at this address.

Proceedings of the 3rd Workshop on Advances in Language and Vision Research, pages 138–154
August 16, 2024 ©2024 Association for Computational Linguistics

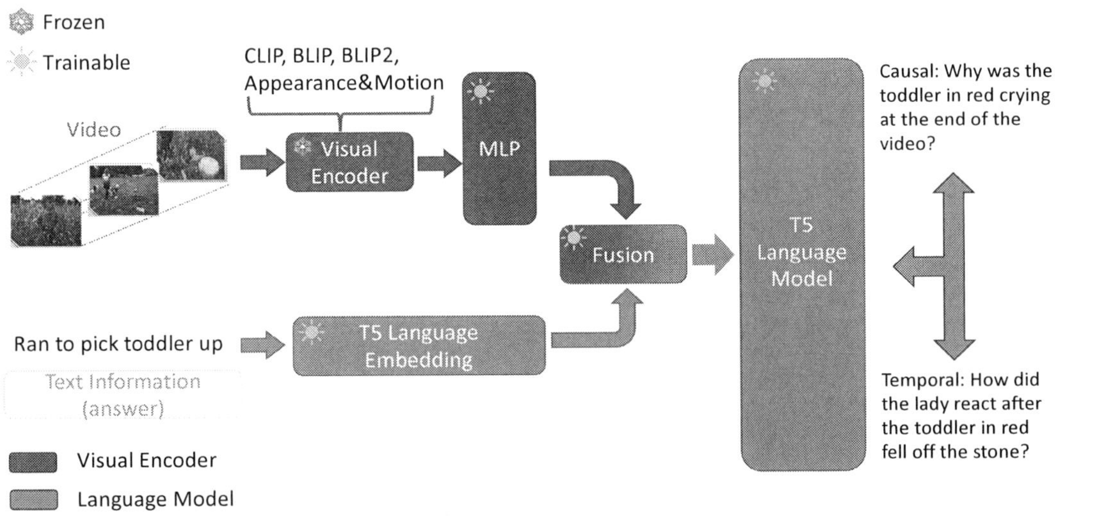

Figure 1: The overall framework for visual question generation. It comprises four essential components: a visual encoder, an auxiliary text encoder (T5), multi-modal interaction, and an output question decoder (T5). Videos and auxiliary text are respectively encoded into embeddings and be concatenated through multilayer perception (MLP) layers. Temporal and causal questions will be generated by the question decoder.

entity relationships within videos. This research suggests the direction of enhancing frame-based consistency in causal and temporal video inference for future work.

2 Background and Related Work

Visual Question Generation: The field of VQG has seen notable progress since its introduction (Mostafazadeh et al., 2016). Existing research has extensively explored single-image VQG (Vedd et al., 2021; Krishna et al., 2019), while multiple-image VQG (Chan et al., 2022) and video VQG (Khurana and Deshpande, 2021), which present promising avenues for inferring causality and temporal relationships between visual elements, remain unexplored. To the best of our knowledge, no prior research has specifically focused on the challenges of generating questions that involve causal and temporal inference in VQG tasks. This represents a critical research gap, as inferential questions have the potential to unlock deeper insights of visual content, going beyond mere factual queries.

Multi-modal Generative Task with Pre-trained Models: Existing research in visual question generation adopts large pre-trained models for tasks like image captioning (Li et al., 2022), visual question answering (Khan et al., 2023), and visual grounding (Peng et al., 2023), showcasing impressive results but facing high computational costs (Dosovitskiy et al., 2020). An alternative, leveraging vision-text matching pre-trained models like CLIP (Radford et al., 2021), BLIP (Li et al., 2022), and BLIP2 (Li et al., 2023), efficiently bridges vision and language domains. Despite success in various generative tasks, no prior research explores these models for vision-based question generation, particularly those involving causal and temporal inference. This research aims to utilize various vision-text matching pre-trained models in capturing causal and temporal relationships.

3 Methods

The overall framework for VQG is displayed in Figure 1. This section introduces our training strategies and inferential relationship abstraction methods.

3.1 Multi-modal Fusion

Visual information and textual context are often complementary in nature. The visual content provides rich details and cues that are not present in the text, and vice versa. The core issues are *how to unify the multi-modal embedding space between vision and language*, and how to *effectively guide the language model in recognizing visual information and generating temporal and causal questions.*

Concatenate Vision and Language: Inspired by one of the latest methods (Liu et al., 2023b,a), we propose a direct but powerful technique to connect vision and language spaces. Specifically, given auxiliary text input words which are "Text Information" shown in Figure 1 $w_V^1, w_V^2, ..., w_V^p$, for a video V, we process them by language models and get a series of word embeddings $t_V^1, t_V^2, ..., t_V^i$. Given a video V, we first divide the video V as separate frames $x_V^1, x_V^2, ..., x_V^m$. Next, after processing the frames by visual encoders, we employ a light mapping network (multilayer perceptron), denoted by F, to map the visual embedding to k embedding vectors (we set the k as 5 in our experiments):

$$p_V^1, p_V^2, ...p_V^k = F(visual\_encoder(x_V^1, ..., x_V^m)). \tag{1}$$

where each vector p_V^k has the same dimension as the word embedding of language models. We then concatenate the obtained visual embedding to the auxiliary input text embeddings:

$$Z_V = p_V^1, ..., p_V^k, t_V^1, ..., t_V^i. \tag{2}$$

During fine-tuning, we feed the language models with the prefix-text concatenation $\{Z_i\}_{i=1}^N$, where N is the number of videos. Our training objective is to predict the temporal and causal question tokens conditioned on the prefix in an auto-regressive fashion. To this purpose, we train the mapping component F using the simple, yet effective, cross-entropy loss:

$$\mathcal{L} = \sum_{i=1}^{N} \sum_{j=1}^{\ell} \log p_\theta(q_j^i | Z_V, q_1^i, ...q_{j-1}^i), \tag{3}$$

where ℓ is the length of the predicted questions, p_θ is the probability of ground-truth tokens,.

Two Stage Fine Tuning: Inspired by prior research (Liu et al., 2023b,a), a two-stage fine-tuning methodology is introduced to tackle the challenge of multi-modal fusion in visual question generation by effectively aligning visual and textual information. In the first stage, we prioritize feature alignment fine-tuning, aligning the visual encoder with the language model through a parameter mapping network F. This ensures alignment between video features and language model word embeddings, streamlining visual tokenizers. In the second stage, a fine-tuning end-to-end strategy takes place after the convergence of the first stage. Visual encoder weights are frozen, and both pre-trained weights of the projection layer and the language model are updated. This two-stage process, acting on the "Fusion model" shown in Figure 1, optimizes the language model's performance.

3.2 Causal and Temporal Inference Abstraction Methods

This section introduces two methods which aim to enhance the abstraction of causal and temporal inference from events and entities within a video.

Vision Projection Matrix Choice: An intuitively straightforward approach is taken by creating distinct MLP layers for individual frames similar to equation 1 (In this experiment we set the number of the MLP layers as 16), aiming to capture nuanced characteristics. Each frame's embeddings are projected onto a linguistic embedding using an additional MLP with a prefix length of 5.

Contradictory Frame Comparison aims to abstract causal and temporal relationships in a video by exploiting differences between consecutive frames. Two strategies are employed using the CLIP vision encoders. (1) *Global Frame Comparison*: 16 frames at uniform intervals are transformed into vision embeddings through the CLIP encoder. Pairs of frames with the lowest cosine similarity represent the most contradictory frames, projected onto the language embedding through an MLP layer. (2) *Local Frame Comparison*: Once again, we select pairs of frames and calculate their cosine similarity. But during training, firstly the CLIP model is invoked to determine the most relevant frame in relation to the given question and answer since at training time we have all relevant inputs. Then, we select the rest frame which displays the lowest cosine similarity with the contextually chosen frame. Again, an MLP layer projects the selected frame pair onto the language embedding.

4 Experiment

4.1 Data and Evaluation

Existing video question-answering datasets primarily address factoid questions with direct visual answers (Xu et al., 2016; Jang et al., 2017) but lack inference questions. To fill this gap and integrate causal and temporal inference, this study opts for the **NExT-QA** dataset (Xiao et al., 2021), which is designed for inferential visual-question-answering, offering about 52K diverse questions (48% causal, 29% temporal, 23% descriptive).

The assessment of visual question generation (VQG) systems traditionally relies on language metrics like BLEU (Papineni et al., 2002), METEOR (Banerjee and Lavie, 2005), ROUGE (Lin, 2004), and CIDEr (Vedantam et al., 2015), designed for machine translation, lacking inference evaluation. To address this gap, our study introduces new metrics—precision, recall, and F1-score grounding—examining word overlap between predicted and ground-truth questions. The grounding metrics consider matching overlaps of content-bearing words and exclude irrelevant words[2]. We define the formula of the grounding metrics:

$$
\begin{aligned}
PG =& N_{\text{matching overlap}} / N_{\text{predicted question tokens}} \\
RG =& N_{\text{matching overlap}} / N_{\text{ground truth question tokens}} \\
FG =& \frac{2 * PG * RG}{PG + RG},
\end{aligned} \tag{4}
$$

Where PG means Precision Grounding, RG means Recall Grounding, FG means F1 score Grounding, $N_{\text{matching overlap}}$ counts matching overlaps between predicted and ground truth questions. $N_{\text{predicted question tokens}}$ and $N_{\text{ground truth question tokens}}$ represent the respective token counts.

4.2 Experiment Setup

Baseline Models: In establishing baseline models for a fair comparison on the NExT-QA datasets, we employ the **Heterogeneous Graph Attention (HGA) model** (Jiang and Han, 2020) and **a pre-trained language model** with text-only input: (1) The HGA model utilizes 3D motion and 2D appearance vectors, abstracted from ResNet (He et al., 2016) and ResNeXt-101 (Xie et al., 2017).(2) The pre-trained language model T5 (Radford et al., 2021) is explored with text-only input as a baseline, to assess its ability to recognize visual content in videos in the following experiments.

Video Encoder: To enhance visual question generation for temporal and causal inference, traditional 2D and 3D convolutional networks face limitations in generative tasks. Leveraging pre-trained vision-text matching models like **CLIP (Radford et al., 2021), BLIP (Li et al., 2022) and BLIP2 (Li et al., 2023)**, we conduct a comprehensive performance comparison against convolutional networks.

Language Model Size Selection: To explore the impact of language model size on recognizing relationships in videos, we employ **T5 Small** and **T5 Large**. In addition, we adopt two tuning strategies. "One Stage" in Table 4 and Table 5 means we directly train the mapping network F in section 3.1 from scratch and "Two Stage" represents the fine-tuning strategy explained in section 3.1.

[2]We exclude the words of POS types "CC", "DT", "IN", "TO" and "UH" in our experiments.

4.3 Experiment Results

4.3.1 Baseline

We evaluated our baseline models with results summarized in Table 1. The HGA model, incorporating video and text input, achieves the highest grounding score but exhibits lower question quality due to stop-word repetition and shorter length generation (Figure 2). Although BLEU has a brevity penalty and METEOR and ROUGEL consider the recall evaluation metrics, with higher precision, the evaluation performance of the HGA model still gets close to that of the T5 model. In addition, as shown in Table 2, since our grounding metric ignores stop-words and considers only relevant words to the vision content such as nouns and verbs, precision will have an advantage in the evaluation compared to recall, thus the HGA model achieves a significant improvement compared to the T5 model. However, HGA has comparatively lower recall than those of T5 in causal and temporal question generation (Table 2). In conclusion, HGA exhibits higher precision and F1-score in the grounding metric but lower performance in BLEU, METEOR, CIDEr, and recall in the grounding metric of causal and temporal questions. *This leads us to choose T5 as the foundation for subsequent experiments.*

Model	B	RL	M	C	Grounding
HGA	0.1248	**0.4128**	0.3101	0.8271	**0.3248**
T5 Small Text Only	**0.1269**	0.3857	**0.3276**	**0.8480**	0.2957
T5 Large Text Only	0.1239	0.3851	0.3237	0.8353	0.2987

Table 1: Baseline Model Evaluation Performance. B is BLEU, RL is ROUGEL, M is METEOR, C is CIDEr, and Grounding is the F1-score grounding metric.

Model	C G-Pre	C G-Re	C G-F1	T G-Pre	T G-Re	T G-F1
HGA	**0.3378**	0.2357	**0.2776**	**0.4126**	0.2763	**0.3310**
T5 Small Text Only	0.2527	0.2541	0.2534	0.3096	**0.2943**	0.3018
T5 Large Text Only	0.2736	**0.2650**	0.2692	0.2998	0.2786	0.2888

Table 2: Baseline Model Grounding Performance in Causal and Temporal Inference. C G represents the grounding metric of causal questions. T G represents the grounding metric of temporal questions. "Pre" represents precision. "Re" represents recall. "F1" represents the F1 score.

4.3.2 Multi-modal Concatenation

Video Encoder Comparison: We assess the performance of different vision video encoders, and

Video:

Ground Truth Question:
1:how did the girl react when she saw that the ball was running at the beginning?
2: why was the girl on the floor in the middle of the video?
3: why does the dog chase the ball?
4: why did the girl run down the slope?
5: why does the child run after the ball?
6: what did the dog do after the girl approached the adult and stood beside him?
7: where is this video taken?
8: what did the girl do after she fell on the ground?
9: what did the girl do after she finished playing with the ball at the end of the video?
10: what did the girl do to the dog when the dog stood beside the man?
11: what did the girl do after the dog took the ball away?
12: why does the child run down the slope after the ball rolls away from him?

T5-small text only: ***27 matching overlap***
"1": "what did the boy do after he walked away from the ball",
"2": "why did the girl in pink hold onto the girl in pink when she is squatting down",
"3": "why did the baby put his hand on the toy in the middle of the video",
"4": "why did the man in black bend down at the start of the video",
"5": "why did the man in black bend down at the start of the video",
"6": "what does the man in black do after the man in black starts talking",
"7": "where is this video taken",
"8": "what did the boy do after he walked to the other side of the room",
"9": "what does the girl do after the girl in pink starts dancing",
"10": "what does the man do after the dog starts running",
"11": "what does the dog do after the dog starts running",
"12": "what does the man in black do after the man in black starts playing the drums"

HGA: ***42 matching overlap***
"1": "what did the boy do after the girl ran away",
"2": "why did the girl in after the girl in the",
"3": "why did the dog run towards the ball",
"4": "why did the boy run to the ball after the ball",
"5": "why did the boy run down the ball",
"6": "what did the boy do after the ball ball",
"7": "where is this video taken",
"8": "what did the dog do after the the ball",
"9": "what did the girl do after the the ball",
"10": "what did the boy do after the dog ran away",
"11": "what did the girl do after the dog ran away",
"12": "what did the dog do after the ball ball"

Figure 2: Baseline Performance. Yellow markup shows the matching overlap compared with the ground truth questions. Red markup shows the repetitive words.

the results are summarized in Table 3. CLIP and BLIP2 stand out, with CLIP excelling in ROUGEL, and Grounding metrics, showcasing good visual content recognition. In contrast, BLIP2 performs well in BLEU, METEOR, and CIDEr, generating detailed questions. Despite BLIP2's detailed questions, CLIP's higher matching overlap with ground truth and its balanced performance led to the *selection of CLIP as the video encoder for subsequent experiments* (Figure 3).

Model	B	RL	M	C	Grounding
None Text Only	0.1269	0.3857	0.3276	0.8480	0.2957
App&Mot	0.1348	0.3958	0.3353	0.8816	0.3092
CLIP	0.1564	**0.4216**	0.3594	1.0366	**0.3505**
BLIP	0.1562	0.4179	0.3584	1.0205	0.3425
BLIP2	**0.1583**	0.4210	**0.3599**	**1.0488**	0.3455

Table 3: Visual encoders performance with T5-small following Section 3.1 fusion method. App&Mot means 2D appearance vectors and 3D motion vectors abstracted from convolution networks. B is BLEU, RL is ROUGEL, M is METEOR, C is CIDEr, and Grounding is the F1-score grounding metric.

Language Model Size Comparison: We evaluate T5's performance across various sizes, presenting results in Table 4. T5 large outperforms T5 small, aligning with expectations due to its larger parameter count. In addition, our observations yield two primary findings that emerge through two-stage tuning: (1) Two-stage tuning enhances T5 large's performance, particularly improving token-level matching overlap such as nouns and verbs (Table 5). This improvement, consistent across T5 sizes, suggests enhanced visual content recognition, attributed to weight initialization and warming-up of the projection matrix. (2) Despite the close total performance,T5 large outperforms T5 small in causal questions by 2%-3% (Table 6), hinting at the potential for guiding language models in recognizing causal relationships.

4.3.3 Causal and Temporal Inference Abstraction

In this section, we present the outcomes of our two methods employed to abstract the causal and temporal relationships embedded within the events and entities within a video, with the ultimate aim of generating inferential questions.

Figure 3: Visual encoder CLIP and BLIP2 performance. Yellow scopes represent matching overlap with ground truth questions. Red scopes represent the more details recognized by the BLIP model compared with the CLIP model.

model	B	RL	M	C	Grounding
T5 Small One Stage	0.1564	0.4216	0.3594	1.0366	0.3505
T5 Small Two Stage	0.1559	0.4181	0.3594	1.002	0.3453
T5 Large One Stage	0.1459	0.4025	0.3459	0.9449	0.3249
T5 Large Two Stage	**0.1572**	**0.4281**	**0.3634**	**1.0657**	**0.3573**

Table 4: Difference Language Size Performance. T5 small has *60M* parameters, with total **135M** parameters for a whole framework, T5 large has *770M* parameters, with total **917M** parameters for a whole framework. B is BLEU, RL is ROUGEL, M is METEOR, C is CIDEr, and Grounding is the F1-score grounding metric.

model	NN	WRB	VBZ	VBD	VB	JJ	VBG	WP	PRP
T5 Small One Stage	4199	**2692**	1121	1154	713	504	248	1038	220
T5 Small Two Stage	4287	2640	1268	**1184**	643	**533**	228	**1091**	**221**
T5 Large One Stage	3927	2664	**1429**	947	719	467	227	1048	187
T5 Large Two Stage	**4478**	2655	1379	1078	**777**	517	**277**	1024	207

Table 5: Number of matching overlaps for various word types based on Spacy about the difference language model sizes. NN means noun, singular or mass, WRB means wh-adverb, VBZ means verb, 3rd person singular present, VBD means verb, past tense, VB means verb, base form, JJ means adjective, VBG means verb, gerund or present participle, WP means wh-pronoun, personal, PRP means pronoun, personal.

Vision Projection Matrix Comparison explores projection matrix techniques, revealing unexpected trends shown in Table 7. Contrary to expectations, the method directly concatenating CLIP encoder and language embeddings ("Video MLP" in Table 7) outperforms that employing the addition of MLP layers to each frame before concatenating with the language embedding ("Video 16to5 MLP" in Table 7), including grounding metrics on causal and temporal questions (Table 8). Findings underscore that the blind proliferation of MLP layers, even on individual frames, *fails to*

Model	C G-Pre	C G-Re	C G-F1	T G-Pre	T G-Re	T G-F1
T5 Small two stage	0.3096	0.3078	0.3087	0.3625	0.3357	0.3486
T5 large two stage	**0.3333**	**0.3115**	**0.3221**	**0.3767**	**0.3374**	**0.3560**

Table 6: Grounding evaluation performance of different sizes of T5 models with the two-stage tuning method in causal and temporal inference. C G represents the grounding metric of causal questions. T G represents the grounding metric of temporal questions. "Pre" represents precision. "Re" represents recall. "F1" represents the F1 score.

capture inferential relationships in visual content.

Model	B	RL	M	C	Grounding
Video MLP	**0.1564**	**0.4216**	**0.3594**	**1.0366**	**0.3505**
Video 16to5 MLP	0.1549	0.4170	0.3574	0.9722	0.3415

Table 7: Vision Projection Matrix Performance. Both experiments are conducted with a CLIP image encoder and T5-small. Video MLP means the vision embedding would be processed by a MLP layer and video 16to5 MLP means we add 16 fine-grained MLP for the frames of the video input. B is BLEU, RL is ROUGEL, M is METEOR, C is CIDEr, Grounding is the F1-score grounding metric.

Model	C G-Pre	C G-Re	C G-F1	T G-Pre	T G-Re	T G-F1
Video MLP	**0.3204**	**0.3072**	**0.3137**	**0.3695**	**0.3331**	**0.3503**
Video 16to5 MLP	0.3028	0.3014	0.3021	0.3589	0.3316	0.3447

Table 8: Vision Projection Matrix Grounding Performance in Causal and Temporal Inference. C G represents the causal grounding metric. T G represents the temporal grounding metric. "Pre" represents precision. "Re" represents recall. "F1" represents the F1 score.

Frame Comparison Based on CLIP evaluates two frame comparison methods using the CLIP-based approach. The summarized evaluations are presented in Table 9 along with an illustrative example shown in Appendix Figure A1, yielding several noteworthy findings:

1. While slightly behind direct vision embedding concatenation (Video MLP) across all evaluation metrics in Table 9, the global frame method with only 73M parameters is less than the direct concatenation approach (135M). In addition, the global frame comparison method outperforms the baseline (Random Select) on all metrics in Table 9 and has a substantial 20% boost compared to its baseline in causal and temporal questions (Table 10). Moreover, the global frame method excels in the direct concatenation approach in the grounding metrics of temporal questions within videos.

2. The local frame comparison method yields inferior results compared to its global counterpart across all evaluation metrics in Table 9. Aligning these findings with the performance of random selection, **we argue that maintaining a consistent relationship between input frames during both training and inference phases is pivotal for enabling the language model to deduce relationships between events and entities within videos effectively.** The method of random selection introduces *the highest level* of inconsistency compared to global and local frame comparison methods between training and inference due to its reliance on random frame selection throughout both phases. Additionally, an examination of CLIP frame selection based on questions and answers in the *local frame comparison method* reveals certain limitations. While instances of accurate frame selection aligned with questions and answers are observed, inherent challenges persist (Challenge examples are provided in Figure 4): (1) Descriptive questions such as "Where is this video happening?" often fail to pinpoint a specific frame, leading to varied frame selections by the CLIP model for identical questions. (2) Given that some videos within the NExT-QA dataset (Xiao et al., 2021) last 1 to 2 minutes, with only 16 available frames for video input, the CLIP model tends to select frames with similar content regardless of chronological time order if the event described in the question has not been captured by the 16 frames. These issues exacerbate inconsistencies and disorderliness in input frames between training and inference, resulting in *comparatively poorer performance of local frame comparison method* compared to the *global frame comparison method.* In conclusion, the global frame method introduces the least inconsistency, consistently measuring cosine similarity and selecting the least similar frame pair for language model input.

3. To further support our argument, we conduct an additional experiment where the initial and final (1&16) frames are consistently selected as the video input for the language model, as outlined in the fifth row of Table 9. Remarkably, the performance of this fixed selection method, while slightly distinct, consistently trails behind that of the global frame selection across all evaluation metrics except causal grounding metrics. This observation lends additional support to our argument, reinforcing the validity of our premise. Moreover, it opens a promising avenue for future exploration — **seeking methods that improve consistent relationships with frame-based techniques.**

model	B	RL	M	C	Grounding
All 16 frames (Video MLP)	**0.1564**	**0.4216**	**0.3594**	**1.0366**	**0.3505**
Two frames (Random Select)	0.0796	0.3128	0.2173	0.2520	0.2082
Two frames (Global Frame Comparison)	0.1538	0.4165	0.3578	1.007	0.3417
Two frames (Local Frame Comparison)	0.1315	0.3946	0.3316	0.8576	0.3095
Two frames (Fixed Selection) Frame 1&16	0.1526	0.4161	0.3549	0.9745	0.3407

Table 9: Frame Comparison Performance. "Video MLP" means the vision embedding would be processed by a MLP layer; "Random Select" means we randomly select two frames embedding within a video as the vision input. B is BLEU, RL is ROUGEL, M is METEOR, C is CIDEr, and Grounding is the F1-score grounding metric.

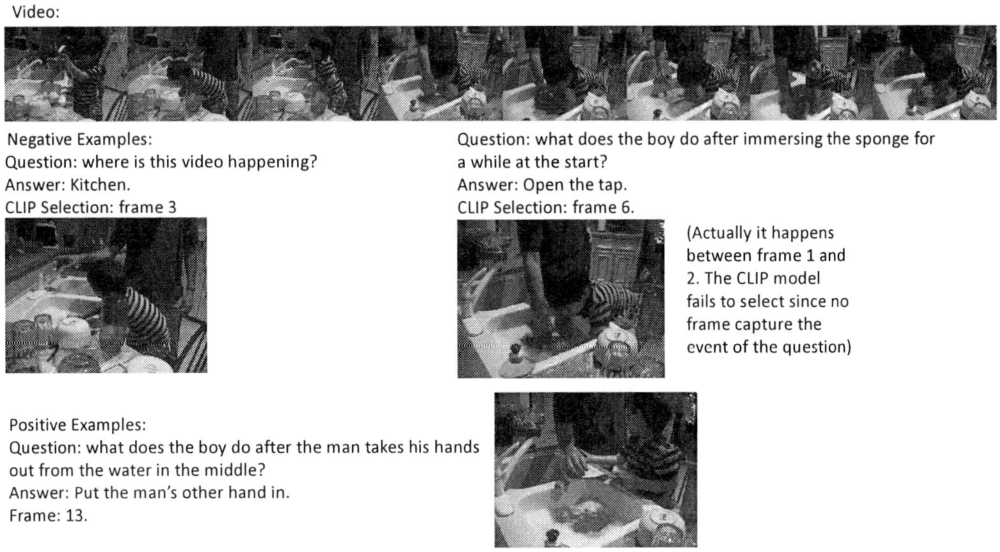

Figure 4: CLIP Selection Performance. The negative example on the left explains the inherent Challenge 1 and another negative example on the right explains the inherent Challenge 2. The positive example displays the correct frame selection.

Model	C G-Pre	C G-Re	C G-F1	T G-Pre	T G-Re	T G-F1
Video MLP	**0.3204**	0.3072	**0.3137**	0.3695	0.3331	0.3503
Random Select	0.3121	0.2340	0.2674	0.2191	0.1375	0.1689
Global Frame Comparison	0.3089	**0.3074**	0.3081	**0.3817**	**0.3509**	**0.3656**

Table 10: Global Frame Comparison Grounding Performance in Causal and Temporal Inference. C G represents the grounding metric of causal questions. T G represents the grounding metric of temporal questions. "Pre" represents precision. "Re" represents recall. "F1" represents the F1 score.

5 Conclusion

This paper bridges the gap in aligning machine-generated visual questions, focusing on inferential questions in video VQG. Our framework utilizes pre-trained models to enhance event-entity inferential relationships and question generation. We additionally introduce a grounding metric and propose techniques for causal and temporal abstraction. Through extensive experiments, we achieve significant improvement across all metrics, highlighting our framework's efficacy in promoting visual content recognition. We underscore the importance of consistent relationships between input frames during training and inference for event-entity relationship inference. This research opens a promising avenue for future work, focusing on methods to enhance consistent frame-based relationships in causal and temporal video inference.

Limitation

We employ the T5 encoder-decoder language model because of its excellent performance within the 500M to 1B parameter scope and limited GPUs. Future research could lie in exploring the inferential video VQG task with larger parameters and decoder-only language model structures. In addition, future research could separately research causal and temporal relationships between entities within videos. We attempted some methods that had negative effects on our framework and experiments. These include applying contrastive learning and visual-semantic arithmetic inferential relations. Details and results of these methods are provided in the Appendix, offering references for future research.

Acknowledgments

This work originated from a dissertation at the University of Edinburgh. We must thank Yijun Yang, Hanxu Hu, Danyang Liu, and Pizhen Chen for giving valuable suggestions on this work. We are grateful to the anonymous reviewers for their advice to further clarify the novelty of this work.

References

Satanjeev Banerjee and Alon Lavie. 2005. METEOR: An automatic metric for MT evaluation with improved correlation with human judgments. In *Proceedings of the ACL Workshop on Intrinsic and Extrinsic Evaluation Measures for Machine Translation and/or Summarization*, pages 65–72, Ann Arbor, Michigan. Association for Computational Linguistics.

Shih-Han Chan, Tsai-Lun Yang, Yun-Wei Chu, Chi-Yang Hsu, Ting-Hao Huang, Yu-Shian Chiu, and Lun-Wei Ku. 2022. Let's talk! striking up conversations via conversational visual question generation. *arXiv preprint arXiv:2205.09327*.

Alexey Dosovitskiy, Lucas Beyer, Alexander Kolesnikov, Dirk Weissenborn, Xiaohua Zhai, Thomas Unterthiner, Mostafa Dehghani, Matthias Minderer, Georg Heigold, Sylvain Gelly, et al. 2020. An image is worth 16x16 words: Transformers for image recognition at scale. *arXiv preprint arXiv:2010.11929*.

Gabriel Goh, Nick Cammarata, Chelsea Voss, Shan Carter, Michael Petrov, Ludwig Schubert, Alec Radford, and Chris Olah. 2021. Multimodal neurons in artificial neural networks. *Distill*, 6(3):e30.

Kaiming He, Xiangyu Zhang, Shaoqing Ren, and Jian Sun. 2016. Deep residual learning for image recognition. In *Proceedings of the IEEE conference on computer vision and pattern recognition*, pages 770–778.

Yunseok Jang, Yale Song, Youngjae Yu, Youngjin Kim, and Gunhee Kim. 2017. Tgif-qa: Toward spatio-temporal reasoning in visual question answering. In *Proceedings of the IEEE conference on computer vision and pattern recognition*, pages 2758–2766.

Pin Jiang and Yahong Han. 2020. Reasoning with heterogeneous graph alignment for video question answering. In *Proceedings of the AAAI Conference on Artificial Intelligence*, volume 34, pages 11109–11116.

Zaid Khan, Vijay Kumar BG, Samuel Schulter, Xiang Yu, Yun Fu, and Manmohan Chandraker. 2023. Q: How to specialize large vision-language models to data-scarce vqa tasks? a: Self-train on unlabeled images! In *Proceedings of the IEEE/CVF Conference on Computer Vision and Pattern Recognition*, pages 15005–15015.

Khushboo Khurana and Umesh Deshpande. 2021. Video question-answering techniques, benchmark datasets and evaluation metrics leveraging video captioning: A comprehensive survey. *IEEE Access*, 9:43799–43823.

Ranjay Krishna, Michael Bernstein, and Li Fei-Fei. 2019. Information maximizing visual question generation. In *Proceedings of the IEEE/CVF Conference on Computer Vision and Pattern Recognition*, pages 2008–2018.

Che-Hao Lee, Tzu-Yu Chen, Liang-Pu Chen, Ping-Che Yang, and Richard Tzong-Han Tsai. 2018. Automatic question generation from children's stories for companion chatbot. In *2018 IEEE International Conference on Information Reuse and Integration (IRI)*, pages 491–494. IEEE.

Junnan Li, Dongxu Li, Silvio Savarese, and Steven Hoi. 2023. Blip-2: Bootstrapping language-image pre-training with frozen image encoders and large language models. *arXiv preprint arXiv:2301.12597*.

Junnan Li, Dongxu Li, Caiming Xiong, and Steven Hoi. 2022. Blip: Bootstrapping language-image pre-training for unified vision-language understanding and generation. In *International Conference on Machine Learning*, pages 12888–12900. PMLR.

Chin-Yew Lin. 2004. ROUGE: A package for automatic evaluation of summaries. In *Text Summarization Branches Out*, pages 74–81, Barcelona, Spain. Association for Computational Linguistics.

Xiao Lin and Devi Parikh. 2016. Leveraging visual question answering for image-caption ranking. In *Computer Vision–ECCV 2016: 14th European Conference, Amsterdam, The Netherlands, October 11-14, 2016, Proceedings, Part II 14*, pages 261–277. Springer.

Haotian Liu, Chunyuan Li, Yuheng Li, and Yong Jae Lee. 2023a. Improved baselines with visual instruction tuning. *arXiv preprint arXiv:2310.03744*.

Haotian Liu, Chunyuan Li, Qingyang Wu, and Yong Jae Lee. 2023b. Visual instruction tuning. *arXiv preprint arXiv:2304.08485*.

Ron Mokady, Amir Hertz, and Amit H Bermano. 2021. Clipcap: Clip prefix for image captioning. *arXiv preprint arXiv:2111.09734*.

Nasrin Mostafazadeh, Ishan Misra, Jacob Devlin, Margaret Mitchell, Xiaodong He, and Lucy Vanderwende. 2016. Generating natural questions about an image. *arXiv preprint arXiv:1603.06059*.

Aaron van den Oord, Yazhe Li, and Oriol Vinyals. 2018. Representation learning with contrastive predictive coding. *arXiv preprint arXiv:1807.03748*.

Kishore Papineni, Salim Roukos, Todd Ward, and Wei-Jing Zhu. 2002. Bleu: a method for automatic evaluation of machine translation. In *Proceedings of the 40th Annual Meeting of the Association for Computational Linguistics*, pages 311–318, Philadelphia, Pennsylvania, USA. Association for Computational Linguistics.

Zhiliang Peng, Wenhui Wang, Li Dong, Yaru Hao, Shaohan Huang, Shuming Ma, and Furu Wei. 2023. Kosmos-2: Grounding multimodal large language models to the world. *arXiv preprint arXiv:2306.14824*.

Alec Radford, Jong Wook Kim, Chris Hallacy, Aditya Ramesh, Gabriel Goh, Sandhini Agarwal, Girish Sastry, Amanda Askell, Pamela Mishkin, Jack Clark, et al. 2021. Learning transferable visual models from natural language supervision. In *International conference on machine learning*, pages 8748–8763. PMLR.

Yoad Tewel, Yoav Shalev, Idan Schwartz, and Lior Wolf. 2022. Zerocap: Zero-shot image-to-text generation for visual-semantic arithmetic. In *Proceedings of the IEEE/CVF Conference on Computer Vision and Pattern Recognition*, pages 17918–17928.

Ramakrishna Vedantam, C Lawrence Zitnick, and Devi Parikh. 2015. Cider: Consensus-based image description evaluation. In *Proceedings of the IEEE conference on computer vision and pattern recognition*, pages 4566–4575.

Nihir Vedd, Zixu Wang, Marek Rei, Yishu Miao, and Lucia Specia. 2021. Guiding visual question generation. *arXiv preprint arXiv:2110.08226*.

Chuhan Wu, Fangzhao Wu, and Yongfeng Huang. 2021. Rethinking infonce: How many negative samples do you need? *arXiv preprint arXiv:2105.13003*.

Junbin Xiao, Xindi Shang, Angela Yao, and Tat-Seng Chua. 2021. Next-qa: Next phase of question-answering to explaining temporal actions. In *Proceedings of the IEEE/CVF conference on computer vision and pattern recognition*, pages 9777–9786.

Saining Xie, Ross Girshick, Piotr Dollár, Zhuowen Tu, and Kaiming He. 2017. Aggregated residual transformations for deep neural networks. In *Proceedings of the IEEE conference on computer vision and pattern recognition*, pages 1492–1500.

Jun Xu, Tao Mei, Ting Yao, and Yong Rui. 2016. Msr-vtt: A large video description dataset for bridging video and language. In *Proceedings of the IEEE conference on computer vision and pattern recognition*, pages 5288–5296.

Min-Hsuan Yeh, Vincent Chen, Ting-Hao Huang, and Lun-Wei Ku. 2022. Multi-VQG: Generating engaging questions for multiple images. In *Proceedings of the 2022 Conference on Empirical Methods in Natural Language Processing*, pages 277–290, Abu Dhabi, United Arab Emirates. Association for Computational Linguistics.

Zhenjie Zhao, Yufang Hou, Dakuo Wang, Mo Yu, Chengzhong Liu, and Xiaojuan Ma. 2022. Educational question generation of children storybooks via question type distribution learning and event-centric summarization. *arXiv preprint arXiv:2203.14187*.

A Appendix

A.1 Causal and Temporal Inference Abstraction

Videos:

Ground Truth Questions:
1: why is the man in green holding onto the shoe as the man in white is cutting it?
2: what does the man in white do after holding the shoe stably?
3: why did the man in green point his hand at the man in white while he is talking?
4: why did the man in white pick up a knife after changing place with the man in green?
5: why does the man in green hold a shoes in his hand at the start?
6: what does the man in white do after cutting the shoes for a while?
7: why did the man in green hold up the shoe as he is speaking?
8: how do the men appear while cutting the shoes?
9: why are the men looking down at the shoe while the man in white is cutting it?
10: why did the man in white stand beside the man in green while he is speaking?
11: why did the man in white move behind after the man in green put down the shoe on the table?

Global Frame Comparison: (***42 matching overlap***)
"1": "why did the man in black hold onto the man in black s hand when he walks ?",
"2": "how did the man in black show that he wants to cut the glass?",
"3": "why did the man in black look at the man in black when he walks to the man in black ?",
"4": "why did the man in black bend down at the start ?",
"5": "why did the man in black put his hand on the glass in the middle of the video?",
"6": "why did the man in black point to the man in black when he is speaking?",
"7": "what did the man in black do after he walked to the man in black ?",
"8": "how does the man in black look while talking ?",
"9": "why did the man in black hold onto the bottle when he walks?",
"10": "why did the man in black walk back to the man in black after he finished talking?",
"11": "why did the man in black change his position after` he sat down"

Video MLP: (***39 matching overlap***)
"1": "why did the man in black hold onto the man in red s hand when he walks?",
"2": "what did the man in black do after he pointed at the grass at the start?",
"3": "why did the man in black look at the man in black after he stops walking?",
"4": "why did the man in black bend down at the start?",
"5": "why did the man in black hold the stick in his hand?",
"6": "why did the man in black point to the man in black when he is talking?",
"7": "why did the man in black bend down at the start?",
"8": "how does the man in black look while talking?",
"9": "why is the man in black holding the stick?",
"10": "why did the man in black walk towards the man in green after he finished talking?",
"11": "why did the man in black move backwards after he has finished talking?"

Figure A1: Frame Comparison Performance. Yellow scopes represent matching overlap with ground truth questions. Red scopes represent more details recognized by the frame comparison method compared with the Video MLP method.

A.2 Negative Methods for Causal and Temporal Inference Abstraction

A.2.1 Contrastive Learning Based on Frame Comparison

Contrastive Learning on Unifying Vision and Language Embedding aims to leverage the nuanced interplay between video frames using contrastive learning. The infoNCE loss function (Oord et al., 2018) is employed for contrastive learning (Wu et al., 2021), maximizing the lower bound of mutual information between pairs of variables. The core framework encompasses a relevance function such as cosine similarity, represented as $f(\cdot,\cdot)$, where each positive sample (x^+, c) is linked with a set of k randomly chosen negative samples denoted as $(x_1^-, c), (x_2^-, c), ..., (x_k^-, c)$. Then, the InfoNCE loss function $\mathcal{L}_k$ is formulated as follows:

$$\mathcal{L}_k = -\log\left(\frac{e^{f(x^+,c)}}{e^{f(x^+,c)} + \sum_{i=1}^{k} e^{f(x_i^-,c)}}\right) \quad (5)$$

Positive samples are derived from two frame pairs: the global contradictory frame pair and the local contradictory frame pair, similar to the methods in the Contradictory Frame Comparison Section. The remaining frames, paired with the second frame from each contradictory set, serve as negative samples. These positive and negative samples, along with the second frame's embedding, are used in the infoNCE loss formula. The contrastive learning loss is integrated with the pre-trained language model loss, defining the total loss function. Formally, the total loss function was defined as:

$$\mathcal{L}_{Total} = \mathcal{L}_{language\ model} + \mathcal{L}_k \quad (6)$$

A.2.2 Visual-Semantic Arithmetic Inferential Relation

Visual-Semantic Arithmetic Inferential Relation Abstraction aims to capture relationships between frames within a video by subtracting frame embeddings. Drawing inspiration from recent findings (Tewel et al., 2022; Goh et al., 2021) on the CLIP multi-modal representation, we develop a loss function which is adapted to guide the language model in recognizing relationships, especially causal and temporal ones. Specifically, we first compute the relevance of frames for potential tokens at length i. Top K token candidates are selected, while the remaining tokens are assigned zero potential to enhance computational efficiency. These candidate sentences, denoted as $s_i^k = (x_1, ..., x_{i-1}, x_i^k)$, correspond to the k-th candidate token and are matched against the frame I. It is pertinent to highlight that the context tokens $x_1, ..., x_{i-1}$ are constant for the current token x_i^k. Subsequently, the frame potential of the k-th token is computed as:

$$D_i^k \propto \exp\left(\frac{F_{cos}(E_{Text}(s_i^k), E_{frame}(I))}{\tau_c}\right), \quad (7)$$

Here, F_{cos} represents the cosine distance between CLIP's embeddings of the text (E_{Text}) and the frame (E_{Image}). The hyperparameter $\tau_c > 0$ is a temperature parameter that adjusts the sharpness of the target distribution. In our experiments, it was set to 0.05. Notably, the frame embedding E_{Image} emerges from subtracting the CLIP image embeddings of two frames. Subsequently, the CLIP loss materializes as the cross-entropy loss between the frame potential distribution and the target distribution of the next token x_{i+1} derived from the language model:

$$\mathcal{L}_{CLIP} = CE(D_i, x_{i+1}). \quad (8)$$

This loss encourages the language model to discern relationships between frames, fostering causal and temporal inferences. The total loss function combines the language model loss and the CLIP loss:

$$\mathcal{L}_{Total} = \mathcal{L}_{language\ model} + \mathcal{L}_{CLIP} \quad (9)$$

A.3 Experiment Results on Negative Methods for Causal and Temporal Inference Abstraction

model	B	RL	M	C	Grounding
Global Frame Comparison baseline	0.1538	**0.4165**	0.3578	1.007	0.3417
Global Frame Comparison Contrast	**0.1555**	0.4164	**0.3601**	**1.010**	0.3383
Local Frame Comparison Contrast	0.1531	0.4165	0.3555	1.001	**0.3426**

Table A1: Contrasting Learning Performance. The baseline is the "Global Frame Comparison" shown in Table 5. B is BLEU, RL is ROUGEL, M is METEOR, C is CIDEr, and Grounding is the F1-score grounding metric.

A.3.1 Experiment Results on Contrastive Learning Based on Frame Comparison

Contrastive Learning Based on Frame Comparison evaluates two contrasting learning methods rooted in global frame comparisons, summarized in Appendix Table A1. Surprisingly, both global frame contrast and local frame contrast methods outperform the baseline in specific metrics, showcasing the potential of contrastive learning in enhancing the language model's ability to discern nuanced details within videos, such as characters, colours, verbs, and tense, as illustrated within Appendix Figure A2's red scope. Despite the marginal overall performance difference, contrasting learning proves beneficial for the language model in understanding video content and generating inferential questions, particularly concerning temporal relationships, shown in Appendix Table A2 and Appendix Table A3. However, the similarity in performance raises considerations about the limited negative sample pool and the constrained parameters of the T5 small model, affecting the model's ability to differentiate between positive and negative samples during contrastive learning. This observation highlights the need for a more extensive negative sample pool and suggests potential limitations in the model's capacity to encompass comprehensive knowledge for effective contrastive learning in continuous video data.

A.3.2 Experient results on Visual-Semantic Arithmetic Inferential Relation

Visual-Semantic Arithmetic Inferential Relation reveals that the visual-semantic arithmetic method's performance closely resembles the baseline approach of directly concatenating vision embeddings, detailed in Table A4. This suggests that supplementing the visual-semantic arithmetic with CLIP loss may not significantly enhance performance. A comparison of questions generated by two frame selection techniques indicates similarities and disparities, with examples presented in Appendix Figure A3. Examination of generated questions in causal and temporal types, along with matching overlap levels with the baseline, is detailed in Appendix Table A5. However, the visual-semantic arithmetic method outperforms in temporal questions, exhibiting a 1-2% increase compared to direct vision concatenation, particularly excelling in recognizing time adverbs. Despite its effectiveness, the method's reliance on multi-model concatenation may fall short in enabling the language model to comprehensively discern the complete spectrum of visual relationships within contrasting frame pairs in a video, as suggested by examples in Appendix Figure A4.

model	NN	WRB	VBD	VBZ	VB	JJ	VBG	WP	PRP
Global Frame Comparison baseline	4166	2571	981	**1489**	776	503	**345**	1131	**247**
Global Frame Comparison Contrast	**4222**	2553	**1157**	1332	592	**558**	224	**1155**	233
Local Frame Comparison Contrast	4196	**2588**	1122	1310	**823**	530	225	1136	244

Table A2: Number of matching overlap for various word types based on Spacy about the frame contrasting methods. NN means noun, singular or mass, WRB means wh-adverb, VBZ means verb, 3rd person singular present, VBD means verb, past tense, VB means verb, base form, JJ means adjective, VBG means verb, gerund or present participle, WP means wh-pronoun, personal, PRP means pronoun, personal.

model	C G precision	C G recall	C G F1-score	T G precision	T G recall	T G F1-score
Global Frame Comparison	0.3089	**0.3074**	**0.3081**	0.3817	0.3509	0.3656
Global Frame Comparison Contrast	**0.3138**	0.2960	0.3046	0.3562	0.3383	0.3470
Local Frame Comparison Contrast	0.3010	0.2939	0.2974	**0.3972**	**0.3599**	**0.3776**

Table A3: Contrasting Learning Methods Evaluation Performance in Causal and Temporal Inference. C G represents the causal grounding metric. T G represents the Temporal causal grounding metric.

model	B	RL	M	C	Grounding
Video MLP	0.1564	**0.4216**	0.3594	**1.0366**	**0.3505**
CLIPloss top word 100	**0.1568**	0.4184	**0.3602**	1.0359	0.3460

Table A4: Visual-semantic arithmetic inferential performance. Video MLP represents the direct vision concatenation method. CLIPloss represents the visual-semantic arithmetic method. B is BLEU, RL is ROUGEL, M is METEOR, C is CIDEr, and Grounding is the grounding metric.

model	C G precision	C G recall	C G F1-score	T G precision	T G recall	T G F1-score
Video MLP	**0.3204**	**0.3072**	**0.3137**	0.3695	0.3331	0.3503
CLIPloss top word 100	0.3107	0.3061	0.3084	**0.3828**	**0.3433**	**0.3620**

Table A5: Visual-semantic Arithmetic Evaluation Performance in Causal and Temporal Inference. C G represents the causal grounding metric. T G represents the Temporal causal grounding metric.

Videos:

Ground Truth Questions:

1: what did the lady in black do after the man next to her gave her a microphone?
2: how did the lady in black reacted when the man in black beside her passed her the microphone?
3: what is the man with white tag on shirt do while man in stripes speaking?
4: why did the man in black with tied up hair turned backwards after he received the microphone?
5: what is the lady in black doing with her hands as she spoke into the microphone at the end of the video?
6: what did the man in grey do after he finished his speech?
7: what did the man in black in front of the man in grey do before the man in grey passed him the microphone?
8: why did the man in black with tied up hair walked towards the man in grey in the middle of the video?
9: why is the lady in black moving her hands at the end of video?
10: why did the lady in black face the man in black beside her before she started talking into the microphone?

Global Frame Contrast Learning: (***58 matching overlap***)

"1": "what does the lady in black do after the man in black points at her at the start?",
"2": "how did the man in black react when the man in black was talking?",
"3": "what did the man in black do as the man in white was talking?",
"4": "why did the man in black walk away after he finished talking?",
"5": "why did the man in black move his hands away from the lady in white?",
"6": "what did the man in black do after he finished speaking?",
"7": "what did the man in black do after the man in grey walked away?",
"8": "why did the man in black walk towards the man in black?",
"9": "why did the man in black raise his hands in the air at the end of the video?",
"10": "what did the lady in black do after she turned to face the man in black?"

Global Frame Baseline: (***40 matching overlap***)

"1": "what does the man in blue do after the man in blue points at him at the start?",
"2": "what does the man in blue do after he finishes talking?",
"3": "what did the man in blue do after he walked away from the man in blue?",
"4": "why did the man in blue walk away after he walked away?",
"5": "why did the man in blue move his hand towards the lady in blue at the end of the video?",
"6": "what did the man in black do after he finished talking?",
"7": "what did the man in black do after the man in grey walked away at the end of the video?",
"8": "why did the man in blue walk towards the man in blue?",
"9": "why did the man in black move his hands as he speaks?",
"10": "what did the man in blue do after he pointed at the man in blue?"

Local Frame Contrast Learning: (***47 matching overlap***)

"1": "what does the man in black do after the man in black starts speaking?",
"2": "what did the man in black do after he took the photo?",
"3": "what does the man in black do as the man in black was talking?",
"4": "why did the man in black walk away after he talked to the man in black?",
"5": "why did the man in black move his hand towards the lady in black?",
"6": "what did the man in black do after he finished singing?",
"7": "what did the man in black do after the man in grey walked away?",
"8": "why did the man in black walk towards the man in black?",
"9": "why did the man in black move his hands as he speaks?",
"10": "what did the man in black do after he walked to the man in black?"

Figure A2: Contrast Learning Performance. Yellow scopes represent matching overlap with ground truth questions. Red scopes represent more details recognized by the frame contrasting methods compared to the global frame comparison method.

Videos:

Ground Truth Questions:
1: where is the man and the girl?
2: how does the man react when the horse plays with the girl?
3: what does the girl do after patting the horse?
4: how does the girl in pink react when the horse licks her?
5: what does the horse do after the girl pats it in the middle of the video?
6: how does the girl react when the horse turns towards her the first time?
7: does the girl seem more scared or excited to play with the horse?
8: what does the horse do after it turns back to the girl the second time?
9: why does the girl move her head away from the horse at the end of the video?
10; what does the man do when the horse plays with the girl?
11: what is the animal show in the video?
12: what does the girl do after tucking her hair behind her ear?

Visual-semantic Arithmetic Method: (***51 matching overlap***)
"1": "where is this video taken?",
"2": "how does the girl react when the man is playing with her?",
"3": "what did the girl do after the man walked away?",
"4": "how does the girl react when the man is playing with her?",
"5": "what does the girl do after the horse approaches her at the end?",
"6": "how does the girl react when the man is playing with her?",
"7": "why did the girl start jumping when the horse is near her?",
"8": "why did the girl put her hand on her face when the horse approached her?",
"9": "why did the girl bend down at the end of the video?",
"10": "how does the man support the girl as she stands on the horse?",
"11": "what is the animal shown in the video?",
"12": "what does the girl do after the man puts her down?"

VideoMLP Baseline: (***44 matching overlap***)
"1": "where is this place?",
"2": "how does the girl react after the horse jumps up?",
"3": "what does the girl do after the man approaches her at the end?",
"4": "how does the girl react after the horse jumps up?",
"5": "how does the dog show affection towards the girl?",
"6": "how does the girl react after the horse jumps up?",
"7": "why did the girl start jumping when the horse approached her?",
"8": "why did the girl put her hand on the horse after the horse jumps up?",
"9": "why did the girl run towards the horse after the horse jumped up?",
"10": "how does the man ensure the girl does not fall?",
"11": "what animal is shown in the video?",
"12": "what does the girl do after the man starts to approach her at the start?"

Figure A3: Visual-semantic arithmetic method performance. Yellow scopes represent matching overlaps with ground truth questions. Red scopes represent more details recognized by the visual-semantic arithmetic method.

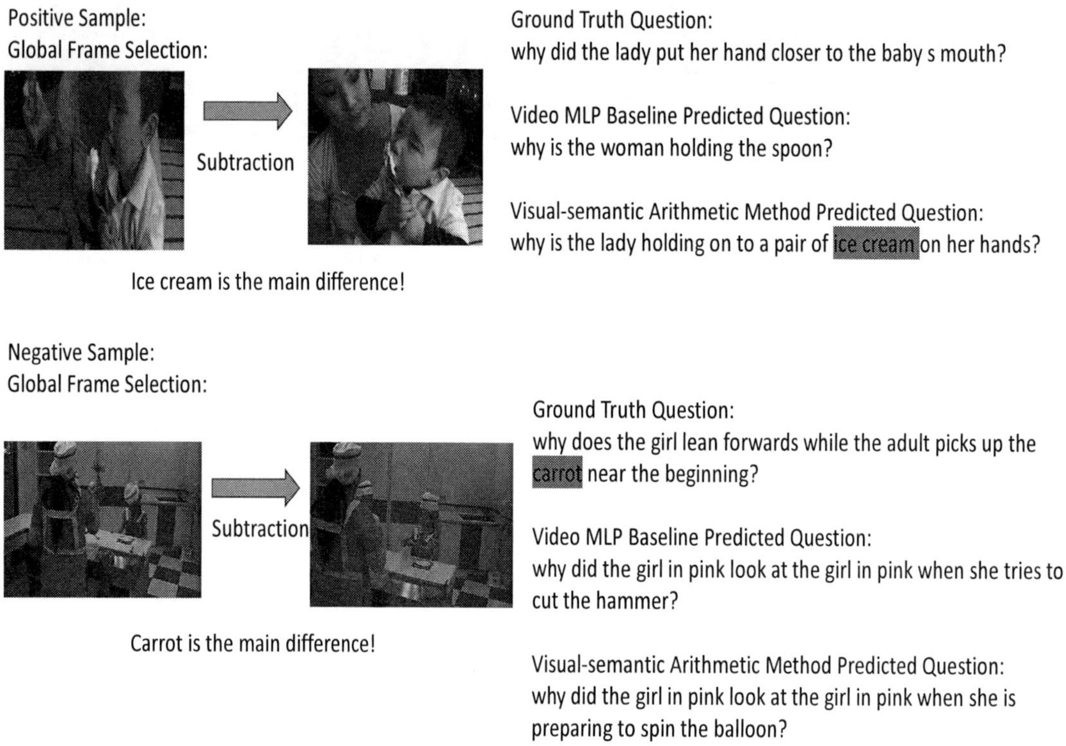

Figure A4: The effectiveness of the Visual-semantic arithmetic method: check if the language model could recognize the difference between two frames.

Improving Vision-Language Cross-Lingual Transfer with Scheduled Unfreezing

Max Reinhardt[1] **Gregor Geigle**[12] **Radu Timofte**[2] **Goran Glavaš**[1]
[1]WüNLP, [2]Computer Vision Lab, CAIDAS, University of Würzburg,
gregor.geigle@uni-wuerzburg.de

Abstract

Large-scale pretraining of vision-language (VL) models brought dramatic improvements across numerous tasks, from visual question-answering to cross-modal retrieval but these gains are mostly limited to English. Massively multilingual VL encoder models (mVLMs) hold promise for other languages: after fine-tuning on only English task data, they can perform the task in other languages in what is termed zero-shot cross-lingual transfer (ZS-XLT). Still, ZS-XLT sees a large performance gap to English, especially for low-resource languages. In this work, we reduce this gap with a fine-tuning strategy known as *Scheduled Unfreezing* (SUF): instead of updating all parameters from the start, we begin with the top layer(s) of the vision-language encoder and gradually unfreeze (i.e., update) its layers top to bottom. SUF forces reliance on encoder's representations from higher layers: the fact that in multilingual models these representations encode higher-level semantics rather than low-level language-specific idiosyncrasies, we hypothesize, should render SUF beneficial for ZS-XLT. Experiments with two mVLMs (UC2 & CCLM) on three downstream tasks (xGQA, XVNLI, xFlickrCo) show that SUF brings consistent gains in ZS-XLT, especially for visual Q&A (xGQA) by up to 10 points.

1 Introduction

Recent vision-language (VL) models (Zhou et al., 2021; Zeng et al., 2022; Li et al., 2023a; Liu et al., 2023c; Geigle et al., 2023, inter alia), trained on massive amounts of image-text data, led to dramatic improvements on virtually all VL tasks (e.g., image-text retrieval or visual Q&A). This progress, however, benefits primarily English. Large Vision-Language models (LVLMs) (Li et al., 2023a; Liu et al., 2023c,b; Dai et al., 2023; Bai et al., 2023)—which align an image encoder to a Large Language Model (LLM)—excel in generalizing *zero-shot* to new tasks (without task-specific fine-tuning). Most LVLMs use English LLMs and are not highly multilingual; they fail to follow instructions in other languages or produce English output (Geigle et al., 2023; Kew et al., 2023; Holtermann et al., 2024; Shaham et al., 2024). Multilingual LVLMs are much less available[1] and generally underperform their English counterparts (Geigle et al., 2023).

The alternative is task-specific fine-tuning of smaller, but massively multilingually pretrained VL *encoder* models (mVLMs) (Ni et al., 2021; Zhou et al., 2021; Zeng et al., 2022). Here, however, task-specific training data exists predominantly in English which forces us to rely on *zero-shot cross-lingual transfer* (ZS-XLT) (Conneau et al., 2020b; Lauscher et al., 2020): due to the massively multilingual pretraining, the encoders fine-tuned on English task data can be used for inference in other languages. Still, ZS-XLT results in substantial performance drops in other languages compared to English, especially for less represented target languages in m(V)LM's pretraining. While few-shot training for specific target languages can reduce this performance gap (Lauscher et al., 2020; Schmidt et al., 2022), annotating sufficient data (for training and model validation) is expensive and does not scale to hundreds of languages.

In this work, we improve ZS-XLT with mVLMs using a training method known as *scheduled unfreezing* (SUF) (Howard and Ruder, 2018a; Liu et al., 2024). SUF, which we apply in task-specific fine-tuning of an mVLM on English data, gradually increases the set of encoder's (i.e., Transformer's) parameters that are being fine-tuned (i.e., updated), starting from the last layer(s) and gradually adding lower layers of the Transformer stack as the training progresses. Multilingual language-only encoders have been shown to encode language-agnostic high-level semantic knowledge in higher layers and language-specific idiosyn-

[1]Powerful multilingual LVLMs such as Google's PaLI models (Chen et al., 2023) are, unfortunately, not public.

Proceedings of the 3rd Workshop on Advances in Language and Vision Research, pages 155–166
August 16, 2024 ©2024 Association for Computational Linguistics

crasies in lower layers (Libovický et al., 2020; Hu et al., 2020). If the same holds for mVLMs, then SUF—by enforcing stronger reliance on representations from higher layers of an mVLM—should facilitate ZS-XLT for VL tasks. Put differently, with SUF fine-tuning on English-only data, idiosyncratic English-specific knowledge from lower layers of the encoder is less available, forcing the model to rely on more language-agnostic knowledge from higher layers of the encoder.

We evaluate the effects of SUF fine-tuning on ZS-XLT for two multilingual vision-language encoders: UC2 (Zhou et al., 2021) and CCLM (Zeng et al., 2022); and on three distinct downstream tasks: visual QA (xGQA (Pfeiffer et al., 2022)), image-text retrieval (xFlickrCo (Bugliarello et al., 2022)), and visual entailment (XVNLI (Bugliarello et al., 2022)). We find that SUF consistently improves performance compared to standard fine-tuning: by up to 3 points in retrieval and entailment and by a massive 10 points for visual QA.

Our further fine-grained analysis of model behavior on xGQA reveals that: (1) in standard fine-tuning the performance for most target languages stagnates or degrades over the course of (English) training, while the English performance steadily improves. (2) in SUF fine-tuning, in contrast, trajectory of target language performance longer mirrors that of English performance, suggesting that the model relies on more language-agnostic representations; this results in massive improvements especially for some languages distant from English, such as Korean and Bengali. Using parallel data, we show that SUF fine-tuning indeed leads to cross-lingually more aligned representations of the sequence start token (`[CLS]`), which is input to the classifier. Finally, we compare SUF against two other strategies that similarly reduce reliance on lower layers of the encoder: (1) layer-wise learning rate decay and (2) fixed training of only the top layers. While both these also yield some performance gains, they underperform SUF. SUF-based fine-tuning not only improves ZS-XLT of mVLMs but is also computationally more efficient than standard fine-tuning: we thus hope that our work motivates broader investigation of SUF strategies in the context of multilingual VL models.

2 Related Work

Cross-lingual Transfer with Vision-Language Models. Bugliarello et al. (2022) created the IGLUE benchmark, which has become the de facto benchmark for evaluating cross-lingual transfer abilities of mVLMs. IGLUE comprises four VL tasks: visual QA (xGQA (Pfeiffer et al., 2022)), visual entailment (XVNLI (Xie et al., 2019)), multi-image reasoning (MaRVL) (Suhr et al., 2019; Liu et al., 2021a), and image-text retrieval (Lin et al., 2014; Plummer et al., 2015). Being designed specifically for ZS-XLT, each dataset in IGLUE comes with a training portion in English and test portions in different target languages.

Bugliarello et al. (2022) compare several multilingual VL encoder models on IGLUE, namely: M3P (Ni et al., 2021), x/mUNITER (Liu et al., 2021a), and UC2 (Zhou et al., 2021)), primarily in ZS-XLT, but also in few-shot cross-lingual transfer (FS-XLT) in which few training instances in target languages are assumed to exist. Crucially, in both setups they demonstrate significant gaps between models' English performance and their performance for other languages. Subsequent models such as CCLM (Zeng et al., 2022), Li et al. (2023b), and Ernie-UniX2 (Shan et al., 2022) improved target-language performance, but since their English performance improved as well, this resulted overall in similar ZS-XLT performance gaps.

For visual question answering in particular, there has been work dedicated to reducing the cross-lingual performance gap. Nooralahzadeh and Sennrich (2023) assessed that a high ambiguity in the label space makes learning more difficult, attempting to remedy for this with several strategies, including addition of a similarity-based loss to standard classification cross-entropy loss, code-switching at the instance level and a sparse fine-tuning approach. Liu et al. (2023a) reduce the ZS-XLT performance gap by replacing the standard single-layer classifier with a deeper two-layer architecture. Observing stark performance differences across different question types, they also introduced a special question-type token.

Finally, Geigle et al. (2023) find that fine-tuning a multilingual LVLM that relies on mT0 (Xue et al., 2021; Muennighoff et al., 2022) as the LLM backbone nearly closes the ZS-XLT gap. Training and fine-tuning billion-parameter LVLMs is, however, much more computationally expensive; crucially, the same is true for inference, which hinders model application for most users. Moreover, Geigle et al. (2023) show that the cross-lingual performance gap is highly dependent on the backbone LLM, ob-

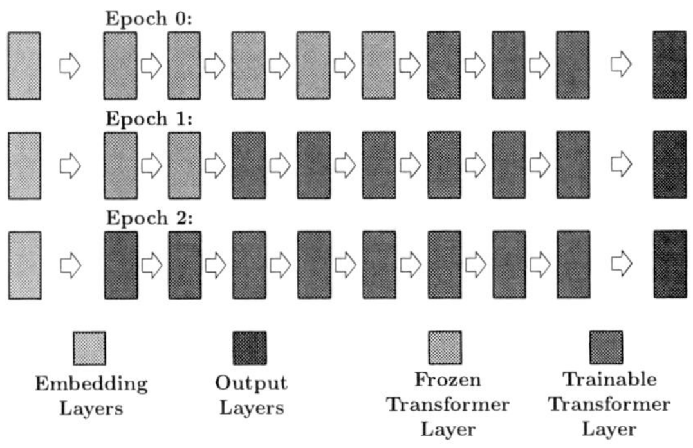

Figure 1: Illustration of Scheduled Unfreezing; each rectangle shows one Transformer layer, green rectangles denote unfrozen layers whereas gray ones indicate frozen layers. The embedding layer (orange) is kept unfrozen along with the task-specific classification head (purple). In every epoch, we unfreeze a fixed number of layers from top to bottom.

serving larger ZS-XLT gaps with BLOOMZ (Scao et al., 2022; Muennighoff et al., 2022).

In this work, we focus on encoder mVLMs, due to their smaller computational footprint and thus broader applicability. To the best of our knowledge, our SUF is the first strategy shown to substantially reduce the ZS-XLT gap for VL encoders.

Unfreezing training strategies. Various strategies for (un)freezing model parts have been proposed in transfer learning scenarios. Howard and Ruder (2018b) introduce Gradual Unfreezing for fine-tuning a pretrained recurrent LM, to avoid catastrophic forgetting across different text classification tasks; in each epoch, starting from the top layer, they unfreeze one layer of the pretrained LM. However, Raffel et al. (2020) find that this underperforms full model fine-tuning for Transformer-based LMs. In the context of XLT with multilingual LMs, in concurrent work Liu et al. (2024) propose a scoring function that dynamically decides when and which layers to unfreeze. In this work, in contrast, we investigate a simpler fixed unfreezing schedule and focus on bimodal vision-language models rather than unimodal language-only models.

3 Scheduled Unfreezing

The exact setup on which we focus in this work is zero-shot cross-lingual transfer (ZS-XLT) for downstream vision-language tasks (e.g., visual QA) with massively multilingual vision-language encoder models (mVLMs) as vehicles of the transfer. In this setup, we fine-tune the mVLM on task-specific data in English only and evaluate its performance on task-specific data in other languages.

Based on the observation (from multilingual language-only encoders) that multilingual encoders encode more language-agnostic higher-order semantics in their upper Transformer layers and language-specific information in their lower layers (Libovický et al., 2020; Hu et al., 2020), we propose fine-tuning based on top-to-bottom **scheduled unfreezing** (SUF) as a method to facilitate cross-lingual transfer with mVLMs. The motivation for SUF in this context is as follows: by (initially) freezing lower Transformer layers, the classification head is forced to solve the task by tuning language-agnostic knowledge from higher Transformer layers of the mVLM first. Contrary, in full fine-tuning, the classifier can additionally leverage language-specific knowledge from lower layers—when fine-tuned on English tasks data only. This means that the classifier is more likely to overfit to English-specific features, harming the effectiveness of cross-lingual transfer to other languages.

To test this hypothesis, we use a fixed-schedule unfreezing in this work, illustrated in Figure 1. The general idea is not to train the full model from the start, but freeze (i.e., not update) all but the top k layers at the beginning and then gradually unfreeze k layers top-to-bottom in every epoch.

Architecture-specific Implementation. Compared to unimodal language-only encoders (Devlin et al., 2019; Conneau et al., 2020b), mVLMs additionally contain components for encoding the visual modality (i.e., images). Moreover, mVLMs come with different architectures, differing primarily w.r.t. where cross-modal information aggregation occurs. As such, we introduce architecture-specific unfreezing schedules for the two mVLMs with which we experiment in this work: UC2 (Zhou et al., 2021) and CCLM (Zeng et al., 2022).

UC2 is an encoder Transformer model, architecturally identical to the language-only XLM-R encoder (Conneau et al., 2020a). UC2 encodes an image offline, relying on an object detection model (Ren et al., 2015)[2]; the features for image regions given by this model are linearly projected and then concatenated with the text embeddings as input to the model. The image region vectors are treated by the Transformer like any other text token. As a result, we can use general SUF without any adjust-

[2]All images are processed prior to training and the detection model is not used during training of UC2.

ments: UC2, using a base-size XLM-R architecture, has 12 Transformer layers. In the first epoch, the task-specific classification head, the embedding layer[3], and the top $k = 3$ Transformer layers remain unfrozen. After every training epoch, we unfreeze 3 additional layers, top to bottom.

CCLM, also a Transformer-based encoder, comprises n layers for processing only the text input, followed by m more cross-modal layers, which additionally have a cross-attention component. Through this cross-attention, the model attends to the image features extracted by a separate Vision Transformer (ViT) (Dosovitskiy et al., 2020). For $\text{CCLM}_{\text{base}}$, which we use in our experiments, there are n=12 layers for pure text encoding (initialized from XLM-R), followed by m=6 cross-modal layers (initialized from X2-VLM (Zeng et al., 2023)). We keep the ViT fully unfrozen during training. The motivation for this is twofold: (i) the resolution of images in fine-tuning is larger (384x384) than in its pretraining (224x224), requiring ViT to adapt; and (ii) we employ SUF to reduce the impact of language-specific (i.e., English) overfitting in fine-tuning and image encoding with ViT is inherently language-agnostic. We thus keep the ViT, task-specific classification head, and embedding layer unfrozen throughout training. In the first epoch, we additionally start with the top $k = 3$ Transformer layers (out of $m + n$=18) unfrozen and then unfreeze 3 more layers after each epoch.

4 Evaluation

We provide details of our experimental setup and then consider results over three downstream tasks with the two architectures (UC2 & CCLM).

4.1 Experimental Setup

Datasets. We evaluate SUF on the multilingual IGLUE benchmark (Bugliarello et al., 2022) for ZS-XLT. IGLUE spans 4 different tasks: visual QA (**xGQA** (Pfeiffer et al., 2022; Hudson and Manning, 2019)), image-text retrieval (**xFlickrCo** (Bugliarello et al., 2022)), visual entailment (**XVNLI**) (Xie et al., 2019; Bugliarello et al., 2022), and multi-image reasoning (**MaRVL** (Liu et al., 2021b)). We exclude MaRVL, because it requires changes to the model architecture in order to support multi-image input.

[3]Initial experiments showed that keeping the embedding layer unfrozen was critical for good performance.

xGQA contains diverse questions over multiple question types – Verify (yes/no), Query (open), Choose (one of two options), Logical (true or false), Compare (across multiple objects) – with nearly 2000 unique labels. This dataset is obtained by extending the monolingual GQA (Hudson and Manning, 2019) with human translations in 7 languages. The English training portion contains 943K examples. We report classification accuracy.

For image-text retrieval, the task is to retrieve the best caption for an image (Text Retrieval, TR) or the corresponding image given a caption (Image Retrieval, IR). We use xFlickrCo which couples 1K images from Flickr30K (Plummer et al., 2015) test portion with 1K images from the COCO (Lin et al., 2014) test portion with human-written captions in 7 languages (plus the original English Flickr30k and MSCOCO captions). For training, we use the Flickr30k training split with 145K examples. As metric, we report recall@1 (R@1)—the proportion of images (in TR) or captions (in IR) for which the matching caption (in TR) or image (in IR) is positioned at the very top of the ranking.

For visual entailment on XVNLI, a model must predict if a statement (i.e., a hypothesis), is entailed, contradicts, or is neutral to an image (as the "premise"). The training portion of the dataset consists of 541K English examples and the test portion covers 4 other languages (Arabic, Spanish, French, and Russian). We report results in terms of classification accuracy.

Training Setup. We mirror the training procedures from IGLUE and (Zeng et al., 2022) for task-specific fine-tuning of of UC2 and CCLM. For xGQA with UC2, we add a 2-layer classification head (with $\sim$ 2000 classes, i.e., valid answers from the training data). CCLM casts VQA as a generation task, adding a full-blown 6-layer decoder Transformer (the input to which is the representation of the `[CLS]` token, output of the last layer of the CCLM's cross-encoder). The decoder Transformer is trained on the task and as such not frozen.

Hyperparameters: We train for the same number of epochs for each task as in IGLUE: 5/10/10 epochs, for xGQA, XVNLI, and xFlickrCo, respectively. Regarding other hyperparameter values, we follow IGLUE for training UC2, using the learning rate of $4 \cdot 10^{-5}$ for xGQA and $2 \cdot 10^{-5}$ for XVNLI and xFlickrCo. We train in batches of size 256 for xGQA, 64 for xFlickrCo, and 128 for XVNLI. For CCLM (the original work did not report fine-tuning hyperparameter values), we use a learning rate of $2 \cdot 10^{-5}$ for the image encoder (i.e., ViT) and $3 \cdot 10^{-5}$ for the rest of the model. We use an effective batch size of 256/128/144 for xGQA, xFlickrCo, and XVNLI, respectively, resorting to gradient accumulation, due to limited GPU VRAM[4]. For both models and in all fine-tuning procedures, we use AdamW (Loshchilov and Hutter, 2019) optimizer, with linear warm-up for 10% of steps and weight decay of 0.01. We use exactly the same hyperparameters for standard and SUF fine-tuning.

Evaluation Setup. We compare SUF fine-tuning against standard full fine-tuning for ZS-XLT. In other words, we fine-tune the model on the task-specific English training split and then evaluate its performance on the same task on the test splits in English and other languages. We evaluate all models, with and without SUF, after the last training epoch. For xFlickrCo, with CCLM, we first pre-filter 128 best image (in IR) or captions (in TR) matches based on the cosine similarity of their image and text representations (computed independently from the other modality using the image encoder and the text-only layers), and then re-rank the candidates by jointly scoring all candidates. With UC2, we directly compute the pairwise similarity of all possible image-text pairs. For xGQA with CCLM, we perform constrained generation to the set of task-specific class labels.

4.2 Results

The overview of the ZS-XLT results (together with English performance), aggregated over all target languages for each task, is given in Table 1. Scheduled unfreezing (SUF) yields consistent ZS-XLT performance gains over standard fine-tuning for all three tasks and both UC2 and CCLM. At the same time, the English performance in SUF is comparable to that of standard fine-tuning. This means that not only does (1) SUF fine-tuning truly reduce the cross-lingual performance gap for mVLMs, but (2) freezing of lower layers does not seem to hurt the source language performance. While SUF fine-tuning of CCLM brings moderate 2-3 point improvements on XVNLI and xFlickrCo, on xGQA we observe a massive 10-point average gain over the 7 target languages. We next investigate the xQGA performance in more detail.

[4]For xFlickrCo, where we use in-batch negatives, this yields lower scores than reported in Zeng et al. (2022).

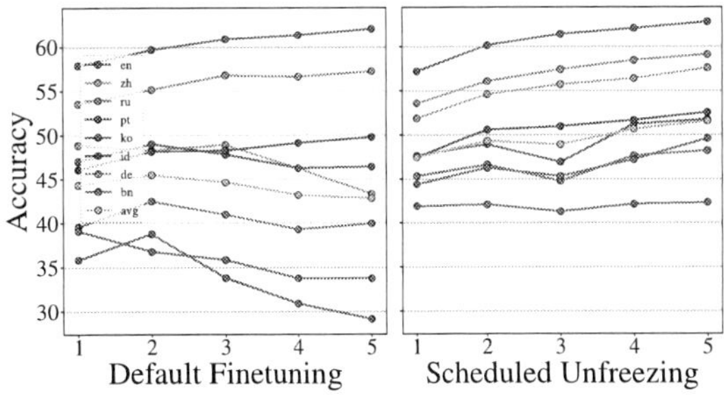

Figure 2: Results on xGQA for $\text{CCLM}_{\text{base}}$ after each epoch for each language. We compare the standard finetuning (left) with scheduled unfreezing (SUF) fine-tuning (right).

In-Depth Analysis for xGQA. Motivated by the large performance gains that SUF fine-tuning brings in ZS-XLT for xGQA, we next inspect model behavior on this task in more detail, across two performance dimensions: (i) individual target languages and (ii) different question types, aiming to unravel factors that specifically contribute to good ZS-XLT performance.

Per-Language Performance. We first analyze how training on English data affects the transfer to other languages for different training duration. In Figure 2, we show the per-epoch accuracy of $CCLM$ for all target languages (and EN as the source language. With standard fine-tuning, English performance improves throughout the training; the performance for most other languages, however, either stagnate or decreases. The only exception to this pattern is German (DE), which is not only a high-resource language but also linguistically closest to English. For languages most distant from English, Korean and Bengali, we observe largest performance drops with prolonged English training. Scheduled unfreezing, on the other hand, prevents this performance decay and most languages benefit from longer English training under SUF fine-tuning. Additionally, we see that most languages also start at a higher accuracy with scheduled unfreezing. This suggests that the freezing of lower layers at the start forces the model to rely on more language-agnostic features that transfer better.

Per-Question Type Performance. GQA is constructed around 5 question types: *Verify* (yes/no), *Query* (open), *Choose* (one out of two options), *Logical* (true or false), and *Compare* (across multiple objects). Figure 3 summarizes the ZS-XLT performance for different question types across the training epochs. We see that SUF fine-tuning pre-

Setup	xGQA		XVNLI		xFlickrCo			
					TR		IR	
	EN	ZS-XLT	EN	ZS-XLT	EN	ZS-XLT	EN	ZS-XLT
UC2	57.1	31.9	77.1	**61.7**	**36.8**	18.0	**43.0**	20.0
UC2+SUF	57.1	**41.3**	77.2	61.2	36.4	**20.0**	41.8	**22.3**
CCLM	62.0	42.8	**81.2**	68.6	77.7	63.4	78.0	64.2
CCLM+SUF	**62.8**	**51.5**	80.6	**70.6**	**78.5**	**66.7**	**78.6**	**67.1**

Table 1: Evaluation of SUF on UC2 and $\text{CCLM}_{\text{base}}$ across multiple V&L tasks. We report results for English (en) and averaged (avg) across all non-English languages. We **bold** the best results. We report accuracy for xGQA and XVNLI, and recall@1 for xFlickrCo for both Text Retrieval (TR) and Image Retrieval (IR).

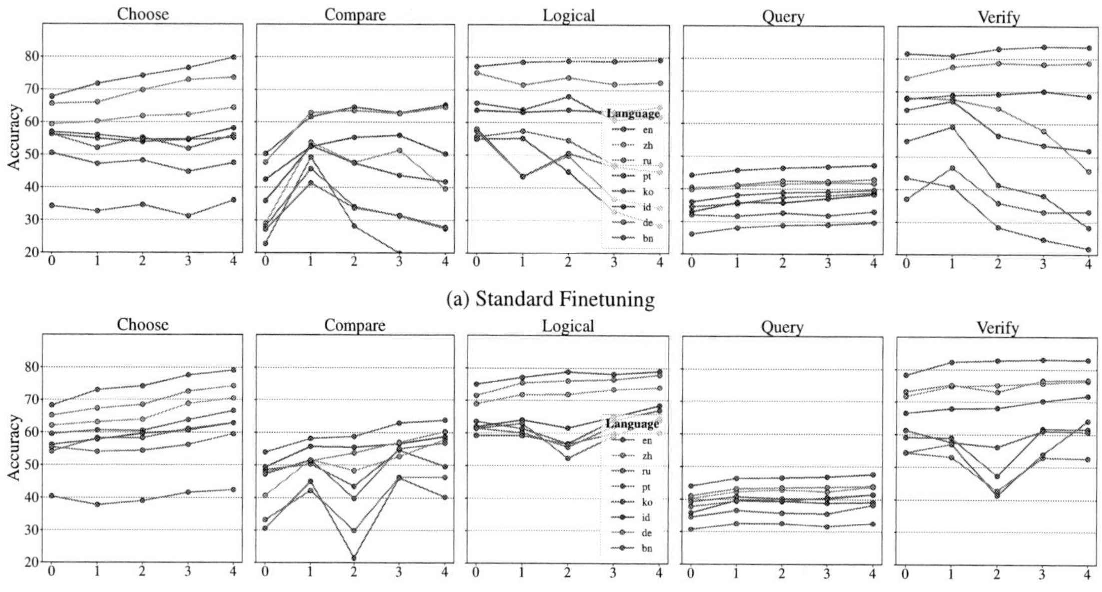

(a) Standard Finetuning

(b) Scheduled Unfreezing

Figure 3: Accuracy every epoch for each question type in xGQA for SUF and standard fine-tuning with $\text{CCLM}_{\text{base}}$.

vents language-specific overfitting to English in particular for *Compare*, *Logical*, and *Verify* questions. It is worth noting that all three question types effectively have only 'yes' and 'no' as answer labels. This means that SUF is not improving ZS-XLT by reducing label space ambiguity (like, e.g., Nooralahzadeh and Sennrich (2023)), but rather by preventing early overfitting to English-specific idiosyncrasies in the questions.

Expectedly, all models generally exhibit the lowest performance on the open-ended *Query* questions, which account for the largest portion of the xQGA data. For both *Query* and *Choose* questions, English training with both standard and SUF fine-tuning generally increases the performance for target languages throughout the training; for SUF fine-tuning, however, the starting accuracy scores are higher than for standard fine-tuning, resulting in overall better scores at the end of training.

5 Further Analysis

We further analyze SUF fine-tuning through the lens of cross-language similarity of [CLS] tokens for parallel data. We then compare SUF with conceptually similar alternatives: (i) layer-wise learning rate decay and (ii) updating only the top layers Transformer layers throughout the whole training. Finally, we report the results of few-shot cross-lingual transfer (FS-XLT).

5.1 Cross-Lingual Semantic Alignment

Our previous findings suggest that SUF can retain the cross-lingual transfer abilities of the mVLM better than standard finetuning. We thus further test cross-lingual semantic alignment for both fine-tuning regimes (with UC2), using parallel data.

SF	bn	de	en	id	ko	pt	ru	zh
bn	100	45	33	48	58	47	55	48
de	45	100	61	58	48	55	60	57
en	33	61	100	53	39	49	52	56
id	48	58	53	100	50	57	60	60
ko	58	48	39	50	100	54	57	56
pt	47	55	49	57	54	100	58	56
ru	55	60	52	60	57	58	100	60
zh	48	57	56	60	56	56	60	100

(a) xGQA: Standard Finetuning (Unpaired similarity: 20)

SUF	bn	de	en	id	ko	pt	ru	zh
bn	100	50	43	54	61	54	55	52
de	50	100	78	71	65	71	74	70
en	43	78	100	69	59	68	70	70
id	54	71	69	100	68	71	72	67
ko	61	65	59	68	100	67	67	66
pt	54	71	68	71	67	100	72	67
ru	55	74	70	72	67	72	100	70
zh	52	70	70	67	66	67	70	100

(b) xGQA: Scheduled Unfreezing (Unpaired similarity: 22)

SF	ar	en	es	fr	ru
ar	100	41	48	47	48
en	41	100	48	70	56
es	48	48	100	49	49
fr	47	70	49	100	58
ru	48	56	49	58	100

(c) XVNLI: Standard Finetuning (Unpaired similarity: 17)

SUF	ar	en	es	fr	ru
ar	100	76	83	79	83
en	76	100	79	89	84
es	83	79	100	82	83
fr	79	89	82	100	85
ru	83	84	83	85	100

(d) XVNLI: Scheduled Unfreezing (Unpaired similarity: 62)

Figure 4: Average pairwise CLS-similarity (in percentage points) between the translation-parallel examples of xGQA and XVNLI, compared between scheduled unfreezing (SUF) and standard fine-tuning (SF), evaluated on the last epoch of fine-tuning with UC2. For a baseline of similarity between unpaired examples, we report the average similarity between all examples over all languages (unpaired similarity).

With UC2, the predictions are made from the transformed vector of the sequence start token [CLS]. We thus analyze how similar representations of the [CLS] token are for parallel sentences (same meaning, but in different languages): The more language-agnostic the representations are, the more aligned should the [CLS] token vectors of parallel sentences be.

For this analysis, we leverage the multi-parallel instances of xGQA and XVNLI. We use simple cosine similarity to quantify the similarity of [CLS] vectors of mutual translations. Given that it is possible that a fine-tuning procedure can make inputs appear generally more similar, we also measure "baseline" average similarity between non-parallel sentences (randomly sampled).

Figure 4 displays the results of this analysis on the multi-parallel xGQA and XVNLI test data. We make two observations. First, the average similarity with English is highly correlated with the relative zero-shot performance between the languages with a Pearson correlation of over 0.9. This, unsurprisingly, means that there are higher cross-lingual similarities between instances, e.g., for English-German in xGQA or English-French for XVNLI, which also means better transfer results. This confirms the common assumption that good semantic alignment between representations of different languages is key for successful cross-lingual transfer: we show that the same is true for mVLMs. Second, we see that for xGQA, the pairwise similarity between the languages increases substantially more for SUF fine-tuning than for standard fine-tuning (also relatively, compared to the baseline similarity). This suggests that scheduled unfreezing yields more language-agnostic final representations for this task. For XVNLI, where SUF yielded no gains for UC2, the pairwise similarity also increases but so does the baseline similarity, suggesting no improvement in cross-lingual semantic alignment.

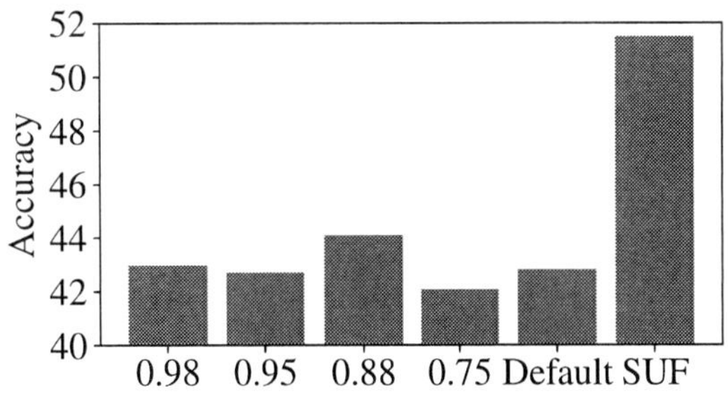

Figure 5: Result of different values for the decay factor d for layer-wise learning rate decay on zero-shot performance for xGQA compared to standard fine-tuning and scheduled unfreezing (SUF). Note that the y-axis starts at 40 to better show performance differences.

5.2 Layer-wise Learning Rate Decay

Our experiments suggest that ZS-XLT, especially with xGQA, profits when the lower layers are trained less. As an alternative to SUF, where a layer is either trained or not (with the same learning rate for all layers), we consider layer-wise learning rate decay. Here, the model is fully trained but we decay the learning rate exponentially between the layers, with a decay factor d, so that parameters of lower layers are trained with much smaller learning rates: For N layers and learning rate l, the actual learning rate $l(i)$ for layer i (counted bottom to top) is: $l(i) = ld^{N-i}$. This means that the top

Setup	en	avg
Standard	62.0	42.8
SUF	**62.8**	**51.5**
CM only	61.9	49.7

Table 2: Results with CCLM on xGQA comparing standard finetuning, scheduled unfreezing (SUF) , and cross-modal layers only (CM only), where we only train the top 6 cross-modal layers and freeze the rest.

layers are trained throughout with the same learning rate as in SUF, but the lower layers, instead of being "flicked-on", after some number of epochs, are instead trained from the start but with a much smaller learning rate. This, in principle, should also limit the overfitting to language-specific knowledge from lower layers.

To evaluate a reasonable range for the decay, we train $\text{CCLM}_{\text{base}}$ on xGQA and choose: $d \in \{0.98, 0.95, 0.88, 0.75\}$ with otherwise the same hyperparameters. As a result, the learning rate of the bottom layer (of 18) is 70% to 0.5% of the learning rate for the top layer.

We present the results in Figure 5. For $d = 0.98$, which decays the least, we see results close to the standard fine-tune setup. For $d = 0.75$, which effectively does not train the lowest layers, performance decreases. We see the best results for $d = 0.88$. While it achieves better results than the standard setup, it underperforms compared to scheduled unfreezing. Looking at per-language results here, we again observe that accuracy for languages like Bengali and Korean, which drop during standard training, are better retained with layer-wise decay.

5.3 Training Top-Layers Only

In Table 2, we test for CCLM, which has 12 XLM-R-initialized text-only layers and 6 cross-modal layers, a setup where we only train the upper 6 cross-modal layers (*CM only* in Table 2). While results are notably better compared to standard finetuning for zero-shot transfer, they are slightly worse than with SUF. Allowing the model to adapt the full model, albeit not fully from the start, is important for best performance though results on English are close to standard finetuning.

5.4 SUF in Few-Shot Training

While the focus of this work is on zero-shot cross-lingual transfer, we want to briefly explore if SUF can also further improve results in a few-shot setup. In a few-shot setup, the model is first trained on the large English train split (as in zero-shot) but then also trained on a few dozen to hundred examples in the target language. This can help reduce the performance gap for multiple IGLUE tasks (Bugliarello et al., 2022; Zeng et al., 2022).

Setup	Zero-Shot	Few-Shot
Standard	31.9	44.3
SUF	**41.3**	**46.7**

Table 3: Results for UC2 on xGQA for zero-shot and few-shot when trained with and without SUF on the English train split (*not* for few-shot step).

Following the few-shot setup in IGLUE for xGQA with UC2 (with the maximum 48 shots), we compare a model trained on the English data with and without scheduled unfreezing. During the few-shot training, both setups are trained identically, that is, scheduled unfreezing is not used. As shown in Table 3, SUF is only around 2 points better after few-shot training. While the more language-agnostic representations learned with SUF might be a slightly better starting point for few-shot training, we also see that with a few examples, the model can 'rectify' the performance drop seen during training on English for most languages.

6 Conclusion

Cross-lingual zero-shot allows us to train massively multilingual vision-language models on English task-specific data and then use them for other languages without additional target language training data. Still, there is a large performance gap to English. In this work, we leverage scheduled unfreezing – a finetuning strategy where we initially keep all but the upper model layers frozen and gradually unfreeze the model top-down during training – as a method for reducing the transfer gap.

Experiments with two different models on three downstream vision-language tasks show that scheduled unfreezing can help improve non-English performance; results in visual question answering are especially promising with massive gains in accuracy. Subsequent analysis suggests that scheduled unfreezing can help the zero-shot transfer by forcing the model to learn more language-agnostic features and overfit less on English-specific idiosyncrasies in the training data.

Acknowledgements

This work was in part supported by the Alexander von Humboldt Foundation.

References

Jinze Bai, Shuai Bai, Shusheng Yang, Shijie Wang, Sinan Tan, Peng Wang, Junyang Lin, Chang Zhou, and Jingren Zhou. 2023. Qwen-VL: A Frontier Large Vision-Language Model with Versatile Abilities. *CoRR*, abs/2308.12966. ArXiv: 2308.12966.

Emanuele Bugliarello, Fangyu Liu, Jonas Pfeiffer, Siva Reddy, Desmond Elliott, Edoardo Maria Ponti, and Ivan Vulić. 2022. Iglue: A benchmark for transfer learning across modalities, tasks, and languages. In *International Conference on Machine Learning*, pages 2370–2392. PMLR.

Xi Chen, Josip Djolonga, Piotr Padlewski, Basil Mustafa, Soravit Changpinyo, Jialin Wu, Carlos Riquelme Ruiz, Sebastian Goodman, Xiao Wang, Yi Tay, Siamak Shakeri, Mostafa Dehghani, Daniel Salz, Mario Lucic, Michael Tschannen, Arsha Nagrani, Hexiang Hu, Mandar Joshi, Bo Pang, Ceslee Montgomery, Paulina Pietrzyk, Marvin Ritter, A. J. Piergiovanni, Matthias Minderer, Filip Pavetic, Austin Waters, Gang Li, Ibrahim Alabdulmohsin, Lucas Beyer, Julien Amelot, Kenton Lee, Andreas Peter Steiner, Yang Li, Daniel Keysers, Anurag Arnab, Yuanzhong Xu, Keran Rong, Alexander Kolesnikov, Mojtaba Seyedhosseini, Anelia Angelova, Xiaohua Zhai, Neil Houlsby, and Radu Soricut. 2023. PaLI-X: On Scaling up a Multilingual Vision and Language Model. *CoRR*, abs/2305.18565. ArXiv: 2305.18565.

Alexis Conneau, Kartikay Khandelwal, Naman Goyal, Vishrav Chaudhary, Guillaume Wenzek, Francisco Guzmán, Édouard Grave, Myle Ott, Luke Zettlemoyer, and Veselin Stoyanov. 2020a. Unsupervised cross-lingual representation learning at scale. In *Proceedings of the 58th Annual Meeting of the Association for Computational Linguistics*, pages 8440–8451.

Alexis Conneau, Kartikay Khandelwal, Naman Goyal, Vishrav Chaudhary, Guillaume Wenzek, Francisco Guzmán, Edouard Grave, Myle Ott, Luke Zettlemoyer, and Veselin Stoyanov. 2020b. Unsupervised Cross-lingual Representation Learning at Scale. In *Proceedings of the 58th Annual Meeting of the Association for Computational Linguistics, ACL 2020, Online, July 5-10, 2020*, pages 8440–8451. Association for Computational Linguistics.

Wenliang Dai, Junnan Li, Dongxu Li, Anthony Meng Huat Tiong, Junqi Zhao, Weisheng Wang, Boyang Li, Pascale Fung, and Steven C. H. Hoi. 2023. InstructBLIP: Towards General-purpose Vision-Language Models with Instruction Tuning. *CoRR*, abs/2305.06500. ArXiv: 2305.06500.

Jacob Devlin, Ming-Wei Chang, Kenton Lee, and Kristina Toutanova. 2019. BERT: Pre-training of Deep Bidirectional Transformers for Language Understanding. In *Proceedings of the 2019 Conference of the North American Chapter of the Association for Computational Linguistics: Human Language Technologies, NAACL-HLT 2019, Minneapolis, MN, USA, June 2-7, 2019, Volume 1 (Long and Short Papers)*, pages 4171–4186. Association for Computational Linguistics.

Alexey Dosovitskiy, Lucas Beyer, Alexander Kolesnikov, Dirk Weissenborn, Xiaohua Zhai, Thomas Unterthiner, Mostafa Dehghani, Matthias Minderer, Georg Heigold, Sylvain Gelly, et al. 2020. An image is worth 16x16 words: Transformers for image recognition at scale. In *International Conference on Learning Representations*.

Gregor Geigle, Abhay Jain, Radu Timofte, and Goran Glavas. 2023. mblip: Efficient bootstrapping of multilingual vision-llms. *CoRR*, abs/2307.06930.

Carolin Holtermann, Paul Röttger, Timm Dill, and Anne Lauscher. 2024. Evaluating the elementary multilingual capabilities of large language models with multiq. *CoRR*, abs/2403.03814.

Jeremy Howard and Sebastian Ruder. 2018a. Universal language model fine-tuning for text classification. In *Proceedings of the 56th Annual Meeting of the Association for Computational Linguistics (Volume 1: Long Papers)*, pages 328–339.

Jeremy Howard and Sebastian Ruder. 2018b. Universal language model fine-tuning for text classification. In *Proceedings of the 56th Annual Meeting of the Association for Computational Linguistics (Volume 1: Long Papers)*, pages 328–339, Melbourne, Australia. Association for Computational Linguistics.

Junjie Hu, Sebastian Ruder, Aditya Siddhant, Graham Neubig, Orhan Firat, and Melvin Johnson. 2020. Xtreme: A massively multilingual multi-task benchmark for evaluating cross-lingual generalisation. In *International Conference on Machine Learning*, pages 4411–4421. PMLR.

Drew A. Hudson and Christopher D. Manning. 2019. GQA: A New Dataset for Real-World Visual Reasoning and Compositional Question Answering. In *IEEE Conference on Computer Vision and Pattern Recognition, CVPR 2019, Long Beach, CA, USA, June 16-20, 2019*, pages 6700–6709. Computer Vision Foundation / IEEE.

Tannon Kew, Florian Schottmann, and Rico Sennrich. 2023. Turning English-centric LLMs Into Polyglots: How Much Multilinguality Is Needed? *CoRR*, abs/2312.12683. ArXiv: 2312.12683.

Anne Lauscher, Vinit Ravishankar, Ivan Vulić, and Goran Glavaš. 2020. From zero to hero: On the limitations of zero-shot language transfer with multilingual transformers. In *Proceedings of the 2020*

Conference on Empirical Methods in Natural Language Processing (EMNLP), pages 4483–4499.

Junnan Li, Dongxu Li, Silvio Savarese, and Steven C. H. Hoi. 2023a. BLIP-2: Bootstrapping Language-Image Pre-training with Frozen Image Encoders and Large Language Models. *CoRR*, abs/2301.12597. ArXiv: 2301.12597.

Zejun Li, Zhihao Fan, Jingjing Chen, Qi Zhang, Xuanjing Huang, and Zhongyu Wei. 2023b. Unifying cross-lingual and cross-modal modeling towards weakly supervised multilingual vision-language pre-training. In *Proceedings of the 61st Annual Meeting of the Association for Computational Linguistics (Volume 1: Long Papers)*, pages 5939–5958, Toronto, Canada. Association for Computational Linguistics.

Jindřich Libovický, Rudolf Rosa, and Alexander Fraser. 2020. On the language neutrality of pre-trained multilingual representations. In *Findings of the Association for Computational Linguistics: EMNLP 2020*, pages 1663–1674, Online. Association for Computational Linguistics.

Tsung-Yi Lin, Michael Maire, Serge Belongie, James Hays, Pietro Perona, Deva Ramanan, Piotr Dollár, and C Lawrence Zitnick. 2014. Microsoft coco: Common objects in context. In *Computer Vision–ECCV 2014: 13th European Conference, Zurich, Switzerland, September 6-12, 2014, Proceedings, Part V 13*, pages 740–755. Springer.

Chen Liu, Jonas Pfeiffer, Anna Korhonen, Ivan Vulić, and Iryna Gurevych. 2023a. Delving deeper into cross-lingual visual question answering. In *Findings of the Association for Computational Linguistics: EACL 2023*, pages 2408–2423.

Chen Cecilia Liu, Jonas Pfeiffer, Ivan Vulić, and Iryna Gurevych. 2024. Fun with fisher: Improving generalization of adapter-based cross-lingual transfer with scheduled unfreezing.

Fangyu Liu, Emanuele Bugliarello, Edoardo Maria Ponti, Siva Reddy, Nigel Collier, and Desmond Elliott. 2021a. Visually grounded reasoning across languages and cultures. In *Proceedings of the 2021 Conference on Empirical Methods in Natural Language Processing*, pages 10467–10485.

Fangyu Liu, Emanuele Bugliarello, Edoardo Maria Ponti, Siva Reddy, Nigel Collier, and Desmond Elliott. 2021b. Visually grounded reasoning across languages and cultures. In *Proceedings of the 2021 Conference on Empirical Methods in Natural Language Processing*, pages 10467–10485, Online and Punta Cana, Dominican Republic. Association for Computational Linguistics.

Haotian Liu, Chunyuan Li, Yuheng Li, and Yong Jae Lee. 2023b. Improved Baselines with Visual Instruction Tuning. *CoRR*, abs/2310.03744. ArXiv: 2310.03744.

Haotian Liu, Chunyuan Li, Qingyang Wu, and Yong Jae Lee. 2023c. Visual Instruction Tuning. *CoRR*, abs/2304.08485. ArXiv: 2304.08485.

Ilya Loshchilov and Frank Hutter. 2019. Decoupled weight decay regularization. In *International Conference on Learning Representations*.

Niklas Muennighoff, Thomas Wang, Lintang Sutawika, Adam Roberts, Stella Biderman, Teven Le Scao, M. Saiful Bari, Sheng Shen, Zheng Xin Yong, Hailey Schoelkopf, Xiangru Tang, Dragomir Radev, Alham Fikri Aji, Khalid Almubarak, Samuel Albanie, Zaid Alyafeai, Albert Webson, Edward Raff, and Colin Raffel. 2022. Crosslingual Generalization through Multitask Finetuning. *CoRR*, abs/2211.01786. ArXiv: 2211.01786.

Minheng Ni, Haoyang Huang, Lin Su, Edward Cui, Taroon Bharti, Lijuan Wang, Dongdong Zhang, and Nan Duan. 2021. M3p: Learning universal representations via multitask multilingual multimodal pretraining. In *Proceedings of the IEEE/CVF conference on computer vision and pattern recognition*, pages 3977–3986.

Farhad Nooralahzadeh and Rico Sennrich. 2023. Improving the cross-lingual generalisation in visual question answering. In *Proceedings of the AAAI Conference on Artificial Intelligence*, volume 37, pages 13419–13427.

Jonas Pfeiffer, Gregor Geigle, Aishwarya Kamath, Jan-Martin Steitz, Stefan Roth, Ivan Vulić, and Iryna Gurevych. 2022. xgqa: Cross-lingual visual question answering. In *Findings of the Association for Computational Linguistics: ACL 2022*, pages 2497–2511.

Bryan A. Plummer, Liwei Wang, Chris M. Cervantes, Juan C. Caicedo, Julia Hockenmaier, and Svetlana Lazebnik. 2015. Flickr30k Entities: Collecting Region-to-Phrase Correspondences for Richer Image-to-Sentence Models. In *2015 IEEE International Conference on Computer Vision, ICCV 2015, Santiago, Chile, December 7-13, 2015*, pages 2641–2649.

Colin Raffel, Noam Shazeer, Adam Roberts, Katherine Lee, Sharan Narang, Michael Matena, Yanqi Zhou, Wei Li, and Peter J. Liu. 2020. Exploring the limits of transfer learning with a unified text-to-text transformer. *J. Mach. Learn. Res.*, 21:140:1–140:67.

Shaoqing Ren, Kaiming He, Ross Girshick, and Jian Sun. 2015. Faster r-cnn: Towards real-time object detection with region proposal networks. *Advances in neural information processing systems*, 28.

Teven Le Scao, Angela Fan, Christopher Akiki, Ellie Pavlick, Suzana Ilic, Daniel Hesslow, Roman Castagné, Alexandra Sasha Luccioni, François Yvon, Matthias Gallé, Jonathan Tow, Alexander M. Rush, Stella Biderman, Albert Webson, Pawan Sasanka Ammanamanchi, Thomas Wang, Benoît Sagot, Niklas Muennighoff, Albert Villanova del Moral, Olatunji Ruwase, Rachel Bawden, Stas Bekman, Angelina

McMillan-Major, Iz Beltagy, Huu Nguyen, Lucile Saulnier, Samson Tan, Pedro Ortiz Suarez, Victor Sanh, Hugo Laurençon, Yacine Jernite, Julien Launay, Margaret Mitchell, Colin Raffel, Aaron Gokaslan, Adi Simhi, Aitor Soroa, Alham Fikri Aji, Amit Alfassy, Anna Rogers, Ariel Kreisberg Nitzav, Canwen Xu, Chenghao Mou, Chris Emezue, Christopher Klamm, Colin Leong, Daniel van Strien, David Ifeoluwa Adelani, and et al. 2022. BLOOM: A 176B-Parameter Open-Access Multilingual Language Model. *CoRR*, abs/2211.05100. ArXiv: 2211.05100.

Fabian David Schmidt, Ivan Vulić, and Goran Glavaš. 2022. Don't stop fine-tuning: On training regimes for few-shot cross-lingual transfer with multilingual language models. In *Proceedings of the 2022 Conference on Empirical Methods in Natural Language Processing*, pages 10725–10742.

Uri Shaham, Jonathan Herzig, Roee Aharoni, Idan Szpektor, Reut Tsarfaty, and Matan Eyal. 2024. Multilingual Instruction Tuning With Just a Pinch of Multilinguality. *CoRR*, abs/2401.01854. ArXiv: 2401.01854.

Bin Shan, Yaqian Han, Weichong Yin, Shuohuan Wang, Yu Sun, Hao Tian, Hua Wu, and Haifeng Wang. 2022. ERNIE-UniX2: A Unified Cross-lingual Cross-modal Framework for Understanding and Generation. *CoRR*, abs/2211.04861. ArXiv: 2211.04861.

Alane Suhr, Stephanie Zhou, Ally Zhang, Iris Zhang, Huajun Bai, and Yoav Artzi. 2019. A Corpus for Reasoning About Natural Language Grounded in Photographs. *arXiv:1811.00491 [cs]*. ArXiv: 1811.00491.

Ning Xie, Farley Lai, Derek Doran, and Asim Kadav. 2019. Visual entailment: A novel task for fine-grained image understanding.

Linting Xue, Noah Constant, Adam Roberts, Mihir Kale, Rami Al-Rfou, Aditya Siddhant, Aditya Barua, and Colin Raffel. 2021. mT5: A Massively Multilingual Pre-trained Text-to-Text Transformer. In *Proceedings of the 2021 Conference of the North American Chapter of the Association for Computational Linguistics: Human Language Technologies, NAACL-HLT 2021, Online, June 6-11, 2021*, pages 483–498. Association for Computational Linguistics.

Yan Zeng, Xinsong Zhang, Hang Li, Jiawei Wang, Jipeng Zhang, and Wangchunshu Zhou. 2023. X 2-vlm: All-in-one pre-trained model for vision-language tasks. *IEEE Transactions on Pattern Analysis and Machine Intelligence*.

Yan Zeng, Wangchunshu Zhou, Ao Luo, and Xinsong Zhang. 2022. Cross-view language modeling: Towards unified cross-lingual cross-modal pre-training. *arXiv e-prints*, pages arXiv–2206.

Mingyang Zhou, Luowei Zhou, Shuohang Wang, Yu Cheng, Linjie Li, Zhou Yu, and Jingjing Liu. 2021. Uc2: Universal cross-lingual cross-modal vision-and-language pre-training. In *Proceedings of the IEEE/CVF Conference on Computer Vision and Pattern Recognition*, pages 4155–4165.

A Per-Language Results

We report the per-language results for all our models and tasks.

Zero-Shot	**en**	**ar**	**es**	**fr**	**ru**	**Ø**
UC2	77.1	**56.6**	58.1	68.1	**64.9**	**61.9**
UC2 + SUF	**77.2**	55.6	**58.5**	**69.2**	63.7	61.7
CCLM	**81.2**	60.9	69.6	75.6	68.5	68.6
CCLM + SUF	80.6	**63.6**	**70.9**	**77.6**	**70.4**	**70.6**

Table 4: Accuracy of SUF compared with our baseline on XVNLI on $CCLM_{base}$ and UC2.

Zero-Shot	**en**	**de**	**bn**	**id**	**ko**	**pt**	**ru**	**zh**	**Ø**
UC2	**57.1**	44.4	20.8	30.7	25.3	34.1	35.4	32.8	31.9
UC2 + SUF	**57.1**	**51.6**	**26.5**	**40.5**	**38.6**	**41.2**	**43.8**	**47.0**	**41.3**
CCLM	62.0	57.2	33.7	49.8	29.1	46.4	39.9	43.3	42.8
CCLM + SUF	**62.8**	**59.0**	**49.5**	**52.5**	**42.2**	**51.7**	**48.2**	**57.5**	**51.5**

Table 5: Zero-shot evaluation of scheduled unfreezing on CCLM and UC2.

Zero-Shot	**en**	**de**	**es**	**id**	**ja**	**ru**	**tr**	**zh**	**Ø**
Text Retrieval									
UC2	**36.8**	25.8	16.0	12.8	21.6	16.9	7.3	25.8	18.0
UC2 + SUF	36.4	**26.0**	**17.8**	**16.3**	**23.5**	**19.7**	**8.2**	**29.0**	**20.0**
CCLM	77.7	68.8	66.4	55.3	69.6	64.5	45.6	73.6	63.4
CCLM + SUF	**78.5**	**71.0**	**69.5**	**58.1**	**71.1**	**68.9**	**50.7**	**73.2**	**66.1**
Image Retrieval									
UC2	**43.0**	39.3	15.9	12.7	26.3	19.7	6.4	33.4	20.0
UC2 + SUF	41.8	**30.2**	**18.7**	**15.1**	**28.1**	**22.8**	**8.0**	**33.5**	**22.3**
CCLM	78.0	69.2	68.6	54.8	72.7	64.8	45.7	73.7	64.2
CCLM + SUF	**78.6**	**70.5**	**70.9**	**60.0**	**74.3**	**68.7**	**50.4**	**74.6**	**67.1**

Table 6: Results of SUF compared with our baseline on text and image retrieval (r@1, xFlickrCo) on $CCLM_{base}$ and UC2.

Automatic Layout Planning for Visually-Rich Documents with Instruction-Following Models

Wanrong Zhu[¶], Jennifer Healey[§], Ruiyi Zhang[§], William Yang Wang[¶], Tong Sun[§]
[¶]UC Santa Barbara, [§]Adobe Research
{wanrongzhu,william}@cs.ucsb.edu, {jehealey,ruizhang,tsun}@adobe.com

Abstract

Recent advancements in instruction-following models have made user interactions with models more user-friendly and efficient, broadening their applicability. In graphic design, non-professional users often struggle to create visually appealing layouts due to limited skills and resources. In this work, we introduce a novel multimodal instruction-following framework for layout planning, allowing users to easily arrange visual elements into tailored layouts by specifying canvas size and design purpose, such as for book covers, posters, brochures, or menus. We developed three layout reasoning tasks to train the model in understanding and executing layout instructions. Experiments on two benchmarks show that our method not only simplifies the design process for non-professionals but also surpasses the performance of few-shot GPT-4V models, with mIoU higher by 12% on Crello (Yamaguchi, 2021). This progress highlights the potential of multimodal instruction-following models to automate and simplify the design process, providing an approachable solution for a wide range of design tasks on visually-rich documents.

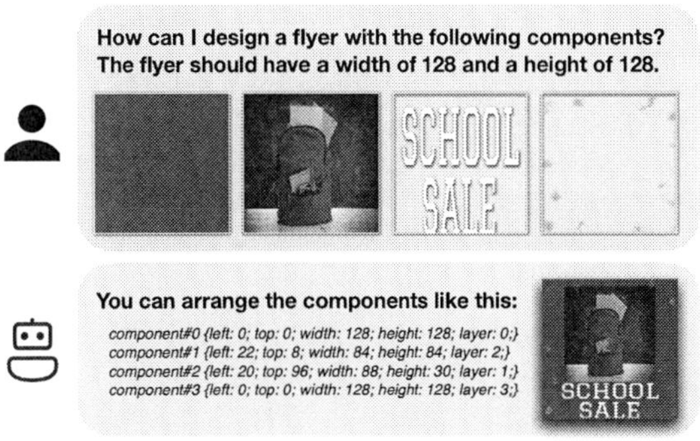

Figure 1: An example of a model conducting automatic layout planning following human-provided instructions and arranging visual contents for design purpose.

1 Introduction

The creation of visually-rich documents (e.g., posters, brochures, book covers, digital advertisements, etc) using available visual components, poses a significant challenge for both professionals and amateurs in the design field. Central to this challenge is the task of arranging these components in an efficient and aesthetically pleasing manner, a process known to be both tedious and time-consuming. Existing toolkits such as Adobe Express[1], Canva[2], and PicsArt[3], usually provide fixed templates to users. These templates, while useful, often fail to fully accommodate the varied and evolving design needs of users, thereby potentially limiting creative expression. Existing research on automatic layout planning (Hsu et al., 2023; Yamaguchi, 2021; Inoue et al., 2023) often requires detailed annotations and poses addition constraints on fixed canvas ratios, thereby diminishing user-friendliness and adaptability.

Recent advancements in large language models (LLMs) have showcased their remarkable ability to follow human instructions and execute specified tasks (Brown et al., 2020; Ouyang et al., 2022; OpenAI, 2023a), introducing a new level of flexibility and control in human-computer interaction. Alongside these developments, we have witnessed the emergence of instruction-tuned multimodal models (Ye et al., 2023; Li et al., 2023a,b; Awadalla et al., 2023; OpenAI, 2023b), extending the capabilities of LLMs to understand and process information across both textual and visual domains. This progression naturally raises the question of the potential application of instruction-following models in the complex domain of multimodal layout planning. However, employing these models for layout planning presents significant challenges, as the task requires intricate reasoning abilities, including but not limited to, cross-referencing multiple images and performing numerical calculations.

[1]https://www.adobe.com/express/
[2]https://www.canva.com/
[3]https://picsart.com/

Proceedings of the 3rd Workshop on Advances in Language and Vision Research, pages 167–172
August 16, 2024 ©2024 Association for Computational Linguistics

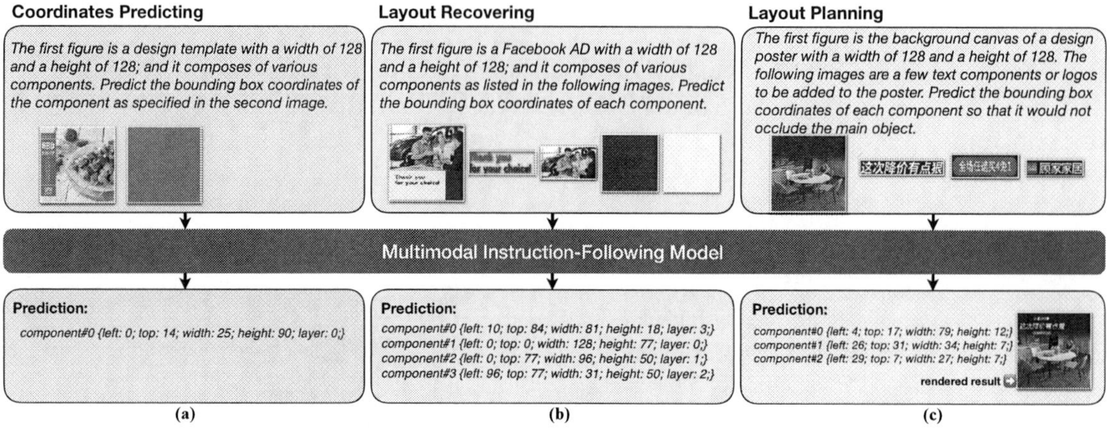

Figure 2: Example inputs and outputs of the three layout reasoning tasks. (a) and (b) are examples from Crello (Yamaguchi, 2021), while (c) is an example from PosterLayout (Hsu et al., 2023).

In this study, we propose DocLap, aiming to address the challenge of visually-rich document layout planning using instruction-following models. To equip these models with the necessary knowledge beyond their primary focus on natural language processing, we have devised three instruction-following tasks focusing on layout reasoning. We evaluated our instruction-tuned DocLap model across two benchmark datasets, and the findings reveal that our approach not only succeeds in this novel application but also outperforms the baseline established by few-shot GPT-4(V). Our main contributions are:

- We propose a novel method for solving the layout planning task using instruction-following models, opening new avenues for research in design automation.
- We develop an instruction dataset featuring three layout reasoning tasks, aiming to enrich the resources available for future research.
- Through experiments on two benchmark datasets, we validate the feasibility of our approach and demonstrate its competitive performance against few-shot GPT-4(V) models.

2 Instruction-Guided Layout Planning for Visually-Rich Documents

Task Definition Visually-rich documents consist of diverse design elements distributed across a canvas. To maintain the integrity of original text designs, text content is converted into images in our setup. The layout planning task involves arranging these design components, provided as a sequence of images $\boldsymbol{i}_1, \boldsymbol{i}_2, ...\boldsymbol{i}_n$, where n represents the component count, onto a canvas for specific application scenarios $\boldsymbol{a}$ (e.g., posters, Instagram posts, book covers) with defined dimensions $\boldsymbol{w}$ (width) and $\boldsymbol{h}$ (height). The canvas may either be blank or have a predefined background.

Instruction-Following Format To offer a more adaptable solution and enhance user experience, we approach this visually-rich layout planning task in an instruction-following manner (Ye et al., 2023; Li et al., 2023a,b; Awadalla et al., 2023; OpenAI, 2023b). The model, in addition to receiving the sequence of design components $\boldsymbol{i}_1, \boldsymbol{i}_2, ...\boldsymbol{i}_n$, will also be given instructions $\mathcal{I}$ detailing the application scenarios $\boldsymbol{a}$ and the canvas size $(\boldsymbol{w}, \boldsymbol{h})$. It is tasked with predicting the layout of each component in a structured format (Feng et al., 2023; Lin et al., 2023). We adopt CSS to encapsulate layout properties including `top`, `left`, `width`, `height`, and another property `layer` that manages the stacking order of potentially overlapping elements.

Instruction-Following Format The task of layout planning encompasses challenges such as following instructions, cross-modal understanding, and numerical reasoning. To equip the model with essential knowledge, we designed three interrelated tasks, as illustrated in Figure 2: (a) *Coordinates Predicting*, where the model predicts the coordinates of a specific component within a given design template; (b) *Layout Recovering*, which involves predicting the coordinates of each component in a template given a sequence of components; and (c) *Layout Planning*, where the model arranges a sequence of components on a canvas by predicting their coordinates. During preprocessing, components smaller than 5% of the canvas size are ex-

		Express	Crello	PosterLayout
	Coordinates Predicting	581k	57k	26k
Train	Layout Recovering	160k	18k	9k
	Layout Planning	160k	18k	9k
Val	Design Layout	-	1493	591

Table 1: Number of examples contained in each training or validation tasks for the datasets used in this study.

cluded, and all templates are resized to ensure the longest edge does not exceed 128. While all three tasks contribute to model training, only the *Layout Planning* task is evaluated during inference.

Model DocLap extends mPLUG-Owl (Ye et al., 2023), a multimodal framework integrating an LLM, a visual encoder, and a visual abstractor module. Specifically, it employs Llama-7b v1 (Touvron et al., 2023) as the LLM and CLIP ViT-L/14 (Radford et al., 2021) as the visual encoder. The visual abstractor module converts CLIP's visual features into 64 tokens that match the dimensionality of text embeddings, allowing for the simultaneous processing of multiple visual inputs. We extended the Llama v1 vocabulary with numerical tokens ranging from 0 to 128. The embeddings of the extended tokens are randomly initialized, and then tuned in further instruction tuning.

3 Experimental Setup

Datasets We conduct experiments on layout planning for visually-rich documents with the following two benchmarks: (1) Crello (Yamaguchi, 2021) is built upon design templates collected from online service. This task begins with an empty canvas, challenging the model to organize the layouts of the provided visual components. (2) PosterLayout (Hsu et al., 2023) starts from non-empty canvas (background image for posters), and requires the model to strategically place text, labels, and logos. Our training data is supplemented with design templates from Adobe Express. Detailed dataset statistics are available in Table 1. To ensure fair comparison, validation examples are limited to no more than 4 images, aligning with the input constraints of GPT-4V at the time of our submission. Illustrative examples from both datasets are presented in Figure 2.

Baselines For Crello, we compare with CanvasVAE (Yamaguchi, 2021) and FlexDM (Inoue et al., 2023). For PosterLayout, we compare with DS-GAN (Hsu et al., 2023). Additionally, we include

	Model	mIoU	Left	Top	Width	Height
#1	CanvasVAE	42.39	29.31	30.97	27.58	29.99
#2	FlexDM	50.08	34.98	34.03	30.04	33.08
#3	GPT-4 0-shot	30.75	24.36	24.07	13.63	15.11
#4	GPT-4 1-shot	29.97	26.09	23.71	13.94	13.33
#5	GPT-4V 0-shot	28.81	19.96	18.09	10.45	10.08
#6	GPT-4V 1-shot	35.17	22.77	20.90	13.16	14.11
#7	DocLap (Ours)	43.75	33.46	35.61	19.18	22.79

Table 2: Automatic evaluation results on Crello showing mIoU and the accuracy for left, top, width and height.

	Model	Occ.↓	Uti.↑	Rea.↓
#1	DS-GAN	21.57	23.92	20.16
#2	GPT-4 0-shot	50.61	43.09	25.87
#3	GPT-4 1-shot	47.92	38.00	25.34
#4	GPT-4V 0-shot	36.67	33.26	24.39
#5	GPT-4V 1-shot	36.39	20.24	26.03
#6	DocLap (Ours)	23.01	22.46	21.00

Table 3: Evaluation results on PosterLayout. *Occ.*: occlusion rate; *Uti.*: utility rate; *Rea.*: unreadability.

comparative evaluations with text-only versions of GPT-4 and GPT-4V (OpenAI, 2023a,b,c; gpt, 2023) across both tasks. For the text-only GPT-4 evaluations, visual components are not directly supplied. Instead, we employ BLIP-2 (Li et al., 2023c) to generate textual descriptions of each component.

Metrics For Crello evaluation, we measure mean Intersection-over-Union (mIoU) between predicted and actual bounding boxes, along with accuracy in width, height, left, and top dimensions following FlexDM (Inoue et al., 2023). Accuracy is quantified by assigning a score of 1 if the predicted value falls into the same 64-bin quantized range as the ground truth; otherwise, it scores 0. In assessing PosterLayout, we follow DS-GAN (Hsu et al., 2023) and employ content-aware metrics, including (1) occlusion rate↓, indicating the percentage of primary objects obscured by design elements; (2) utility rate↑, reflecting the extent to which design components cover non-primary object areas; and (3) unreadability↓, measuring the uniformity of areas where text-containing elements are placed.

4 Results & Analysis

Quantitative Results Table 2 shows the automatic evaluation results on Crello dataset. The first two lines are results from models that are trained with supervised learning. Line #3−#6 show few-shot GPT-4(V) results, in which we notice that GPT-4V surpasses text-only GPT-4, and that providing demonstrative examples leads to better results com-

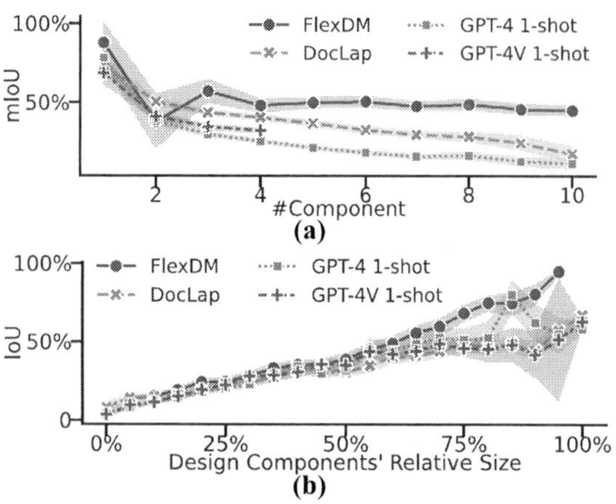

Figure 3: (a) mIoU variation with the number of visual components in design templates. (b) IoU correlation with the relative size of a single visual component. Both plots pertain to Crello.

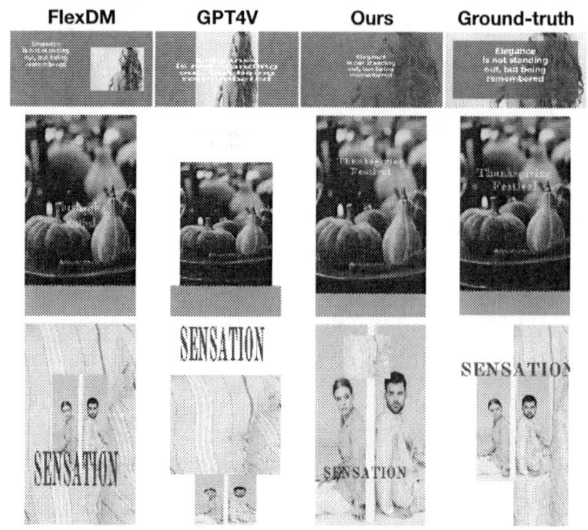

Figure 4: Qualitative comparisons for layout planning results on Crello. GPT-4V w/ 1-shot learning.

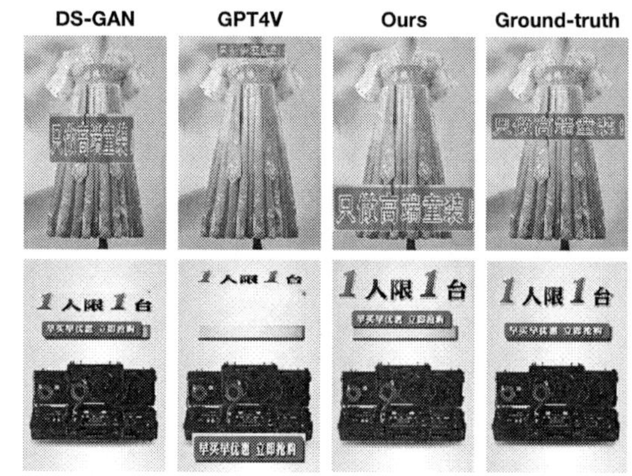

Figure 5: Qualitative comparisons for layout planning results on PosterLayout. GPT-4V w/ 1-shot learning.

pared to zero-shot prompting. Our DocLap's performance (#7) surpass the few-shot GPT-4(V) on both mIoU and aspect accuracies, but still falls behind a bit compared to FlexDM (#2).

Table 3 presents the PosterLayout evaluation results, which reveals a trade-off between occlusion rate and utility rate across models. GPT-4(V) models (#2−#5) exhibit high occlusion and utility rates, indicating a propensity for predicting larger bounding boxes. Our DocLap shows a reduced occlusion rate, accompanied by a decrease in utility rate. Regarding unreadability, DocLap outperforms GPT-4(V), though DS-GAN (#1) achieves the highest performance, underscoring the efficacy of supervised models in this context.

Effects of #Component Figure 3(a) reveals that all listed models exhibit high mIoU for templates with a single component. FlexDM's mIoU shows slight fluctuations, stabilizing around 50%. In contrast, mIoU for DocLap and GPT-4(V) decreases as the number of components increases, indicating that more complex scenarios involving more visual components might pose challenges to current instruction-following models.

Effects of Component Size Figure 3(b) demonstrates a linear correlation between the relative size of a single visual component and the IoU of the model prediction with the ground truth for all models assessed. This suggests that smaller visual components pose a greater challenge for precise placement in accordance with the ground truth during layout planning. Typically, these small components, such as logos, small text boxes, or decorative elements, have a degree of positional flexibility, allowing for multiple valid placements.

Demonstrative Examples Figure 4 shows examples from Crello while Figure 5 shows examples from PosterLayout.

5 Conclusion

This study demonstrates the potential of instruction-following models in addressing the intricate task of layout planning for visually rich documents. The positive outcomes observed from our experiments on two distinct benchmarks affirm the viability and effectiveness of our methodology. This research paves the way for future explorations into the application of instruction-following models across various domains, highlighting their potential to revolutionize tasks that require a nuanced understanding of both language and visual elements.

Limitations

This study, while pioneering in its approach to simplifying the graphic design process through instruction-following models, acknowledges several limitations. First, the performance of our model, DocLap, and GPT-4(V) diminishes as the complexity of the layout increases, particularly with the addition of more visual components. This suggests a need for improved model robustness and adaptability in handling more intricate design scenarios. Additionally, the evaluation metrics, such as mIoU and the binary accuracy measurement for layout attributes, may not fully capture the nuances of aesthetic and functional design quality. The reliance on these metrics might overlook the subjective and context-specific nature of effective design, indicating a potential area for developing more comprehensive evaluation frameworks.

Ethics Statement

Our work on instruction-following models for layout planning, while innovative, introduces potential risks including over-reliance on automation, which may impede the development of design skills and creativity. Importantly, our model does not generate new visual content; all predictions are based on existing components provided by users. The outputs are solely layouts in text formats, mitigating risks related to copyright infringement and originality. However, the reliance on automated tools could lead to a homogenization of design aesthetics and potentially amplify biases present in the input data. Addressing these challenges requires careful consideration of the ethical implications of automated design tools and the promotion of responsible usage to complement human creativity. Noted here that we utilize ChatGPT to polish the writing and ensure clarity and conciseness in the presentation of our research, without altering the fundamental nature of the work or its implications.

References

2023. Chatgpt can now see, hear, and speak. https://openai.com/blog/chatgpt-can-now-see-hear-and-speak.

Anas Awadalla, Irena Gao, Josh Gardner, Jack Hessel, Yusuf Hanafy, Wanrong Zhu, Kalyani Marathe, Yonatan Bitton, Samir Yitzhak Gadre, Shiori Sagawa, Jenia Jitsev, Simon Kornblith, Pang Wei Koh, Gabriel Ilharco, Mitchell Wortsman, and Ludwig Schmidt. 2023. Openflamingo: An open-source framework for training large autoregressive vision-language models. *ArXiv*, abs/2308.01390.

Tom Brown, Benjamin Mann, Nick Ryder, Melanie Subbiah, Jared D Kaplan, Prafulla Dhariwal, Arvind Neelakantan, Pranav Shyam, Girish Sastry, Amanda Askell, Sandhini Agarwal, Ariel Herbert-Voss, Gretchen Krueger, Tom Henighan, Rewon Child, Aditya Ramesh, Daniel Ziegler, Jeffrey Wu, Clemens Winter, Chris Hesse, Mark Chen, Eric Sigler, Mateusz Litwin, Scott Gray, Benjamin Chess, Jack Clark, Christopher Berner, Sam McCandlish, Alec Radford, Ilya Sutskever, and Dario Amodei. 2020. Language models are few-shot learners. In *Advances in Neural Information Processing Systems*, volume 33, pages 1877–1901. Curran Associates, Inc.

Weixi Feng, Wanrong Zhu, Tsu-Jui Fu, Varun Jampani, Arjun Reddy Akula, Xuehai He, S Basu, Xin Eric Wang, and William Yang Wang. 2023. LayoutGPT: Compositional visual planning and generation with large language models. In *Thirty-seventh Conference on Neural Information Processing Systems*.

Hsiao-An Hsu, Xiangteng He, Yuxin Peng, Hao-Song Kong, and Qing Zhang. 2023. Posterlayout: A new benchmark and approach for content-aware visual-textual presentation layout. *2023 IEEE/CVF Conference on Computer Vision and Pattern Recognition (CVPR)*, pages 6018–6026.

Naoto Inoue, Kotaro Kikuchi, Edgar Simo-Serra, Mayu Otani, and Kota Yamaguchi. 2023. Towards flexible multi-modal document models. *2023 IEEE/CVF Conference on Computer Vision and Pattern Recognition (CVPR)*, pages 14287–14296.

Bo Li, Yuanhan Zhang, Liangyu Chen, Jinghao Wang, Fanyi Pu, Jingkang Yang, C. Li, and Ziwei Liu. 2023a. Mimic-it: Multi-modal in-context instruction tuning. *arXiv preprint arXiv:2306.05425*.

Bo Li, Yuanhan Zhang, Liangyu Chen, Jinghao Wang, Jingkang Yang, and Ziwei Liu. 2023b. Otter: A multi-modal model with in-context instruction tuning. *arXiv preprint arXiv:2305.03726*.

Junnan Li, Dongxu Li, Silvio Savarese, and Steven C. H. Hoi. 2023c. Blip-2: Bootstrapping language-image pre-training with frozen image encoders and large language models. In *International Conference on Machine Learning*.

Jiawei Lin, Jiaqi Guo, Shizhao Sun, Zijiang James Yang, Jian-Guang Lou, and Dongmei Zhang. 2023. Layoutprompter: Awaken the design ability of large language models. In *Thirty-seventh Conference on Neural Information Processing Systems*.

OpenAI. 2023a. Gpt-4 technical report.

OpenAI. 2023b. Gpt-4v(ision) system card.

OpenAI. 2023c. Gpt-4v(ision) technical work and authors. https://cdn.openai.com/contributions/gpt-4v.pdf.

Long Ouyang, Jeffrey Wu, Xu Jiang, Diogo Almeida, Carroll Wainwright, Pamela Mishkin, Chong Zhang, Sandhini Agarwal, Katarina Slama, Alex Ray, John Schulman, Jacob Hilton, Fraser Kelton, Luke Miller, Maddie Simens, Amanda Askell, Peter Welinder, Paul F Christiano, Jan Leike, and Ryan Lowe. 2022. Training language models to follow instructions with human feedback. In *Advances in Neural Information Processing Systems*, volume 35, pages 27730–27744. Curran Associates, Inc.

Alec Radford, Jong Wook Kim, Chris Hallacy, Aditya Ramesh, Gabriel Goh, Sandhini Agarwal, Girish Sastry, Amanda Askell, Pamela Mishkin, Jack Clark, Gretchen Krueger, and Ilya Sutskever. 2021. Learning transferable visual models from natural language supervision. In *International Conference on Machine Learning*.

Hugo Touvron, Thibaut Lavril, Gautier Izacard, Xavier Martinet, Marie-Anne Lachaux, Timothée Lacroix, Baptiste Rozière, Naman Goyal, Eric Hambro, Faisal Azhar, Aurelien Rodriguez, Armand Joulin, Edouard Grave, and Guillaume Lample. 2023. Llama: Open and efficient foundation language models. *ArXiv*, abs/2302.13971.

Kota Yamaguchi. 2021. Canvasvae: Learning to generate vector graphic documents. *2021 IEEE/CVF International Conference on Computer Vision (ICCV)*, pages 5461–5469.

Qinghao Ye, Haiyang Xu, Guohai Xu, Jiabo Ye, Ming Yan, Yi Zhou, Junyan Wang, Anwen Hu, Pengcheng Shi, Yaya Shi, Chenliang Li, Yuanhong Xu, Hehong Chen, Junfeng Tian, Qiang Qi, Ji Zhang, and Feiyan Huang. 2023. mplug-owl: Modularization empowers large language models with multimodality. *ArXiv*, abs/2304.14178.

SEA-VQA: Southeast Asian Cultural Context Dataset For Visual Question Answering

Norawit Urailertprasert, Peerat Limkonchotiwat,
Supasorn Suwajanakorn, Sarana Nutanong
School of Information Science and Technology, VISTEC, Thailand
{norawit.u_s18,peerat.l_s19,supasorn.s,snutanon}@vistec.ac.th

Abstract

Visual Question Answering (VQA) is a critical task requiring the simultaneous understanding of visual and textual information. While significant advancements have been made with multilingual datasets, these often lack cultural specificity, especially in the context of Southeast Asia (SEA). In this paper, we introduce SEA-VQA, aiming to highlight the challenges and gaps in existing VQA models when confronted with culturally specific content. Our dataset includes images from eight SEA countries, curated from the UNESCO Cultural Heritage collection. Our evaluation, comparing GPT-4 and GEMINI models, demonstrates substantial performance drops on culture-centric questions compared to the A-OKVQA dataset, a commonsense and world-knowledge VQA benchmark comprising approximately 25,000 questions. Our findings underscore the importance of cultural diversity in VQA datasets and reveal substantial gaps in the ability of current VQA models to handle culturally rich contexts. SEA-VQA serves as a crucial benchmark for identifying these gaps and guiding future improvements in VQA systems. Our code and dataset are publicly available at https://wit543.github.io/sea-vqa

1 Introduction

Visual question answering (VQA) is the task of answering questions based on an image. As exemplified in Figure 1, one may ask a question involving an object or an action in an image. The VQA system accepts the question and picture as input and answers the questions based on the image's contents. Therefore, the performance of VQA depends on the ability of the model to understand textual and visual information simultaneously. Given its applications in various domains, such as healthcare, autonomous driving, and assistive technologies, VQA is pivotal in advancing human-computer interaction by enabling machines to comprehend and respond to complex visual content and textual queries.

Past efforts in VQA evaluation datasets have generally focused on measuring the reasoning, common knowledge, and image understanding of models. Initially, these datasets (Agrawal et al., 2016) used real-world images paired with straightforward questions, requiring direct answers based on visible elements. Over time, the emphasis shifted towards complex reasoning with datasets like CLEVR (Johnson et al., 2017) and GQA (Hudson and Manning, 2019), which present questions that demand comprehension of relationships, quantities, and spatial awareness. More recent datasets focus on improving generalization across various visual data types and question formats, testing the capabilities of VQA models from multiple perspectives and reasoning tasks (Lu et al., 2022; Yue et al., 2023; Liu et al., 2023; Li et al., 2023; Yu et al., 2023; Wu et al., 2024; Fu et al., 2024).

Although these datasets have been instrumental in advancing VQA, they often lack multicultural aspects. Multilingualism is typically achieved by translating existing queries into multiple languages, which does not fully capture cultural specificities (Gao et al., 2015; Raj Khan et al., 2021; Pfeiffer et al., 2022; Tran et al., 2023). This approach overlooks the nuances and contextual knowledge unique to different cultures, limiting the robustness of VQA systems in diverse settings. For instance, xGQA (Pfeiffer et al., 2022) introduces cross-lingual VQA but focuses more on language translation rather than cultural context. Vi-CLEVR (Tran et al., 2023) explores visual reasoning in Vietnamese, but it is limited to a single culture and language. Table 1 provides a comprehensive comparison of existing VQA datasets by country, highlighting the diversity in answer types, image sources, languages, and question types across different datasets.

To address this gap, we propose developing a

Proceedings of the 3rd Workshop on Advances in Language and Vision Research, pages 173–185
August 16, 2024 ©2024 Association for Computational Linguistics

Dataset	Answer Type	Image Source	Coverage		Question Types		
			Languages	Countries in SEA	General	Reasoning	Culture-centric
General VQA dataset							
A-OKVQA	mc	COCO	1	0	✓	×	×
Multilingual VQA dataset							
xGQA	y/n, open	GQA	8	1	✓	×	×
MaXM	y/n, open	cross3600	7	1	✓	×	×
EVJVQA	open	Self-sourced	3	1	✓	×	×
Our dataset							
SEA-VQA	mc	UNESCO	1	8	×	✓	✓

Table 1: Comparison of existing VQA dataset. Given 'y/n' represents yes/no answer types, 'Open' denotes free-form answer types, and 'mc' indicates multiple-choice questions.

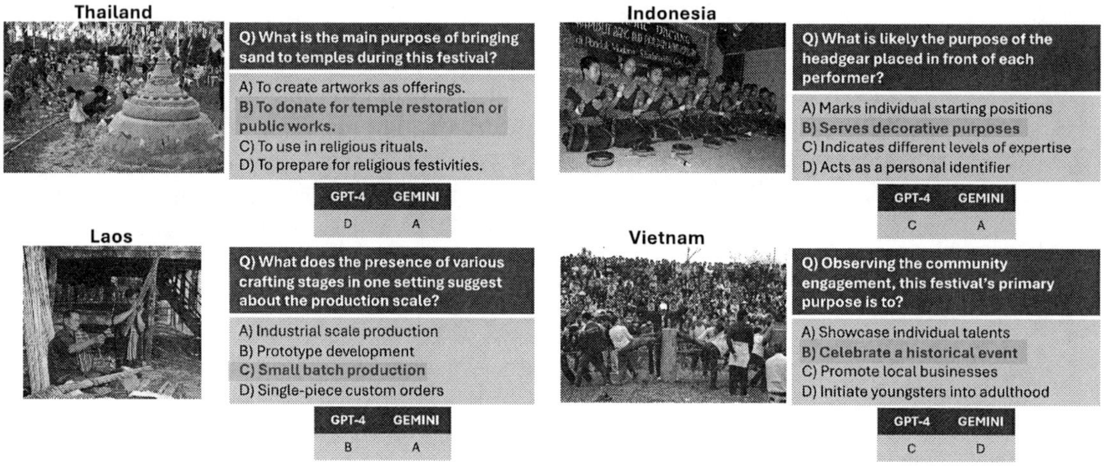

Figure 1: Examples of questions from the SEA-VQA dataset that require an understanding of cultural context. Each question is paired with an image from a specific Southeast Asian country (Thailand, Indonesia, Laos, Vietnam).

VQA dataset that challenges models in comprehending three distinct levels of concepts:

- General world knowledge, e.g., recognizing common entities such as people and animals.
- Specific cultural knowledge unique to each country.
- Understanding the contents of the image itself.

In particular, we develop a culturally specific dataset tailored to the region depicted in the image, incorporating a wider range of languages, including low-resource languages, particularly from Southeast Asia. This approach aims to improve the generalizability of VQA systems and address the current limitations in evaluating VQAs on SEA languages, which remains an open question in the field.

Our approach involves designing a data-gathering pipeline based on the utilization of large language models, such as GPT-4, to formulate questions and answers based on culturally specific images. To ensure quality in question generation, we leverage metadata for cultural questions, including cultural names, countries, and image descriptions, to assist the multi-modal large language model (MLLM) system in generating accurate questions. Additionally, human oversight in the quality-checking process ensures the integrity of the data. Our dataset comprises 515 images, 1,999 questions, and 53 cultures from 8 countries, focusing on the traditions of each culture and the reasoning behind each answer. This culturally specific approach aims to improve the generalizability of VQA systems and address the current limitations in evaluating VQAs on SEA languages, thereby ensuring robustness across diverse cultural and linguistic contexts.

2 Methodology

To formulate our dataset, the data creation pipeline consists of four steps: (i) image curation, (ii) attribute extraction, (iii) QA generation, and (iv) data quality assurance.

2.1 Image Curation

To obtain images from SEA cultures, we curate images from the UNESCO Cultural Heritage collection[1]. This collection is ideal for our purpose as it encompasses a diverse range of culturally significant sites and practices, ensuring that our dataset reflects Southeast Asia's cultural heritage and diversity. Our dataset includes images from 8 countries, totaling 515 images: Cambodia (55 images), Indonesia (139 images), Laos (18 images), Malaysia 64 images), the Philippines (69 images), Singapore (8 images), Thailand (40 images), and Vietnam (122 images). For more information about cultures in each country, please refer to Appendix A.1. We base the number of cultures on those recognized and registered by UNESCO. This approach ensures that the selected cultures are officially recognized. To address the imbalance, we identify the culture each question pertains to and treat the set of questions about a particular culture as a single unit. This method helps avoid cultural imbalance in our dataset.

2.2 Attribute Extraction

The purpose of this step is to enhance the quality and relevance of the QA generation process by providing rich contextual information. Instead of using the image alone to generate questions as proposed by Agrawal et al. (2016); Schwenk et al. (2022), we found that adding more attributes extracted from images is more beneficial. To achieve this, we utilize each image's description, cultural name, and country. These attributes are generated and verified by humans in the next step, ensuring that the information provided contains insightful context for each image. This comprehensive attribute extraction process significantly improves the effectiveness of the QA generation.

2.3 QA Generation

One straightforward method to compose these pairs is by utilizing human annotators (Agrawal et al., 2016; Schwenk et al., 2022; Nguyen et al., 2023). While the human method demonstrates the best data quality, it poses challenges in terms of scalability and broader applicability. Given our goal of introducing a dataset with cultural diversity, it is crucial to develop a repeatable and economically viable approach. Our objective is to balance cost and quality in generating question-answer pairs. Therefore, in our work, we have employed a machine-human collaborative approach in which QA pairs are generated by GPT-4, while humans are employed for quality assurance (see Section 2.4).

We composed a specific instruction prompt for GPT-4 to generate questions that require understanding the depicted culture and reasoning based on detailed descriptions of the image, including cultural and geographical context. To perform an assessment of an MLLM on our dataset, we opted for a multiple-choice format comprising four options: one correct answer and three plausible but incorrect alternatives. Furthermore, to minimize the occurrence of redundant questions, we generate batches of 20 questions simultaneously. We experimented with generating between 1 and 30 questions and found that 20 questions resulted in a diverse set that remained on the topic of culture. Our goal was to determine the maximum number of questions that could still stay relevant to the topic, and we concluded that 20 questions provided the best outcome. Additionally, we instruct GPT-4 to create a question that involves reasoning, and the answers require thought rather than simple observation 1. This strategy significantly improves the diversity and complexity of the dataset. For QA generation analysis, please refer to Appendix A.2.

An example prompt: *"Create 20 challenging multiple-choice questions based on this image that require multi-step reasoning. These questions should be culturally relevant but not explicitly mention the culture in the questions themselves. Each question should have four options: one correct answer and three nearly correct alternatives. Highlight the correct answer in each set with a '<' at the end of the correct answer. Use the descriptive context provided to enhance the complexity of each question. The culture and country depicted in the image are provided below. culture:{culture} Description: {description} country: {country}"*

2.4 Data Quality Assurance

To ensure the quality and validity of our questions, we employ human reviewers to assess and filter out those that are nonsensical, unanswerable, or incorrect. This approach keeps humans in the loop, ensuring that the questions are coherent and appropriate at a reduced cost. Using GPT-4, the total cost for question generation is less than \$15, which averages out to about \$0.008 per question. This is significantly cheaper compared to a local labeling platform, charging more than \$0.28 per question, and even Amazon Mechanical Turk, where the fee starts at \$0.01, excluding the reward per question.

[1] https://whc.unesco.org/en/list/

We provide reviewers with detailed guidelines to evaluate the choices and answers in relation to the image, its cultural context, and its description. If reviewers are uncertain about an answer, they are permitted to access external knowledge sources such as a search engine to ascertain the correct response. This process requires the reviewers to consider general world knowledge, the cultural significance of the image, and its content, ensuring that the dataset maintains high standards of accuracy and cultural relevance. To ensure accuracy, we provide images, country names, culture names, and descriptions. If this information is insufficient, reviewers can use additional resources to verify each question. We also provide examples of acceptable and unacceptable questions. Reviewers are graduate students specializing in computer vision (CV) and natural language processing (NLP) from Southeast Asia to ensure familiarity with regional cultures. Table 2 provides a comprehensive overview of the dataset statistics and comparisons.

3 Experimental Results

3.1 Evaluation Setting

Test Models. We use GPT-4-TURBO and GEMINI-PRO-VISION for testing. We use the same prompt for both models. The prompt: *"Answer the following question and provide only the letter output, for example: a, b, c, d. Choose only one option, output only the choice. question:{question} choice: a) {a} b) {b} c) {c} d) {d}"*

We evaluate each question individually by inputting the prompt and image one at a time. In addition, we evaluate MLLMs on the A-OKVQA dataset (Schwenk et al., 2022) to observe the performance changes compared to our VQA dataset.

Evaluation Metrics. We use accuracy scores as the primary metric. In addition, we also demonstrate the performance of each language separately.

3.2 Main Results

Table 3 shows the performance of the two models on two datasets: A-OKVQA (Schwenk et al., 2022), a VQA dataset that requires commonsense reasoning and world knowledge to answer and our proposed dataset, SEA-VQA. We can see that with SEA-VQA, the performance of both models drastically drops compared to A-OKVQA. The results also show that GPT-4 outperforms GEMINI in both datasets, and the gap is larger for SEA-VQA. The table also provides a breakdown in terms of countries. Indonesia is the only dataset portion where GEMINI performs better than GPT-4. Another interesting point to note is that the performance of GPT-4 on the Singapore portion of the dataset (0.688) is substantially higher than the second-highest one, i.e., the Philippines (0.523). One possible explanation is due to the urbanized nature of the city-state. In the big picture, our findings demonstrate the need for improvement and adaptation in VQA systems to handle broader cultural contexts from diverse sources.

3.3 Error Analysis

We organize the error analysis into two parts: errors made by both models and errors made by only one of the models. Both models perform poorly on questions requiring the ability to differentiate subtle variations of cultures originating from the same region or cultures that exist across multiple SEA nations with local variations. Such questions require the knowledge and understanding of differences in attires, musical instruments, and cultural performances that look similar even for humans who are not from this region. For example, the Thai cultural performances of Nora and Khon may look similar to those unfamiliar with the SEA cultural context. Additionally, cultural diffusion across the Southeast Asian region historically means that similar cultures can exist in different countries. This is evident in the Royal Ballet of Cambodia and Thai Khon, which may seem similar to outsiders, but locals can distinguish them by their costumes and dance patterns.

Furthermore, the models struggle particularly with questions that require recognizing specific cultural elements in an image to determine the reasoning behind the action or role of the subjects depicted. Neither model performs well on questions involving musical performance, requiring the ability to recognize musical instruments. For example, consider this question: "This instrument is a part of which traditional performance art?" When shown a canang, which is typically used in Mak Yong theatre, both models incorrectly answer "Wayang Kulit."

In addition to commonly occurring errors found in GEMINI and GPT-4, there are also error patterns specific to either model.

- GEMINI often fails to adhere to instructions to select one answer, frequently outputting multiple choices, e.g., (a, b), or (a, b, c).
- GPT-4 struggles with the determination of a per-

Country	Total			Images/Culture		Questions/Culture		Questions/Image	
	Cultures	Images	Questions	Avg.	Std.	Avg.	Std.	Avg.	Std.
Cambodia	6	55	304	9.17	1.17	50.67	3.56	5.53	2.85
Indonesia	12	139	752	11.58	7.12	62.67	40.22	5.41	3.92
Laos	2	18	72	9.00	1.41	36.00	15.56	4.00	4.24
Malaysia	7	64	189	9.14	1.57	27.00	5.86	2.95	1.46
Philippines	6	69	153	11.50	4.14	25.50	6.72	2.22	1.33
Singapore	1	8	32	8.00	0.00	32.00	0.00	4.00	1.69
Thailand	4	40	184	10.00	0.00	46.00	13.04	4.60	3.12
Vietnam	15	122	313	8.13	3.23	20.87	9.71	2.57	0.73
Over All	53	515	1999	9.57	2.33	37.59	11.83	3.91	2.42

Table 2: The dataset statistics on the number of cultures, images, and associated questions. The table provides metrics on the average number of images per culture and questions per culture and image, complete with standard deviations.

Language	GEMINI	GPT-4
Proposed Dataset, SEA-VQA		
Cambodia	0.257	0.467
Indonesia	0.453	0.336
Laos	0.278	0.375
Malaysia	0.360	0.492
Philippines	0.307	0.523
Singapore	0.219	0.688
Thailand	0.348	0.478
Vietnam	0.176	0.495
Average (Macro)	0.300	0.482
Average (Micro)	0.275	0.365
Existing VQA Benchmark		
A-OKVQA (Micro)	0.760	0.822

Table 3: Accuracy of GEMINI and GPT-4 on culture-specific questions from the SEA-VQA dataset and the general knowledge-based A-OKVQA dataset. The table presents model performance across various Southeast Asian countries.

son's age, the length of objects, and actions within a cultural context. For instance, when asked about the typical range of diameters for instruments shown in an image (an image of a gong in Vietnam), the model incorrectly suggested 15 to 35 centimeters, whereas the correct answer is 25 to 80 centimeters. In response to a question about an image showing a traditional ensemble, the correct label should have been "A khene orchestra concert." However, due to a focus only on visible actions and objects, GPT-4 answer was "A bamboo dance."

These examples highlight areas where the model's accuracy can be improved.

4 Conclusion and Future Work

In conclusion, we propose a VQA dataset for the Southeast Asian cultural context called *SEA-VQA*. Our dataset is generated from MLLM while using humans in the data quality assurance process. Using this approach, we are able to generate 1,999 questions from 8 countries and 53 cultures with limited human efforts. Results from assessments using our SEA-VQA dataset reveal that, although MLLMs demonstrate reasonable performances in standard VQA benchmarks, there is a gap in understanding local cultural knowledge.

In future work, we aim to apply this process to other underrepresented languages and dialects from the region. We plan to explore more languages and images from open-source projects in SEA, i.e., SEACrowd (Lovenia et al., 2024), to extend from monolingual to multilingual VQAs. Additionally, we will explore generating VQAs using multiple models to improve accuracy and robustness. We also plan to add more attribute extraction methods to create more variation in VQAs. In addition, we also plan to explore the integration of virtual reality technology to enhance the richness of the dataset.

5 Limitations

One limitation is the quality of image data and description. Expanding the dataset size requires a greater source of image data; however, ensuring that these images accurately represent the relevant cultures is challenging, thus limiting the number of usable images. For the selection of cultures, we rely on those officially recognized and registered with UNESCO. This approach may restrict the scope of represented cultures, as many local cultures that are not registered or are in the process of registration are excluded. Despite these limitations, using UNESCO as a source allows us to extend our research beyond Southeast Asia, incorporating cultures from around the globe.

References

Aishwarya Agrawal, Jiasen Lu, Stanislaw Antol, Margaret Mitchell, C. Lawrence Zitnick, Dhruv Batra, and Devi Parikh. 2016. VQA: Visual Question Answering.

Chaoyou Fu, Peixian Chen, Yunhang Shen, Yulei Qin, Mengdan Zhang, Xu Lin, Jinrui Yang, Xiawu Zheng, Ke Li, Xing Sun, Yunsheng Wu, and Rongrong Ji. 2024. MME: A Comprehensive Evaluation Benchmark for Multimodal Large Language Models.

Haoyuan Gao, Junhua Mao, Jie Zhou, Zhiheng Huang, Lei Wang, and Wei Xu. 2015. Are You Talking to a Machine? Dataset and Methods for Multilingual Image Question Answering.

Drew A. Hudson and Christopher D. Manning. 2019. GQA: A New Dataset for Real-World Visual Reasoning and Compositional Question Answering. In *2019 IEEE/CVF Conference on Computer Vision and Pattern Recognition (CVPR)*, pages 6693–6702, Long Beach, CA, USA. IEEE.

Justin Johnson, Bharath Hariharan, Laurens Van Der Maaten, Li Fei-Fei, C. Lawrence Zitnick, and Ross Girshick. 2017. CLEVR: A Diagnostic Dataset for Compositional Language and Elementary Visual Reasoning. In *2017 IEEE Conference on Computer Vision and Pattern Recognition (CVPR)*, pages 1988–1997, Honolulu, HI. IEEE.

Bohao Li, Yuying Ge, Yixiao Ge, Guangzhi Wang, Rui Wang, Ruimao Zhang, and Ying Shan. 2023. SEED-Bench-2: Benchmarking Multimodal Large Language Models.

Yuan Liu, Haodong Duan, Yuanhan Zhang, Bo Li, Songyang Zhang, Wangbo Zhao, Yike Yuan, Jiaqi Wang, Conghui He, Ziwei Liu, Kai Chen, and Dahua Lin. 2023. MMBench: Is Your Multi-modal Model an All-around Player?

Holy Lovenia, Rahmad Mahendra, Salsabil Maulana Akbar, Lester James V. Miranda, Jennifer Santoso, Elyanah Aco, Akhdan Fadhilah, Jonibek Mansurov, Joseph Marvin Imperial, Onno P. Kampman, Joel Ruben Antony Moniz, Muhammad Ravi Shulthan Habibi, Frederikus Hudi, Railey Montalan, Ryan Ignatius, Joanito Agili Lopo, William Nixon, Börje F. Karlsson, James Jaya, Ryandito Diandaru, Yuze Gao, Patrick Amadeus, Bin Wang, Jan Christian Blaise Cruz, Chenxi Whitehouse, Ivan Halim Parmonangan, Maria Khelli, Wenyu Zhang, Lucky Susanto, Reynard Adha Ryanda, Sonny Lazuardi Hermawan, Dan John Velasco, Muhammad Dehan Al Kautsar, Willy Fitra Hendria, Yasmin Moslem, Noah Flynn, Muhammad Farid Adilazuarda, Haochen Li, Johanes Lee, R. Damanhuri, Shuo Sun, Muhammad Reza Qorib, Amirbek Djanibekov, Wei Qi Leong, Quyet V. Do, Niklas Muennighoff, Tanrada Pansuwan, Ilham Firdausi Putra, Yan Xu, Ngee Chia Tai, Ayu Purwarianti, Sebastian Ruder, William Tjhi, Peerat Limkonchotiwat, Alham Fikri Aji, Sedrick Keh, Genta Indra Winata, Ruochen Zhang, Fajri Koto, Zheng-Xin Yong, and Samuel Cahyawijaya. 2024. Seacrowd: A multilingual multimodal data hub and benchmark suite for southeast asian languages.

Pan Lu, Swaroop Mishra, Tony Xia, Liang Qiu, Kai-Wei Chang, Song-Chun Zhu, Oyvind Tafjord, Peter Clark, and Ashwin Kalyan. 2022. Learn to Explain: Multimodal Reasoning via Thought Chains for Science Question Answering.

Ngan Luu-Thuy Nguyen, Nghia Hieu Nguyen, Duong T. D. Vo, Khanh Quoc Tran, and Kiet Van Nguyen. 2023. VLSP2022-EVJVQA Challenge: Multilingual Visual Question Answering. *Journal of Computer Science and Cybernetics*, pages 237–258.

Jonas Pfeiffer, Gregor Geigle, Aishwarya Kamath, Jan-Martin Steitz, Stefan Roth, Ivan Vulić, and Iryna Gurevych. 2022. xGQA: Cross-Lingual Visual Question Answering. In *Findings of the Association for Computational Linguistics: ACL 2022*, pages 2497–2511, Dublin, Ireland. Association for Computational Linguistics.

Humair Raj Khan, Deepak Gupta, and Asif Ekbal. 2021. Towards Developing a Multilingual and Code-Mixed Visual Question Answering System by Knowledge Distillation. In *Findings of the Association for Computational Linguistics: EMNLP 2021*, pages 1753–1767, Punta Cana, Dominican Republic. Association for Computational Linguistics.

Dustin Schwenk, Apoorv Khandelwal, Christopher Clark, Kenneth Marino, and Roozbeh Mottaghi. 2022. A-OKVQA: A Benchmark for Visual Question Answering using World Knowledge.

Khiem Vinh Tran, Hao Phu Phan, Kiet Van Nguyen, and Ngan Luu Thuy Nguyen. 2023. ViCLEVR: A Visual Reasoning Dataset and Hybrid Multimodal Fusion Model for Visual Question Answering in Vietnamese.

Haoning Wu, Zicheng Zhang, Erli Zhang, Chaofeng Chen, Liang Liao, Annan Wang, Chunyi Li, Wenxiu Sun, Qiong Yan, Guangtao Zhai, and Weisi Lin. 2024. Q-Bench: A Benchmark for General-Purpose Foundation Models on Low-level Vision.

Weihao Yu, Zhengyuan Yang, Linjie Li, Jianfeng Wang, Kevin Lin, Zicheng Liu, Xinchao Wang, and Lijuan Wang. 2023. MM-Vet: Evaluating Large Multimodal Models for Integrated Capabilities.

Xiang Yue, Yuansheng Ni, Kai Zhang, Tianyu Zheng, Ruoqi Liu, Ge Zhang, Samuel Stevens, Dongfu

Jiang, Weiming Ren, Yuxuan Sun, Cong Wei, Botao Yu, Ruibin Yuan, Renliang Sun, Ming Yin, Boyuan Zheng, Zhenzhu Yang, Yibo Liu, Wenhao Huang, Huan Sun, Yu Su, and Wenhu Chen. 2023. MMMU: A Massive Multi-discipline Multimodal Understanding and Reasoning Benchmark for Expert AGI.

A Appendix

A.1 Cultures List

Table 4 catalogs diverse cultural practices across Southeast Asia and adjacent regions. Organized by country, the table highlights traditional cultural heritage, such as Cambodia's Kun Lbokator and Indonesia's Wayang puppet theatre, demonstrating each nation's commitment to preserving its cultural identity. Noteworthy, entries like Tugging rituals and games are shared between countries, indicating cultural ties that transcend national borders.

A.2 QA Generation Analysis

We can use a language model like GPT-4 to automate the generation of questions, choices, and answers. However, the generated contents may contain inaccuracy, irrelevant information, and formatting inconsistencies. To combat these issues, human involvement is still necessary to ensure the dataset quality.

We observe that nearly 15% of all questions generated from GPT-4 cannot be used for VQA purposes. These are questions lacking definitive answers, e.g., the determination of the time of day the image was captured (e.g., morning, evening, noon, night), the emotion of a person depicted in the image (e.g., happy, excited, stressed, sad). This observation indicates that a significant portion of these questions require further refinement and human oversight to ensure they are appropriate and useful for VQA tasks.

Country	Culture
Cambodia	Kun Lbokator, traditional martial arts in Cambodia
Cambodia	Lkhon Khol Wat Svay Andet
Cambodia	Chapei Dang Veng
Cambodia	Royal ballet of Cambodia
Cambodia	Sbek Thom, Khmer shadow theatre
Cambodia, Philippines, Republic of Korea, Viet Nam	Tugging rituals and games
Indonesia	Jamu wellness culture
Indonesia	Gamelan
Indonesia	Traditions of Pencak Silat
Indonesia	Pinisi, art of boatbuilding in South Sulawesi
Indonesia	Three genres of traditional dance in Bali
Indonesia	Noken multifunctional knotted or woven bag, handcraft of the people of Papua
Indonesia	Saman dance
Indonesia	Indonesian Angklung
Indonesia	Indonesian Batik
Indonesia	Education and training in Indonesian Batik intangible cultural heritage for elementary, junior, senior, vocational school and polytechnic students, in collaboration with the Batik Museum in Pekalongan
Indonesia	Indonesian Kris
Indonesia	Wayang puppet theatre
Indonesia, Malaysia	Pantun
Laos	Traditional craft of Naga motif weaving in Lao communities
Laos	Khaen music of the Lao people
Malaysia	Mek Mulung
Malaysia	Songket
Malaysia	Silat
Malaysia	Dondang Sayang
Malaysia	Mak Yong theatre
Malaysia, China	Ong Chun/Wangchuan/Wangkang ceremony, rituals and related practices for maintaining the sustainable connection between man and the ocean
Philippines	Aklan piña handloom weaving
Philippines	The School of Living Traditions (SLT)
Philippines	Buklog, thanksgiving ritual system of the Subanen
Philippines	Darangen epic of the Maranao people of Lake Lanao
Philippines	Hudhud chants of the Ifugao
Singapore	Hawker culture in Singapore, community dining and culinary practices in a multicultural urban context
Thailand	Songkran in Thailand, traditional Thai New Year festival
Thailand	Nora, dance drama in southern Thailand
Thailand	Nuad Thai, traditional Thai massage
Thailand	Khon, masked dance drama in Thailand
Viet Nam	Art of pottery-making of Chăm people
Viet Nam	Art of Xòe dance of the Tai people in Viet Nam
Viet Nam	Practices of Then by Tày, Nùng and Thái ethnic groups in Viet Nam
Viet Nam	The art of Bài Chòi in Central Viet Nam
Viet Nam	Xoan singing of Phú Thọ province, Viet Nam

Continued on next page

Country	Culture
Viet Nam	Practices related to the Viet beliefs in the Mother Goddesses of Three Realms
Viet Nam	Ví and Gim folk songs of Ngh Tĩnh
Viet Nam	Art of Đn ca tài t music and song in southern Viet Nam
Viet Nam	Worship of Hùng kings in Phú Th
Viet Nam	Gióng festival of Phù Đông and Sóc temples
Viet Nam	Ca trù singing
Viet Nam	Quan H Bc Ninh folk songs
Viet Nam	Nha Nhac, Vietnamese court music
Viet Nam	Space of gong culture

Table 4: **Table of Cultures**: The table organizes the cultures used in the dataset by country, providing a comprehensive overview of diverse cultural elements across different nations.

A.3 More Culture Examples

We provided more examples of challenging cultural elements to elevate the visual question-answering (VQA) capabilities of our dataset. The text highlighted in green represents the correct answer, while the responses from GPT-4 and GEMENI are displayed in the box below.

These examples feature Khaen music of the Lao people, a traditional form of music recognized by UNESCO for its unique use of bamboo pipes; Songket weaving from Malaysia, a luxurious fabric interwoven with gold and silver threads; Aklan piña handloom weaving from the Philippines, known for its intricate process of weaving pineapple leaf fibers; and children playing the Suling, a key instrument in the Gamelan ensemble of Indonesia. Each example has been carefully selected to challenge the understanding and appreciation of these unique cultural expressions.

Example: Laos

Figure 2: **Culture:** Khaen music of the Lao people

What type of traditional ensemble performance is shown in the image?
A. A choir concert
B. A bamboo dance
C. A khene orchestra concert
D. A traditional puppet show

GPT4	GEMINI
B	C

Example: Malaysia

Figure 3: **Culture:** Songket

What is the name of the fabric pattern used in this headgear?

A. Batik

B. Pua Kumbu

C. Songket

D. Tenun

GPT4	GEMINI
B	A

Example: the Philippines

Figure 4: **Culture:** Aklan piña handloom weaving

What characteristic makes the tool in the image appropriate for fiber extraction?
A. Flexibility
B. Sharpness
C. Weight
D. Porosity

GPT4

B

GEMINI

A

Example: Indonesia

Figure 5: **Culture:** Gamelan

Which musical instrument is predominantly played by the children in the image?

A. Angklung

B. Kendang

C. Suling

D. Bonang

GPT4	GEMINI
C	A

Wiki-VEL: Visual Entity Linking for Structured Data on Wikimedia Commons

Philipp Bielefeld[*1], **Jasmin Geppert**[*1], **Necdet Güven**[*1], **Melna Treesa John**[*1], **Adrian Ziupka**[*1], **Lucie-Aimée Kaffee**[2], **Russa Biswas**[3], **Gerard de Melo** [1]

[1]Hasso Plattner Institut / University of Potsdam, Potsdam, Germany,
[2]Hugging Face, [3]Aalborg University, Copenhagen, Denmark
lucie.kaffee@huggingface.co, rubi@cs.aau.dk, gdm@demelo.org

Abstract

Describing images using structured data enables a wide range of automation tasks, such as search and organization, as well as downstream tasks, such as labeling images or training machine learning models. However, there is currently a lack of structured data labels for large image repositories such as Wikimedia Commons. To close this gap, we propose the task of *Visual Entity Linking (VEL) for Wikimedia Commons*, which involves predicting labels for Wikimedia Commons images based on Wikidata items as the label inventory. We create a novel dataset leveraging community-created structured data on Wikimedia Commons. Additionally, we fine-tune pre-trained models based on the CLIP architecture using this dataset. Although the best-performing models show promising results, the study also identifies key challenges of the data and the task.

1 Introduction

Wikimedia Commons is a service that hosts around 100 million community-contributed, openly licensed images and media files, including metadata, multilingual textual descriptions, and categories similar to Wikipedia categories. At the same time, Wikimedia's Knowledge Graph (KG), *Wikidata*, offers detailed structured knowledge descriptions of over 100 million entities. In 2017, the *Commons: Structured Data* project was initiated to organize and search images by better connecting the two efforts. Community members tag relevant Wikidata items in images, adding them to Commons as structured data via new `depict` statements, enabling machine-friendly association of images with universal, language-independent concepts. In Wikimedia Commons, structured data unlocks the full potential of its image repository, providing users with a more enriching and productive experience. Yet, as of November 2023, only 15% of Wikimedia Commons images are accompanied by structured data, suggesting that a considerable portion of this vast resource remains unexplored. This lack of structured data poses a challenge for users seeking to extract meaningful information from the extensive collection. Structured data is crucial for modern information retrieval systems, providing a systematic framework for describing entities and their attributes, and enhancing discoverability and interoperability across platforms and applications.

This gap in the coverage of Commons image annotations can be addressed by automatically suggesting depicted items using ***Visual Entity Linking (VEL)***, a multi-modal task of linking visual items in an image with corresponding entities in a KG.

This paper proposes the ***Wiki-VEL*** framework, applying the task of VEL to Wikimedia Commons using the structured data of Wikidata. This allows users to perform targeted searches and explore images based on specific topics, events, or attributes, enhancing the usability and utility of Wikimedia Commons. Further, integrating VEL on Wikimedia Commons opens opportunities for automation and innovation in content management and analysis. Images annotated with structured data can be used for visual question answering, search algorithms, image classification, object detection, semantic segmentation, and recommender systems (de Melo and Tandon, 2016; Shutova et al., 2015; Li et al., 2017). Our contributions are as follows:

- A novel image dataset[1] for Visual Entity Linking extracted from Wikimedia Commons.
- A framework for Visual Entity Linking (Wiki-VEL) connecting entities in the images of Wikimedia Commons with the KG, Wikidata.
- Human evaluation of Wiki-VEL annotations.

[*]In alphabetical order, as these authors contributed equally to this work.

[1]`https://huggingface.co/datasets/aiintelligentsystems/vel_commons_wikidata`

Proceedings of the 3rd Workshop on Advances in Language and Vision Research, pages 186–194
August 16, 2024 ©2024 Association for Computational Linguistics

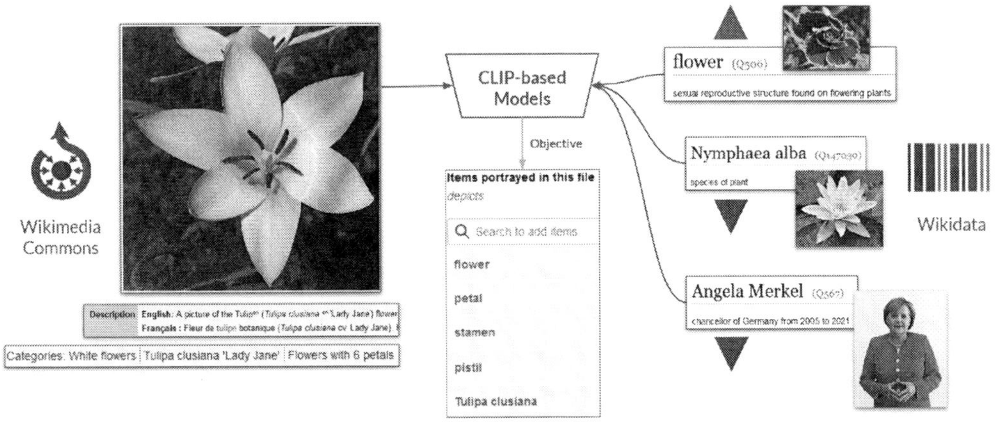

Figure 1: Overview of the Wiki-VEL framework.

2 Related Work

2.1 Visual Entity Linking

Visual Entity Linking (VEL; Weegar et al., 2014; Tilak et al., 2017) is the task of linking entities detected in images to their corresponding entities in a KG. VEL works across different modalities: the images that entities are detected in, the labels of entities in a KG, and the KG entities themselves. Some studies (Müller-Budack et al., 2021; Gan et al., 2021; Dost et al., 2020) focus on coarse-grained entity linking of items in the images to a KG by leveraging the entity mentions in the corresponding textual information. Recent years have also witnessed entity linking models that use visual information to identify entity mentions in social media texts (Moon et al., 2018; Adjali et al., 2020; Zhang et al., 2021; Lu et al., 2018; Biten et al., 2019). Wang et al. (2022) propose a multimodal entity linking dataset based on Wikipedia, emphasizing text input as the primary component, complemented by visual input. However, the entity types are limited to only persons and organisations.

Sun et al. (2022) aim to link the visual mention in the image with the entire image as the context to the corresponding named entity in KGs without textual descriptions. This model focuses mostly on images of persons. For this, they create a human-annotated dataset and then finetune a variety of models that are partly based on CLIP, adding output heads on top of pre-trained models such as CLIP to obtain more task-specific features.

In their *OVEN* task, Hu et al. (2023) aim to link over 6 million open domain images to (English) Wikipedia, given also a natural language question as input. They, too, finetune composed models with CLIP as a backbone along with another much larger multimodal model named PaLI (Chen et al., 2023), and achieve state-of-the-art results on visually-situated text understanding and object localization tasks.

The contributions of this paper close a gap in the aforementioned efforts: Given our goal of applying the VEL process on Wikimedia Commons, we do not provide additional textual queries as input, as we would not have a source for them on Commons. Instead, we aim to predict the depicted items only from the image itself, which gives rise to a multi-label problem, i.e., multiple entities depicted in one image. Additionally, we are not limited to a certain group of items but seek to provide a domain-independent solution. This combination makes it a very difficult problem worth exploring.

2.2 Pre-trained CLIP

Modern deep learning models, such as ResNet-50 (He et al., 2015), excel in computer vision tasks such as image classification, achieving an accuracy of around 80% across the 1,000 different pre-defined candidate classes of the ImageNet dataset. OpenAI introduced Contrastive Language-Image Pre-training (CLIP; Radford et al., 2021) to address the limitation of being confined to predefined classes. CLIP is a multimodal model trained to map images and natural language text to high-dimensional embeddings close to each other based on cosine similarity. It uses two separate encoders for image and text input, allowing for inference comparing image embeddings against text embeddings of freely chosen labels. Different experimental settings for CLIP are investigated in depth by Shen et al. (2021) and Gao et al. (2024).

3 Dataset

On Wikimedia Commons, the community contributes meta-data for the uploaded images. This includes descriptions and licensing information as well as structured data in the form of Wikidata items. In our work, we focus on the structured data describing entities in the images. To express this relation, the property `depicts` is used on Wikimedia Commons.

3.1 Collection

Wikimedia regularly publishes database dumps of its projects[2], including Commons structured data and Wikidata entities. These dumps[3] are used in this project, providing basic information on all Commons images, descriptions and categories, and labels for all current Wikidata items. The advantage of using dumps is that they only need to be downloaded once, and all processing can be done offline afterwards. The following initial data preprocessing is employed to extract relevant information for the dataset:

- For Commons images, we only retain the unique image ID (Commons page ID), description, categories, and list of depicted items. Images without any annotated depicted item are discarded completely at this stage. Also, we only consider images with the (case-insensitive) file name extensions *.jpg*, *.jpeg*, *.png*, and *.svg*.
- For Wikidata, we only keep the unique item ID (known as *QID*), label (short descriptive name), and description. Along with these, the ID of the first linked image from the *image* property (if any) is saved. Items that are never annotated as *depicted* across the entire Commons dump are discarded completely at this stage.

We employ a heuristic filtering strategy to retain only commonly depictable items in the Wikidata dumps, removing other items such as scholarly articles or metadata items. This further ensures that all textual input is in English. Commons categories are assumed to be in English but are filtered to only include categories descriptive of the image. For example, categories merely relating to specific users or upload dates are eliminated via simple pattern matching, using patterns such as *User:* or *Photographs by:*.

[2]`https://dumps.wikimedia.org/commonswiki/`
[3]extracted as of November 7, 2023

Additional information on the `depicts` statements such as the prominence flag or item qualifiers (e.g., *"color: blue"*) is omitted.

A data structure is built while parsing Wikidata to capture the item hierarchy according to Wikidata's *subclass of* and *instance of* properties. This allows for the association of items of differing granularity, as subclassed or instantiated items can also be considered as their respective superclass(es). The data structure is a mapping of an item's QID to all QIDs of its superclasses, for different numbers of hops (for up to three hops).

3.2 Hierarchy-Aware Item Filtering

The distribution of `depicts` annotations across all 2.3 million items is severely skewed, as shown in Figure 3a, with around 50% occurring merely once as ground-truth, and 90% occurring fewer than ten times. This suggests poor model performance on rare items among the large pool of candidates. To mitigate this, we promote the long-tail items to more frequent and generic Wikidata items using Wikidata's class hierarchy and a threshold f. This filtering removes items depicted fewer than f times in the training split generated from the intermediate data. However, item appearances accumulate across three hops in the Wikidata hierarchy, potentially affecting generic items. This accumulation is relevant for more generic Wikidata items such as *human*, for which specific people are often annotated using the `depicts` statement, but rarely annotated as *human*.

To adjust the images' ground-truth, we check if every original ground-truth item fulfils the threshold. If so, it is kept, otherwise, we probe the KG hierarchy for more generic substitute items. Once one or more items fulfil f, they are taken as replacements for the original ground-truth item. To retain as many images as possible and their distribution, an image is only discarded if no replacement item can be found within three hops.

3.3 Experimental Dataset

In the following experiments, we use a dataset consisting of 1 million Commons images. It is created by randomly shuffling the order of the intermediate file to eliminate biases such as by upload date or batch uploads. The dataset is split into 80% training, 10% validation, and 10% testing splits, as shown in Table 1. It also illustrates that the number of rows for train and validation splits is higher than the number of images, as many images have multi-

	f = 0	f = 10
#images train	800,000	800,000
(#rows)	(1,377,684)	(1,498,026)
(#gt_items)	(490,876)	(17,287)
#images validation	100,000	100,000
(#rows)	(195,535)	(212,885)
(#gt_items)	(72,055)	(14,253)
#images test	100,000	100,000
(#rows)	(100,000)	(100,000)
(#gt_items)	(72,271)	(14,351)
#Wikidata items	2,305,611	18,522

Table 1: Statistics of the Experimental Dataset. #rows = no. of labels available for the images, #gt_items = no. of unique Wikidata items as ground-truth labels.

f=0		f=10	
Label	Freq.	Label	Freq.
road	34,615	human	119,233
village	16,186	painting	55,213
agriculture	16,117	taxon	44,461
path	15,601	village	37,040
house	14,943	road	36,159

Table 2: Most frequent items in the training split.

ple ground-truth labels, which are used in the experiments for training and validation mini-batches. Most experiments use an item frequency of $f = 10$. Figure 2 and Table 2 show the item super-category distributions and most frequent items in the entire dataset for $f = 0$ and $f = 10$.

The super-categories are arbitrary selections of generic classes an item can belong to, inferred from the Wikidata dump by certain properties. Figure 2 shows many items that depict humans, animals, plants, or natural objects. Following the skewed distribution as illustrated in Figure 3a, the most frequent items in the train split without applying a threshold are highly overrepresented and fairly generic, as shown in Table 2.

With a threshold of $f = 10$, we have 18,522 items left that are depicted often enough in the train split. Still, only 6,034 images were discarded because of lacking suitable ground-truth items, showing that the KG hierarchy helps in retaining most images. Overall, with one ground-truth item per datapoint, there are about 1.5 million train datapoints and 213,000 validation datapoints, averaging roughly two ground-truth items per image.

This also causes the super-category distribution in the dataset to change, with *human* becoming the most frequent item and *painting* or *taxon* being assigned to specific paintings or species. As shown in Figure 3b, every remaining item occurs ten times or more (across three hops) in the training dataset. This implies that a few items are highly overrepresented among candidates (see Table 2). Instead of balancing the frequencies in the dataset, this work intends to produce a dataset that is a reasonably representative sample of all Commons images. This approach allows fine-tuned models to work well on the generality of Commons images, rather than ensuring similar performance across all depictable items, many of which are very rare. Therefore, the experiments conducted in this work are on an imbalanced real-world dataset.

3.4 Challenges

While preparing the dataset, we identified the following challenges:

Depicts statements. The guidelines for the `depicts` statement, as many community guidelines, vary across the project, e.g., sometimes suggesting not to add generic items if more specific ones are already marked[4], while with others the recommendation is to add *both* generic and specific items.[5] Therefore, different images with similar content might be annotated differently.

Depicted items. The number of items marked in images on Commons varies considerably, as shown in Figure 4a, due to differing understanding of the guidelines on adding `depicts` statements. Figure 4b contrasts two images that both have *tree* marked, while the red house in the background is very prominent. This inconsistency in ground-truth data can lead to inconsistencies in the diversity of images, making it difficult for models to predict the correct items accurately.

Specific items. Even after filtering with our threshold of 10, there are items that appear overly specific. For example, the item *Flintenweg 8, Orvelte* (Q17447776) is still present in the dataset, as relatively many images are annotated with this item despite it not even having a description on Wikidata.

Similar and Dissimilar Items. The KG hierar-

[4] https://commons.wikimedia.org/wiki/Commons:Depicts#What_items_not_to_add

[5] https://commons.wikimedia.org/wiki/Commons:Depiction_guidelines#Depicts_level_of_detail (marked as disputed)

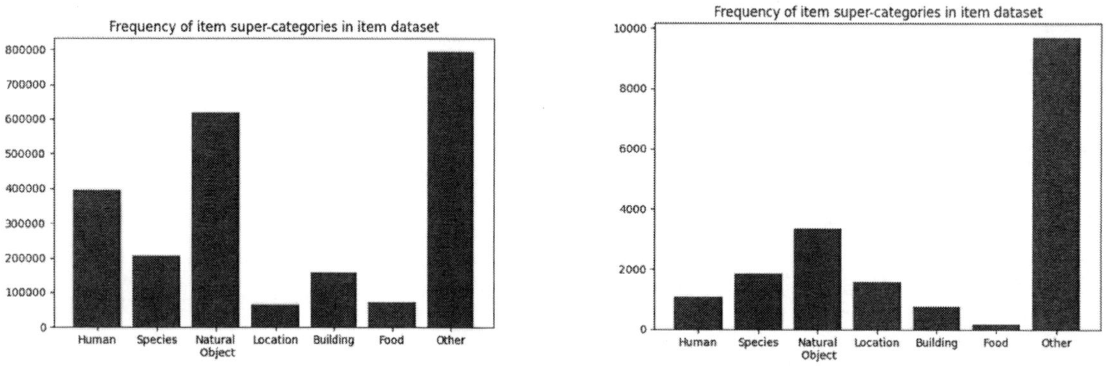

(a) $f = 0$: 2.3 million items

(b) $f = 10$: 18,522 items

Figure 2: Distribution of inferred item super-categories.

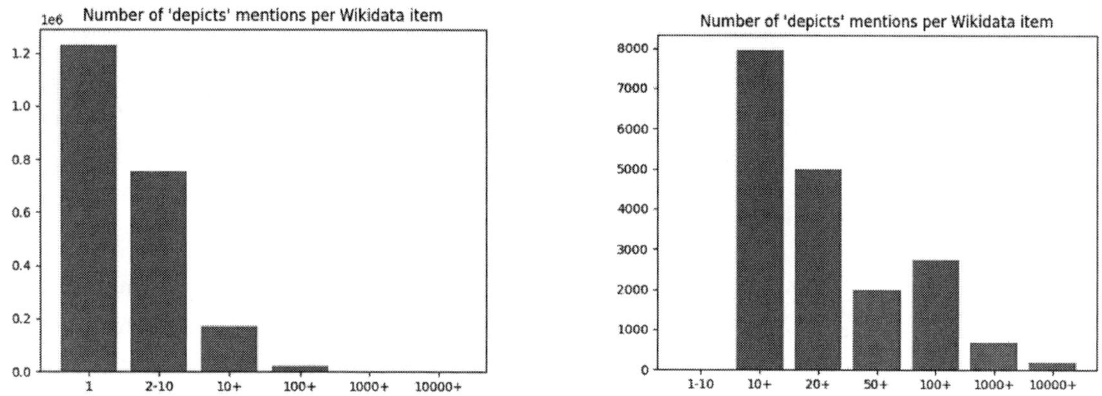

(a) $f = 0$: 2.3 million items (no hops)

(b) $f = 10$: 18,522 items (over three hops)

Figure 3: Number of `depicts` mentions across items.

QID	Label
Q466066	BMW Series 3
Q608824	BMW Series 3
Q730915	BMW Series 3
Q756792	BMW Series 3 (E46)
Q838837	BMW Series 3

Table 3: Excerpt of highly similar items.

chy captures candidate items of varying granularity, while multiple items with QIDs and statements share labels and descriptions. For example, Table 3 lists an excerpt of Wikidata items related to the same car model series. However, there are many near-identical items, describing similar concepts with different labels.

4 Experimental Setup

In the following, we describe the CLIP variants used in the proposed Wiki-VEL framework to link the WikiCommons images to Wikidata entities.

4.1 Naive CLIP

Our Naive CLIP model (see Figure 5) is a multimodal approach to the VEL task, leveraging the CLIP's image encoder for the Wikimedia Commons images and each item's label concatenated with its description is passed through CLIP's text encoder. The resulting image and text embeddings are then normalized and compared by their cosine similarity to determine a relevance score. Additional multi-layer perceptron (MLP) heads are added to the image and text encoders to adjust the semantically rich CLIP features to the task. Each MLP head consists of a linear layer of double the input dimensionality, followed by a ReLU activation function, a dropout layer with probability 0.5, and a final linear layer mapping back to the input dimensionality. A residual connection is added to the CLIP embeddings to facilitate training. This model is named Naive CLIP because it does not utilize all

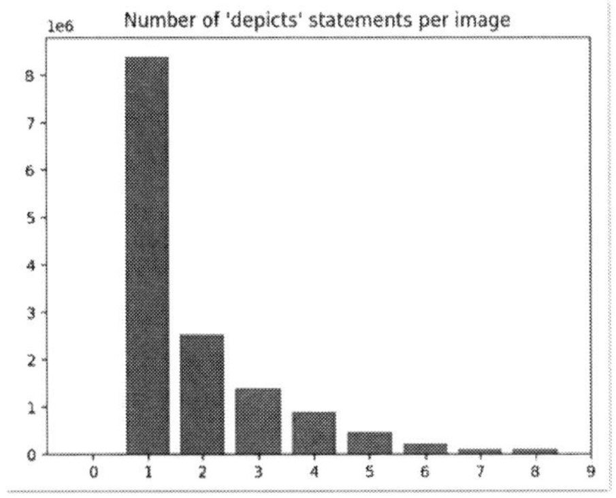

(a) Greatly varying number of `depicts` statements.

(b) Contrary ways on how to add *depicts* statements.

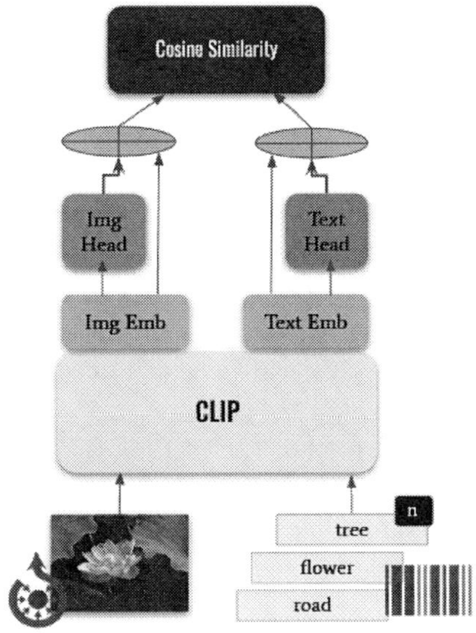

Figure 5: Architecture of the Naive CLIP model.

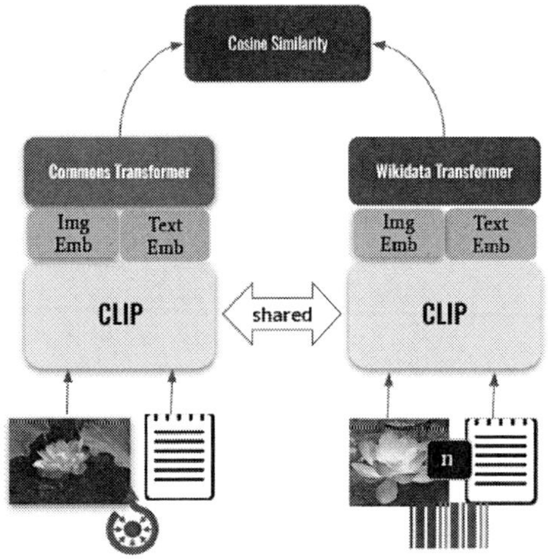

Figure 6: Architecture of the CLIP Fusion model.

available information, such as image descriptions and categories.

4.2 CLIP Fusion

The CLIP Fusion architecture (Hu et al., 2023) uses two separate encoders for the query and the entity, each relying on a CLIP backbone for image and text embeddings. A transformer-model head outputs a single embedding per encoder, which can be matched against each other. We adopt this architecture, with the CLIP backbone shared by both encoders, referred to as Commons encoder and Wikidata encoder, as shown in Figure 6. For the Commons encoder, the Wikimedia Commons image description and categories are concatenated to form the textual input. In the Wikidata encoder, in addition to the Wikidata labels, we use their item images. Since Wikidata item images also come from Commons, there is a risk that item images could be part of the test dataset. To avoid leaking test data, we removed these images from the test dataset, which was the case for 74 items in the $f = 10$ dataset.

4.3 Loss Targets

The in-batch contrastive loss function of CLIP's pre-training assumes all matching pairs (the loss targets) of images and texts to lie on the diagonal of the input matrix. The composed loss function is: $0.5 \times$ (image_to_text_loss + text_to_image_loss), where both the individual loss functions are the cross-entropy loss. We aim to relax the diagonal requirement by allowing all combinations of images to be set as loss targets. This means that the same Wikidata item can be depicted in multiple images and potentially multiple ground-truth items. This means that each batch must determine the corresponding matches before setting them as equally weighted loss targets. Our method also allows the loss targets to be dependent on the number of hops between a ground-truth item and another item in the batch, using the Wikidata item hierarchy. This is to force the model to move embeddings of related specific and generic items closer together.

4.4 Experimental Details

The models described in Section 4 are trained with two validation loops per epoch and early stopping before evaluation on the test split. The optimal hyperparameters for our model include a learning rate of 0.001, a batch size of 1,024, and AdamW optimization. We also rescale item gradients by inverse batch frequency and set one loss target hops. The inverse batch frequency accounts for the fact that Wikidata items like *human* occur frequently. The train split contains 800,000 small images, which creates a massive IO overhead during finetuning. However, at the cost of increased memory usage, latency is reduced, speeding up finetuning. Due to resource limitations, the experiments use *ViT-B/32* as CLIP's image encoder, limiting the batch size to 256, despite a larger batch size being preferable in contrastive learning (Chen et al., 2022) for finetuning experiments. The study focuses on testing common learning rates and optimizer values without sophisticated hyperparameter tuning, retaining those that initially yielded good results. We use the following evaluation metrics to analyse the models. **Recall@k** measures the proportion of relevant items retrieved within the *top-k* results. **Diversity Recall@k** measures the percentage of the relevant items matched by the *top-k* predictions. **Mean Average Precision@k (mAP)** measures the percentage of predictions matching any relevant item for every rank up to *k*, considering their order.

5 Results

5.1 Empirical Evaluation

Zero-shot model & baseline algorithms. The zero-shot CLIP model, without output head, performs poorly on the test split, but achieves a recall score of over 15 at the tenth rank. In a qualitative analysis, we find that the model predicts more specific items, e.g., people in an image often get predicted with their specific names. We believe this results from CLIP's pre-training, where the ground-truth texts were more specific to the image compared to our dataset's labels. The random baseline algorithm randomly picks items from the candidate pool with a probability equal to their frequency in the train split, but results are comparably poor compared to the zero-shot model. The top-k baseline algorithm predicts the same ten items for every image, namely the most frequent ones in the train split, which performs well based on metrics. However, no rare item is predicted correctly, which is the main shortcoming of this baseline.

MLP Naive CLIP model. The Naive CLIP model with both CLIP encoders frozen and a simple MLP head performs well with a recall score of over 50 at rank ten. It suggests a correct item on every second image, making it the best Naive CLIP model. However, the precision is lower at the top rank. The recall scores at ranks 20, 50, and 100 increased, with rank 100 still being among the first 0.5% of all candidate items. The actual prediction scores are close to each other, with an average of 0.29 at rank one and 0.25 at rank 100. The model achieves a good balance between more specific and generic items, considering image content instead of outputting specific persons' names. This makes it a good choice for predicting diverse kinds of items. For example, it accurately predicts *presenters*, *microphones*, *awards*, and *human*[6] instead of suggesting specific names of people.

CLIP Fusion model. The CLIP Fusion model outperforms all tested models, with double precision and recall and a recall value of 92.4 at rank 100. We found that this is due to the Commons category input often revealing the correct answer, especially for infrequent items. The corresponding image category in some cases may be named almost or even exactly the same as the name of the item, such as "*London Victoria station*"[7].

However, the effectiveness of the model drops when no descriptive text input is available for the existing Wikicommons images or when a new image is uploaded. Combining categories and a threshold dataset can make tasks harder when specific categories are provided but mapped to generic items with little in common in textual representation. While fitting the model on the full pool of candidate items might be promising, it does not address the issue of input dependency.

5.2 Human Evaluation

We evaluated the model performance of the Naive CLIP model with a human evaluation study. The simplicity of the Naive CLIP model, and its reduced reliance on large amounts of training data,

[6]https://commons.wikimedia.org/?curid=28127864
[7]https://commons.wikimedia.org/?curid=12289864

Model	Recall			Div. Recall			mAP		
	@1	@5	@10	@1	@5	@10	@1	@5	@10
Zero-shot	4.7	11.5	15.9	4.7	7.5	10.3	4.7	4.7	5.1
Random baseline	2.1	9.6	17.2	2.1	6.5	11.5	2.1	3.1	3.7
Top-k baseline	12.4	29.8	40.8	12.4	20.5	29.8	12.4	14.3	15.9
MLP Naive CLIP	16.2	**40.5**	**51.8**	16.2	**27.5**	**37.2**	16.2	17.1	18.7
TE Naive CLIP BS 256	**20.6**	37.5	45.0	**20.6**	26.0	31.8	**20.6**	**19.0**	**20.0**
MLP Naive CLIP BS 256	14.2	38.8	49.8	14.2	26.3	35.6	14.2	15.7	17.3
CLIP Fusion	36.4	62.4	71.8	36.4	45.5	56.3	36.4	32.3	34.3

Table 4: Comparison of the performance of various model setups on our test split (zero hops in the metrics). Default batch size is 1,024. "MLP" = CLIP encoders frozen, "TE" = finetuned text encoder, "BS" = batch size.

	CC	TG	OR	CI	IDK
k=1	**43.1**	5.2	20.7	24.8	6.2
k=5	**34.3**	6.6	28.0	24.4	6.7
k=10	**29.8**	6.8	28.7	26.4	8.3

Table 5: Human Evaluation Results in %. CC = completely correct, TG = too general, OR = only related, CI = completely incorrect, IDK = I don't know.

make it more realistic for this model to be deployed on Wikimedia Commons.

With this study, we aim to understand to what extent a model genuinely predicts reasonable items. Given the large variety in data, and the data challenges enumerated in Section 3, we believe the actual model output may be more useful than is evident from the metrics relying on the ground-truth data. To this end, we set up a website using a subset of test split images, their ground-truth items, and the top 10 model predictions. For each prediction, participants choose between four qualitative ratings (*"completely correct"*, *"too generic"*, *"only related"*, or *"completely incorrect"*), as well as an alternative *"I don't know"* option. In our human evaluation study, 100 random images from the test split were annotated, each image by three people.

Our study focuses on quantifying the inter-annotator agreement in image evaluations using Fleiss' Kappa measure (Fleiss, 1971). The average agreement across all images for rank one is 0.54. To estimate model performance, the chosen options are aggregated over all users and images. We calculate distributions across ranks $k = 1$, $k = 5$, and $k = 10$ to compare previous metric-based evaluation results. The results illustrated in Table 5 show a value of 43.1 for the top prediction being completely correct, which is over 2.5 times the precision/recall value of 16.2 (cf. Table 4) with MLP Naive CLIP, indicating better model performance than the metric-based evaluation results.

The value for *"completely correct"* decreases for later ranks, as only a few completely correct answers per image are predicted for later ranks. The option with the highest percentage is *"only related"*, as it is the model's best next guess. *"Too general"* predictions occur in certain model setups, and completely incorrect and obscure predictions are observed at rank ten.

6 Conclusion

In this paper, we propose the Wiki-VEL framework, linking the items portrayed in images with structured knowledge stemming from Wikidata. We create a dataset from community-contributed, open-licensed Wikimedia Commons images labeled with the depicted entities in the form of Wikidata entities. In our VEL experiments, we show that the Naive CLIP model shows promising performance by outperforming the zero-shot model and simple baselines. The performance of the CLIP Fusion model also improved with more input data. However, all setups reached a plateau in learning due to the noisy real-world data. In our human evaluation, we show that the data quality also affects the metrics to evaluate model performance – humans perceive the model to be correct more than the automated metrics.

Looking towards the future, our results are promising for automatically providing structured labels for Wikimedia Commons images. To realise this vision, the Wikimedia community could participate in a large-scale human evaluation to assess the integration of the model into Commons to support contributors on image uploads and achieve the desired benefits from the structured data project. Further, the dataset can easily be extended to a multilingual dataset by extracting the image description and item names in different languages from structured data.

References

Omar Adjali, Romaric Besançon, Olivier Ferret, Hervé Le Borgne, and Brigitte Grau. 2020. Multimodal entity linking for tweets. In *European Conference on Information Retrieval*, pages 463–478. Springer.

Ali Furkan Biten, Lluis Gomez, Marçal Rusinol, and Dimosthenis Karatzas. 2019. Good news, everyone! context driven entity-aware captioning for news images. In *Proceedings of CVPR 2019*.

Changyou Chen, Jianyi Zhang, Yi Xu, Liqun Chen, Jiali Duan, Yiran Chen, Son Dinh Tran, Belinda Zeng, and Trishul Chilimbi. 2022. Why do we need large batchsizes in contrastive learning? a gradient-bias perspective. In *Advances in Neural Information Processing Systems*.

Xi Chen, Xiao Wang, Soravit Changpinyo, AJ Piergiovanni, Piotr Padlewski, Daniel Salz, Sebastian Goodman, Adam Grycner, Basil Mustafa, Lucas Beyer, Alexander Kolesnikov, Joan Puigcerver, Nan Ding, Keran Rong, Hassan Akbari, Gaurav Mishra, Linting Xue, Ashish Thapliyal, James Bradbury, Weicheng Kuo, Mojtaba Seyedhosseini, Chao Jia, Burcu Karagol Ayan, Carlos Riquelme, Andreas Steiner, Anelia Angelova, Xiaohua Zhai, Neil Houlsby, and Radu Soricut. 2023. PaLI: A jointly-scaled multilingual language-image model. *Preprint*, arXiv:2209.06794.

Gerard de Melo and Niket Tandon. 2016. Seeing is believing: The quest for multimodal knowledge. *ACM SIGWEB Newsletter*, (Spring 2016):4:1–4:9.

Shahi Dost, Luciano Serafini, Marco Rospocher, Lamberto Ballan, and Alessandro Sperduti. 2020. VT-LINKER: visual-textual-knowledge entity linker. In *ECAI 2020*, pages 2897–2898. IOS Press.

Joseph Fleiss. 1971. Measuring nominal scale agreement among many raters. *Psychological Bulletin*, 76:378–.

Jingru Gan, Jinchang Luo, Haiwei Wang, Shuhui Wang, Wei He, and Qingming Huang. 2021. Multimodal entity linking: a new dataset and a baseline. In *Proceedings of ACM Multimedia 2021*.

Peng Gao, Shijie Geng, Renrui Zhang, Teli Ma, Rongyao Fang, Yongfeng Zhang, Hongsheng Li, and Yu Qiao. 2024. Clip-adapter: Better vision-language models with feature adapters. *International Journal of Computer Vision*, 132(2):581–595.

Kaiming He, Xiangyu Zhang, Shaoqing Ren, and Jian Sun. 2015. Deep residual learning for image recognition. *Preprint*, arXiv:1512.03385.

Hexiang Hu, Yi Luan, Yang Chen, Urvashi Khandelwal, Mandar Joshi, Kenton Lee, Kristina Toutanova, and Ming-Wei Chang. 2023. Open-domain visual entity recognition: Towards recognizing millions of Wikipedia entities. *Preprint*, arXiv:2302.11154.

Huadong Li, Yafang Wang, Gerard de Melo, Changhe Tu, and Baoquan Chen. 2017. Multimodal question answering over structured data with ambiguous entities. In *Proceedings of WWW 2017*. ACM.

Di Lu, Leonardo Neves, Vitor Carvalho, Ning Zhang, and Heng Ji. 2018. Visual attention model for name tagging in multimodal social media. In *Proceedings of ACL 2018*.

Seungwhan Moon, Leonardo Neves, and Vitor Carvalho. 2018. Multimodal named entity disambiguation for noisy social media posts. In *Proceedings of ACL 2018*.

Eric Müller-Budack, Jonas Theiner, Sebastian Diering, Maximilian Idahl, Sherzod Hakimov, and Ralph Ewerth. 2021. Multimodal news analytics using measures of cross-modal entity and context consistency. *International Journal of Multimedia Information Retrieval*, 10(2):111–125.

Alec Radford, Jong Wook Kim, Chris Hallacy, Aditya Ramesh, Gabriel Goh, Sandhini Agarwal, Girish Sastry, Amanda Askell, Pamela Mishkin, Jack Clark, Gretchen Krueger, and Ilya Sutskever. 2021. Learning transferable visual models from natural language supervision. *Preprint*, arXiv:2103.00020.

Sheng Shen, Liunian Harold Li, Hao Tan, Mohit Bansal, Anna Rohrbach, Kai-Wei Chang, Zhewei Yao, and Kurt Keutzer. 2021. How much can CLIP benefit vision-and-language tasks? *arXiv preprint arXiv:2107.06383*.

Ekaterina Shutova, Niket Tandon, and Gerard de Melo. 2015. Perceptually grounded selectional preferences. In *Proceedings of ACL 2015*, pages 950–960.

Wen Sun, Yixing Fan, Jiafeng Guo, Ruqing Zhang, and Xueqi Cheng. 2022. Visual named entity linking: A new dataset and a baseline. In *Findings of the Association for Computational Linguistics: EMNLP 2022*.

Neha Tilak, Sunil Gandhi, and Tim Oates. 2017. Visual entity linking. In *2017 International Joint Conference on Neural Networks (IJCNN)*. IEEE.

Xuwu Wang, Junfeng Tian, Min Gui, Zhixu Li, Rui Wang, Ming Yan, Lihan Chen, and Yanghua Xiao. 2022. WikiDiverse: a multimodal entity linking dataset with diversified contextual topics and entity types. *arXiv preprint arXiv:2204.06347*.

Rebecka Weegar, Linus Hammarlund, Agnes Tegen, Magnus Oskarsson, Kalle Åström, and Pierre Nugues. 2014. Visual entity linking: A preliminary study. In *Workshops at the Twenty-Eighth AAAI Conference on Artificial Intelligence*.

Li Zhang, Zhixu Li, and Qiang Yang. 2021. Attention-based multimodal entity linking with high-quality images. In *Database Systems for Advanced Applications: 26th International Conference, DASFAA 2021, Taipei, Taiwan, April 11–14, 2021, Proceedings, Part II 26*, pages 533–548. Springer.

VerbCLIP: Improving Verb Understanding in Vision-Language Models with Compositional Structures

Hadi Wazni, Kin Ian Lo, Mehrnoosh Sadrzadeh
University College London
{hadi.wazni.20, kin.lo.20, m.sadrzadeh}@ucl.ac.uk

Abstract

Verbs describe the dynamics of interactions between people, objects, and their environments. They play a crucial role in language formation and understanding. Nonetheless, recent vision-language models like CLIP predominantly rely on nouns and have a limited account of verbs. This limitation affects their performance in tasks requiring action recognition and scene understanding. In this work, we introduce VerbCLIP, a verb-centric vision-language model which learns meanings of verbs based on a compositional approach to statistical machine learning. Our methods significantly outperform CLIP in zero-shot performance on the VALSE, VL-Checklist, and SVO-Probes datasets, with improvements of +2.38%, +3.14%, and +1.47%, without fine-tuning. Fine-tuning resulted in further improvements, with gains of +2.85% and +9.2% on the VALSE and VL-Checklist datasets.

1 Introduction

Trained on extensive datasets of image-caption pairs, current vision-and-language models (VLMs) excel in various applications, yet stall in tasks that require structural knowledge and compositional reasoning (Thrush et al., 2022; Liu et al., 2023). Research by (Yuksekgonul et al., 2023; Lin et al., 2024) demonstrates some of the difficulties they face in understanding attributes, relationships, and order information. More specifically, (Hendricks and Nematzadeh, 2021) points out that VLMs often fail to distinguish between different verbs, instead relying predominantly on noun understanding. One possible reason for this issue is the inherent biases within the training datasets. These datasets host a limited number of examples where captions share similar contexts but differ in verbs. As a result, they focus on specific objects and subjects, with minimal emphasis on verbs. This tendency is a form of shortcut learning, a phenomenon in deep neural networks where models opt for simpler, superficial solutions over a deeper understanding (Geirhos et al., 2020).

Conversely, Compositional Distributional Semantic models (CDSMs) (Erk and Padó, 2008; Mitchell and Lapata, 2008; Baroni and Zamparelli, 2010; Coecke et al., 2010) learn meaning representations of sentences by considering their compositional linguistic structures, such as the relationships between verbs and their subjects and objects. In the model proposed by (Baroni et al., 2014), verbs are represented as tensors that take lower-order word representations, typically vectors, as arguments. This means that intransitive verbs are represented as matrices, transitive verbs as cubes, and ditransitive verbs as hypercubes. These tensor-based representations have shown promising results in tasks such as verb disambiguation and sentence similarity (Kartsaklis and Sadrzadeh, 2013; Grefenstette et al., 2013). CDSMs have primarily been applied to text-only data and tasks, and have recently been used as text encoders for CLIP (Lewis et al., 2023).

The novel contribution of this paper lies in integrating VLMs with CDSMs within a framework called VerbCLIP to enhance verb understanding. We implement various methods for learning verb tensors on an image-caption matching task and evaluate these methods on VALSE, VL-Checklist, and SVO-Probes datasets. Our best tensor learning method achieves improvements of +2.38%, +3.14%, and +1.47% over CLIP. Beyond these quantitative improvements, a significant advantage of VerbCLIP is that it does not require training from scratch. Our code and data are available at `https://github.com/lanlos-lab/verbclip`.

2 Methodology

We present an overview of our framework, illustrated in Figure 1. It utilises frozen CLIP as the backbone. Initially, we input the original sentence

Proceedings of the 3rd Workshop on Advances in Language and Vision Research, pages 195–201
August 16, 2024 ©2024 Association for Computational Linguistics

and image into CLIP's encoders to obtain a similarity score, reflecting the overall alignment between the general semantics of the text and the image. Simultaneously, we extract the subject-verb-object triplet from the sentence. These components are encoded separately: the subject and object as vectors, and the verb as matrices, forming a compositional text embedding that captures the detailed semantic relationships. We then calculate a similarity score between the compositional text embedding and the image embedding. We add the two scores to produce the final matching score.

2.1 Compositional Distributional Semantics Models (CDSMs)

We consider a number of compositional distributional semantics models, which have been proposed in past work but have not been applied to a visually grounded language setting. Table 1 represents the algebraic formulas used in our experiments.

Vector-based Models Following the work of (Mitchell and Lapata, 2008), vector-based models compute a sentence vector as a mixture of the original word vectors, using simple operations such as element-wise multiplication and addition. Multiplication can be seen as the intersection of features, while addition resembles the union. The main characteristic of these models is that they do not distinguish between the type-logical identities of different words. For example, an intransitive verb is considered of the same order as its subject (a noun), and both will contribute equally to the composite sentence vector.

Tensor-based Models Following the work of (Baroni and Zamparelli, 2010) and (Coecke et al., 2010), relational words such as verbs and adjectives are represented by multilinear maps (tensors). Meanings of words are composed through the application of these maps to vectors representing the arguments (usually nouns). These models offer a more linguistically motivated solution to the problem of composition, effectively addressing the 'bag of words' issue. However, a practical difficulty is that the creation and usage of third-order tensors can be computationally expensive. One solution is to first create a matrix presentation of the verb, which is then expanded to a tensor by applying the Frobenius coproduct (copying) map to either the left or right axis, resulting in the *Copy-Subject* and *Copy-Object* methods (Kartsaklis et al., 2012; Kartsaklis and Sadrzadeh, 2014). This map can be visualised as placing a matrix along a specific diagonal of a tensor. In this work, we propose a new method: *Copy-Add*.

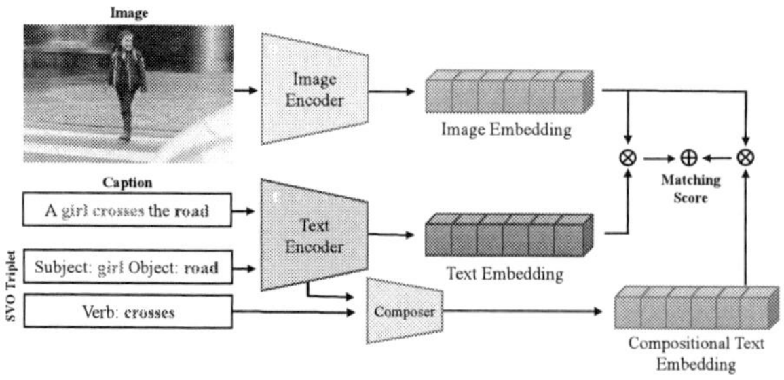

Figure 1: The VerbCLIP framework makes use of two types of text embeddings: the *Text Embedding*, which captures the meaning of the entire caption; and the *Compositional Text Embedding*, which captures the syntactically sensitive meaning by combining word-level embeddings of the subject, verb, and object.

Copy-Subject The semantic interpretation of a transitive sentence involves a two-step compositional process. Initially, the verb's meaning is applied to the object, creating an intermediate representation that highlights how the verb's action targets the object. This result is then applied to the subject, integrating the roles of both subject and object with the verb's action to construct the overall sentence meaning. This approach effectively combines the individual meanings to reflect the sentence's complete semantic structure.

$$\overrightarrow{subj\ verb\ obj} = \overrightarrow{subj} \odot \left(\overline{verb} \times \overrightarrow{obj}\right)$$

Copy-Object The meaning of a transitive sentence is derived by first applying the verb's meaning to the subject, and then combining the result with the meaning of the object. Similarly, this process helps form a coherent semantic output by sequentially engaging the subject and object with the verb.

$$\overrightarrow{subj\ verb\ obj} = \left(\overrightarrow{subj} \times \overline{verb}\right) \odot \overrightarrow{obj}$$

Copy-Add Combining the *Copy-Subject* and *Copy-Object* methods provides a more comprehensive representation of the verb and enhances the sentence meaning. Here the parameters α and β can be trained to balance and optimise the combination, reducing biases and improving overall semantic interpretation.

$$\overrightarrow{subj\ verb\ obj} = \alpha \left[\overrightarrow{subj} \odot \left(\overline{verb} \times \overrightarrow{obj}\right)\right] + \beta \left[\left(\overrightarrow{subj} \times \overline{verb}\right) \odot \overrightarrow{obj}\right]$$

Method	Algebric Formula
Add	$\overrightarrow{T_{sent}} \cdot \overrightarrow{I_{img}} + (\overrightarrow{s} + \overrightarrow{v} + \overrightarrow{o}) \cdot \overrightarrow{I_{img}}$
Mult	$\overrightarrow{T_{sent}} \cdot \overrightarrow{I_{img}} + (\overrightarrow{s} \odot \overrightarrow{v} \odot \overrightarrow{o}) \cdot \overrightarrow{I_{img}}$
Copy-Subject	$\overrightarrow{T_{sent}} \cdot \overrightarrow{I_{img}} + (\overrightarrow{s} \odot (\mathbf{V} \times \overrightarrow{o})) \cdot \overrightarrow{I_{img}}$
Copy-Object	$\overrightarrow{T_{sent}} \cdot \overrightarrow{I_{img}} + ((\overrightarrow{s} \times \mathbf{V}) \odot \overrightarrow{o}) \cdot \overrightarrow{I_{img}}$
Copy-Add	$\overrightarrow{T_{sent}} \cdot \overrightarrow{I_{img}} + (\alpha[\overrightarrow{s} \odot (\mathbf{V} \times \overrightarrow{o})] + \beta[(\overrightarrow{s} \times \mathbf{V}) \odot \overrightarrow{o}]) \cdot \overrightarrow{I_{img}}$

Table 1: Compositional methods used in this study with their corresponding algebraic formulas. We make use of element-wise product $\odot$, matrix multiplication $\times$, and $\cdot$ dot product. The vectors $\overrightarrow{s}$, $\overrightarrow{v}$, and $\overrightarrow{o}$ are text embeddings for the subject, verb, and object entities respectively. $\overrightarrow{T_{sent}}$ and $\overrightarrow{I_{img}}$ are holistic embeddings for the input text and image. By default, we let $\alpha, \beta = 1$.

2.2 Creating verb tensors

We review several proposals for constructing tensors for verbs and opt to use matrices in our work. Matrices often perform as well as, or even better than, full tensors, thereby reducing the number of parameters needed in our framework (Polajnar et al., 2014).

Kronecker In work of (Grefenstette and Sadrzadeh, 2011b), the verb matrix is created as the outer product[1] of the verb vector with itself:

$$\overline{verb} = \overrightarrow{verb} \otimes \overrightarrow{verb}$$

Relational Following ideas from the set-theoretic view of formal semantics, (Grefenstette and Sadrzadeh, 2011a) suggest that the meaning of a verb is the sum of the outer product of its arguments (subject, object) over all occurrences of the verb in a corpus. This is represented as:

$$\overline{verb} = \frac{1}{N} \sum_{i=1}^{N} \overrightarrow{subj}_i \otimes \overrightarrow{obj}_i$$

where N is the number of examples. The intuition is that the matrix encodes higher weights to the contextual features of subjects and objects that are frequently observed together.

Linear Regression Building on the concept introduced by (Baroni and Zamparelli, 2010) of creating adjective matrices, we propose a verb matrix A, when applied to the vector representation of a noun (as either a subject or object), yields a vector that effectively captures the distributional semantics of the combined subject-verb or verb-object phrase. For example, for the verb-object compound "eat food", we compute the verb matrix A_{eat}, such that $\overrightarrow{y} = A_{eat} \times \overrightarrow{food}$, where $\overrightarrow{food}$ represents the distributional vector of "food" and $\overrightarrow{y}$ reflects the semantic composition of "eat food". To find matrix A, we minimise the discrepancy between the predicted vectors and the actual distributional vectors. This optimisation can be achieved through gradient descent or analytically[2], $A_{eat}^T = (X^T X)^{-1} X^T Y$, where the rows of matrix X are vectors of objects found in the corpus as arguments of the verb, and the rows of Y are the vectors of the corresponding verb-object phrases. A similar procedure is used to create matrices for subject-verb phrases.

3 Experiment

We focus on the task of matching images with correct captions. An image is described by both a positive and a negative caption; the negative caption differs from the positive only by a verb. Our aim is to achieve a higher matching score between the image and the positive caption compared to the negative one.

Evaluation Datasets We test our methods on VALSE (Parcalabescu et al., 2022), VL-Checklist (Zhao et al., 2023), and SVO-Probes (Hendricks and Nematzadeh, 2021). Detailed descriptions of the datasets are in the above papers; however, for this study, we selected only those entries where the verb differs between the positive and negative captions, while the subjects and objects are the same. For the SVO-Probes, we create negative captions by substituting the verb in the positive caption with its corresponding negative form from the given negative (SVO) triplet. For example, given a positive caption *'a woman is **running** in the field'* and a

[1]It is the tradition in the literature to use the Kronecker product to form a vector in a tensor-product space. In this work we use the outer product to obtain a matrix instead.

[2]The analytical formula fails when X is not full rank. In such cases, the Moore-Penrose pseudoinverse shall be used.

Method	VALSE			VL-Checklist			SVO-Probes		
	Kron	**Rel**	**Reg**	**Kron**	**Rel**	**Reg**	**Kron**	**Rel**	**Reg**
Copy-Subject	74.76	74.29	74.29	59.53	58.80	58.49	78.74	**78.90**	69.28
Copy-Object	72.86	72.86	73.33	58.53	56.62	52.56	78.35	78.85	70.63
Copy-Add	**75.24**	72.86	75.24	**60.41**	57.85	59.53	77.30	78.44	69.27
Copy-Add FT	75.71	74.29	77.62	66.47	65.47	62.90	77.30	78.49	69.28

Table 2: Comparison of accuracy (%) across three datasets using tensor-based methods. Verb matrices are built with Kronecker (Kron), Relational (Rel), and Regression (Reg) methods using the ViT-B/32 variant of CLIP.

Method	VALSE	VL-Checklist	SVO-Probes
Add	**74.76**	**60.00**	77.64
Mult	73.33	57.83	**78.68**
CLIP	72.86	57.27	77.43

Table 3: The accuracies (%) of vector-based methods using ViT-B/32. For CLIP, image embeddings are generated by CLIP's vision encoder (ViT-B/32); and text embeddings are generated by CLIP's text encoder. We compute the dot product between the image and the text embeddings to obtain the matching score.

negative verb *'walk'*, the resulting negative caption would be *'a woman is **walking** in the field'*. Out of the 14,097 images in the SVO-Probes dataset, 11,769 images were accessible from the internet in February 2024.

Data We extracted all subject-verb-object (SVO) triplets associated with each verb in the three datasets from the March 2022 English Wikipedia dump, using the dependency parser in spaCy. Then, we removed entries with pronouns, stop-words, and tokens that were less than three characters long. We prioritised the triplets, selecting only the top 2,000 subject-object pairs based on the frequency of occurrence. We ensured that for each verb, there were sufficient corresponding entries to build high-quality representation matrices. Verbs that failed to meet all the criteria were dropped. We ended up experimenting with 100 unique verbs in 210 entries from VALSE, 274 unique verbs in 9,407 entries from VL-Checklist, and 290 unique verbs in 14,544 entries from SVO-Probes.

4 Results and Discussion

The compositional tensor-based methods significantly outperform CLIP and vector-based models, with Copy-Add showing the highest performance in most cases. Copy-Add appears capable of utilising information from the combination of subject-verb and verb-object, and incorporating further information from the object and subject. This highlights the importance of ordering and syntactic information in the compositional methods. Upon fine-tuning the weights, α and β, we noticed further improvement (+2.85% and +9.2% on the VALSE and VL-Checklist datasets respectively).

We noticed lower performance improvements on the SVO-Probes dataset compared to VALSE and VL-Checklist. This discrepancy is likely due to the nature of the SVO-Probes dataset, which contains sketchy samples and tends to be noisy, with significant issues such as object mismatches, as detailed in (Castro et al., 2023; Jiang et al., 2024).

In terms of learning verb matrices, regression methods demonstrated lower accuracies, whereas the Kronecker (Kron) and Relational (Rel) methods performed better. The fact that Kron requires no training data makes it an effortless choice for constructing verb matrices, while still providing competitive performance.

In terms of verb-type performance, the Copy-Add model significantly improved accuracy for interaction-based verbs such as "hang" (+12.5%), "hold" (+11.6%), "attached" (+3.7%), and "take" (+29.62%). However, while it struggled with some visually static verbs like "stand" (-5.8%) and "sit" (-6.0%), it showed improvement in others such as "observe" (+50%) and "look" (+10.87%). Furthermore, we tested sentence pairs where the subject and object nouns are swapped, such as *"A **man** lies on the **sofa**"* vs *"A **sofa** lies on the **man**"*. CLIP often misinterprets these as equally plausible, reflecting its approach of processing text as independent words, similar to a bag-of-words approach. In contrast, Copy-Add model correctly identifies *"A **man** lies on the **sofa**"* as the correct caption by capturing structured detailed semantics. Overall, VerbCLIP

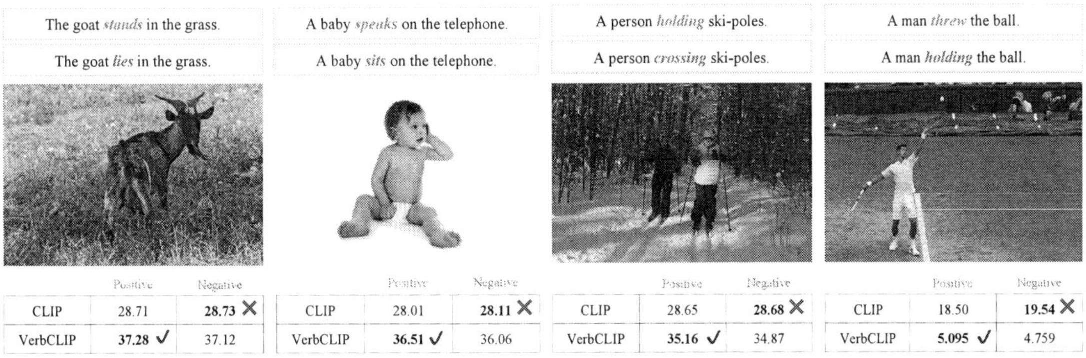

Figure 2: Examples where CLIP pairs images with incorrect text captions, as indicated by higher similarity scores for negative captions. In contrast, our framework achieves more accurate matching. The positive captions (marked in green) and negative captions (marked in red) are semantically very close, with the verb being different.

incorporates syntactic and semantic structures, allowing it to better understand context and dynamic actions.

5 Limitations

Creating verb matrices or tensors is computationally intensive, which poses a significant challenge when scaling to very large pretraining datasets. Additionally, our approach assumes a fixed linguistic structure, typically the subject-verb-object format, which does not account for the varied and flexible ways verbs are used in natural language. However, tensors are natural components of quantum systems, and quantum computing resources can efficiently learn them. The Quantum Natural Language Processing (QNLP) framework (Lorenz et al., 2023; Wazni and Sadrzadeh, 2023), inspired by categorical quantum mechanics and the DisCoCat (Distributional Compositional Categorical) framework, uses string diagrams to translate grammatical structures into quantum processes. This advanced option could offer a promising solution.

6 Conclusion

The CLIP model is noted for its limited ability to understand verbs, often relying heavily on nouns. Our approach seeks to mitigate this issue by introducing verb-focused compositional methods, which have demonstrated enhanced performance across the SVO-Probes, VL-Checklist and VALSE datasets. Our framework can boost the zero-shot inference capability of other models, such as SLIP (Mu et al., 2021) and BLIP (Li et al., 2022), without the need for further training or fine-tuning. Scaling to longer and more complicated sentences with varied grammatical structures is a work in progress.

7 Acknowledgement

The authors gratefully acknowledge the two anonymous reviewers for their valuable comments. Hadi Wazni would like to thank the UCL CS department for the PhD scholarship that supported this work. Kin Ian Lo was supported by the Engineering and Physical Sciences Research Council [grant number EP/S021582/1]. Mehrnoosh Sadrzadeh is grateful to the Royal Academy of Engineering for the Research Chair/Senior Research Fellowship RCSRF2122-14-152 on Engineered Mathematics for Modelling Typed Structures.

References

Marco Baroni, Raffaella Bernardi, and Roberto Zamparelli. 2014. Frege in space: A program for composition distributional semantics. *Linguistic Issues in Language Technology*, 9.

Marco Baroni and Roberto Zamparelli. 2010. Nouns are vectors, adjectives are matrices: Representing adjective-noun constructions in semantic space. In *Proceedings of the 2010 Conference on Empirical Methods in Natural Language Processing*, pages 1183–1193, Cambridge, MA. Association for Computational Linguistics.

Santiago Castro, Oana Ignat, and Rada Mihalcea. 2023. Scalable performance analysis for vision-language models. *Preprint*, arXiv:2305.18786.

Bob Coecke, Mehrnoosh Sadrzadeh, and Stephen Clark. 2010. Mathematical foundations for a compositional distributional model of meaning. *Preprint*, arXiv:1003.4394.

Katrin Erk and Sebastian Padó. 2008. A structured vector space model for word meaning in context. In *Proceedings of the 2008 Conference on Empirical*

Methods in Natural Language Processing, pages 897–906, Honolulu, Hawaii. Association for Computational Linguistics.

Robert Geirhos, Jörn-Henrik Jacobsen, Claudio Michaelis, Richard Zemel, Wieland Brendel, Matthias Bethge, and Felix A. Wichmann. 2020. Shortcut learning in deep neural networks. *Nature Machine Intelligence*, 2(11):665–673.

E. Grefenstette, G. Dinu, Y. Zhang, M. Sadrzadeh, and M. Baroni. 2013. Multi-step regression learning for compositional distributional semantics. In *Proceedings of the 10th International Conference on Computational Semantics (IWCS 2013) – Long Papers*, pages 131–142, Potsdam, Germany. Association for Computational Linguistics.

Edward Grefenstette and Mehrnoosh Sadrzadeh. 2011a. Experimental support for a categorical compositional distributional model of meaning. In *Proceedings of the 2011 Conference on Empirical Methods in Natural Language Processing*, pages 1394–1404, Edinburgh, Scotland, UK. Association for Computational Linguistics.

Edward Grefenstette and Mehrnoosh Sadrzadeh. 2011b. Experimenting with transitive verbs in a discocat. *Preprint*, arXiv:1107.3119.

Lisa Anne Hendricks and Aida Nematzadeh. 2021. Probing image-language transformers for verb understanding. *Preprint*, arXiv:2106.09141.

Kenan Jiang, Xuehai He, Ruize Xu, and Xin Eric Wang. 2024. Comclip: Training-free compositional image and text matching. *Preprint*, arXiv:2211.13854.

Dimitri Kartsaklis and Mehrnoosh Sadrzadeh. 2013. Prior disambiguation of word tensors for constructing sentence vectors. In *Proceedings of the 2013 Conference on Empirical Methods in Natural Language Processing*, pages 1590–1601, Seattle, Washington, USA. Association for Computational Linguistics.

Dimitri Kartsaklis and Mehrnoosh Sadrzadeh. 2014. A study of entanglement in a categorical framework of natural language. In Proceedings of the 11th workshop on *Quantum Physics and Logic,* Kyoto, Japan, 4-6th June 2014, volume 172 of *Electronic Proceedings in Theoretical Computer Science*, pages 249–261. Open Publishing Association.

Dimitri Kartsaklis, Mehrnoosh Sadrzadeh, and Stephen Pulman. 2012. A unified sentence space for categorical distributional-compositional semantics: Theory and experiments. In *Proceedings of COLING 2012: Posters*, pages 549–558, Mumbai, India. The COLING 2012 Organizing Committee.

Martha Lewis, Nihal V. Nayak, Peilin Yu, Qinan Yu, Jack Merullo, Stephen H. Bach, and Ellie Pavlick. 2023. Does clip bind concepts? probing compositionality in large image models. *Preprint*, arXiv:2212.10537.

Junnan Li, Dongxu Li, Caiming Xiong, and Steven Hoi. 2022. Blip: Bootstrapping language-image pre-training for unified vision-language understanding and generation. *Preprint*, arXiv:2201.12086.

Zhiqiu Lin, Xinyue Chen, Deepak Pathak, Pengchuan Zhang, and Deva Ramanan. 2024. Revisiting the role of language priors in vision-language models. *Preprint*, arXiv:2306.01879.

Fangyu Liu, Guy Emerson, and Nigel Collier. 2023. Visual spatial reasoning. *Transactions of the Association for Computational Linguistics*, 11:635–651.

Robin Lorenz, Anna Pearson, Konstantinos Meichanetzidis, Dimitri Kartsaklis, and Bob Coecke. 2023. Qnlp in practice: Running compositional models of meaning on a quantum computer. *Journal of Artificial Intelligence Research*, 76:1305–1342.

Jeff Mitchell and Mirella Lapata. 2008. Vector-based models of semantic composition. In *Proceedings of ACL-08: HLT*, pages 236–244, Columbus, Ohio. Association for Computational Linguistics.

Norman Mu, Alexander Kirillov, David Wagner, and Saining Xie. 2021. Slip: Self-supervision meets language-image pre-training. *Preprint*, arXiv:2112.12750.

Letitia Parcalabescu, Michele Cafagna, Lilitta Muradjan, Anette Frank, Iacer Calixto, and Albert Gatt. 2022. Valse: A task-independent benchmark for vision and language models centered on linguistic phenomena. In *Proceedings of the 60th Annual Meeting of the Association for Computational Linguistics (Volume 1: Long Papers)*. Association for Computational Linguistics.

Tamara Polajnar, Luana Făgărăşan, and Stephen Clark. 2014. Reducing dimensions of tensors in type-driven distributional semantics. In *Proceedings of the 2014 Conference on Empirical Methods in Natural Language Processing (EMNLP)*, pages 1036–1046, Doha, Qatar. Association for Computational Linguistics.

Tristan Thrush, Ryan Jiang, Max Bartolo, Amanpreet Singh, Adina Williams, Douwe Kiela, and Candace Ross. 2022. Winoground: Probing vision and language models for visio-linguistic compositionality. In *CVPR*.

Hadi Wazni and Mehrnoosh Sadrzadeh. 2023. Towards transparency in coreference resolution: A quantum-inspired approach. In *Proceedings of The Sixth Workshop on Computational Models of Reference, Anaphora and Coreference (CRAC 2023)*, pages 15–27, Singapore. Association for Computational Linguistics.

Mert Yuksekgonul, Federico Bianchi, Pratyusha Kalluri, Dan Jurafsky, and James Zou. 2023. When and why vision-language models behave like bags-of-words, and what to do about it? *Preprint*, arXiv:2210.01936.

Tiancheng Zhao, Tianqi Zhang, Mingwei Zhu, Haozhan Shen, Kyusong Lee, Xiaopeng Lu, and Jianwei Yin. 2023. Vl-checklist: Evaluating pre-trained vision-language models with objects, attributes and relations. *Preprint*, arXiv:2207.00221.

Evolutionary Reward Design and Optimization with Multimodal Large Language Models

Ali Emre Narin
Kabatas Erkek High School
aliemre2024@gmail.com

Abstract

Designing reward functions is a pivotal yet challenging task for Reinforcement Learning (RL) practices, often demanding domain expertise and substantial effort. Recent studies have explored the utilization of Large Language Models (LLMs) to generate reward functions via evolutionary search techniques (Ma et al., 2023). However, these approaches overlook the potential of multimodal information, such as images and videos. In particular, prior methods predominantly rely on numerical feedback from the RL environment for doing evolution, neglecting the incorporation of visual data obtained during training. This study introduces a novel approach by employing Multimodal Large Language Models (MLLMs) to craft reward functions tailored for various RL tasks. The methodology involves providing MLLM with the RL environment's code alongside its image as context and task information to generate reward candidates. Then, the chosen agent undergoes training, and the numerical feedback from the environment, along with the recorded video of the top-performing policy, is provided as feedback to the MLLM. By employing an iterative feedback mechanism through evolutionary search, MLLM consistently refines the reward function to maximize accuracy. Testing on two different agents points to the preeminence of our approach over previous methodology, which themselves outperformed 83% (Ma et al., 2023) of reward functions designed by human experts.

1 Introduction

Large Language Models (LLMs) have shown remarkable success in distinct tasks. State-of-the-art models such as Gemini (Anil et al., 2023), Palm (Chowdhery et al., 2023), and GPT-4 (OpenAI et al., 2023) have achieved results comparable to human experts on different benchmarks. In this paper, we are specifically interested in their capabilities in designing Reward functions for Reinforcement Learning practices. Recent studies have shown that GPT-4 can autonomously generate reward functions for multiple agents in IsaacGYM by taking the environment code as context and employing evolutionary search (Ma et al., 2023). Impressively, it achieved results similar to and sometimes even better than those of human experts.

This result is very important for two reasons: firstly, the task of designing effective reward functions is notoriously challenging and time-consuming, and this approach streamlines the process by creating an end-to-end pipeline; secondly, by requiring no additional task-specific modifications, it showcases the generalization capabilities of evolutionary search on reward design.

However, a significant shortcoming of this approach, and LLMs in general, is that they can only operate on textual and numerical data. In contrast, when designing reinforcement learning strategies, human experts often leverage visual data to gain a deeper understanding of the problems that can be solved and improvements that can be made. It is our hypothesis that incorporating visual data could provide the model with enhanced comprehension, thus leading to improved accuracy.

We introduce EROM: "**E**volutionary **R**eward Design and **O**ptimization with **M**ultimodal Large Language Models (MLLMs)" method as a novel way to generate reward functions. In the EROM method, we utilize MLLMs' zero-shot coding abilities to generate reward functions. First, we provide the MLLM with the environment as context by providing the source code; then, we give it the description of the task, guidelines for reward function generation, and an image of the idle agent. After it generates the first iteration of the reward function, we provide feedback from the environment both numerically and visually by providing the video of the agent . Using evolutionary search, it generates a better set of reward functions, and this process iteratively continues.

Proceedings of the 3rd Workshop on Advances in Language and Vision Research, pages 202–208
August 16, 2024 ©2024 Association for Computational Linguistics

Our contributions with the EROM method are as follows:

1. To the best of our knowledge, this is the first work that tests the MLLMs' abilities on reward function generation using evolutionary search.
2. We show that capturing the video (or image of an idle agent) of the top-performing policy and providing it to the MLLMs as feedback helps the performance, compared to just providing textual reflection.
3. By enhancing the qualities of an autonomous method that outperformed 83% human experts, we contribute to the advancement of autonomous reward design techniques without introducing significant computational cost or expenses.

Due to budget limitations, we mostly aimed to show a proof-of-concept of our approach. All the contributions listed above held true for our tests, but without more experiments, the (2) and (3)' rd contributions above should be approached tentatively.

2 Background

2.1 Reward Design

Reward design plays a pivotal role in reinforcement learning, where a well-crafted reward function is instrumental in achieving optimal outcomes. It guides agents toward actions aligned with the desired outcomes. Specifically, they provide positive feedback for actions conducive to achieving specific goals, while also providing negative feedback for actions that lack purpose or have a detrimental impact on the situation.

2.2 Evolutionary Search with LLMs

Evolutionary search algorithms, drawing inspiration from biological evolution, involve the generation of outputs by a generator, such as a LLM (Lehman et al., 2024). The generated outputs undergo evaluation, leading to feedback that informs subsequent iterations of output generation. This iterative process includes the generation of outliers, thereby mitigating the risk of the algorithm converging to a local optimum.

A recent study demonstrated notable success in leveraging Evolution with LLMs for the design of reward functions, incorporating textual feedback and information from the environment (Ma et al., 2023). In the present research, we extend this approach by introducing an additional modality of feedback—visual feedback—into the evolutionary process.

3 Methods

3.1 Environment as Context

The model needs to have a comprehensive understanding of the environment to generate a task-specific reward design for that environment. To achieve this, we give the environment source code as context to the model (Ma et al., 2023). This helps because providing the environment code gives the MLLM essential information about the variables used in the environment code and in what format we expect an output. Additionally, we augment the contextual information by presenting the MLLM with visual representations of the environment and agent. We believe this helps MLLM better understand the environment's visual cues and agent characteristics.

3.2 Evolutionary Search

We employ Evolutionary search for the iterative refinement of reward design. Initially, the model generates random samples of reward candidates, which are then evaluated on the task, and the top performer is selected. Subsequently, both reward feedback and the top performers are collected and fed back into the model for further enhancement. This iterative process is crucial, as evidenced by studies on LLMs demonstrating their capacity for self-improvement over time (Madaan et al., 2023). Moreover, this approach aligns with human intuition, as trial-and-error is a common strategy employed in the design of reward functions (Booth et al., 2023).

3.3 Reward Reflection

Previous studies utilizing LLMs to generate reward samples have primarily relied on textual feedback provided by the environment for evolutionary search (Ma et al., 2023). However, capturing the visual behavior of an agent can also yield valuable insights into necessary adaptations. For instance, visual feedback can aid in identifying instances of reward hacking or pinpointing areas where the agent is not performing as intended. To address this, following the initial iteration of reward sampling, each reward function is individually tested, and both textual feedback from the environment and video recordings of the agent's performance are collected. Subsequently, for the subsequent iteration of evolution, the MLLM is provided with the code of the best-performing reward function, along with its numerical and video feedback gathered during training. The MLLM then reasons over this information to iteratively design improved reward functions. Through this process of reward reflection, the accuracy of designed rewards consistently improves, leading to notable outcomes in our experiments.

4 Experiments

4.1 Baselines

4.1.1 Environment

IsaacGYM (Makoviychuk et al., 2021) is a GPU-Accelerated Physics Simulation for robotics tasks. It enables hundreds of trainings to run at the same time, thus making it faster to conduct experiments. Also, we can capture videos during training, which is a prerequisite for our experiment. We picked humanoid and ant agents on two different tasks for our experiments on this simulator. The reason for selecting these agents was the GPU memory limit of our hardware.

4.1.2 Multimodal Large Language Model

GPT-4V(Vision) (OpenAI et al., 2023) is a MLLM that can take both visual and textual input. Its multimodal capabilities will allow it to reason over videos and images, and its natural language and programming capabilities will allow it to understand tasks and generate reward functions as Python codes, making it suitable to use in our experiments.

4.1.3 Eureka Method

Evolution-driven Universal Reward Kit for Agents (Eureka) (Ma et al., 2023) is a method that inspired us and the method that we built upon. The Eureka method involves providing the environment source code as context, evolutionary search to improve rewards, and using reward reflection. The only difference we made in our method is that we added visuals to the feedback loop and the environment as context part. We used very similar prompts to those of Eureka, with only minor changes indicating to the MLMM that we have added visuals. Also, Eureka has been shown to outperform 83% of human-expert-designed reward functions, which makes being able to outperform it a remarkable achievement.

4.2 Experimental Setup

We conducted three different tests to evaluate the effectiveness of our approach. Following the experiments originally described in the Eureka paper, we ran both EROM and Eureka for five iterations, generating 8 samples of reward function codes in each iteration. Due to the stochastic nature of MLLMs, when none of the codes worked in the first iteration, we reran it until at least one worked, resulting in guaranteed four rounds of feedback. We refer to this as "general testing" in the results subsection of our research.

We separately assessed the importance of providing an image of an agent in the first generation. We ran EROM and Eureka for one iteration, generating 32 samples. We have increased the sample size to have more examples to lower the chance factors that could effect results. We refer to this as "Image Testing" in the results subsection of our research.

We also separately assessed the importance of providing video during the feedback loop by providing the MLLM with the same reward codes generated in another iteration: one with only numerical feedback and the other with video feedback alongside numerical feedback. We generated 32 samples for both methods and compared them. We refer to this as "Video Testing" in the results subsection of our research.

Unless otherwise specified, when making experiments with EROM method, we provided the MLLM with a one-minute video of the agents training on the best policy generated during the training process (divided into 200 frames due to the context length of GPT-4V). In the reward sampling process, we trained the ant agent for 1500 epochs and the humanoid agent for 1000 epochs. In each training, the environment size was set to default for both agents. Each reward that achieved the best success rate in the initial training process was chosen to seed the next generation. We refer to the success rate obtained by reward functions in the initial iteration as "training-success" in the rest of the research. We evaluated the final best reward by retraining it over 5 different seeds and taking the average. We refer to this average as "average success."

4.3 Results

All the "average-success" results can be found in Table 1. Firstly, we observed that our method per-

Table 1: Average Success Rates

Test Type	Ant-EROM	Ant-Eureka	Humanoid-EROM	Humanoid-Eureka
General Testing	$7.27\|0.36\sigma$	$3.68\|0.71\sigma$	$5.26\|0.29\sigma$	$4.21\|0.53\sigma$
Video Testing	$6.13\|0.95\sigma$	$3.38\|0.39\sigma$	$5.42\|0.27\sigma$	$4.81\|0.70\sigma$
Image Testing	$6.38\|1.89\sigma$	$1.76\|0.87\sigma$	$3.17\|0.30\sigma$	$5.33\|0.39\sigma$

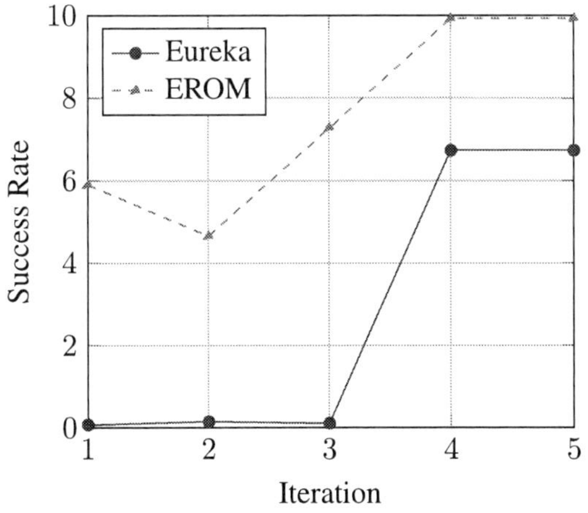

Figure 1: Comparison of success rates in General Testing on Ant agent.

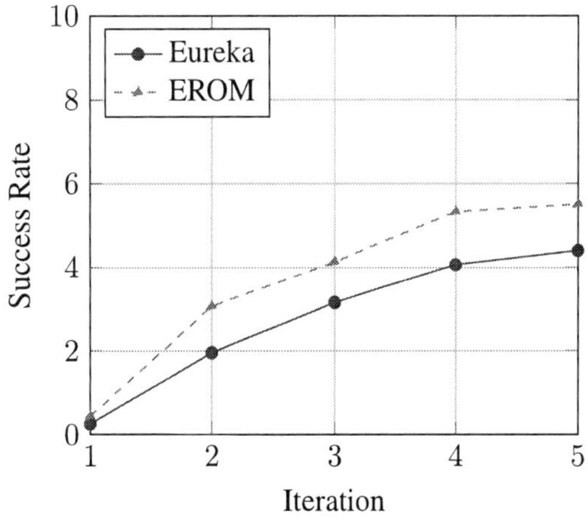

Figure 2: Comparison of success rates in General Testing on Humanoid agent.

formed better on general testing, where we ran both codes for 5 iterations with 8 samples generated in each iteration. On ant and humanoid agents, EROM achieved an average-success rate of 7.27 and 5.26, while Eureka achieved an average-success rate of 3.68 and 4.21, respectively. We have also plotted the difference between EROM and Eureka over the "training-success" of each iteration on Fig. 1, 2. These graphs effectively demonstrate the effectiveness of evolutionary search for both methods, as well as the value of video feedback and providing the image of the agent.

Secondly, to test the importance of providing the image of an agent in the first generation, we generated 32 samples using each method to increase the sample size and obtain a better average. As shown in Table 1, providing an image has shown to increase the average success rate for the ant agent, but not for the humanoid agent.

Lastly, by seeding the MLLM with the same reward functions and reward reflection, one with video and the other with only numerical feedback, we generated 32 samples with each method. We observed that providing the video also improved the average success for both of the agents.

5 Conclusion and Discussion

Designing effective reward functions is a laborious task that requires expertise and time. Recent researchers have sought to address this problem by utilizing Large Language Models (LLMs) to generate reward functions by taking the environment as context, employing evolutionary search, and utilizing reward reflection (Ma et al., 2023). However, they have only used numerical feedback and textual information for reward sampling and the reward reflection process. In this work, we address this limitation by incorporating videos of agents in training and their idle images into the evolutionary process with the help of Multimodal Large Language Models (MLLMs). Our aim is to enhance the success rate of previous methodology, which have already outperformed 83% (Ma et al., 2023) of human experts in their focused tasks. Experiments conducted with two agents across two distinct tasks have indicated that our approach is more effective than solely utilizing textual information.

Limitations

Since we utilized GPT-4V (OpenAI et al., 2023) in our experiments, results largely depend on its capabilities. Alongside that, the real-life applications of our method might not be as successful as in online simulation environments because of the complexity of the real world that is superficially present in simulations.

Another limitation of our work was that, due to the lack of GPU memory, we could only make tests on two agents in IsaacGYM. An experiment on more agents and different environments would better show our approach's generalization capabilities and effectiveness.

References

Rohan Anil, Sebastian Borgeaud, Yonghui Wu, Jean-Baptiste Alayrac, Jiahui Yu, Radu Soricut, Johan Schalkwyk, Andrew M. Dai, Anja Hauth, Katie Millican, David Silver, Slav Petrov, Melvin Johnson, Ioannis Antonoglou, Julian Schrittwieser, Amelia Glaese, Jilin Chen, Emily Pitler, and ... Oriol Vinyals. 2023. Gemini: A family of highly capable multimodal models.

Serena Booth, W. Bradley Knox, Julie Shah, Scott Niekum, Peter Stone, and Alessandro Allievi. 2023. The perils of trial-and-error reward design: Misdesign through overfitting and invalid task specifications. *Proceedings of the AAAI Conference on Artificial Intelligence*, 37(5):5920–5929.

Aakanksha Chowdhery, Sharan Narang, Jacob Devlin, Maarten Bosma, Gaurav Mishra, Adam Roberts, Paul Barham, Hyung Won Chung, Charles Sutton, Sebastian Gehrmann, Parker Schuh, Kensen Shi, Sasha Tsvyashchenko, Joshua Maynez, Abhishek Rao, Parker Barnes, Yi Tay, Noam Shazeer, Vinodkumar Prabhakaran ..., and Noah Fiedel. 2023. Palm: Scaling language modeling with pathways. *Journal of Machine Learning Research*, 24(240):1–113.

Joel Lehman, Jonathan Gordon, Shawn Jain, Cathy Yeh, Kenneth Stanley, and Kamal Ndousse. 2024. *Evolution Through Large Models*, pages 331–366.

Yecheng Jason Ma, William Liang, Guanzhi Wang, De-An Huang, Osbert Bastani, Dinesh Jayaraman, Yuke Zhu, Linxi Fan, and Anima Anandkumar. 2023. Eureka: Human-level reward design via coding large language models.

Aman Madaan, Niket Tandon, Prakhar Gupta, Skyler Hallinan, Luyu Gao, Sarah Wiegreffe, Uri Alon, Nouha Dziri, Shrimai Prabhumoye, Yiming Yang, Shashank Gupta, Bodhisattwa Prasad Majumder, Katherine Hermann, Sean Welleck, Amir Yazdanbakhsh, and Peter Clark. 2023. Self-refine: Iterative refinement with self-feedback. In *Advances in Neural Information Processing Systems*, volume 36, pages 46534–46594. Curran Associates, Inc.

Viktor Makoviychuk, Lukasz Wawrzyniak, Yunrong Guo, Michelle Lu, Kier Storey, Miles Macklin, David Hoeller, Nikita Rudin, Arthur Allshire, Ankur Handa, and Gavriel State. 2021. Isaac gym: High performance gpu-based physics simulation for robot learning.

OpenAI, :, Josh Achiam, Steven Adler, Sandhini Agarwal, Lama Ahmad, Ilge Akkaya, Florencia Leoni Aleman, Diogo Almeida, Janko Altenschmidt, Sam Altman, Shyamal Anadkat, Red Avila, Igor Babuschkin, Suchir Balaji, Valerie Balcom, Paul Baltescu, Haiming Bao, Mo Bavarian, Jeff Belgum, Irwan Bello, and ... Barret Zoph. 2023. Gpt-4 technical report.

A Prompts

In this subsection, we provide the prompts used in our research. We have used the same prompts used in (Ma et al., 2023), with marginal changes regarding visuals.

```
The Python environment is
 ↪ {task_obs_code_string}. Write a
 ↪  reward function for the following
 ↪  task: {task_description}.
Here is an image of the agent.
 ↪  Carefully analyze it for better
 ↪  understanding.
<img src="{image_src}"
 ↪  alt="{image_alt}">
```

Figure 3: User Prompt

```
You are a reward engineer trying to
 ↪  write reward functions to solve
 ↪  reinforcement learning tasks as
 ↪  effective as possible.
Your goal is to write a reward function
 ↪  for the environment that will help
 ↪  the agent learn the task described
 ↪  in text.
Your reward function should use useful
 ↪  variables from the environment as
 ↪  inputs. As an example,
the reward function signature can be:
 ↪ {task_reward_signature_string}
Since the reward function will be
 ↪  decorated with @torch.jit.script,
please make sure that the code is
 ↪  compatible with TorchScript (e.g.,
 ↪  use torch tensor instead of numpy
 ↪  array).
Make sure any new tensor or variable
 ↪  you introduce is on the same device
 ↪  as the input tensors.
```

Figure 4: System Prompt

```
We trained a RL policy using the
 ↪  provided reward function code
 ↪  and tracked the values of the
 ↪  individual components in the
 ↪  reward function as well as
 ↪  global policy metrics such as
 ↪  success rates and episode
 ↪  lengths after every
 ↪ {epoch_freq} epochs and the
 ↪  maximum, mean, minimum values
 ↪  encountered:
{Reward Reflection}
Please carefully analyze the policy
 ↪  feedback and provide a new,
 ↪  improved reward function that
 ↪  can better solve the task. Some
 ↪  helpful tips for analyzing the
 ↪  policy feedback:
    (1) If the success rates are
     ↪  always near zero, then you
     ↪  must rewrite the entire
     ↪  reward function
    (2) If the values for a certain
     ↪  reward component are near
     ↪  identical throughout, then
     ↪  this means RL is not able to
     ↪  optimize this component as
     ↪  it is written. You may
     ↪  consider
        (a) Changing its scale or
         ↪  the value of its
         ↪  temperature parameter
        (b) Re-writing the reward
         ↪  component
        (c) Discarding the reward
         ↪  component
    (3) If some reward components'
     ↪  magnitude is significantly
     ↪  larger, then you must
     ↪  re-scale its value to a
     ↪  proper range
Please analyze each existing reward
 ↪  component in the suggested
 ↪  manner above first, and then
 ↪  write the reward function code.
```

Figure 5: Feedback Prompt

B Computational Resources and Additional Expenses

We utilized an RTX 2060 6GB graphics card to execute all experiments. None of the experiments exceeded a runtime of 16 hours. We could only train one policy at a time for the humanoid agent, while two for the ant agent. The total cost of GPT-4V(ision) API calls, to run all the experiments, amounted to approximately $40.

C Task Details

In this section, we provide task details. For task details, we follow the structure from (Ma et al., 2023). We provide the task description, environment, observation and action dimensions, and the task fitness function F.

Table 2: Task Details and Descriptions

Environment	Obs. Dim.	Act Dim.	Task Description
Ant	60	8	To make the ant run forward as fast as possible (Fitness Function: $cur\_dist - prev\_dist$)
Humanoid	108	21	To make the humanoid run as fast as possible (Fitness Function: $cur\_dist - prev\_dist$)

Author Index

Association for Computational Linguistics
209 N. Eighth Street
Stroudsburg, Pennsylvania 18360

ISBN 979-8-3313-0155-2

CURRAN ASSOCIATES INC.
proceedings.com